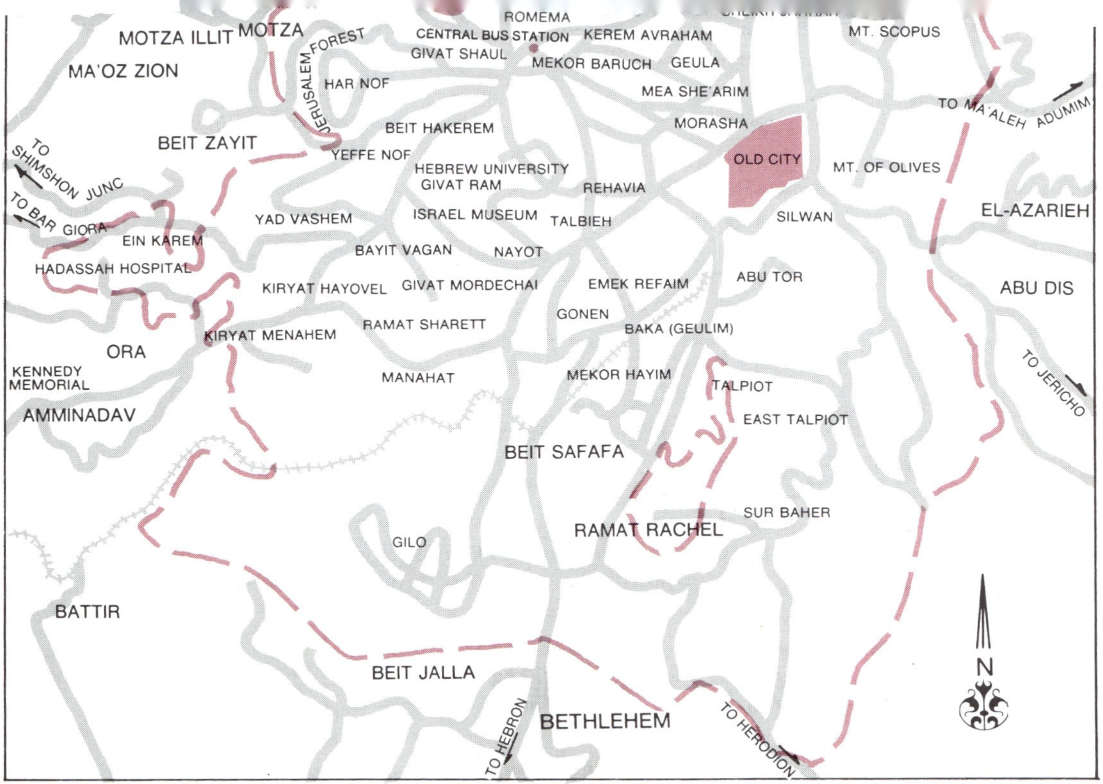
MOTZA ILLIT
MOTZA
MA'OZ ZION
JERUSALEM FOREST
ROMEMA
CENTRAL BUS STATION
GIVAT SHAUL
KEREM AVRAHAM
MEKOR BARUCH
GEULA
MEA SHE'ARIM
MT. SCOPUS
HAR NOF
BEIT HAKEREM
MORASHA
OLD CITY
MT. OF OLIVES
TO MA'ALEH ADUMIM
BEIT ZAYIT
YEFFE NOF
HEBREW UNIVERSITY
GIVAT RAM
REHAVIA
TO SHIMSHON JUNC
TO BAR GIORA
EIN KAREM
HADASSAH HOSPITAL
YAD VASHEM
ISRAEL MUSEUM
TALBIEH
SILWAN
EL-AZARIEH
BAYIT VAGAN
NAYOT
KIRYAT HAYOVEL
GIVAT MORDECHAI
EMEK REFAIM
ABU TOR
ABU DIS
GONEN
BAKA (GEULIM)
RAMAT SHARETT
KIRYAT MENAHEM
ORA
KENNEDY MEMORIAL
MANAHAT
MEKOR HAYIM
TALPIOT
TO JERICHO
EAST TALPIOT
AMMINADAV
BEIT SAFAFA
SUR BAHER
RAMAT RACHEL
GILO
BATTIR
N
BEIT JALLA
BETHLEHEM
TO HEBRON
TO HERODION

illustrated guide to
jerusalem

illustrated guide to jerusalem

Eliyahu Wager

The Jerusalem Publishing House

Keter Publishing House, Jerusalem

Editorial	*Georgette Corcos* *Susan Fogg*
Translation	*Shlomo Ketko* *Stephanie Nakache* *Asher Arbit*
Photography	*Moshe Caine*
Maps	*Chaim Eytan*
Cover Design	*Studio Ehud Avishai, Tel Aviv*
Layout	*Elisse Goldstein*
Paging	*Margalit Bassan*
Production	*Rachel Gilon*

©1988 by G.G. The Jerusalem Publishing House, Ltd.
P.O.B. 7147, Jerusalem, Israel

No part of this book may be reproduced or transmitted in any form or by any means, electronic or mechanical, including photocopying, recording or by any information storage and retrieval system, without the written permission of the Publishers.

Catalog No. 258445

1   2   3   4   5   6   7   8

For sale in the State of Israel only.

Plates by Prizma, Jerusalem
Typeset, printed and bound by Keterpress Enterprises, Jerusalem

Printed in Israel

Table of Contents

FOREWORD BY TEDDY KOLLEK **9**

TOUR No. 1 . . . . **10**
The Early Days of Jerusalem: The Ophel □ City of David Archaeological Garden □ Area G □ Warren's Shaft □ Walls of the City of David □ Gihon Spring □ Siloam Channel □ Hezekiah's Tunnel □ Pool of Siloam (Shiloah) □ Excavation above the southern slope □ En Rogel □ First Temple period tombs □ Zechariah's Tomb □ Tomb of the House of Hezir □ Monument of Absalom □ Tomb of Jehoshaphat.

TOUR No. 2 . . . . **24**
The Temple Mount: The Cup □ the Summer Pulpit □ Yussuf Dome □ Dome of Learning □ Dome of the Rock □ Dome of the Prophet □ Dome of the Ascension □ Elijah's Dome □ Dome of the Spirits □ Dome of the Chain □ Golden Gate □ Solomon's Throne □ Gate of the Tribes □ Gate of Atonement □ The Dark Gate □ Dome of Solomon □ Gate of the Inspector □ The Iron Gate □ Gate of the Cotton Merchants □ Gate of the Bath □ Madrassa el-Uthmanyya □ Fountain of Qayt Bey □ Fountain of Qasem Pasha □ Fig Tree Area □ Dome of Moses □ Gate of the Chain □ Solomon's Stables □ El-Aksa Mosque □ Women's Mosque □ Dome of Yussuf Agha □ Madrassa el-Fakhryya □ The Islamic Museum.

TOUR No. 3 . . . . **42**
Western Wall Excavations

TOUR No. 4 . . . . **52**
The Jewish Quarter: Zion Gate □ Observation point □ Batei Mahseh Square □ Nea Church □ Memorial □ Sephardi synagogues □ Ramban Synagogue □ Hurva Synagogue □ Heart of the Jewish Quarter □ Ashkenazi Compound □ The Cardo □ The Broad Wall □ The Israelite tower □ Western Wall Observation Point □ German Hospice □ Burnt House □ Tiferet Israel Synagogue □ Karaite Synagogue □ Herodian residential quarter □ Old Yishuv Court Museum □ Bikur Holim Hospital □ Other sites in the Jewish Quarter.

TOUR No. 5 . . . . **72**
The Muslim Quarter: Khan es-Sultan □ Tashtimuryya □ Khalidi Library □ Tazyya □ Turkan Khatun □ Tankizyya-Mahkama □ Square of the Gate of the Chain □ Ashrafyya □ Shomrei Hahomot building □ Hammam el-Ein □ Cotton Market □ Iron Gate Street □ Ala ed-Din Street □ HaGai Street □ Harat Sa'adyya □ Havatzelet building □ Sitt Tunshuk □ Takyya □ Rasasyya □ Hebron Street — El-Khalidyya □ Es-Sarayya Street □ Es-Sarayya □ Kirami Street □ The buildings around the markets.

TOUR No. 6 . . . . **86**
From St Stephen's Gate to the Church of the Holy Sepulcher: St Stephen's Gate □ Church of St Anne □ Pool of Bethesda compound □ Via Dolorosa (including nine stations of the Cross along this street and other sites) □ Church of the Holy Sepulcher (including the last five stations of the Cross).

TABLE OF CONTENTS

TOUR No. 7 104
The Christian Quarter: New Gate □ Monastery of Saint Savior □ Latin Patriarchate □ Casa Nova □ Greek Catholic Patriarchate □ Greek Orthodox Patriarchate Museum □ Greek Orthodox Patriarchate □ Ethiopian Patriarchate □ Coptic Patriarchate □ Church of the Redeemer □ Muristan □ Church of St John the Baptist □ Coptic Khan □ Roman Column.

TOUR No. 8 113
The Armenian Quarter: The Kishla □ Cathedral of St James □ Mardigian Museum and Gulbenkian Library □ Church of the House of Annas □ The Armenian Garden □ Church of St Thomas □ St Mark's Church and Convent □ Watson House □ Maronite Church □ Christ Church.

TOUR No. 9 121
From Jaffa Gate to Mount Zion: Jaffa Gate □ The Citadel □ Along the ramparts □ House of Caiaphas □ Dormition Abbey □ The Cenacle □ Tomb of David □ Holocaust Chamber □ Palombo Museum □ Church of St Peter in Gallicantu □ Franciscan Convent □ Greek Orthodox Monastery □ Gobat School.

TOUR No. 10 138
The Ramparts Walk: From Jaffa Gate to Damascus Gate □ From Damascus Gate to St Stephen's Gate □ From the Citadel to Zion Gate □ From Zion Gate to Dung Gate □ Dung Gate □ Zion Park (Beit Shalom Park).

TOUR No. 11 147
From the Tombs of the Kings to Zedekiah's Cave: Kikar Pikud Merkaz (Central Command Square) □ American Colony □ Tombs of the Kings □ St George Cathedral □ The Third Wall □ St Etienne □ Garden Tomb □ Hospice of St Paul □ Damascus Gate □ Zedekiah's Cave.

TOUR No. 12 155
The Mount of Olives: Viri Galilaei □ Russian Church of the Ascension □ Church of the Ascension □ Pelagia Cave □ Eleona Church (Pater Noster) □ Moriah Observation Point □ Jewish cemetery □ Tombs of the Prophets □ War Monument □ Dominus Flevit Church □ Church of Mary Magdalene □ Gethsemane and Church of the Agony □ Grotto of Gethsemane □ Church of the Assumption □ Tomb of Mujir ed-Din □ Church of St Stephen □ Paratroopers' Memorial.

TOUR No. 13 168
The Hinnom Valley: Mamilla Mall □ Huzot Hayozer (Artisans' Quarter) □ Sultan's Pool □ Cinematheque □ Ancient tombs □ The Karaite cemetery □ Later tombs □ Monastery of St Onuphrius.

TOUR No. 14 174
The Beginnings of the New City: Montefiore Windmill □ Mishkenot Sha'ananim □ Yemin Moshe □ Herod family tomb □ Pontifical Biblical Institute □ Hebrew Union College □ Mahaneh Israel □ Agron Street □ Mamilla Cemetery □ Nahalat Shiva □ Buildings in Jaffa Road □ Russian Compound.

TOUR No. 15 185
The Street of the Prophets and Vicinity: Herut (Liberty) Square–the Davidka □ English Hospital □ Kamenitz Hotel □ The Pasha's house □ Joseph Navon Bey house □ Evangelical Church □ Bikur Holim Hospital □ Israel Medical Association

TABLE OF CONTENTS

building □ German Hospital □ St Joseph Convent □ William Holman Hunt's residence □ Thabor House □ Ethiopia Street □ Ethiopian Church □ B'nai B'rith building □ Yad Sarah □ Ticho House □ Beit David neighborhood □ Rothschild Hospital □ German Evangelical School □ O.R.T. School–Probst Building □ Ethiopian Consulate □ Italian Hospital □ Mahanaim House □ Armenian Mosaic □ Nissan Bak neighborhood.

TOUR No. 16 197
From Gan Daniel to Mea She'arim: Gan Daniel □ The Armenian buildings □ Former French Consulate □ Bergheim Houses □ Bible Society building □ Town Hall □ Feil Hotel building □ Tsahal Square □ St Louis (French) Hospital □ Notre Dame □ Morasha Quarter (Musrara) □ Church of St Paul □ Mea She'arim.

TOUR No. 17 205
From Nahalat Zvi to the Bukharan Quarter: Nahalat Zvi □ Sha'ar Hapinah □ Beit Yisrael □ New Beit Yisrael □ Bukharan Quarter.

TOUR No. 18 211
From Sanhedria to the Tomb of Simon the Just: Tombs of Sanhedria □ Eshkolot Cave □ Givat HaTahmoshet (Ammunition Hill) □ Tomb of Simon the Just.

TOUR No. 19 215
Upper Jaffa Road to Mahaneh Yehuda: Jaffa Road–King George V Avenue intersection □ Ezrat Yisrael □ Even Yisrael □ Sephardi Orphanage □ Sukkat Shalom □ Mishkenot Yisrael □ Mazkeret Moshe □ Ohel Moshe □ Mahaneh Yehuda Market □ Etz-Hayim Yeshiva □ Sundial Building □ District Health Office □ Mahaneh Yehuda Police Station □ Alliance Israelite Universelle □ Clal Center.

TOUR No. 20 221
From Beit Ya'akov to the Laemel School: Beit Ya'akov □ Mahaneh Yehuda neighborhood □ Sha'arei Zedek, Ohel Shlomo and Sha'arei Yerushalayim □ Batei Sayidoff □ Sha'arei Zedek building □ Mekor Baruch □ Ohalei Simha □ Kerem □ Schneller □ Kerem Avraham □ Yegia Kapayim □ Ahva □ Zikhron Moshe □ The Laemel School.

TOUR No. 21 227
From Zion Square to Sha'arei Hessed: Zion Square □ Ben Yehuda Street □ Schmidt School □ Religious Teachers' Seminary □ Histadrut building □ Talitha Kumi □ Artists' House □ Beit Ha'am □ Knesset Yisrael □ Shevet Ahim □ Nahalat Zion □ Zikhron Ahim and Nahalat Ya'akov □ Nahalat Ahim □ Neveh Bezalel □ Nahalat Zadok □ Sha'arei Hessed.

TOUR No. 22 234
From Rehavia to the German Colony: Rehavia □ Talbieh (Komemiut) □ German Colony.

TOUR No. 23 245
From the Railway Station to Ratisbonne Monastery: Railway Station □ The Khan □ St Andrew's Church □ Ketef Hinnom □ Liberty Bell Garden □ King David Hotel □ Y.M.C.A. □ Convent of the Soeurs du Rosaire □ Center for Conservative Judaism □ Terra Sancta College □ Hechal Shlomo □ The Great Synagogue □ The National Institutions □ Yeshurun Synagogue □ St Pierre de Ratisbonne Monastery.

TABLE OF CONTENTS

TOUR No. 24 255
The President's Residence and Vicinity: Van Leer Institute ◻ Israel Academy of Science and Humanities ◻ The President's residence ◻ L.A. Mayer Memorial — Institute for Islamic Art ◻ Jerusalem Theater ◻ Hansen Hospital.

TOUR No. 25 258
Sites in West Jerusalem: The Military Cemetery ◻ Mount Herzl ◻ Yad Vashem Memorial ◻ Hadassah Medical Center, Ein Karem ◻ Model of Jerusalem in the Second Temple period at the Holyland Hotel ◻ Romema ◻ Givat Shaul ◻ Lifta

TOUR No. 26 270
Givat Ram and Vicinity: North Givat Ram (Binyanei Ha'uma-Convention Center, Hilton Hotel, Wohl Rose Garden, the Menorah, the Knesset, HaKirya–David Ben-Gurion Government Center, Beit Yad Labanim) ◻ Hebrew University Campus ◻ Israel Museum ◻ Monastery of the Cross.

TOUR No. 27 279
Ein Karem: Church of St John the Baptist ◻ Sisters of Zion Convent ◻ Tour of the village ◻ Church of the Visitation ◻ Russian Convent ◻ St John in the Desert Monastery.

TOUR No. 28 283
Sites in the Northeast of the City: The Hebrew University Campus, Mount Scopus ◻ Hadassah Hospital Center, Mount Scopus ◻ The Jerusalem War Cemetery ◻ The Rockefeller Museum.

TRIPS BY CAR OR BUS

TOUR No. 29 289
Sites in the Southeast of the City: Gilo ◻ Talpiot ◻ Arnona ◻ Ramat Rachel ◻ East Talpiot ◻ The Promenade ◻ Abu Tor (Givat Hananya) Observation Point.

TOUR No. 30 296
Givat Shapira — Neveh Ya'akov

TOUR No. 31 299
Ramot Allon — Nebi Samwil

TOUR No. 32 301
Ora — Amminadav — Kennedy Memorial

TOUR No. 33 303
Bethany (El-Azarieh)

INDEX 305

ACKNOWLEDGMENTS 312

ראש העיריה
رئيس البلدية
MAYOR OF JERUSALEM

Jerusalem is a city of beauty, of ancient monuments, of sites holy to three great religions, venerated by Jews, Christians and Moslems throughout the world. At the same time, it is a growing and thriving modern city.

The growth of Jerusalem in the past two decades together with exciting archaeological discoveries have added many new sites linking the past, present and future of our city. It was often said that Jerusalem is the only city for which the Bible is the guidebook. But the fact is that to experience Jerusalem today, one also needs a companion guide.

Eliahu Wager's guide introduces the visitor to Jerusalem from the time of King David to today. It gives the opportunity of acquiring an intimate knowledge of the Holy City by carefully planned itineraries of tours and excursions covering the Old City and the New. Every place of interest is described, its history brought to life through vivid descriptions. All practical details are listed, including bus lines.

The large collection of illustrations highlights the beauty of Jerusalem and enhances the special character of this colorful, vibrant, many-faceted city where black caftans, kaffiyehs, punk hairstyles or staid business suits are all part of the scenery. But however Jerusalemites differ, they have one thing in common: their pride in their city.

Teddy Kollek

TOUR No. 1

THE EARLY DAYS OF JERUSALEM

Details of tour: Includes the City of David, the Kidron Valley and the burial sites in the valley. The focal point of the tour is the remains of the earliest times of Jerusalem via the City of David Archaeological Garden. We shall also see part of the Kidron Valley and the "City of Tombs" from the First Temple period and end with the Jewish burial monuments of the Second Temple period.

Distance covered: 2 km (1½ miles)
Time: approx. 5 hours (including 1 hour walking in water through a tunnel, using flashlights)
Transportation: Buses No 1, 38 and 99 (to the Dung Gate)
Parking lot opposite Dung Gate for private vehicles
Starting point: Ophel Road
End of tour: at the starting point or at Jericho Road
The Sites: 1. The Ophel; 2. The City of David Archaeological Garden: Area G; 3. Warren's Shaft; 4. Walls of the City of David; 5. Gihon Spring; 6. Siloam Channel; 7. Hezekiah's Tunnel; 8. Pool of Siloam (Shiloah); 9. Excavation above the southern slope; 10. En Rogel; 11. First Temple period tombs; 12. Zechariah's Tomb. 13. Tomb of the House of Hezir; 14. Monument of Absalom; 15. Tomb of Jehoshaphat.

FOREWORD

Jerusalem is one of the most ancient cities in the world. It was founded some 5000 years ago near the Gihon Spring in the Kidron Valley. King David conquered the city from the Jebusites in 1000 BCE, established the "City of David" and made it his capital, the capital of the united Kingdom of Israel. The site contains the remains of Biblical Jerusalem, and has attracted many archaeologists since the middle of the 19th century when the exploration of the Holy Land began. In 1867, the first excavations were undertaken by the British Palestine Exploration Fund conducted by C. Warren and were followed by seven other expeditions. In 1977, one hundred and ten years after the first excavation, The City of David Association was founded, with the purpose of expanding archaeological research of the City of David. Seven seasons of digs headed by Prof. Y. Shiloh have taken place between 1978 and 1984. In two out of the six sites excavated the surveys have been completed, and they are included in The City of David Archaeological Garden, which was opened to the public in 1985.

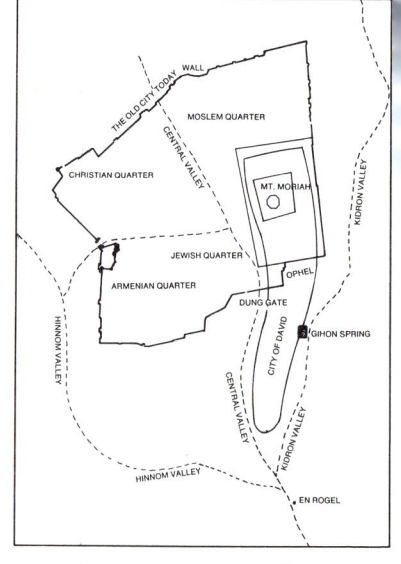

City of David and Ancient Jerusalem. ▲

Map of the tour. ▶

THE EARLY DAYS OF JERUSALEM

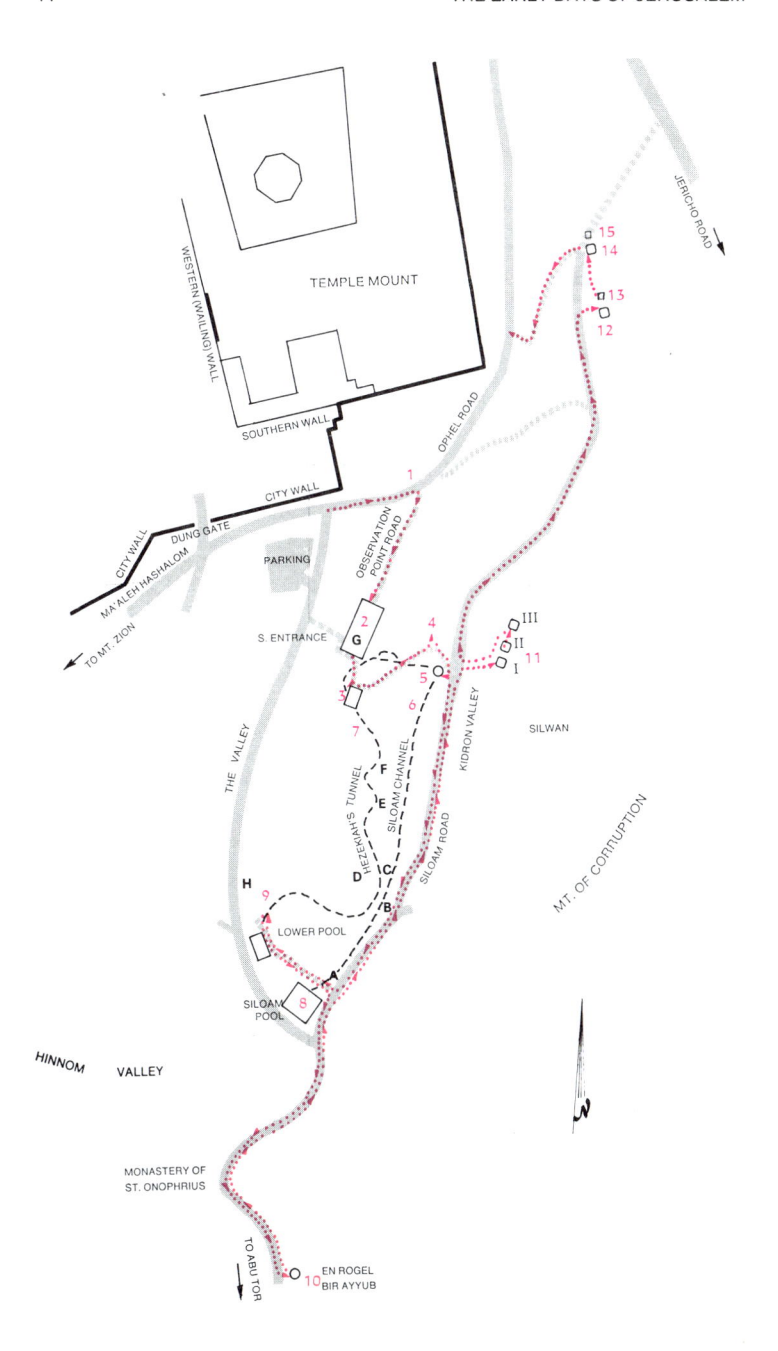

11

THE TOUR

1. The Ophel where the tour begins is the plain north of the City of David where the road passes between the wall of the Temple Mount to the north and the southern slope of the City of David. The Ophel is 720 m (2360 ft). above sea level (as compared to the Temple Mount which is 734 m (2408 ft). It is mentioned in the Bible as "wall" or "tower" of Ophel in the City of David (II Chr. 27:3; Neh. 3:27). The fenced area, which can be seen from the road, south of the Temple Mount wall, contains many remains from the First Temple period and from later periods. (See Tour No. 3, Temple Mount excavations.) From the Ophel, the hill of the City of David slopes southward to its lowest point (625 m — 2050 ft) near the Pool of Siloam. It is protected in the east, west and south by deep river beds. In the east, by the Kidron Valley, in the west and south, by the Central Valley. (In the time of King David the city covered approx. 60000 sq m (15 acres). After the building of the Temple it expanded to about 160000 sq m (40 acres). (See map.)

2. The City of David Archaeological Garden — Area G. Visiting hours: daily from 9.00 am to 5.00 pm.

From the Ophel we walk southward and stop on the path from which we have a panoramic view: to the east towards the Kidron Valley and the village of Silwan, are the burial sites from the First Temple period; to the north, up the Kidron Valley, we can see monumental structures of the Second Temple period. We then go southward, down the paved Observation Path to the northern entrance of Area G. On our way down we can see to the east the steep slope of the hill where the houses of the City of David stood, just like the houses of the village of Silwan, on the opposite slope of the Kidron Valley, today.

Between the houses of the village, the square openings of burial caves from the First Temple period can be seen.

From the entrance of the fenced Archaeological Garden (Area G) the excavated site is surrounded by a path which allows the visitor to get a better view of the various structures, some of which have been reinforced and some reconstructed. From

General view of the Ophel showing the southern wall of the Temple Mount, the Archaeological Garden and the Ophel Road in the forefront.

THE EARLY DAYS OF JERUSALEM

the Garden entrance we go down several iron steps leading to a part of the path opposite the structures of Area G (they have been given numbers and are explained in detail on signs at the site). These structures include:

① **The city wall** built during the time of the Hasmoneans (Second Temple period). It is mentioned by Josephus Flavius as the "First Wall".

② **The northern tower of the wall.**

③ **The southern tower of the wall.** The wall and its towers were used also during the Byzantine period.

④ **The stone stepped structure** which was built in King David's time and was in use until the destruction of the Kingdom of Judah by the Babylonians (in 586 BCE). This is probably what remained of "David's Fortress" from the period of the Judean kings. It is 17 m (56 ft) high and its remains were used as a foundation for the Second Temple period wall.

⑤ **The House of Ahiel,** a typical Israelite house from the time of the late Judean kings, which was destroyed during the Babylonian conquest and reconstructed by the Shiloh archaeological mission. Its name derives from the inscription on a pottery fragment found in the house. The entrance in the southern wall leads to a hall with four pillars that supported the partially-reconstructed ceiling. The house is adjacent to two cubicles, one of which had a toilet, testifying that the houses in the area belonged to wealthy residents.

⑥ **The Burnt Room,** part of the remains of an Israelite house of the time of the First Temple, burnt down by the Babylonians during the destruction of Jerusalem. Traces of soot left by the fire are still visible. Several iron arrowheads (Israelite) and bronze ones (Babylonian) were found on the floor as well as furniture, identified as imported from Syria by the kind of wood it is made of. This is the first discovery of that period of this kind ever made in Israel).

⑦ **The House of the Bullae** from the time of the late Judean kings in which were found 51 clay seal impressions (*bullae*, in Greek), bearing well-known Biblical names such as "Gemaryah son of Shaphan", King Jehoiakim's scribe mentioned in the Book of Jeremiah 36:10. Forty

Clay seals from the end of the Judean Kirlgdom found in the destruction level of the City of David, bearing personal names from that period.

TOUR No. 1

Area G: city wall; southern tower; stepped structure; House of Ahiel.

three of the names are of high officials. The clay impressions were attached to documents which were burnt. This is the largest collection of seal impressions ever found in Israel. It is now on show at the Israel Museum.

⑧ **The Canaanite Fortress** includes remnants of the walls and stones of the base structure (the podium) of the Canaanite city's fortress (the acropolis), dating to the 14th and 13th centuries BCE. It could be the "stronghold of Zion" conquered by King David, mentioned in the Second Book of Samuel (5:7).

3. Warren's Shaft Visiting hours: daily from 9.00 am to 5.00 pm. Entrance fee. (An explanatory sheet and detailed pamphlet are on sale at the site.)

From Area G we walk along a paved and sign-posted path down to the bottom of the Kidron Valley. Turning right, we come upon a stone structure bearing a sign with an arrow and the indication "Warren's Shaft". The site is named after the British scholar Charles Warren, who was the first to bring it to light in 1867 while excavating for the British Palestine Exploration Fund. The site was explored again by Charles Parker of Britain between 1909 and 1911. Warren's Shaft was uncovered again in 1978 by the City of David Expedition, cleared, and made accessible to visitors. This is the city's water conduit which was dug during the First Temple period and used by the residents of the northern section of the city. In time of siege it was possible to draw water from the Gihon Spring from here without having to go outside the city walls. Similar water systems were uncovered in Megiddo, Hazor, Gezer and Gibeon, all dating from the period of the Israelite and Judean kings. What distin-

THE EARLY DAYS OF JERUSALEM

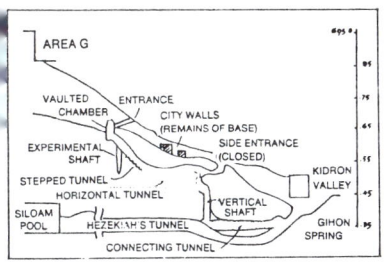

Section of Warren's Shaft.

guishes the Warren Shaft is a natural vertical shaft which the hewers encountered and used to complete their water system. We then go down a spiral iron staircase to a vaulted chamber (2) and continue to a stepped oblique tunnel (3). On the left we can see an unfinished shaft, which was probably an attempt to dig another channel (4). On the right is a side entrance (5) which was dug during the Second Temple period. Through a horizontal tunnel (6) we reach a vertical shaft (7), from which buckets were lowered by ropes, 13 m (43 ft) down to the tunnel (8) connecting the lower shaft to the water of the Gihon Spring (9).

The City of David Archaeological Garden will, in its final stage, encompass other archaeological sites for which there will then be more details available. Since these sites are accessible today, we thought it useful to give some information concerning them (4 and 8 below):

4. Walls of the City of David Coming out of Warren's Shaft, we continue down the paved path. On the left are large rough stone blocks arranged in the form of an L. They are part of the wall and tower of the Canaanite city which stood here during the 2nd millennium BCE. They were discovered by Professor Kathleen Kenyon, the British archaeologist who excavated here between 1961 and 1967, and had a retaining wall built to prevent possible landslides. The Canaanite city is mentioned as "Ursalimum" in the Egyptian Execration Texts (18th–19th centuries BCE, the Period of the Patriarchs). Above the Canaanite wall are the remains of another wall from the period of the Judean kings, whose stones are smaller and cut differently. A projection in this wall may have been part of a gate tower facing the spring. The perimeter of the city at each period can be determined by the line of the walls. The

Staircase leading down to Warren's Shaft.

lower walls, on the eastern slope, belong to the Canaanite period. The wall of the City of David is higher up and the Hasmonean (Hellenistic) walls are at the highest point (in Area G). Other walls of the City of David were uncovered near the Pool of Siloam (See 8).

5. The Gihon Spring Visiting hours: Sunday through Thursday 9.00 am to 5.00 pm. A flashlight is needed for the visit.

We continue walking along the paved path until it joins the road which follows the Kidron riverbed. Turning right (southward) we find twelve steps leading down under a small stone building to a wide vaulted entrance. From this point one can hear and see, on the right, the water running from the spring in a dark cave under the steps.

The Gihon was the main source of water for Jerusalem and the first settlement of the city was located near the spring. Pottery fragments from this period were found in holes in the bedrock.

The Gihon is mentioned in the Bible in connection with the anointing of King Solomon (I Kings 1:45). The spring is also called the Fountain of the Virgin and in Arabic Umm ed-Daradj or Ein Sit Maryam.

The original entrance was closed up in the time of the king of Judah Hezekiah, so that the spring would be hidden from the enemy during the siege of Jerusalem by Sennacherib, king of Assyria. It was rediscovered following an earthquake in the 15th century, at which time the steps and the entrance as it is today were built. The spring originates in a natural cave and gushes forth intermittently (karstic syphon spring) for periods of 30 to 40 minutes, an average of five times a day, and supplied the city with between 200 to 1100 cubic meters of water a day.

Steps leading down to the Gihon Spring.

6. Siloam Channel From the Gihon Spring a channel runs south at the foot of the hill of the City of David. Part of it is a rock-hewn tunnel and the roof is blocked by large masses of stone. This channel, dating from the First Temple period (before Hezekiah's time), carried the water from the spring to the Pool of Siloam, south of the City of David. "Windows" were cut along the channel through which the water was directed to irrigate the area along the Kidron Valley (this is the "King's Garden" mentioned several times in the Bible).

The Siloam Road runs beside the channel. Those walking through the tunnel will return by this road upon leaving the tunnel. (See 7)

We walk on from the Gihon southward to the Pool of Siloam. On the way we can see several interesting sites within the areas that are still being excavated:

1. Part of the Siloam Channel in which are three "windows" for irrigating the King's Garden.

2. Remains of a round tower (in Area A), above the channel. This could be the "Tower of Siloam" mentioned in Luke 13:4.

3. Further south, we can see part of a long supporting wall, above which are remains of a structure from the days of the Kingdom of Judah, where a Hebrew inscription was brought to light (Area D).

7. The Tunnel (Hezekiah's Tunnel, also known as the Siloam Tunnel). We enter the tunnel just left of the outflow point of the Gihon Spring. The tunnel is cut in the rock and the water of the spring flows along its floor to the Pool of Siloam to the south of the City of David. The tunnel is dark and a flashlight is needed to walk through it. It is also advisable to wear clothes and shoes suitable for walking in water. The tunnel was dug during the reign of King Hezekiah, as part of his preparations to withstand the siege of the Assyrians in 701 BCE (II Chr. 32:2–3; II Kings 20:20). The tunnel, 533 m (581 yd) long, is S-shaped (the distance between the spring and the pool is only 320 m (350 yd). The reason for the twisting route is probably related to the types of rock or natural cracks in the rock.

View of the tunnel.

The height of the tunnel ranges from 1.45 m to 5 m (1.6 to 5.5. yd). Its average width is 60 cm (24 in) and its slope is only 6 per thousand (a total of 30 cm — 12 in throughout its length). The level of the water in the tunnel at present is between 20–80 cm (8 in–32 in), depending on the season. The tunnel was hewn by two teams of workers starting at opposite ends, working toward each other. The moment when the two teams met is described in an inscription found on the wall of the tunnel in 1880. It is known as the Siloam Inscription and was examined by Prof. C. Schick; it is now in the Istanbul Museum. This inscription, dating to the reign of Hezekiah, is the longest ever found of the First Temple period. It is written in ancient Hebrew script and provides a lively description: "...when (the tunnel) was driven through... (were still... (axe)s, each man toward his fellow, and while there were still three cubits to be cut through (there was heard) the voice of a man calling to his fellow, for there was an overlap in the rock on the right (and on the left). And the tunnel was driven through, the quarrymen hewed (the rock), each man toward his fellow, axe against axe, and the water flowed from the spring toward the reservoir for 1200 cubits and the height of the rock above the head(s) of the quarrymen was 100 cubits."

8. The Pool of Siloam King Hezekiah's tunnel which conveys the water of the Gihon Spring opens into a small pool in which the remains of stone columns are visible. This may be the pool mentioned in Isaiah 22:9 as "the lower pool". It has been erroneously called the Siloam Pool since the Second Temple period. The pool from the days of Hezekiah, which the Siloam channel reached, and whose name was preserved until the period of the return from the Babylonian exile in 536 BCE, is located further down the valley. The site of the pool is now planted with fruit trees, and is called Birket el-Hamra (the Red Pool). The water of the Pool of Siloam was used for irrigating the "King's Garden" (II Kings 25:4, Jer. 39:4; Neh. 3:15). During the Second Temple period, Herod built a bathhouse surrounded by columns in the lower pool. Later a Roman bathhouse *(tetranympheum)* was built here; it could be reached by steps from the level of the present road near the Dung Gate. The Byzantine empress Eudocia built a church over the bathhouse to commemorate the miracle of the blind man who was healed by washing with the water of the Pool of Siloam at Jesus's command (John 9:7). During the Ottoman period a mosque — whose minaret still exists today — was built on the remains of the church.

During the Second Temple period, the beginning of the tunnel was called the Spring of Shiloah (Siloam) since the opening of the Gihon had been blocked during Hezekiah's reign, and the spring itself was forgotten. Water was drawn from the opening of the tunnel for the Temple for the "water libation ceremony" during the Feast of Water Drawing. On the eve of the Feast of Tabernacles, the Temple priests went down to the spring and drew water in

The Siloam inscription.

a golden vessel. They would then pour the water on the altar and proceed with the Prayer for Rain. There was a procession down to Siloam and back accompanied by joyful songs and dancing. It was said: "He who has not seen the celebration of the Feast of Drawing Water has never seen real joy". The surplus of the Gihon water flowed through a channel from the small pool at the end of the tunnel opening to the orchards across the road. The channel is visible as we walk down an unpaved track to the Kidron Valley road. It was cut in the rock at the ridge of the City of David, and conveyed the surplus water from the two pools. Today, the Pool of Siloam is not in use and the channel conducts the surplus water from the lower pool only. A path above the pool leads north to an excavation site above the slope (9). Those interested in visiting it can climb the path and return the same way.

9. The excavations on the southern slope The French archaeologist R. Weill explored in the southern part of the City of David above the Pool of Siloam in 1913–1914 on a plot of land purchased by Baron de Rothschild. Weill uncovered two

The Pool of Siloam.

Weill excavations: quarry and cave openings.

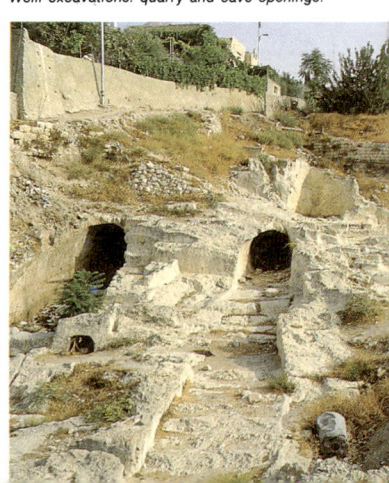

large caves in the rock which had been used as quarries during the Roman period. He believed that these were the tombs of the kings of the House of David — an opinion which has been rejected today. He also found a Greek inscription, which was the first evidence that a synagogue existed here in the first century CE, in the Second Temple period (probably after Herod's reign).

The inscription reads "Theodotos son of Vettenos, priest and head of the synagogue, son and grandson of the head of the synagogue...". It is on display at the Rockefeller Museum.

Remains of several walls of the City of David from the Second Temple period were discovered by the British archaeologists C. Bliss and A. Dickie in 1894. Y. Shiloh's expedition discovered remains from the First Temple period nearby (Area H). Remains of a wall of the same period were also found south of the eastern slope (Areas D and E). The 1928 expedition of J. Crowfoot and G. Fitzgerald discovered remains of a wall and a gate (identified as the Valley Gate) dating to the First Temple period, in the northwest of the City of David area.

10. En Rogel We shall go another 150 m (165 yd) south along the Kidron Valley road, turning left after the second bend. The spring of En Rogel, outside the City of David, was on the border between Judah and Benjamin, and is mentioned frequently in the Bible. Adonijah's abortive attempt to succeed his father King David (Kings I, 1:9) took place at En Rogel. The spring became a well, called Bir-Ayyub ("Job's Well") by the Arabs, who believe that Job was cured of his leprosy after bathing here.

In 1888 Jews from the Yemen settled in the southern part of the village of Silwan, opposite the spring of En Rogel, but were obliged to abandon their homes during the Arab riots of 1929 and 1936. Some of the abandoned houses still stand. North of these structures, is a two storey-house with a tiled roof, built by the Meyuhas family in 1873, which remained their home until the time of the British Mandate. Going back to the road, we shall continue northward until we are opposite the Gihon Spring.

11. Tombs from the First Temple Period The village of Silwan stands on the slopes of the south part of the Mount of Olives, originally called the Mount of Anointing since the priests were anointed here. In Isaiah's time pagan altars were built there and it became known as the Mount of Offence (Kings II, 23:13). The Arab name Silwan is a corruption of the New Testament name Siloam, which in turn is a corruption of the Hebrew name Shiloah. Between the houses we glimpse

The village of Silwan and the Kidron Valley.

the mouths of caves and several prominent monolithic buildings, some of which we saw from the observation path at the beginning of this tour. One of the sole vestiges of Jerusalem in the period of the Kings of Judah is a magnificent cemetery for the well-to-do and notables. The burial caves were hewn in the virgin rock on the east slope of the Kidron Valley, facing the City of David. Most of the burial structures were destroyed in the Roman-Byzantine period, and the caves were occupied by priests who engraved crosses and Greek inscriptions on the walls. Many of the burial chambers today are incorporated into the village houses and serve as storerooms, wells, hen-houses, etc. Three famous burial structures should be visited:

I **The tomb of "... Yahu who is over the house"** On the main street of the village, behind the flight of steps leading to a house, appears to be a square hewn from the rock foundation. The ancient Hebrew inscriptions, originally in its upper part, have been transferred to the British Museum. This may have been the tomb of "Shebna who is over the house", mentioned in Isaiah (22:15–17).

II **Tomb incorporated into a house** The steps before the tomb of Yahu lead to the entrance of this tomb. Traces of the ancient inscription are still visible. The wording is similar to that on the tomb of Yahu.

III **The Tomb of Pharaoh's Daughter** Hewn in the rock, this impressive square, monolithic structure, at the north end of the village, was investigated in the 19th century. The remnants of ancient Hebrew characters found on its facade, probably part of the names of those buried there, are no longer visible. The tomb is Egyptian in style; it was surmounted by a pyramid, traces of which can still be seen.

Further north along the Kidron Valley, on the slopes of the Mount of Olives, to our right, are many Jewish tombs. Some are ancient and some date from the last hundred years. This is the lower edge of the large Jewish cemetery (that extends from here to the top of the Mount). This part of the Kidron Valley is called the Valley of Jehoshaphat. According to the prophecy in the Book of Joel (3:2), here the Last Judgment will take place. Popular belief holds that the resurrection of the dead will also take place here. These traditions and legends are shared by Jews, Christians and Muslims, who all have holy places in the valley.

12. The Tomb of Zechariah The first monument on the right, built towards the end of the Second Temple period, is a cube-shaped structure crowned by a pyramid, standing 12 m (39 ft) high. Along its four sides run columns adorned with Ionic capitals topped by an Egyptian-style cornice, a style widespread in the late Second Temple period. The monument has no burial chamber. A late 15th-century tradition connects the monument with the prophet Zechariah whom Joash, king of Judah had stoned to death (Chronicles II, 24:20–22). The first holy books printed in Jerusalem contain an illustration of the monument. Jews in Jerusalem see great merit in being buried near the tomb of Zechariah and this has contributed to the development of the cemetery from here to the top of the Mount of Olives.

13. The Tomb of the Sons of Hezir The next monument to the north, hewn in the rock, is the tomb of the Hezir family. A Hebrew inscription, discovered here in 1854, gives the names of the six brothers buried here. The priestly Hezir family is mentioned in the Book of Nehemiah (10:21) and in Chronicles I (24:15). The

Tomb of Pharaoh's Daughter.

21   THE EARLY DAYS OF JERUSALEM

Valley of Jehoshaphat: on the right, the Tomb of Zechariah.

Tomb of the Sons of Hezir.

façade of the monument has Doric columns; the architrave above them bears the inscription. The monument is in the Hellenistic-Egyptian style, of the Hasmonean period (mid-2nd century BCE). There are two closed-off entrances to the monument: one on the side of the Tomb of Zechariah, and the other, on the side of the Jewish cemetery above the monument. Steps lead from the entrances to a first chamber, and from there to a central chamber. This opens on to three burial chambers. On the walls of the rooms are hewn niches where the coffins were placed.

The monument is popularly known as the "leper chamber", since it is said that it sheltered King Uzziah when he was struck with leprosy (Kings II, 15). According to Christian tradition, St Joseph is buried here, together with Jesus' brother, James, and Simon the Just.

Top: Gable with frieze above the Tomb of Jehoshaphat.
Bottom: Monument of Absalom.

THE EARLY DAYS OF JERUSALEM

14. The Monument of Absalom The most impressive of the burial monuments on the slope of the Mount of Olives is the one popularly known as the Tomb of Absalom, King David's son. The Bible relates that "in his lifetime (he) had taken and reared up for himself a pillar... and he called the pillar after his own name..." (Samuel II, 18:18). However, this monument is of the first century BCE — nearly a thousand years later than the time of Absalom. Because Absalom rebelled against his father, King David, the popular belief that the monument is associated with him had the curious effect that devout Jews, Muslims and Christians would throw stones at it whenever they passed by, with the result that in time the stones almost hid the edifice.

The base of the monument is a square, 8 m (26 ft) high monolith topped by a round drum rising into a concave conical roof, built from hewn stones. The monument reaches a height of over 20 m (66 ft). The base is fronted by Ionic half-columns topped by an architrave with Doric friezes, and an Egyptian-style cornice. At the top of the cone is a lotus flower calyx engraved in the stone. Two burial chambers are hewn in the lower part with an opening in the ceiling. In the 1950s some archaeologists excavated at the foot of the Tomb of Absalom and of the Cave of Jehoshaphat (15) searching for a treasure mentioned in the "Copper Scroll" (one of the Dead Sea Manuscripts found in the Judean desert).

15. The Tomb of Jehoshaphat is slightly to the north of the Monument of Absalom. Steps lead up to the wide entrance, over which is a triangular gable with a frieze decorated with acanthus leaves, vines and fruit motifs. The opening (barred today) leads to the entrance hall, and here a passage branches off to seven other chambers containing burial niches.

The tomb, as the name implies, is believed to be that of King Jehoshaphat who, it is said in the Bible, "was buried with his fathers in the city of David his father" (Kings I, 22:50).

This part of the Kidron is called the "Valley of Jehoshaphat". Our tour ends here. We can take the path up to the Ophel Road, to reach the Dung Gate and the car park opposite, or we can go up to the Jericho-Jerusalem road.

TOUR No. 2

THE TEMPLE MOUNT

Details of tour: This is a Muslim holy place; modest attire is required. Visitors are requested to remove their shoes before entering the mosques.
Distance covered: 800 m (1½ mile)
Time: approx. 3 hours
Transportation: Buses Nos 1, 38, 99 from the Central Bus Station
Parking lot near the Dung Gate for private vehicles
Starting point and end of tour: Moghrabi Gate (Moors' Gate)
Visiting hours: 8 am to 3 pm, closed on Fridays
Admission to the esplanade: free; to the mosques: tickets to be bought at ticket office near the Moghrabi Gate (Moor's Gate)
The Sites: 1. The Cup; 2. the Summer Pulpit; 3. Yussuf Dome; 4. Dome of Learning; 5. Dome of the Rock; 6. Dome of the Prophet; 7. Dome of the Ascension; 8. Elijah's Dome; 9. Dome of the Spirits; 10 Dome of the Chain; 11. Golden Gate; 12. Solomon's Throne; 13. Gate of the Tribes; 14. Gate of Atonement; 15. The Dark Gate; 16. Dome of Solomon; 17. Gate of the Inspector; 18. The Iron Gate; 19. Gate of the Cotton Merchants; 20. Gate of the Bath; 21. Madrassa el-Uthmanyya; 22. Fountain of Qayt Bey; 23. Fountain of Qasem Pasha; 24. Fig Tree Area; 25. Dome of Moses; 26. Gate of the Chain; 27. Solomon's Stables; 28. El-Aksa Mosque; 29. Women's Mosque; 30. Dome of Yussuf Agha; 31. Madrassa el-Fakhryya; 32. The Islamic Museum.
A sign indicates that Jews should not enter the Temple Mount area (this is forbidden by the *halacha* because of ritual impurity).

FOREWORD

The Temple Mount area (Haram esh-Sharif — The Noble Sanctuary) is the rectangular esplanade in the southeastern corner of the Old City, at the top of Mount Moriah (about 740m — 2427 ft) high. It is bounded on all sides by walls, those on its east and south sides forming part of the rampart of the Old City. The lower part of all the walls is from Herod's time (1st century BCE). The Temple Mount covers approximately 144,000 sq m — 35.5 acres), about a sixth of the area of the Old City. At its center is a platform about 4 m (13 ft) higher than the surrounding area, which occupies approximately 23,000 sq m (9.2 acres). The Dome of the Rock (famous for its golden dome), built over the Foundation Stone *(Even Shetyyah)*, is at the center of the raised platform. Eight large staircases lead up to this area, one, two, or three on each of the four sides. There are two other structures in the Temple Mount area: the el-Aksa Mosque and the Islamic Museum. In addition, there are about a hundred other open structures from different periods, starting from the 7th century CE. At present, there are eleven entrance gates to the esplanade: three in the northern wall, seven in the western wall, and the sealed Mercy Gate (or Golden Gate) in the eastern wall. With the exception of the Mercy Gate, all the other gates were planned and built during the Mameluke period (from the 13th to the 16th century) and were restored by the Ottoman Sultan, Suleiman the Magnificent (1520–1566).

The Temple Mount is identified with Mount Moriah, the site of the Sacrifice of Isaac (Genesis 22:2). Here also was the threshing floor purchased by King David from Arauna the Jebusite to erect an altar to the Lord (II Samuel 24:18–25). It was on Mount Moriah that King Solomon built the First Temple in c. 950 BCE (II Chronicles

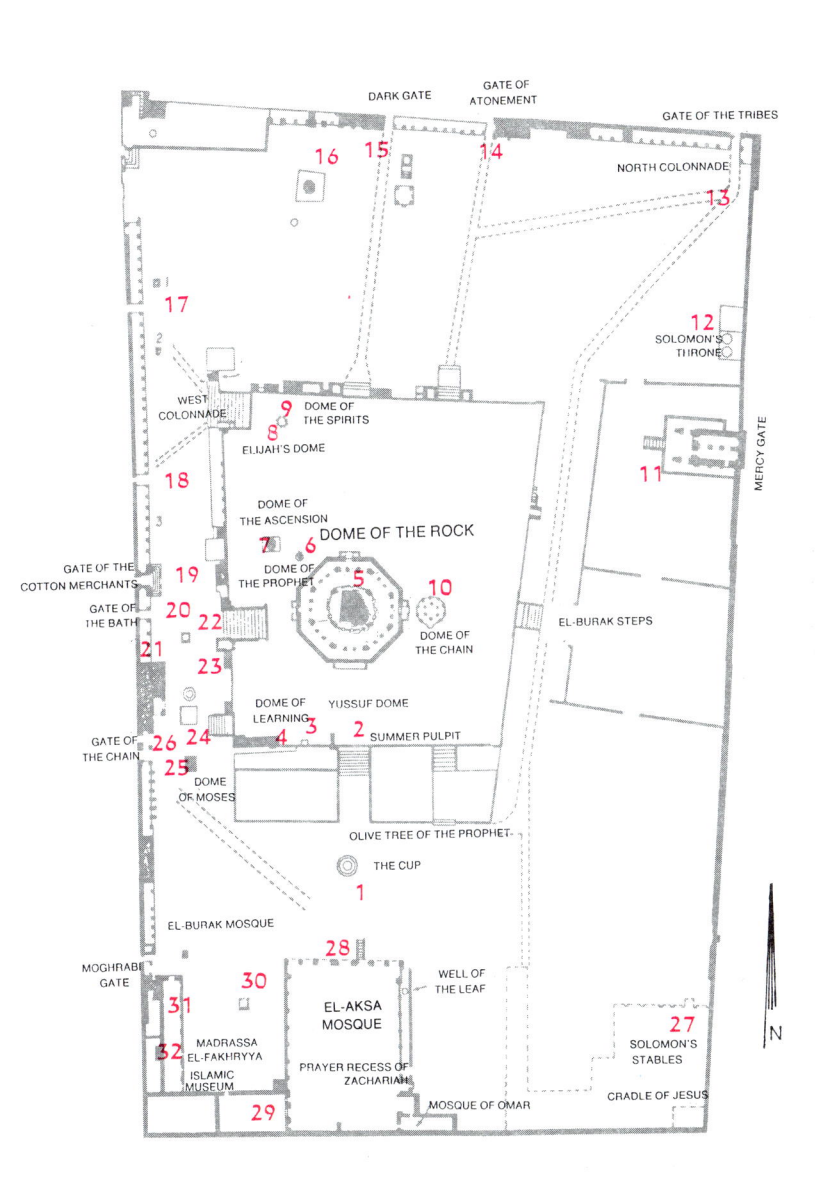

THE TEMPLE MOUNT

Map of the tour.

3:1). Its construction took seven years; thousands of woodcutters, stonemasons and porters were employed as well as craftsmen and Phoenician wood and metal workers sent by Hiram, King of Tyre. The Temple became the religious, spiritual and national center of the Jewish people. In 586 BCE the king of Babylon, Nebuchadnezzer, attacked Jerusalem, destroyed the Temple and deported its inhabitants to Babylon.

In 536 BCE Cyrus II of Persia allowed the Jews to return to their homeland and to rebuild the Temple. This Temple, completed twenty-one years later, was built on the ruins of Solomon's Temple and according to the same plan. In the reign of Antiochus IV of Syria, religious freedom was denied the Jews, the daily offering in the Temple was suspended and a pagan altar was erected there. The Hasmonean revolt of 167 BCE was a direct result of this coercion.

Judah Maccabee purified the Temple (165 BCE) and the daily offerings were resumed (this resanctification is commemorated by the Jews in the Festival of Hanukka). The Hasmonean kings who succeeded Judah Maccabee reconstructed the temple walls, destroyed the *acra* (Greek fortress) that threatened the Temple, and built the citadel outside the northwest corner of the Temple Mount. Internecine strife between the Hasmoneans led to Roman intervention and in 63 BCE Pompey conquered Jerusalem and entered the sanctuary.

Herod, named king of the Jews by the Romans, ruled from 37 BCE to 4 CE. He enlarged the Temple Mount area, embellished the Temple and constructed impressive buildings in Jerusalem. The Jews that had settled throughout the Roman Empire also saw Jerusalem as their spiritual capital, and the Temple as the religious center of the Jewish people and a symbol of their faith. Tens of thousands of Jews made the pilgrimage to the Temple. Herod's construction enterprise was one of the most extensive in the ancient world in his day. He doubled the Temple Mount area with the addition of new support walls in the south, the west and the north (details are given in the Western Wall Excavations Tour). The area was elevated, turrets were built in its corners, porticos were constructed around it, and magnificent gates, passages and entrances were inserted in its walls. The Antonia Fortress replaced the Hasmonean citadel. On the 9th of Av, 70 CE, the Romans razed the Temple to the ground, and to this day it is commemorated as a day of mourning by pious Jews throughout the world.

The enlarged area and parts of its walls are still standing today, including the western and southern walls. Vestiges of Herod's constructions remaining in the Temple Mount area include the foundations, the inner part of Barclay's Gate, other passages and gates, and the gatehouse of the two Hulda Gates, below the el-Aksa Mosque (see Western Wall Excavations Tour).

The Bar-Kochba Revolt (132–135 CE). Daily offerings on the Temple Mount were resumed temporarily. With the suppression of the revolt, Jewish possession of the Temple ended. In its place, the Roman emperor Hadrian erected a temple to Jupiter (135). Jerusalem, now a Roman town, became known as "Aelia Capitolina".

The Byzantine Period (325–638). With Christian rule over Jerusalem, Jupiter's temple was destroyed and the Temple Mount was left in ruins, demonstrating the supremacy of Christianity and the fulfilment of Jesus's prophecy regarding the destruction of the Temple. Building stones and columns were removed from the site and used in the construction of churches in Jerusalem.

Emperor Julian the Apostate encouraged the Jews to reconstruct the Temple (362) but the work was stopped on his death. (See Western Wall Excavations Tour; the inscription on one of the stones refers to this episode.)

The Early Arab Period (638–1099). The Temple Mount is identified with the place from which Mohammed ascended to heaven (Koran, Sura 1, 17). Immediately upon the Arab conquest (638), Caliph Omar decided to make Jerusalem a Muslim religious center — "El-Kuds" (the Holy). He had this area cleared of rubbish and debris and ordered the construction of a mosque there. The edifice, constructed out of wood, was located in the southern part of the Temple Mount.

In 691 Caliph Abd-el-Malik commenced construction of the Dome of the Rock over the Foundation Stone. His son, El-Walid, erected the El-Aksa Mosque, marking the site of the "furthermost sanctuary" mentioned in the Koran account of Mohammed's Night Journey to heaven.

The Crusader Period (1099–1187). The sanctity of the Temple Mount was maintained. The Dome of the Rock, converted into a church, was called "Templum Domini" (Temple of the Lord). The El-Aksa Mosque served as the residence of the Crusader kings and later was converted into a church named "Templum Salomonis" (Solomon's Temple). The Crusaders established their headquarters on the Temple Mount. The Knights Templars built stables for their horses in the cellars of the so-called Solomon's Stables. Elements of Crusader construction are visible in the El-Aksa Mosque and in the Dome of the Rock.

The Ayyubid Period (1187–1229). After the conquest of Jerusalem by the Muslims under the command of Saladin, the Temple Mount buildings again served the Muslims. Many of the Crusader embellishments were removed and extensive renovations were carried out.

The Mameluke Period (1260–1517). Many structures were built in the Temple Mount area, most of the entrance gates were restored and the main structures were renovated.

The Ottoman Period (1517–1917). Many repair works were carried out, buildings were added and the walls of the Dome of the Rock were adorned with ceramic tiles. Until after the Crimean War (1867) entry to the area was forbidden to non-Muslims. In the British Mandatory period this ban applied only to the Jews.

Extensive restoration work was effected in the Dome of the Rock between 1948 and 1967. Its heavy lead dome was replaced by a gold-colored aluminum dome. Many repairs were also carried out in the El-Aksa Mosque.

In 1967 the site was opened to all visitors. In 1969 a Christian fanatic set fire to the El-Aksa Mosque, causing serious damage; the Mosque was closed to visitors for two years while repairs were effected. In 1986 the silver-colored dome was replaced by a black dome.

THE TOUR

We shall start our tour south of the Western Wall Esplanade, and take the path going up an elevation to the Moghrabi Gate (Moors' Gate, because of its proximity to the quarter of the Maghreb Muslims until 1967). This is the main gate for tourists and for worshippers from the southern neighborhoods.

Passing through the gate into the Temple Mount area, we cannot fail to be impressed by the great number of trees covering about a third of the esplanade. The small paved areas *(matztaba)* are intended for prayer, and the alcoves *(mihrab)* to the south indicate the direction to face in prayer. The fountains *(sabil)* are used for washing prior to worship.

1. The Cup (El-Kas) As we proceed northwards to the raised platform we shall pass a large circular stone basin, 2 m (6.58 ft) in diameter. In its center is an ornamental fountain in the form of a cup, made out of one block of stone, surrounded by an ornamental railing. The structure has a series of taps all around and here the Mus-

The Cup.

Sundial at the southern arcade.

Yussuf Dome.

lims wash face, hands and feet before praying. The Cup was constructed in 1320 by the Mameluke Emir Tankiz, ruler of Damascus. The mosaic in the center and the taps round the Cup were restored in the Ottoman period. To our left (to the west) is the ancient and sacred Olive Tree of the Prophet *(Zetunat an-Nabi)*.

Eight sets of steps lead up to the raised platform, one, two or three on each side, delicate arcades standing at the head of each flight — the Arcades of the Scales (in Arabic: *mawazin* — scales; in Muslim tradition, each man's deeds will be weighed on these scales on the Day of Judgement). At the head of the main south flight of steps is an arcade in which a sundial is set, restored by Sultan Abdul Hamid II in 1893.

2. The Summer Pulpit, a marble platform reached by several steps, with pillars, a domed roof and the preacher's seat. The capitals of the pillars are re-used ones from the Crusader period. Different styles of construction can be distinguished, from Saladin's time (late 12th century), from the 14th century, and from the time of the Ottoman Emir Mohammed Rashid in 1843.

3. Yussuf Dome (Qubbat Yussuf), near the Summer Pulpit, a small cube-shaped structure, open on three sides. It is named after two people: Saladin Yussuf, who ordered its construction in 1191, and Yussuf Agha (chief officer at the sultan's palace in Constantinople), who restored it in 1681, as indicated in the Turkish inscription carved on a stone tablet. On the facade are two pairs of small marble columns, and on its south side is a prayer niche *(mihrab)* inlaid with mother-of-pearl.

4. Dome of Learning (Qubbat Nahawyya), next to the Yussuf Dome, a long building comprising three rooms and an underground chamber, extending to the corner of the area. It is also known as *Er-Rasasyya* because of its lead cupola *(rasas* in Arabic). Its marble pillars are vestiges of a more ancient building, probably Crusader. The Ayyubid ruler of Damascus, who called for more intensive study of the Arabic language, ordered its construction in 1207. The marble pillars were brought from another structure to their present location in 1891.

5. The Dome of the Rock is the central edifice of the Temple Mount, built over the "Rock" (the Foundation Stone which was incorporated into the Temple). It is the third holiest site in Islam (after Mecca and Medina), one of the most famous and most impressive architectural achievements in the world, and a magnificent example of early Islamic art. The structure has come to symbolize Jerusalem, appearing on postage stamps, postcards and various popular artifacts. Since its construction in

691 by the Omayyad Caliph Abd-el-Malik, the original form of the structure has not been modified. The mosque was built for several reasons: because of the sanctity of the Rock in Islamic tradition, as the place from which Mohammed ascended to heaven; because Islam recognizes its sanctity in the Scriptures. The third reason was that Abd-el-Malik wanted a Muslim shrine that would counterbalance the Church of the Holy Sepulcher; and in the light of the internal strife between the Muslim rulers in Jerusalem and those in the Arabian Peninsula, he wished to divert pilgrims away from Mecca and Medina. The structure is remarkable for its architectural beauty, the harmony of its proportions and its splendor. On the exterior the mosque is an octagon above which rises a drum, supporting a huge dome. The entire edifice stands 43 m (141 ft) high. The plan is Byzantine and the decorations obviously executed by Byzantine craftsmen. Until the 16th century the structure was faced with mosaics, but they have been severely damaged by weather conditions (a part of the mosaic is on display in the Islamic Museum — see 32. below). Today the structure is faced with marble, decorated with glazed tiles imported from Turkey by Suleiman the Magnificent in the 16th century.

Each of the 8 sides is 20 m (65.8 ft) long and has 7 high, arched windows, decorated with geometrical pieces of colored glass and short Arabic inscriptions praising God. Most of the windows date from the time of Suleiman the Magnificent. The cupola is coated with gilded aluminum sheets which were installed during Jordanian rule (until then the dome was heavily coated with lead). A plaque to the right of the entrance commemorates the restorations carried out by King Hussein between 1958 and 1967. Beneath the external cupola is an inner cupola, formed by a wooden frame and covered with stucco work and arabesques. The frame is attached to a palm-fiber ceiling. Between the two cupolas is a weatherproof insulation space. The cupola has the same diameter as that of the Church of the Holy Sepulcher. It rests on a drum with sixteen colored-glass windows. A crescent, symbol of Islam, tops the cupola. The inscription adorning the upper part of the walls is taken from the story of Mohammed's Night Journey in the Koran.

The structure has four portals, at the four cardinal points. The north door is called the Door of Paradise *(Bab el-Jenneh)*. The inscription over it records the restoration of the Dome of the Rock during the reign of Sultan Suleiman the Magnificent. The east door, leading to the Dome of David's Judgement (Dome of the Chain), is known as David's Gate *(Bab Daud)*. The south door is called the Angel's Gate *(Bab*

Dome of the Rock viewed from the south.

Ceiling of the Dome of the Rock.

Israfil) referring to the angel (Raphael) who will announce the resurrection of the dead and blow the ram's horn to assemble the faithful to be judged. Next to it is a prayer niche *(mihrab)*. The west door was known as the Women's Gate. Today it serves as the main entrance.

Shoes will be removed before entering. No bags or cameras are allowed inside the mosque.

Interior of the Dome of the Rock: the shape and interior decorations are breathtaking. Two concentric colonnades surround the Rock in the center. The outer colonnade is formed by eight pillars corresponding to the eight angles of the building. Between two of these pillars are two round columns. The colonnade is parallel to the octagon of the outer walls. Alternating dark and light-colored stones, bearing decorations and inscriptions, are dovetailed into the arches. The inner colonnade comprises a circle of arches, resting on four pillars and twelve columns. The pillars support the inner cupola, and the drum with sixteen windows. The pillars are faced with marble. The columns are adorned with glass mosaics with geometric and floral designs, symbolizing the Garden of Eden. Most of the columns have been taken from other buildings and are unequal. They are made of marble and granite and have gilded capitals. The colonnades encompassing the Rock were constructed in order to enable the faithful to encircle it. The cupola is decorated with loop-shaped arabesques around circles and inscriptions. It is painted red and gold. A gold chain hangs down from the center. The inscription over the inner arches attributes the construction of the Dome of the Rock to el-Mamun. El-Mamun (who reigned from 813 to 833) in fact inserted his name in the original text but did not change the date (691). The actual founder was Abd el-Malik.

Even Hashetyya (Foundation Stone): In the center of the structure stands the Rock (12 × 15 m, 39.3 × 49.2 ft). It is surrounded by an ornamental wooden balustrade from the Ottoman period. This is the summit of Mount Moriah where tradition places the Sacrifice of Isaac. It was the site of the Holy of Holies in the Temple. Here is the center of the world and the foundation upon which the universe was created according to Jewish tradition. In Islamic tradition it was Ishmael who was to be sacrificed here, and from here also Mohammed ascended to heaven in his Night Journey. He encountered seven people there: Adam, Jesus, Joseph, Enoch, Aaron, Moses and Abraham, and received the commandment of praying five times a day. Each fissure, hole and mark on the rock has its own legend — one being that it marked the places where prophets prayed, another that it was the mark of Idris's (Enoch's) footprint, and Mohammed's footprint. An 80 cm (2.62 ft) diameter cavity in the Rock opens onto the grotto beneath, which is reached by marble-faced steps cut in the rock. The grotto contains four prayer niches where, according to tradition, David, Solomon, Abraham and the Angel Gabriel prayed. It is known as the Well of the Spirits because Muslims believe that all the spirits come first here to salute the Rock. Near the southwest corner is an urn shaped like a tower with a silver box containing two hairs from the beard of the Prophet. Once a year, on the Day of the Prophet's Ascension, these hairs are displayed to the faithful.

6. Dome of the Prophet (Qubbat en-Nabi) This is the dome closest to the Dome of the Rock. The cupola, 3 m (9.8 ft) in diameter, is coated with lead and is supported by eight small marble columns supporting arches constructed with alternating white and red stones. Below it is a stone circle used for prayer. The Dome was built by the Turkish ruler Mohammad Bek.

7. Dome of the Ascension (Qubbat el-Miraj) West of the Dome of the Rock, this cupola surmounts an octagonal edicule consisting of arches and columns. The structure was at one time open, but marble walls were constructed and it became a prayer room with a niche in its south. On the dome is a turret with a small cupola, in Crusader style. According to Muslim tradition, Mohammed prayed here before his ascent to heaven. This Crusader edifice served as a baptistery close to the Templum Domini. The structure was destroyed by the Mamelukes in 1200 and restored a few years later.

8. Elijah's Dome (Qubbat el-Khadr), close to the northwest arcade, is supported by a hexagonal drum resting on six columns with capitals joined to arches. *El-Khadr* (the Green) refers to the prophet Elijah ("the Evergreen"). Another tradition says it is here that King Solomon confined the spirits. Dervishes used to assemble at this site for their rituals.

10. Dome of the Chain (Qubbat es-Silsilah) About 4 m (13 ft) east of the Dome of the Rock is an 11-sided open structure, with a cupola resting on a hexagonal drum. The structure has two rows of round columns supporting arches; there are 11 columns in the outer colonnade and 6 columns within. This dome looks like a miniature version of the Dome of the Rock. The colored clay tablets in the niche were inserted during the reign of Suleiman the Magnificent. According to Muslim tradi-

Elijah's Dome on the right of the northwest arcade.

9. Dome of the Spirits (Qubbat el-Arwah), an octagonal structure with a cupola, in the northwest of the elevated area. The cupola rests on arches between eight marble columns. It is 4 m (13 ft) in diameter and about 2.5 m (8.2 ft) high. At the top of the round cupola is a half crescent. The natural stone of its floor is bare. According to Muslim tradition the spirits of the dead gather here.

tion, King David sat in judgement here, hence the alternative name, *Mahkamat Daud*. It is said that a chain hung from the ceiling at the time of judgement. Anyone telling the truth could touch it, whereas anyone who lied could not reach it, since it rose up out of reach. Some think that this was the seat of the tribunal in the Second Temple period, and the Muslim tradition strengthens this belief. In other traditions, this was the site of the Treasury. During the Crusader period the structure was turned into a chapel dedicated to the Apostle James the Lesser (brother of Jesus and the first bishop of Jerusalem).

According to Jewish tradition, the tablets of the Covenant and Aaron's rod were kept here; this is the site of the altar of Melchizedek king of Salem, and of Jacob's dream.

East of the Dome of the Chain is an arcade with five arches upon four columns, with a pillar on each side. From here a flight of 20 11 m (36 ft) wide steps leads down to the lower area. These are the El-Burak Steps, named after the miraculous horse ridden by Mohammed on his Night Journey from Mecca to Jerusalem. According to an earlier Islamic tradition, Mohammed led his horse to the Temple Mount through the Gate of Mercy, also called El-Burak Gate. It is also believed to be the site where Mohammed prayed with the prophets and the messengers who came to meet him on the night of his ascension to heaven. Those who welcomed him also included his daughter Fatima, and the Angel Gabriel, hence the other names of the Dome (Qubbat Fatima, Makam Gibril).

We shall now proceed to the northeast section of the lower level. Within the three arches between four columns in the upper arcade are two small rooms built under the Mameluke sultan Ibn Kala'un (in 1325). From the flight of steps a path leads to the Gate of Forgiveness and to the Gate of the Tribes, the north colonnade and the Minaret of Israel within it (details below). We shall first go to the east.

11. The Golden Gate — Gate of Mercy (Bab el-Rahmeh) This is the only gate in the east wall of the Temple Mount, which is also the city wall. It is a double gate. One part is called the Mercy Gate and the other the Gate of Repentance. From the Temple Mount esplanade we see its interior part. The structure is striking, with high twin portals. A flight of steps leads down from the Temple Mount area to the twin gates.

Inside the structure is a high chamber which has a row of four round columns with magnificent capitals, in the center. Between the columns are arches supporting a vaulted ceiling. On the second floor of the gate structure is a prayer room, and the two domes constitute its roof. The gate was built during the Omayyad period (7th century). Over the centuries several changes were made; the Turks effecting the last change, converted the gate into a watchtower.

Many legends and traditions are linked with the Gate of Mercy. The Jews believe that it will be opened upon the advent of the Messiah. The Muslims placed a cemetery in front (since the Messiah would be prevented by Jewish laws of ritual purity from passing through a cemetery) and they believe that the Day of Judgement will take place here. In the Middle Ages Jews prayed and mourned the destruction of the Temple at this spot.

In Christian tradition this is the Golden Gate through which Jesus entered Jerusalem on Palm Sunday (Mark 11:8, John 12:13.) From here the Byzantine emperor Heraclius entered Jerusalem in 631, returning with the True Cross which had been taken by the Persians. In Crusader times the gate was opened on the feast of the Exaltation of the Cross (commemorating the event) and on Palm Sunday. When the Muslims returned to power, they blocked the gate. Until the 15th century it served as a Muslim prayer house and a place for study of the Koran. Today it serves as a storehouse and is closed to visitors.

Arcade east of the Dome of the Chain, leading to the El-Burak Steps.

The Golden Gate with the Muslim cemetery in front.

12. Throne of Solomon (Kursi Suleiman) Near the Gate of Mercy (to the north), against the wall, is a square structure with two cupolas, dating from the Omayyad period (638–750). Legend holds that King Solomon sat here during the construction of the Temple, watching the spirits which he controlled.

13. Gate of the Tribes (Bab el-Asbat): the northeast gate of the Temple Mount. To reach it we shall take the path leading to the corner of the east rampart and the north wall of the precint. According to Muslim legend, the gate is named after the tribes of Israel who passed through it after visiting the sanctuary. The gate, simple in form, was constructed in the Ottoman period. To the west begins the north colonnade, a roofed corridor, open to the south, with arches supported by square pillars. The colonnade continues in sections along the entire north wall. Along its length the Mamelukes built twelve *madrassa* (colleges) in the 14th and 15th centuries. On one of the columns is an inscription recording a restoration effected by an Ayyubid ruler in 1213.

In the middle of the colonnade is the Turret of Israel *(Manarat Israil)* built in 1367 on the foundations of an earlier minaret; it takes its name from the Israin or Israil Pool to its north, outside the Temple Mount. In form, it resembles David's Tower.

14. Gate of Atonement (Bab Hitta) The first gate west of the Israel Minaret; an inscription on it ascribes its construction to the 10th century and its renovation to 1220 under Ayyubid Sultan El-Mu'azzam. It takes its name from a story based on a verse of the Koran. The Children of Israel were required to say *hitta* (atonement) in order to atone for their sins, and only then were they allowed to enter Jerusalem. (In the 8th century, in the Omayyad period, the Gate of Atonement was the sealed gate in the Western Wall, now known as Barclay's Gate. (See Western Wall Excavations Tour.)

15. The Dark Gate (Bab el-Atim) The most westerly of the gates in the north wall of the Temple Mount; it is named after the dark passage leading to it. The gate is Mameluke, and another of its names relates to the nearby Mameluke college. It is also called the Gate of the Glory of the Prophets, and Muslim legend tells that it was through here that Caliph Omar came to pray when the first entered Jerusalem. The outer gate leading to the Lions' Gate (St. Stephen's Gate) and the path leading to the Dark Gate are named after King Faisal, king of Iraq whose father, Hussein, is buried in a nearby room.

16. Dome of Solomon (Qubbat Suleiman) Southwest of the Dark Gate is an octagonal structure from the Omayyad period, with 8 windows, over which is a cupola. Steps lead up to the prayer area in the structure. In its south part is a prayer niche, and in the west part is a rock fenced in by an iron railing. According to tradition the rock is a splinter from the Foundation Stone. The structure is also known as the Small Dome of the Rock. According to Arab tradition, Solomon prayed on this rock when the Temple was completed.

We shall continue eastward, to the south wall of the Madrassa el-Jawilyya (Omaryya College). Here we shall observe the edge of the Rock area where the citadel and the Antonia Fortress were built in the Second Temple period. In the corner of the building are steps going up to the Temple Mount from the 'Anum Gate (after the beautiful minaret in the northwest corner of the Temple Mount, visible from here).

Turning south we shall come to the Ala ed-Din el-Basir Fountain, a square drinking structure supporting a flat cupola with a scalloped edge. Three steps on its south side lead down to the water outlet. Originally the water was brought from Solomon's Pools to the Temple Mount through the Gate of the Chain (see below). The fountain was built in the 12th century and renovated in the 15th century by the Mameluke Sultan El-Ashraf Barsbay "for the use of the poor and the needy", as recorded in the inscription.

17. Gate of the Inspector (Bab en-Natir) The gate close to the above fountain is named after the inspector of the sanctuaries of Hebron and Jerusalem, who also built a house nearby. The house later

Dome of Solomon with the Madrassa el-Jawilyya and the Dome of Suleiman Pasha on the right.

Bani 'Anum minaret and northern end of the Dome of Suleiman

became a jail, and the gate became known as the Jail Gate *(Bab el-Habs)*. This was the name in general use under Mameluke ruler Baybars (13th century). The gate was built under the Ayyubid Sultan El-Mu'azzam in 1203 (on the foundations of the Crusader Michael's Gate); a memorial inscription is fixed at the top of the gate. The offices of the Supreme Muslim Council are close to this gate, also known as the Gate of the Council *(Bab el-Majlis)*.

Continuing to the south we shall pass by the esh-Sheikh Budeir Fountain, a structure topped by a small stone cupola on small octogonal marble columns, supporting arches. The bases and capitals of the columns are Turkish. The fountain was built in 740 by the governor of Jerusalem, and is named after Budeir ed-Din who is buried nearby.

We shall continue southwards along the west colonnade, which begins at the Gate of the Inspector (see above) until we come to the Moghrabi Gate. The colonnade is made up of square pillars supporting 60 arches. It is about 6 m (19.7 ft) wide and 34 m (111.5 ft) long and built against the west wall. The colonnade and the college within it were built by the Mamelukes.

18. The Iron Gate (Bab el-Hadid), the next gate in the west wall, has a horseshoe arch. It was built in the 14th century by the ruler of Damascus. In the alley leading from the gate to the outside are Mameluke buildings. Close to the gate is the Ar'unyya College.

19. Gate of the Cotton Merchants (Bab el-Qattanin). This gate is one of the most beautiful of the Temple Mount. From here steps lead up to the Temple Mount area. Over the gate entrance is a stone rosette with "rays of the sun" made from alternating black and white stone. The inscription, engraved on a copper strip over a wooden door, records the construction by Tankiz, ruler of Damascus, between 1336 and 1337 in the reign of the Mameluke Sultan Ibn Kala'un. The gate opens onto the Cotton Market, which has its entrance on HaGai Street.

TOUR No. 2

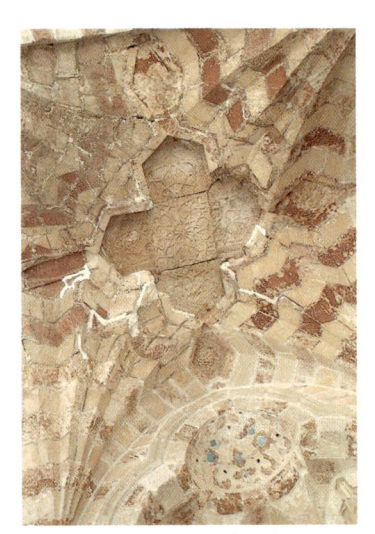

Ornamented dome, western colonnade.

20. Gate of the Bath Next to the Gate of the Cotton Merchants. The two gates are joined by a passage from outside the Temple Mount. It derives its name from the nearby bath-house (in use until the end of the Ottoman period). There were also bathing facilities here in the Second Temple period. This gate, also known as the Gate of the Place of Purification *(Bab el-Mat'hara)*, was built by Emir Ala ed-Din Aidugdai, under the Mameluke Sultan Baybars (1260–1277).

21. Madrassa el-Uthmanyya, beyond the west colonnade, south of the Gate of the Bath, is called after a rich Anatolian lady who built it (1436–1437) during the Mameluke period, and is buried in the structure next to the college. The magnificent entrance is decorated in the style characteristic of that period: alternating light and dark stones and stone benches on each side of the entrance.

22. Fountain of Qayt Bey, opposite Madrassa el-Uthmanyya, before the steps going up from the west of the raised platform. This attractive structure is a drinking fountain of the Mameluke period. On its square lower part, which measures 5 × 5 m (16 × 16 ft), is an octagonal, sculptured drum with small openings, beneath a dome decorated with magnificent carved floral designs. There is a crescent at the summit of the cupola. The structure stands 14 m (46 ft) high. The inscription on the fountain invites the righteous servants of Allah to quench their thirst with its sweet water.

Circular steps at the east lead to the entrance of the fountain. On the three other sides are barred windows with a marble sill. The drinking taps are in the cistern, on the east side of the fountain. The water in fact came from Solomon's Pools through a conduit entering via the Chain Gate (see below).

The fountain is named after Sultan Qayt Bey who renovated it in 1482 in the same style as the mosque bearing his name in Cairo. It was restored in 1883.

23. Fountain of Qasem Pasha This is an octagonal structure south of the Qayt Bey Fountain, with a broad-rimmed, lead-plated dome resting on eight columns. Inside the well is a square, marble-clad cistern, surrounded by an iron railing. The fountain was built in 1527 by Qasem Pasha, as recorded in the inscription on the west facade. The railing was added in 1922 by the Supreme Muslim Council.

Fountain of Qayt Bey.

THE TEMPLE MOUNT

24. The Fig Tree Area (Matztabat et-Tein) A prayer area south of the Qasem Pasha Fountain, measuring 9 ×9 m (29.5 × 29.5 ft). It takes its name from a fig-tree which stood here at the time of its construction (in 1760). On its south side is a prayer niche with an inscription recording the name of its founder.

25. Dome of Moses (Qubbat Musa) South of the Fig Tree area and opposite the Chain Gate (see below), is a square room (7 × 7 m; 23 × 23 ft) under an octagonal drum supporting a cupular roof. By the entrance, which is at the north, is an inscription commemorating the Ayyubid Sultan Saladin who built it in 1249. The dome is probably called after Moses, who is also a holy prophet for the Muslims. By the structure is a large prayer area (15 ×19 m; 49.2 × 62.3 ft), with a small prayer niche in the south.

26. Gate of the Chain (Bab es-Silsileh) This is the main gate to the Temple Mount on the west side. It has two entrances: the north entrance, known as the Divine Gate (Bab es-Sakina), is sealed; and the south entrance, the Gate of the Chain, which is open. These gates are at the end of the Street of the Chain, the eastern continuation of David Street, and were called Solomon's Gate and David's Gate (since they faced David Street which begins at Jaffa Gate — known at that time as David's Gate). The gates were built close to the site of a gate dating from the Second Temple period. This may have been the Casistos Gate mentioned by Josephus in *The Jewish Wars 6,3*.

In the square inside the gate, in the Temple Mount precinct, are heavy columns and a minaret. The square and the columns were restored under Mameluke Sultan Ibn Kala'un (1329–1330). On the columns are 15th-century Mameluke inscriptions, with instructions from the sultans to the city rulers warning then not to impose exorbitant taxes. The outside part of the gate was built by the Crusaders (for details of the outside square, see Tour of the Moslem Quarter).

From the Gate of the Chain we shall go to the south-east of the Temple Mount. In the east wall is a stone column about 1.5 m (4.9 ft) below the crenellations of the wall. The column, which can also be seen on the outside of the wall, is below a semi-circular stone that blocks the entrance. According to Muslim tradition, Mohammed will sit here on the Day of Judgement. The site is known as the Seat of Mohammed (Kursi

The Fig Tree area and the Dome of Moses.

Mohammed). In the southeast corner of the wall, a steel door closes the entrance to the steps leading down to subterranean vaults under the Temple Mount. The door is locked and the key held by the Temple Mount custodians. These vaults are known as Solomon's Stables.

27. Solomon's Stables (Istabil Suleiman) By the top of the flight of steps leading down to the underground area is a shell decoration above a stone niche, where an idol probably stood in the Roman period. The site is known as the Cradle of Jesus. In Muslim tradition Jesus was born here. According to another tradition, this is the niche of the Virgin Mary (Mihrab Maryam) mentioned in the Koran (Sura 3, 37).

The steps lead to a subterranean hall beneath the Temple Mount, covering an area of 55 × 100 m (181.5 × 328 ft). The place is divided into aisles by 12 rows of square pillars (a total of 88), supporting vaults and arches upon which the roof rests.

Herod, when expanding the Temple Mount area, built support walls here with spaces between them, to prevent pressure on the south wall. The Temple Mount area was then 3 m (9.9 ft) higher than today. Above the empty spaces were drainage channels for rainwater. These spaces may have been used as storerooms in Herod's time.

The present vaults were built in the time of the Fatimid rulers (10th century). Some of the building stones are from Herod's time. The holes in the arches may have served for scaffolding during the construction, and for additional storage space.

In the Crusader period the aisles served as stables for the horses of the Templars, who had their residence in the nearby El-Aksa Mosque. The horses entered through the Single Gate in the south wall. Many vestiges remain of this gate, which was blocked in the Ayyubid period. In the excavations of the south wall a tunnel was discovered under the gate, which may have been an emergency exit. On the west side, Solomon's Stables border on a tunnel going up from the east Hulda Gate (Triple Gate) to the Temple Mount level (see Western Wall Excavations Tour).

28. El-Aksa Mosque This is the large and impressive edifice at the south of the Temple Mount, with a dark dome visible from afar. It is the oldest mosque in the Holy Land and one of the holiest and largest in the Muslim world. It is identified with the "furthermost sanctuary" mentioned in the Koran in the description of Mohammed's Night Journey (Sura 17, 1).

According to Muslim tradition, Omar built here a wooden structure when he came to Jerusalem in 638. The Omayyad Caliph El-Walid (whose father Abd el-Malik built the Dome of the Rock in 692) built the first stone structure on the site in 705.

The mosque was designed for the tens of thousands of pilgrims who flocked here from all over the Muslim world. The original structure was far larger than today's. It was destroyed and restored after two earthquakes, in 747 and 1033. The Fatimid Caliph Ez-Zahir rebuilt it as it stands today. After the Crusader conquest of Jerusalem (1099) the mosque became the royal palace of the Crusader kings, who called it Solomon's Temple (Templum Salomonis). The Jews, in the Middle Ages, called it

Solomon's Stables

Solomon's College. Later it became the headquarters of an order of Crusader Knights who became known as the Knights Templars. Vestiges remain of the modifications and additions that the Crusaders effected in the structure. After Saladin's conquest of Jerusalem in 1187 the structure once again became a mosque. A magnificent pulpit *(minbar)* was erected, dedicated to the commander Nur ed-Din. The pulpit, constructed in Haleb, Syria, was made of carved ebony inlaid with arabesques and mother-of-pearl. It was destroyed by the fire in 1969.

Earthquakes in 1927 and 1936 damaged the structure. Since then extensive restoration work has been carried out: in 1943, with the aid of King Farouk of Egypt; and under King Abdallah of Jordan (grandfather of King Hussein) from 1948 to 1951, the year in which he was murdered at the entrance to the mosque. King Hussein continued the restorations commenced by his grandfather.

After the heavy damage caused by the 1969 fire the mosque was closed for repairs for several years.

The style of the mosque is not uniform due to the many modifications and restorations effected thoughout its history. It is essentially a basilica with a central nave divided by a row of columns from the side aisles. There are three aisles on each side (in the first building there were seven on each side) facing north-south, and a large aisle in the north and in the south parts. In the center of the south wall is a prayer niche. East of the south section is the Mosque of Omar, against the south wall. To the north is the Mosque of the Forty Martyrs and beside it the Prayer Recess of Zachariah.

View of El-Aksa Mosque from the Islamic Museum courtyard.

In the facade of the structure there are seven arches: the center arch, which is the highest and widest, embellished with a number of arches resting on pillars with recessed round columns, creating an impression of depth. Over the central arch are small columns, and between them arches (a typical Mameluke decoration); above these is the front of the roof. The main style is Gothic, incorporating Crusader remains. The nave is flanked on both sides by a row of round marble columns with Corinthian-style capitals. The two rows of columns support a decorated architrave, over which arches support a wall with two rows of windows. The upper row of windows faces outward, from over the roof of the side sections. Between the arches are decorations containing quotations from the Koran. On the arch over the end of the south section (containing the prayer niche) are decorated golden mosaics. The capitals of the two pillars are also gilded (11th century, according to the inscription). The decorations and the inscription were uncovered under the plaster during the restorations of 1927. The west side aisles are formed by square columns bearing cross vaults (built in the 14th century in the Mameluke period). The east aisles were renovated in 1938, and it is possible to enlarge the structure to the east if necessary. The south section of the mosque is the most ancient part of the building. The prayer niche *(mihrab)* in the center of its south wall is decorated with mosaics. On each side it has three columns, and a graceful arch over them, with an inscription above relating the restoration of the *mihrab* and of the mosque by Saladin, after his conquest of the city from the Crusaders in 1187. There are two small *mihrabs* west of the central *mihrab*, one dedicated to Moses and one to Jesus. The dome of the mosque was built under Caliph Taher in the 11th century, and its upper part decorated under Ibn Kala'un in the 14th century (as we can see from the

Facade of El-Aksa Mosque.

inscriptions). The dome is constructed on a marble drum with vaulted windows, and columns over them. The plant decorations in its mosaic are the most beautiful in the mosque. The dome was restored in 1927.

The Mosque of Omar, another structure east of the nave, goes from east to west and measures 6 × 25 m (19.8 × 82.5 ft). Its south wall is against the south wall of the Temple Mount. In its center is a prayer niche, and on both sides are round Crusader columns. The mosque was built in the Omayyad period, and underwent many modifications, up until the Ottoman period.

The Mosque of the 40 Martyrs, to the north of the Mosque of Omar, is a small chamber (8 × 7 m; 26.2 × 22 ft) opening to the west. It was originally a Crusader chapel and has no *mihrab*. The lower part of the walls is marble faced. There are several columns in the mosque and an inscription on a wooden tablet recounting Mohammed's Night Journey. A wooden door leads from the east portico to the Prayer Recess of Zachariah. This room measures 4 m by 5.5 m (12.8 × 17.6 ft). The apse on its east side has a round window with six glass panes shaped like lily petals, in a style characteristic of 12th-century French churches. The upper part of the prayer niche in the south wall is shaped like a clover leaf and is decorated in typical Crusader style. The room has a high ceiling (10 m; 33.2 ft) and serves as a place for prayer for distinguished guests (one of whom was Jordan's King Abdallah). The room received the name of Zachariah in the Crusader period and the Muslims identify him with Zachariah, the father of John the Baptist, who is mentioned in the Koran. The inscription over the *mihrab* reproduces the prayer of the High Priest Zachariah for a son from his barren wife.

29. Women's Mosque is a rectangular room to the west of the El-Aksa Mosque, built by the Knights Templars, and served as an arms store and living quarters. The room measures 12 × 75 m (39.4 × 240 ft), and is formed by deep arches resting on pillars. This structure is also known as the White Mosque. The entire ground-floor of the Crusader building has remained intact; the second floor has been destroyed. The room is divided lengthwise by a wall and its west part is attached to the Islamic Museum (see below).

30. Dome of Yussuf Agha Between the Moghrabi Mosque and the El-Aksa Mosque is a small structure (5 × 5 m; 16 × 16 ft) with a cupola. Next to it is a niche bearing the inscription: "Yussuf Agha, in the 17th century, ordered the restoration of the Yussuf Dome". Today the structure serves as a ticket-booth.

31. Madrassa el-Fakhryya Against the southern part of the Western Wall, by the Moghrabi Gate. The college is surrounded by living quarters with courtyards. In the back courtyard there is a platform with a row of columns under six cupolas. To the south of the platform is a niche decorated with Crusader marble columns. The place served as a hostel from 1330, and is named after a Copt judge who converted to Islam and was finance inspector under the Mamelukes. Above the Madrassa is the el-Fakhryya Minaret.

32. Islamic Museum is a rectangular structure (10 × 50 m; 32 × 160 ft) to the west of the Women's Mosque. It was probably built in the Omayyad period. In the Ayyubid period, it was given to the North African Muslim community in Jerusalem who lived near here (in the area now forming the Western Wall esplanade). The mosque was restored under the Turkish Sultan Abdul Aziz (in 1871). Since 1923 it houses the Islamic Museum, where are displayed illustrated Korans, inscriptions, reliefs, utensils and vestiges from the El-Aksa Mosque and from other Temple Mount sites. The entrance to the Museum is on the east side, close to the Moghrabi Gate. There is a charge for admission.

Before concluding our tour we shall have a quick look at the steps of the El-Burak Mosque, on the north side of the Moghrabi Gate. These steps lead up to the Temple Mount from the ancient, blocked gate (Barclay's Gate) in the Western Wall. They date back to Herod's time and the gate is identified with the Coponius Gate mentioned in Second Temple period sources. Our tour ends here.

TOUR No. 3

WESTERN WALL EXCAVATIONS

Details of tour: It consists of the following sections of the excavations at the Western Wall: 1. the northern area of the Western Wall. 2. Ophel Archeological Garden.
(This tour may be divided into two separate visits.)
Distance covered: approx. 2 km (1½ miles)
Time: 4 hours
Transportation: Buses No 1, 38, 99
Parking lot across from the Dung Gate for private vehicles
Starting point and end of tour: Dung Gate
The Sites: included in the route descriptions
Note: The tour may be complemented by a visit to the model of the Second Temple at the Holyland Hotel, highly recommended. (For further details see the sites included in the tour of the west side of the city.)

FOREWORD

Excavations in the area surrounding the Temple Mount began between 1867 and 1869 under the direction of Wilson and Warren of the Palestine Exploration Fund. The archaeologists sunk shafts along the length of the western and southern walls. The shaft system was adopted because permission for digging openly from the ground surface was not granted. Despite the inherent limitations of this system, these excavations made substantial contributions to the initial research of the area, namely uncovering the relief of the original area, the depth of the Western Wall as well as the surrounding structures. (The shafts were later found and reexamined during Professor Mazar's excavations.)

In 1968 an extensive archaeological project was undertaken in the area of the western and southern walls. The excavations were carried out under the auspices of the Society for the Exploration of the Land of Israel and its Antiquities, and the Hebrew University, headed by Professor Mazar and followed up by his assistant M. Ben Dov. In excavations begun in 1970, the northern and subterranean sections of the Western Wall were unearthed under the supervision of Ben Dov and the sponsorship of the Ministry of Religion.

The new excavations uncovered 25 settlement strata, bringing to life the area's history from the time of King Solomon (10th century BCE) to the time of Sultan Suleiman (16th century CE). The discoveries included structures and finds previously unknown and others which supplemented the accounts described in the *Mishna* and by Josephus Flavius. The restoration of many structures and the installation of visitors' facilities presents the tourist with an impressive and comprehensive picture. Excavations of the northern area of the Western Wall have yet to be completed, and only some of the finds are open to the public (see below). In the Ophel Archaeological Garden, paths and stairs have been built to facilitate access in and around the sites. Signs have also been posted offering relevant information in English, Hebrew, and Arabic.

Before beginning the actual tour a brief account will be given of the Herodian construction project on the Temple Mount. The remains of this project are the most impressive and oustanding of the Western Wall excavations. Herod almost doubled the area of the Temple Mount platform on which the Temple stood.

After five years of preparations, the actual construction began, continuing for

WESTERN WALL EXCAVATIONS

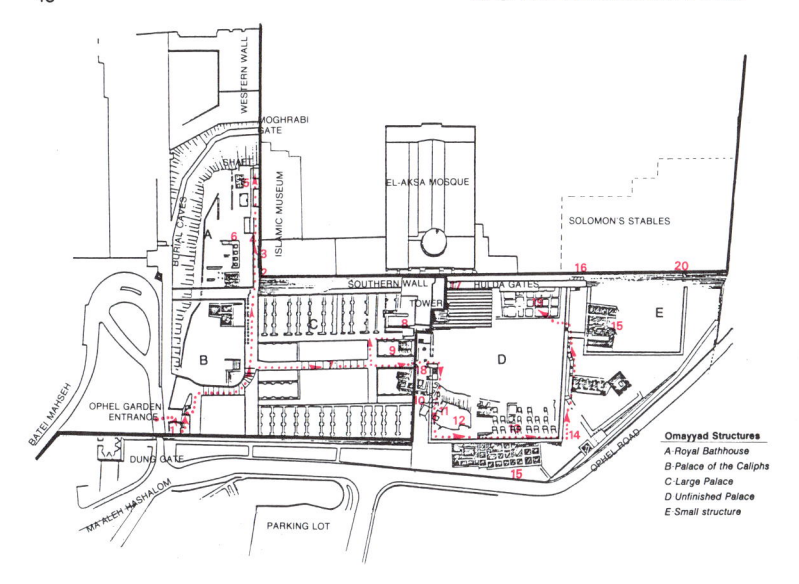

Omayyad Structures
A - Royal Bathhouse
B - Palace of the Caliphs
C - Large Palace
D - Unfinished Palace
E - Small structure

1. Guard Room: entrance/exit to Ophel Garden
2. Southwest corner of Temple Mount wall
3. Robinson's Arch
4. The Hebrew inscription
5. Exposed section of paved street
6. Pillars of Robinson's Arch overpass
7. Omayyad palace courtyard
8. Observation point
9. Byzantine rooms
10. Herodian house
11. Cisterns
12. Open pool
13. Omayyad structure
14. First Temple period public building
15. Byzantine neighborhood
16. Triple Gate — eastern Hulda Gate
17. Double Gate — western Hulda Gate
18. Excavations gate
19. Pillared courtyard
20. Single Gate

Map of the tour of the Ophel Archaeological Garden.

three years and carried out by 11,000 people. The stones were cut in Zedekiah's Cave, in the Matarah Garden across from the cave, and in other quarries in the Jerusalem area. The use of very large stones offers numerous advantages, one of which being to contribute to the wall's stability. Precise chiselling ensured total alignment of the stones and facilitated construction without the use of cement or other such materials, and made possible a quick completion of the construction. The design was daring and complex. The Temple Mount platform was expanded in three directions, north, west, and south. In the north, the naturally high surface area obviated the need for retaining structures. In the west, however, the wall was built for precisely that purpose. A series of arches were built in the south to ease the pressure applied on the southern wall. Empty space between the arches was used for storage areas and water cisterns. This system of construction also limited expenses on building materials and protected the living from the impurity of contact with the dead buried in the ground below. (The southeastern area of the space is today known as Solomon's Stables.) The addition can be clearly seen on the eastern wall where a joint marking the border between the eastern wall of the ancient platform and the addition made in the southern section is evident. In this way, a new level was created, higher than the natural surface, and 2 m (6 ft) higher than today.

In the Western Wall, above the prayer plaza, 11 courses of large ashlar stones can be seen dating from the Herodian period. Two lower courses were uncovered after 1967, during the construction of the prayer plaza. The total length of the Western Wall is 485 m (1552 ft — the longest of the walls) of which 60 m (69 ft) are along the length of plaza. In the southern corner of the prayer plaza (the edge of the women's prayer section) a long stone can be seen which is the lintel of Barclay's Gate (named after the researcher who discovered the gate). The gate has been identified as the Coponius Gate mentioned in the *Mishna*. (Today the gate is located beneath the Moors' Gate.)

The following finds were uncovered in the northern area of the Western Wall. The large vault, known as Wilson's Arch, was built apparently in the Omayyad period, on the ruins of the earlier arch. It is possible that the original arch was an overpass similar to the one located in the southern wall (see below), or the bridge connecting the upper city to the Temple Mount. West of the later arch lie the remains of a hall dating from the Second Temple period identified as part of the larger structure. The tunnel excavated along the length of the Western Wall, in a northerly direction, uncovered once again Warren's Gate. Today, we can therefore be certain of the location of the four gates in the Western Wall, as described by Josephus Flavius, namely, two gates on top of the overpass, the Coponius Gate (Barclay's Gate), and finally Warren's Gate.

In the south of the Western Wall columns and vestiges of arches have been uncovered upon which an overpass was built, crossing over the road parallel to the wall. The overpass led to the Triple Gate, described in detail by Josephus Flavius. There were three porticos against the Temple Mount walls, on the east, the north, and the west side. On the south side was a high basilica, known as the Triple Portico, comprising of 160 gigantic pillars, arranged in four rows, supporting the sloping roof. There were windows on both sides of the elevated central part of the roof. The basilica housed a tribunal which dealt with financial and commercial matters, administrative rooms, and official reception halls, and it was also used temporarily by the Sanhedrin, while repairs were being carried out at their permanent seat

Wilson's Arch.

which was in the Chamber of Hewn Stone.

By the southern wall, (the shortest of the walls), which is 280 m (310 yd) long, steps in the Temple Mount were discovered, as well as a road running along it. Two gates in the south of the Temple Mount are mentioned in the *Mishna*: "the two Hulda Gates on the south, that served for coming in and for going out" *(Middot, 1.3)*. The meaning of the name "Hulda Gates" is now clear: these were entrance gates to the sloping tunnel which began beneath the ground in the south, inside the gate, and ended above ground in the north of the Temple Mount precinct. Anyone passing through the gates looked like a mole (*hulda* in Hebrew) digging a tunnel. The east Hulda Gate was the main entrance gate and the west Hulda Gate was the main exit gate. Pilgrims entered through the eastern gate and left through the western gate. Mourners and outcasts entered through the western gate and left by way of the eastern gate, so that those passing them could comfort them. Both these gates are sealed today. In the eastern (Triple) gate no original vestiges remain. Most of the gatehouse of the western (Double) gate is preserved beneath the floor of the El-Aksa Mosque. Before the facade of the El-Aksa Mosque is a doorway and steps leading down to the Double Gate tunnel. Entrance is prohibited but some scholars have been allowed access and have given descriptions of the gate house, drawings and photographs, showing its pillars, its ornate stone cupolas, arches, steps and beautiful decorations. This is the only architectural vestige of the Temple Mount compound from the time of Herod that has been preserved in its entirety. Today the tunnel is used for storage.

At the foot of the steps, outside the southern wall, ritual baths have been unearthed. Below the surface of the steps, passages and tunnels hewn in the rock were revealed, which led from within the Temple Mount to the exterior. These may have served as a passage through which the priests could leave the precinct and proceed to the ritual baths.

THE TOUR

1. Northern area of the Western Wall.

Open: Sunday, Tuesday, Wednesday 8.30 a.m.–3.00 p.m.; Monday, Thursday, 12.00 a.m.–3.00 p.m.; Friday, *Rosh Hodesh*, (beginning of Hebrew month) Hanukka and Purim, 8.30 a.m.–12.00 a.m. Closed on Jewish holidays. The site is reached through a door in the building at the northwest of the Western Wall prayer plaza, beside the signpost: "Western Wall Caves and Arches".

We enter the underground corridor, which turns north and comes to a system of vaulted areas and rooms close to the Wall. This system is about 100 m (320 ft.) long and continues in an east–west direction. Turning right (east), we see the rooms leading off from the main corridor, as we proceed towards the end of the system. Under the Fatimids (10th–11th centuries), the structure served as the storerooms and stables of an army camp. After it was destroyed by war or by an earthquake, it was used to collect the sewage of the structures above it.

Through a gap in the wall we see, on a lower level, a large Second Temple period room, known as the **Hasmoneans Room.** Three of its walls are the original walls; the south wall and the ceiling vault date from

The water tunnel.

a later period. The structure was discovered by Warren and Wilson about one hundred years ago, and was then called the Masonic Hall, because the Freemasons used it as a meeting place. In the new excavations the place was cleaned up and half columns were discovered in its corners and along the walls. A double portal was revealed in the eastern wall. The structure seems to have been a magnificent hall on the ground floor of an important public building situated close to the Temple Mount.

From the end of the eastern corridor we reach the **Wilson's Arch Room**, against the Western Wall. After removal of the cistern which originally occupied one third of the area, the room was fitted out for prayer. The stones used in the construction of this large vault are smaller than the Herodian building stones visible in the Western Wall and in Robinson's Arch in the south of the Western Wall. The present vault was built apparently in the Omayyad period (7th–9th centuries), on the site of the original arch which was about 3 m (10 ft) higher. Over Wilson's Arch is the Gate of the Chain, at the end of the Street of the Chain. Near the Wall, in the Wilson's Arch Room, is the opening of one of the shafts dug by Wilson and Warren. The shaft goes down to the base of the wall, about 12.5 m (40 ft) below the level of the present floor. At the bottom of the shaft a section of the paved street which ran along the Western Wall was discovered. Large stones, identified as vestiges of the original arch, were discovered on the flagstones of this road. The arch, like the Temple Mount arch, was apparently part of an overpass.

Excavations are still under way in the northern part of the Western Wall, and are proceeding with extreme caution to avoid damage to the stability of the surface buildings; while at the same time concrete and wooden walls, and stone are being employed in the excavation area as reinforcements. Passages, lighting arrangements, and a drainage system are also being installed. Up until today about 350 m (1100 ft) of the Wall have been uncovered, up to the northern edge, which is the northwest corner of the Temple Mount. In a tunnel to the north of Wilson's Arch, the largest stones in the Wall were found, including a gigantic stone about 60 m (66 yd) long, 3 m (10 ft) high, 4 m (13 ft) wide and weighing approximately 400 tons. Approximately 60 m (66 yd) north of Wilson's Arch, is a Second Temple period gate, named after Warren, who first uncovered it. Its dimensions are identical to those of Barclay's Gate, but its arched lintel is probably a Muslim reconstruction from the Omayyad period. The gate is sealed, and the flight of steps over it, beneath the level of the Temple Mount, was plastered and made into a cistern. Warren discovered the inside of the gate when investigating the cistern. At the north end of the tunnel the bedrock was uncovered, hewn in the form of a boss to serve as the foundation of a structure — a vestige of the corner of the Antonia Fortress. After the corner, a Hasmonean period tunnel was uncovered in March 1987. It was hewn in the rock to allow rainwater to flow to a cistern in the depths of the Temple Mount esplanade. The section discovered continues for a distance of 80 m (87 yd) below the Via Dolorosa and comes to a pool in the cellars of the Convent of the Sisters of Zion, where it was sealed off during construction of the convent in the nineteenth century.

The existence of the water tunnel was known from the investigations of Conder, the head of a British expedition, one hundred years ago. It passes beneath the

Robinson's Arch in a model showing the overpass to the Triple Portico.

2. Ophel Archaeological Garden. Open: Sun.–Thurs., 9.00 a.m.–5.00 p.m., Fri. and eve of holidays, until 3.00 p.m. (closed on Sabbaths and holidays). Admission fee. Visits can be organized as proposed in the booklet on sale at the entrance.

The Archaeological Garden is named after Mount Ophel, where the government buildings stood during the First Temple period. It extends southwest of the Western Wall and south of the southern wall. Entrance to the garden is from the Guard Room by the Dung Gate. Going down from the entrance, at a junction of the paths we turn north (left) between two walls built from large ashlar stones. Several courses remain in the east wall, while only one or two remain in the wall opposite. These are the walls of buildings erected by the Omayyad caliphs (7th–8th centuries), incorporating Herodian stones. The east wall and the south wall of the large palace served as a foundation for the Turkish wall east of the Dung Gate (for further details on the palace, see below). From the roof of the palace a bridge was built over the south wall of the Temple Mount, to the El-Aksa Mosque. The place of junction of the bridge is visible on top of the wall, and it was covered with smaller stones. Opposite the palace was the government building, and to its north an enormous royal bath-house used by the residents of all the Omayyad buildings. The floors of the bathhouse were made of burnt bricks, some of which bear the imprint of the seal of the Tenth Roman Legion.

We continue to where the corner of the west and south walls of the Temple Mount have been uncovered, exposing the beautiful Herodian construction to view: the very large stones, dressed with margins, are laid crosswise. On average each stone is about 10 m (33 ft) long, 5 m (16.5 ft) thick and weighs between 30 and 50 tons. The foundations of the wall are dug in the bedrock. From bottom to top there are twenty-two courses, each of which is equally spaced in retreat from the one below, imparting stability to the entire structure (like that of a pyramid). A stone bearing the words "to the place of the trumpeting" was found in the excavations, and is on display at the Israel Museum. The complete inscription was deciphered thanks to Josephus' description of how the priests used to blow trumpets from the towers at the corners of the Temple Mount wall, to announce the beginning of the Sabbath *(Jewish Wars 4, 9, 12)*. This is a "cornerstone" which stood on top of the southwest tower, and which must have fallen from the tower from where the trumpeting was heard.

We continue along the path by the western wall. About 12 m (39 ft) north of the corner, a round stone pier projects, like the beginning of an arch, about 8 m (26 ft) above the path. This is known as **Robinson's Arch** since it was first noticed by the American scholar Edward Robinson in 1838, when the wall was covered with earth almost to the pier, which he thought to be a vestige of a bridge joining the Temple Mount to the Upper City over the Central Valley (the Tyropoeon, mentioned by Josephus). In 1867, Wilson and Warren discovered a column opposite the pier, which they thought to be a vestige of the base of the arch that was the first in the row of arches of the bridge. In the new excavations this column was again uncovered. Opposite it, to the south, vestiges were found of seven arches, each higher than the next, parallel to the Western Wall. It appears that this was not the site of a

Robinson's Arch and the column which were connected by an overpass.

Inscription from the Book of Isaiah.

bridge, but of an overpass. The upper part of the overpass rests on a large arch which extended high over the street. Steps led from the street level over the arches to the north. Finally the overpass turned eastward over the large arch, to the gate of the Triple Portico, the basilica built by Herod, high up in the Western Wall. Part of the paved street which passed beneath the arch in a north-south direction has been uncovered. Vestiges of shops which stood on both sides have also been unearthed: the eastern shops were against the western wall and the western shops were between the columns of the arch and small structures west of it. This was one of the central markets — Jerusalem's lower market. The street, which here ran parallel to the Western Wall, began in the region of today's Damascus Gate and continued southward to the Siloam Pool (its last section, in the area of David's Citadel, was uncovered by a British expedition in the late 1920s). Near Robinson's Arch, an inscription of two lines, in square Hebrew characters, was discovered engraved on a stone in one of the lower courses of the Western Wall. Thought to date from about the 4th century CE., this inscription is part of a verse from Isaiah: "And when you see this, your heart will rejoice and your bones like a herb. . ." (Isaiah, 66:14; "And when you see this, your heart will rejoice and your bones shall flourish like a herb") and could be an expression of the joy the Jews felt at the preparations for construction of the Temple by the Byzantine Emperor Julian the Apostate. In the courses of the wall at this point we can see two conduits which were hewn along the length of the wall in the Byzantine period, apparently for the conveyance of rainwater, and which also served in the Omayyad period.

We shall continue north along the wall until we come to a shaft going down to the wall's foundations. This shaft, which was sunk by Wilson and Warren, uncovers nineteen courses. Opposite it, west of the path, is a section of the 10 m (33 ft) wide Herodian street paved with large, smooth flagstones, which runs parallel to the wall. A raised kerb at the edges of the road was designed to prevent rainwater from flowing into the shops that bordered it. There was a 3 m (9.5 ft) wide row of shops between the road and the wall. In the western part of the area of excavation, which is the west bank of the bed of the Central Valley, First Temple period graves were discovered hewn into the solid rock. Called "skylight graves" because of the additional entry cut in the ceiling, they resemble the Phoenician burial sites known from the time of Ahab, king of Israel. The graves were found empty and are thought to have been cleared as early as the First Temple period under Hezekiah, when the city was expanded to the western hill.

We shall go back south along the path, to the corner of the walls. Beneath the Omayyad period street, stone steps were discovered and a section of a paved Herodian street that turned east and continued along the south wall, alongside the Hulda Gate. The section that turns west went up

Remains of the medieval tower.

to the western hill and its vestiges were found there, in the Jewish Quarter excavations.

Going back to the junction, we shall take the wide path going eastward which will take us through the area of the palace of the Omayyad caliphs. This palace was built on the entire area which today is in the corner of the Ottoman wall, and its walls are thought to have served as a foundation for two sections of this wall. Vestiges of the perpendicular clay gutter in the western wall of the palace show that the structure was two storeys high. The palace occupied 8 hectares (2 acres) and was 13 m (43 ft) high. In its center was a square inner courtyard (20 m × 20 m — 66 ft × 66 ft) where trees, bushes and flowers grew. Around the courtyard were porticos, rooms and halls with pillars and arches. This was a complex of palaces, built in the 8th century by Caliph Mu'awiyya and his successors (Abd el-Malik and his son Walid), who also constructed the Dome of the Rock and the El-Aksa Mosque. The palaces were built partly from stones in secondary use, taken from the ruins on the Temple Mount and from stones of churches (including the Nea Church which was also built from the ruins on the Temple Mount). The Omayyad palaces were destroyed under the Fatimids (10th–11th centuries) and many of the building stones were burnt for lime.

We go into one of the palace rooms, north of the path, and up a flight of steps to the top of a medieval tower. This tower was apparently built by the Crusaders, who fortified the city wall (possibly the first tower on this site was built by the Fatimids, and the Mamelukes renovated the Crusader tower). The eastern part of the tower (which is outside the Turkish wall section) blocks the western side of the Double Gate. The top of the tower affords a view of the surrounding landscape and a passage from there leads along the Ottoman wall up to the Dung Gate.

We leave the tower and turn west, to another room of the Omayyad palace, from which a spiral staircase leads down to a 6th-century Byzantine residential building. Some of the many rooms here belong to an earlier structure, the cisterns of which served as cellars in the Byzantine period. The wooden ceilings and mosaic floors in the rooms have been renovated and repaired. A narrow, roofed passage leads us to a second Byzantine structure, similar to the first. From here a passage, with steps hewn in the rock, takes us outside the wall. Retracing our steps, we can leave by the double gate, opened in 1970 by the archeological expedition digging on the site, in order to create a link between the two parts of the excavations.

The area east of the Ottoman wall is identified with the Ophel, the area which was between the City of David and the Temple Mount in the First Temple period. In the Bible it is mentioned on several occasions as an elevated, fortified area at the top of the City of David. In the excavations 13 m (43 ft) of debris were removed and 25 Jewish, Roman, Byzantine, and Muslim layers of settlement were uncovered. The discoveries from the Second Temple period are particularly interesting. After removal of the interior of the Omayyad structures, which covered most of the surface of the Ophel, the vestiges of an earlier construction were uncovered, reaching down to the bedrock. The important structures were partially restored, including another large Omayyad palace, similar to the palace of the governors, and a smaller structure to the east. The walls of

Pool, ritual baths and Herodian house.

the palace have remained in their place, and their size and the scope of the palace are breathtaking.

The tour of this site is circular and involves many ascents and descents. From the Excavations gate, it is possible to go down south, continue east, and go up to the south wall by the stone steps, returning finally to the gate. It is also possible to take the opposite direction, starting at the stone steps.

We go down the steel steps south of the gate to the excavations and pass through rooms with mosaic floors. One of the floors on the upper level boasts a Greek inscription: "Happy are those who live in this house." Another floor is decorated with geometrical designs. The rooms were part of Byzantine residential structures, a continuation of the neighborhood west of today's city wall.

Continuing our descent, we pass through ritual baths and stuccoed cisterns, and vestiges of a house from the time of Herod. We come to a stuccoed area encompassed by walls, which was a pool in the 2nd century BCE. The Akra (citadel), built by Antiochus in Jerusalem and destroyed by Simon the Hasmonean, may have been on this site.

We continue east along the path and the steps until we come to a rock wall with signs of quarrying. This was a stone quarry from the early Ottoman period (16th century), from which building stones were hewn for the present city wall. Turning southeast along the path and steps, we come to the vestiges of a Byzantine house, with a central hall containing pillars and twelve rooms leading off the hall. Further east along the path, we find vestiges of the southern wing of a public building from the Omayyad period. This large structure is part of the network of palace buildings from the Omayyad period, construction of which began in the early 8th century and which was never completed. The path passes over the wall of the building (the lower part of the wall was reinforced and prepared for this purpose). Further along on the opposite side are vestiges of a public building with many ritual baths, dating from the late Second Temple period. This may have been a hostel for the pilgrims who visited Jerusalem, or it may have been part of the complex of palaces of the kings of Adiabene and their mother, Queen Helena (mentioned by Josephus), who had the so-called Tombs of the Kings hewn.

Turning left we see a wall belonging to a First Temple period public building, and another wall parallel to the main road (the Ophel Road). Three stages of construction have been distinguished here, the first dating from the time of King Solomon in the 10th century BCE. This structure is the most ancient in the Ophel area. Continuing

Stairs leading up to the Hulda Gate.

along the path we again pass by columns of the Omayyad structure. Proceeding west towards the south wall, we go up stone steps along a road from the Byzantine period (4th–6th centuries CE), which goes from the Siloam Gate to the Triple Gate in the south wall. Opposite is another Byzantine neighborhood.

On our left is a courtyard with pillars of a public building from the Omayyad period. Some of these round marble and red granite pillars have been restored, but most of them are lying on the ground. This structure belonged to the complex of **Omayyad** palace buildings, and incorporated pillars from the remains of churches and houses. Crosses are engraved on some pillars, and scholars think that they were brought from the Byzantine Nea Church and before that from the ruins of the Temple — and in this way the pillars were returned close to their original site.

From the courtyard of pillars we shall go up into the plaza and series of stone stairs which lead to the western Hulda Gate. The complex, which was built under Herod, is not mentioned in the ancient sources; it was uncovered in the excavations. The steps have been restored, with reconstruction on the pattern of those uncovered whole. They are alternately wide (90 cm — 29.5 ft) and narrow (40 cm — 13 ft), planned in such a way as to ensure an easy, but slow ascent, to intensify the feeling of reverence. The steps end in the Hulda Gate Road which continues along the south wall at the top of the steps.

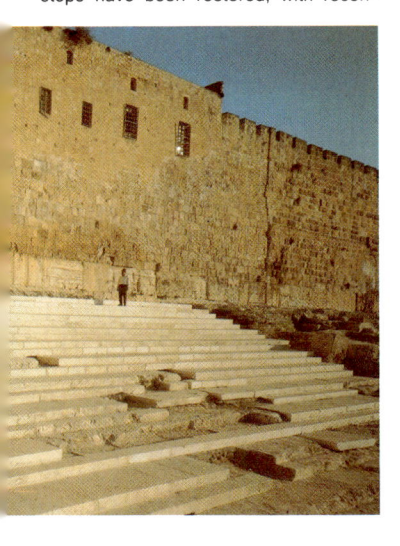

The western (double) Hulda Gate, which continues on below the el-Aksa Mosque, is sealed today. Its original doorjamb is preserved in the first course of the wall, which is double the height of the other Herodian courses (about 2 m — 6.7 ft). The arch in its lintel is from the Omayyad period, when the gate, which was known as the Gate of the Prophet, was open. Over the upper right corner of the arch, a stone in secondary usage was placed upside down; upon it is a now barely visible Latin inscription: "Titus Elius Hadrianus Antoninus Augustus Pius, father of the homeland, the priest who tells the future, by order of the head of the city".

Continuing along the road at the foot of the southern wall, the Hulda Gate Road, where some of the original flagstones have been preserved, we reach the (Triple) eastern gate, recognizable by its three sealed portals. These portals are from the Omayyad period and were built on the site of the original gate. During the Second Temple period this was the main entrance gate for pilgrims. It consisted of a high central portal and a lower portal on each side in the accepted form for a ceremonial gate. Beautiful engraved stones were found in the wall beside it, on the threshold and in the doorjamb. The narrower flight of steps which is thought to have led up to it (but which has not been uncovered in the excavations) was suited for the ascent and entry, since here it was ascertained that all who entered had purified themselves in the ritual bath. Below the Hulda Gate, tunnels hewn in the rock were discovered with niches in the sides, for placing candles for lighting. Possibly these were the staircases described in the *Mishna* as passages for the priests who became ritually unclean. The passages led to ritual purification baths outside the Temple Mount. Along the Hulda Gate Road, up to the Triple Gate only one original course of the south wall (which here is the city wall) is preserved. East of the Triple Gate additional courses are preserved. In the southeast corner of the wall all nineteen of the original courses are preserved. Today the Hulda Gate Road ends by the Triple Gate, but in the Second Temple period it continued to the eastern corner of the southern wall and from there to another overpath that went over the top of the eastern wall. In this section of the southern wall we see traces of the Crusader Single Gate, which was sealed in the Ayyubid period.

Our tour ends here.

TOUR No. 4

THE JEWISH QUARTER

Details of tour: Our first visit to the Jewish Quarter provides a general impression of its sites and the various historical periods. (A special visit can be made separately to view the exhibits at the Museum.)

Distance covered: approx. 3 km (2 miles)

Time: approx. 6 hours (including 4 hours devoted to the Museum and the exhibits)

Transportation: Buses No 1 to Dung Gate, 38 into the Quarter, 99 to Mount Zion and the Dung Gate

Parking lots outside Jaffa Gate and Zion Gate for private vehicles

Starting point: Zion Gate

End of tour: Jaffa Gate

Please note that the tour includes visits to synagogues and holy places — appropriate dress is desirable.

The Sites: 1. Zion Gate; 2. Observation point; 3. Batei Mahseh Square; 4. Nea Church; 5. Memorial; 6. Sephardi synagogues; 7. Ramban Synagogue; 8. Hurva Synagogue; 9. Heart of the Jewish Quarter; 10. Ashkenazi Compound; 11. The Cardo; 12. The Broad Wall; 13. The Israelite tower; 14. Western Wall Observation Point; 15. German Hospice; 16. Burnt House; 17. Tiferet Israel Synagogue; 18. Karaite Synagogue; 19. Herodian residential quarter; 20. Old Yishuv Court Museum; 21. Bikur Holim Hospital; 22. Other sites in the Jewish Quarter.

FOREWORD

The Jewish Quarter is situated in the southeast section of the Old City. To the south it borders on the city wall, between Zion Gate and Dung Gate; to the east on the Western Wall; to the north with Hashalshelet Street (the Street of the Chain); and to the west, the Armenian Quarter.

The quarter can be reached in a number of ways.

By car: from Jaffa Gate along the Armenian Patriarchate Road to the quarter's parking lot, or through Zion Gate to the parking lot outside the wall (this road is closed to traffic on Saturdays); or along Hativat Yerushalayim (Jerusalem Brigade) Road, starting at Mount Zion, leading to the parking lot.

On foot: from Jaffa Gate along the Armenian Patriarchate Road, turn left, into St James Street to Ararat Street and then to Or Hahayim Street.

From Jaffa Gate down David Street, turn right into Habad Street or at the Cardo, or Hayehudim St. We can also continue along Hashalshelet Street (Street of the Chain) and then turn right at Plugat Hakotel Street or at Misgav Ladach Street.

From Damascus Gate through HaGai Street to the Western Wall and then up the Yehuda Halevy steps to the Jewish Quarter. Or: from Zion Gate to the east or north.

From Dung Gate by walking up to Batei Mahseh Street.

From the Western Wall plaza up the Yehuda Halevy steps, or up the narrow stairs leading to the quarter.

The area of the Jewish Quarter was first inhabited during the First Temple period in the 8th century BCE (apparently with the increase in the population of Jerusalem, after the fall of the towns of Judah to Sennacherib, King of Assyria). At first the area was an open city, but a wall was built around it in 701 BCE, during the reign of Hezekiah, King of Judah, when the Assyrians threatened Jerusalem.

Jerusalem was laid in ruins during the conquest of Jerusalem and the destruc-

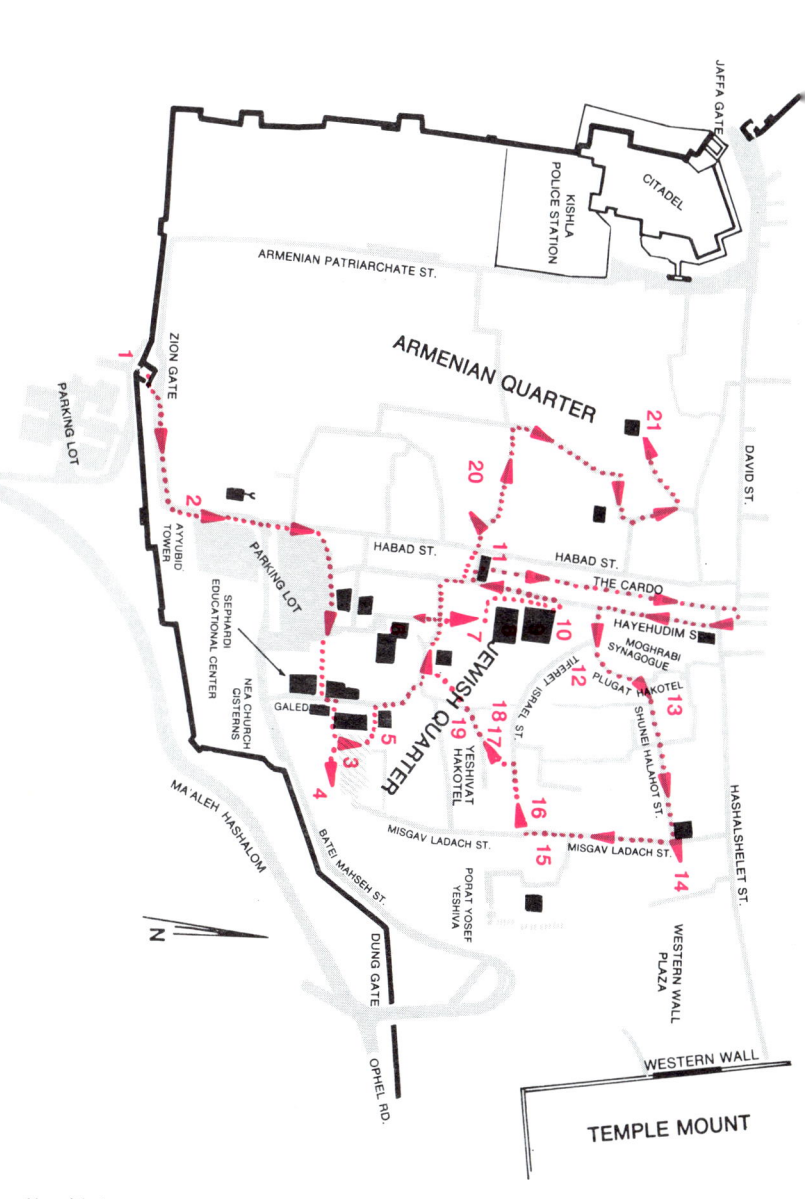

THE JEWISH QUARTER

Map of the tour.

tion of the First Temple in 586 BCE by Nebuchadnezzar, King of Babylon. After the Return to Zion from the Babylonian exile during the Persian period and the early Hellenistic period (538–165 BCE), the area remained desolate. It was only in the Hasmonean (late Hellenistic) period that the Jews returned to the area, built houses and rebuilt the city wall. During the Herodian period a residential suburb for the aristocracy, the wealthy and the priests who served in the Temple sprang up. It reached its climax with Herod the Great but, it was followed by disaster when Rome destroyed the Second Temple (in 70 CE), and the area was razed to the ground. Under Roman and Byzantine rule (70–638) Jews were forbidden to settle in Jerusalem. The Romans set up a military camp in the area; the Byzantines built a large new church (the Nea) and paved a road — the Cardo (the heart) — that ran through the center of the city leading to the church.

After the Arab conquest, in 638, Jews settled in Jerusalem again, at first in the vicinity of Haram esh-Sharif and later in the area north of it. The conquering Crusaders massacred the Jews and Arabs (1099), and built churches and monasteries. After Saladin's victory over the Crusaders (1187) he permitted the Jews to return to Jerusalem. In 1267 the Ramban (Nahmanides) reached Jerusalem and reorganized the Jewish community on Mount Zion.

It was only in the 15th century that the Jewish community moved from Mount Zion to the present site. Jewish communal life was well-organized: synagogues, institutions for education, health and welfare were built there. Jews from many countries settled and followed their community lifestyles, and leading personalities lived in the quarter or visited it. The Jewish population increased during the 19th century, and Jews settled in the Muslim Quarter as well. From 1880 to 1914 the Jews constituted a majority in the Old City. During the British Mandate (1918–1948) the Jewish population decreased as a result of the riots of the 1920s and 1930s. When Israel's War of Independence broke out there were about 1700 Jews in the quarter.

Immediately after the reunification of Jerusalem in 1967, the Israeli government decided to renew Jewish life in the quarter. Restoration and development projects continued over a period of fifteen years. Archaeological excavations under the auspices of the Hebrew University, headed by Prof. N. Avigad, brought to light finds of inestimable scientific value.

As the quarter was restored, streets were paved, houses reconstructed and modern buildings erected — all the while the planners sought to preserve its original character. Some of the synagogues and *Yeshivot* (Talmudic schools) have been restored and new *Yeshivot* and public institutions built. The Porat Yosef Yeshiva has been rebuilt according to the plan of the Israeli architect Moshe Safde who has used numerous arches in his design. Yeshivat Hakotel, situated above the Porat Yosef Yeshiva, is today the tallest building in the quarter. Some of the housing complexes and lanes which were destroyed during the years of Jordanian rule have been restored.

Approximately 5000 Jews live in the quarter, involved in study, teaching and tourism. Studios of artists who have settled there attract visitors and tourists on their way to the Western Wall. The important sites in the quarter are signposted and a guidebook published by the Jerusalem municipality is available at bookstores. New institutions have been established; artifacts used in the daily life of the inhabitants since the mid-19th century are on show at the Old Yishuv Court Museum, and two synagogues in its courtyard have been restored. Literary sessions are held at the Hayim Hazaz Writers' House; workshops on aspects of Judaism are run at the Sapir Jewish Heritage Center, and guided tours and lectures for youth take place at the Rachel Yanait Ben-Zvi Center for Jerusalem Studies.

THE TOUR

We enter the Jewish Quarter through Zion Gate.

1. Zion Gate The western gate in the southern wall of the city is named after Mount Zion. In Arabic it is also called "The Prophet David's Gate" because one

Zion Gate: decorated arch and turret.

passes through it to King David's tomb on Mount Zion. Riddled with bullet holes, it bears testimony to the fighting during the War of Independence (1948). The gate was restored and rebuilt after the Six Day War.

Above the gate is a decorated arch surmounted by a stone rosette. Above that is a turret supported by stones in the form of leaves. The wall itself consists of stone blocks dating from the Crusader period, and stones from earlier periods have been used in the lower courses. On both sides of the gate are embrasures decorated with carved arches from the Mameluke period surmounted by rosettes. The entrance to the gate turns at a sharp right angle, differing in this from the other gates, evidence that this may not be the original structure. Additional proof of this is given by the embrasures in the western and northern walls of the gate entrance, which do not seem to be strategically placed as they face towards the inside. The gate had two double doors (like St Stephen's Gate). Climb the stairs to reach the top of the wall where you can join (for a fee) the Rampart Walk. Above the entrance to the inner gate is a Turkish inscription in honor of the builder of the wall, the Ottoman Sultan Suleiman the Magnificent.

2. Observation Point We leave Zion Gate, enter the Old City and continue along the road to the Tiferet Yerushalayim Square leading to the Jewish Quarter. The area nearest us, between the wall and the parking lot, once served as a refuse dump on the outskirts of the quarter. The archaeological excavations carried out after 1967 at the eastern boundary of this site exposed impressive water cisterns (which can be visited) belonging to the Byzantine Nea Church, and an inscription in Greek refers to Emperor Justinian who ordered the church to be built. (The inscription is on display at the Israel Museum.) The church spread over an area of 75 m × 115 m (245 ft × 373 ft). In the middle of the site alongside which we are standing, between the road and the wall, are the remains of a Crusader church, partly restored, and the basis of an entrance tower (restored) built in 1212 by El-Mu'azzam, the Ayyubid governor (according to an inscription found in the ruins). He also destroyed the gate in 1219 for fear that the Crusaders would fortify themselves within the city once again. It is surmised that in the vicinity was the Nea Gate which stood at the extremity of the Byzantine Cardo. On this site is now an archaeological garden open to visitors.

From here, we can see the southwestern border of the Jewish Quarter. At the corner is the Sephardi Educational Center. North of the parking lot an old building houses the Imreh Bina Yeshiva, and behind it is the new building of the Sapir Jewish Heritage Center. Opposite is a domed low building — the site of four Sephardi synagogues.

3. Batei Mahseh Square We continue in the direction of the Sephardi Educational Center and go along Hahatsotsrot Street (the lane between the buildings) and enter the courtyard to the right. Built in 1874, the design of the original Sephardi Talmud Torah is characteristic of that period: a courtyard enclosed by a series of rooms for study, living accommodation and service rooms. The building was restored after 1967, and the Center's new quarters were constructed opposite.

At the end of the lane we turn left into Galed Street and reach an archway on whose lintel is engraved: "Shelter for the poor on Mount Zion, may it be built and reestablished". We go through the archway and between Beit Hasofer (the Writers' House), on the right, and the Rothschild House, on the left, and come into Batei Mahseh Square. The houses encompassing the paved square were constructed between 1860 and 1890 by an association of Jews from Holland and Germany. The approximately 100 two-room apartments were allocated to poor families for a period of three years free of charge or at a low rental.

To the west of the square is the Rothschild House — a two-storey building with arches. It was built in 1871 with funds provided by Baron Wolf Rothschild of Frankfurt to house poor families, and the Rothschild family coat of arms is still at the top of the building. Today it houses the offices of the Jewish Quarter Development Company.

A giant monumental column found about a 100 m (110 yd) north of the square has been placed there by archaeologists. The Corinthian capital is adorned with carved rose petals, the base is Herodian and the entire column is estimated to have been about 10 m (33 ft) high. Its original site is unknown.

The modern structures surrounding the square were erected on the ruins of buildings destroyed in the War of Independence. Today the square serves as a playground for children and attracts residents of the quarter and visitors. On the wall to the north of the square a new inscription has been carved: "Thus saith the Lord of hosts: There shall yet old men and old women dwell in the streets of Jerusalem. . . the city shall be full of boys and girls playing in the streets thereof" (Zechariah 8:4–5).

3. Nea Church Visiting hours: Sunday through Thursday 9.00 a.m.–5.00 p.m., Friday till 1.00 p.m.

South of Batei Mahseh Square we

The Rothschild House and Batei Mahseh Square.

descend the steps to Nahamu Lane, down a few more steps to a basement of a house which is signposted and numbered. Here are the remains of a Byzantine church built in the 6th century by Emperor Justinian. We see part of the northern apse leading from the eastern wall. This was the new (Nea in Greek) church dedicated to the Virgin Mary. The large building extended from Batei Mahseh Square up to the parking lot alongside the Sephardi Educational Center. Its water cisterns are situated in the area to the south. The church was destroyed when the Persians conquered Jerusalem in 614. It is believed that ancient columns were used in the construction of the church, possibly from the colonnade on Haram esh-Sharif which was destroyed at the time of the destruction of the Temple. These columns and other remains of the Nea Church were discovered in the excavations of the Muslim houses at the south of Haram esh-Sharif.

5. The Monument We return to Batei Mahseh Square and turn into the lane at the northern corner of the Rothschild House. On the wall of the corner house to the right is a memorial plaque and below it a small stone platform enclosed by a fence commemorating the last defenders of the quarter who fell here prior to the surrender to the Jordanians.

We enter Galed Street where we see a two-storey building with an ornamented balcony and arched windows which housed the Sha'ar Hashamayim Ashkenazi Yeshiva. We turn right into Bet-El Street and enter a cul-de-sac and at the end, to the left, we reach the rear entrance of the Stambuli Synagogue. Above the entrance are ancient carved stone decorations, but the doors are new. The synagogue can be visited during services. We retrace our steps and continue along Bet-El Street until we reach Mishmeret Hakehuna Street.

6. Sephardi synagogues Visiting hours: Sun.–Thurs. 9.00 a.m.–4.00 p.m., Fri. till 1.00 p.m. Entry fee. Booklets in Hebrew and in English are available.

Four adjoining synagogues are situated in a compound below the level of Mishmeret Hakehuna Street because,

Rear entrance of the Stambuli Synagogue.

when they were first constructed, in 1588, the Ottoman sultan forbade that synagogues be higher than mosques. Over the centuries the street level has risen and thus the compound is now much lower. The four synagogues were built by members of the Sephardi community who originally came from Spain in the 15th century. After the conquest of Jerusalem by the Ottoman Turks in 1517, Jews immigrated from Italy, Greece and Turkey (where they had settled after the expulsion from Spain and Portugal in 1492 and 1497). Up to the mid-19th century, these communities also included Jews from North Africa, Egypt and Syria. The synagogues are designed in accordance with the traditions of each community, and the Sephardis constituted the largest community for a considerable time, the Chief Sephardi Rabbi being the leading personality in Jerusalem. These synagogues were central to the life of the Jews of Jerusalem from 1721 to 1836, the period when the Ashkenazi Compound (see below) lay in ruins. Originally the four synagogues were separate but in 1835 they were grouped as the Yohanan Ben Zakkai Sephardi Synagogue

As the battle for Jerusalem during the War of Independence drew to an end, most of the Jewish inhabitants of the Old City found refuge in these synagogues. Under Jordanian rule the synagogues were plundered and used as storerooms and stables. After 1967 they were restored by the architect Dan Tannai and reopened in 1972. Some of the furniture and fittings were brought from old Italian synagogues destroyed in World War II and the doors and adornments are the work of Israeli craftsmen, although some of the original decorations were found intact.

From the outside the building looks like an ordinary housing structure. There are no windows facing outwards, but only inwards towards the compound. On the roof are two domes built out of small stones above octagonal turrets in which there are skylights. The floor is 3 m (9 ft) below street level. We descend the stairs into the courtyard and go in through the main entrance of the Yohanan ben Zakkai synagogue.

Yohanan Ben Zakkai Synagogue The largest and most embellished of the four (8.2 m × 20 m — 26 ft × 66 ft). It was built at the beginning of the 17th century. Its present name was given to it in 1893, based on a late tradition that before the destruction of the Second Temple this was the site of Rabbi Yohanan ben Zakkai's religious academy *(Beit Hamidrash)*. From then on the Chief Sephardi Rabbi — the *Rishon-le-Zion* — has been ordained here. The original building had a wooden ceiling held aloft on pillars. In 1835 the pillars were removed, and the stone walls reinforced with crossing vaults. In the southern wall there are three arched windows within a recess, surmounted by a square window. On this window lie a pitcher of oil and a *shofar* (ram's horn) which, according to tradition, will be used to announce the coming of the Messiah. The Holy Ark has been restored on the basis of the original. Above it is a new mural by Jean David of "the celestial Jerusalem". Between the Ark and the mural are marble slabs inscribed with the Ten Commandments brought from a

Yohanan Ben Zakkai Synagogue.

synagogue in Livorno (Leghorn) in Italy.

We go through the doorway at the western end of the hall and enter the **Elijah Synagogue**. Opened in 1586 this is the first synagogue in the complex. It had earlier served as a *Talmud Torah* (Talmudic school) and was first called the Kahal Zion community. After the completion of the Sephardi Talmud Torah in 1874, the building was used solely as a prayer house. According to a tradition, the prophet Elijah once completed a *minyan* (10 man-quorum required by Jewish practice as a minimum for public prayer) on Yom Kippur and at the end of the service disappeared. The legend probably was based on the fact that only a handful of Jews lived here during the first years after the synagogue was built. The original building was made of wood and only in 1835 was the square hall (6.5 m — 21 ft) constructed in stone, capped by a dome on an octagonal turret with skylights. Stairs lead up to the women's gallery, which has new windows in the western wall facing Mishmeret Hakehuna Street, and the new door is opened only for services. On the northwest corner there are steps leading down to a small cellar with an "Elijah's Chair," on which tradition has it the Prophet sat during the service. The original chair was stolen in 1948 and the present one is a replica. The present furniture was brought from a synagogue in Livorno, Italy. The impressive Holy Ark is made of dark wood adorned with carved leaves and flowers. A new "Bridegroom's Chair" and a bench remaining from the original furniture stand beside it.

We return to the Yohanan Ben Zakkai Synagogue and through another doorway enter the small (12.8 × 3.7 m — 39 × 12 ft) **Middle Synagogue** also known as Kahal Katan (the small congregation). It was built in the mid-18th century and for a period served as the women's section of the Yohanan Ben Zakkai Synagogue. Legend has it that a concealed tunnel led to the tomb of King David on Mount Zion. During its reconstruction in 1835, a number of crossing vaults centered on a rosette were added and a new wall at its western extremity formed an internal courtyard common to the adjoining two synagogues. The western wall ends in a pointed arch with a round window, below which are two rows of arched windows. On either side of the door are rectangular windows surmounted by carved stone vents through which the sunlight penetrates. Above the doorway in the southern wall through which we entered is a square plaque bearing part of a dedicatory inscription to a donor by the name of Joseph. The area now serves solely as a passage between the Yohanan Ben Zakkai and Stambuli synagogues.

Stambuli Synagogue was the last to be built in 1764 by immigrants from Istanbul, Turkey. It is similar in style to the Elijah Synagogue and it, too, has a stone dome on whose inner side can be seen a fragment of an inscription giving the year (1835 in Hebrew) in which all four synagogues were renovated. The Stambuli Synagogue is the simplest of the four synagogues and served the Ashkenazi community when it was evicted from its compound, as well as the Moghrabi community before it built its own. After the latest renovation, furniture was brought from Ancona, Italy, including a 17th-century gilded, carved wooden Ark. The *bimah* (raised prayer platform) has four wooden pillars painted to look like marble. Two pillars on either side of the Ark, bearing inscriptions from the books of Proverbs and Psalms, were brought from Pesaro in Italy. Below the synagogue a large cistern was discovered which was used on the first day of *Rosh Hashana* (the Jewish New Year) for the *Tashlich* prayers. Above the original doorway which leads to Bet-El Street is another inscription. This entrance is closed on weekdays and is opened only for services on the Sabbath and Jewish holidays. We return to the main entrance of the Yohanan Ben Zakkai Synagogue, mount the steps to Mishmeret Hakehuna Street and turn right (north) to the entrance to the Hurva Synagogue plaza.

7. Ramban Synagogue open for services. On weekdays it is accessible from Hayehudim Street through the Beit Midrash.

Rabbi Moses ben Nahman (Nahmanides, known as Ramban) immigrated to Jerusalem in 1267 and helped rehabilitate the Jewish community. He wrote to his son as follows: ". . . Jerusalem is in greater ruin than the entire land. . . there is no Jewish congregation within it. . . only two brothers who are dyers. . . and they are joined by a *minyan* of men who pray in their house on the Sabbath. . . we found a ruined house constructed upon marble pillars with a beautiful dome and we took it for our synagogue, for the city is lawless, and whosoever wishes to benefit from the ruins can do so." As this description fits the

Stambuli Synagogue, the bimah and Ark.

synagogue it was presumed that this was the site; however, scholars are now of the opinion that Nahmanides established a synagogue on Mount Zion.

This was the first synagogue to be constructed in the Jewish Quarter, and Jews began to settle around it when they moved from Mount Zion in approximately 1400. The nearby mosque was built later; the synagogue was destroyed by zealous Muslims in 1474. A year later permission was granted to the Jews to rebuild it, and it served all the Jewish communities until 1586 when prayer services were prohibited. From that time on the building was used as a cheese factory and Jews who were unaware of its past also ran a store there. The building was restored after 1967 and since then has served as a synagogue and Beit Midrash.

We go down steps from the plaza to a repaved courtyard. A solitary stone pillar stands at the eastern side of the entrance. An additional entrance from Hayehudim Street leads to a passage and to the right we find the rooms of the Beit Midrash and to the left a women's gallery leading into the prayer hall. The synagogue is divided by a row of four pillars. The fifth pillar in the row (now in the courtyard) was removed to enable construction of the *bimah*. The names Abraham, Isaac and Jacob are carved on the westernmost pillar. The four pillars had been placed upside down, and when the building was being restored their capitals were unearthed.

From the Ramban Synagogue we mount the new stairway to a square overlooking the ruins of the Hurva Synagogue under its reconstructed arch. We can enter the Hurva by returning to the Ramban Synagogue courtyard and then walking along Hayehudim Street.

8. The Hurva Synagogue called Beit Yaacov (after Baron James de Rothschild who provided funds for its completion) but is commonly known as the Hurva (of Rabbi Yehuda Hassid) Synagogue. Built within the confines of the Ashkenazi compound, this synagogue was completed in 1705 following the death of Rabbi Yehuda Hassid, but was destroyed in 1721 together with the entire compound. This is the derivation of the name Hurva ("ruin") given to the synagogue erected by Ashkenazi Jews in its place from 1856 to 1864, and which remained intact for 84 years. Its construction was made possible through donations from Jews throughout the world and especially Yehezkiel ben Reuven Menashe of Baghdad. It was the tallest (25 m — 82 ft) building in the Jewish Quarter — even higher than the minaret of the nearby mosque. The synagogue served as the center of Jewish life throughout the country, and many assemblies were held there.

From Hayehudim Street we go through an iron door, mount a few steps and go through the high, wide entrance into the hall. We can see the remains of the *bimah* in the center and the recess in the eastern wall which housed the Ark. To the left of the stairs are photographs of the building in its original form and of the building permit granted in 1855 through the intervention of the British consul in Constantinople. The architect Assad Bey, engaged by Moses Montefiore, planned the building in oriental style. It had four arches, one in each direction, rising above the walls. Above the arches a turret was built supporting a dome with a dozen windows. The turret was surrounded by a large balcony with an iron railing decorated with verses from the Psalms and illustrations of musical instruments. From the balcony the visitor could view the entire Old City as well as the Temple Mount and the surrounding hills. The hall, covering an area of

Reconstructed arch of Hurva Synagogue.

13.7 m × 15 m (46 ft × 49 ft) and 24 m (79 ft) high, seated 150 men, and in the gallery were seats for 50 women. Light filtered through the turret windows and two rows of large windows in the walls. In the eastern wall there was a Torah Ark reached by wide steps flanked by pillars decorated with gilded baroque-style knop and flowers brought from the synagogue of the Russian city of Kherson. Golden crystal candelabra hung from the ceiling.

9. Lev Harova (Heart of the Jewish Quarter) Visiting hours: Sun.–Thurs. 9.00 a.m. to 5.00 p.m., Fri., till 1.00 p.m. Entry fee. A 20 minute audiovisual program on the history and reconstruction of the quarter is presented in Hebrew and English throughout the day.

North of the Hurva Synagogue, at the corner of Hayehudim Street and Lohamei Harova Street (Defenders of the Quarter Street), a number of sites recount the history of the Quarter. The *Lev Harova* was part of the Ashkenazi compound. An exhibition by the English photographer John Phillips who accompanied the Jordanian Legion, graphically traces developments in the quarter from the day it surrendered. In a cellar below, an illuminated map shows the defense posts and the battles in the Jewish Quarter during the War of Independence.

10. The Ashkenazi Compound We mount the steps to a courtyard enclosed by a number of restored buildings. The compound was bought by the Ashkenazi community in Jerusalem about the year 1400. Rooms were built as accommodation for pilgrims, the poor and widows. At the beginning of the 17th century a synagogue was built, and in 1700 a Beit Midrash (academy) was completed containing 40 rooms and four water cisterns. That year Rabbi Yehuda Hassid arrived in Jerusalem from Poland with some 200 of his followers and settled in the compound. Five years later Rabbi Yehuda died and donations ceased to arrive from Poland. The community sank into debt and in 1721 Arab creditors set fire to the compound and most of the Ashkenazi community was forced to leave Jerusalem. The compound, named the Hurva, lay in ruin for

Facade of Hurva Synagogue with minaret behind.

about 90 years. In 1812 a group of Ashkenazis from Galilee succeeded in obtaining the cancellation the old debts. They moved to Jerusalem and began to restore the compound. In 1837 the Menachem Zion Synagogue was inaugurated and in 1841 the Etz Hayim housing project, a public soup kitchen and a Yeshiva (1862) were set up. (The Etz Hayim Yeshiva was transferred to the new city in 1910.)

During the War of Independence the compound was destroyed completely, but was reconstructed between 1980 and 1985, including the northern section which had been razed to the ground during the 1939 riots. The renovated Menachem Zion Synagogue is open to visitors. The 18th-century furniture and Ark were brought from the Saluzzo community in Italy.

11. The Cardo We retrace our steps southward along Hayehudim Street (Jews' Street) to the mosque next to the Hurva. On the western side of the street is a courtyard below street level enclosed by an iron fence. We go down the stairs into the paved courtyard where six columns (five of them intact) stand in a row. This is the open section of "the Street of Pillars," the main street of Roman and Byzantine Jerusalem, running north to south. The street is depicted in the Madaba map (a 6th century map discovered in 1896 in the floor of a Byzantine church in the Jordanian city of Madaba portraying sites in Palestine). In the course of the renovation of the Bazaar (below) in Hayehudim Street, archaeological excavations exposed 150 m (164 yd) of a street 22.5 m (24 yd) wide between two rows of columns which supported arches. In this section we can see only remains of the western colonnade, a little above street level. A channel for draining rain water ran between the street and the colonnade. To the west of the raised street is a wall hewn into the rock which served as the western wall of a series of shops along the colonnade. Remains of the arches of two of the shops can be seen on the rock wall.

We continue north and go through a narrow passage into a hall with benches in descending rows. A 10-minute audiovisual program, "The Story of a Street," describes the history of the Cardo. A reproduction of the Madaba map is seen on the eastern wall. At the top of the map is an inscription in Greek: "The holy city of Jerusalem." The Cardo appears in the center of the map as a white strip with white pillars running down both sides. The Cardo begins at the northern (left) extremity of the city with a wide plaza in which stands a column. A gate in the wall is where the Damascus Gate stands today and a colonnaded side street leads south. The central street running along the north to south axis is called Cardo Maximus. At the southern extremity of the street we can see the Nea Church with its red-tiled roof and double doors. To the west, at the end of the street, is the Holy Zion Church on Mount Zion. The western wall, which at this time also encompassed Mount Zion, can be seen at the western (lower) part of the city. A small gate in the western wall is the beginning of a short street which at first runs east and then south. This is a section of the "Decumanus" which runs along the course of the present-day David Street and Hashalshelet Street (Es-Silsila Street, Street of the Chain.) To the left and opposite the center of the Cardo is an inverted building at whose base is a yellow dome and next to it a triangular tiled roof and a gate at the eastern end. This is the Holy Sepulcher. All the buildings west of the central street are depicted upside down on the map.

The colonnaded side street which begins at the northern gate is called Cardo Secundus (secondary) or Cardo Valensis (of the valley) which ran along the course of the present-day HaGai Street (its paved continuation to the south has been exposed outside the southern wall near the Dung Gate). In the eastern wall of the city a gate can be seen on the site of the present-day Lions Gate. A short street leads up to it. The Gate of Mercy can be seen south of the eastern wall.

The Cardo built in the reign of the Emperor Justinian (527–565) is elegant and impressive, as in all large Roman cities. The capitals of the pillars were Corinthian, typical of the Byzantine period. The Cardo was the main street of Aelia Capitolina, the Roman city. After this section of the street was exposed, it became apparent that only the northern section (from Damascus Gate to the Holy Sepulcher) was built in Roman times, and its southern section was built in the Byzantine period.

The paved road provided access for pilgrims to the Holy Sepulcher, the Nea Church and the churches on Mount Zion.

We continue northwards to the restored section of the Cardo. There is a row of ten pillars, three of which are intact, bearing the girders of the roof of the western colonnade. Part of the original paving is *in situ*. On the western side of the colonnade

The Cardo — open section.

can be seen the remains of the supporting wall with holes into which the roof girders were fitted. The ceiling of the new hall built to protect the Cardo consists of new concrete arches and above them a building has been constructed. A plaque commemorating the renovation of the Cardo has been fixed into the wall of the hall.

We continue to the north to the hall and come to an open courtyard. To the right are sections of two pillars from the eastern row of the Cardo's columns. To the left, the Lipshitz Information Center provides information on the Jewish Quarter. We climb the stairs from the courtyard to Hayehudim Street. On its eastern side we can see remains of arches of the Cardo's shops and behind them a section of a wide wall, which we will visit later.

We return to the Cardo, continue to the north and reach the Crusader Bazaar, whose shops on both sides were found almost intact and all that was required was to remove the rubble that had accumulated over the centuries. The shops have been renovated and the majority are designed to appeal to the tourist trade.

Two observation shafts appear above the floor between the shops. Through the southern shaft we can see a section of the wall and tower dating to the end of the First Temple period (7th century BCE). On both sides light brown stones show the continuation of the wall. Through the northern shaft we can see the connecting point between the first Hasmonean wall (1st century BCE) and the First Temple period wall. Here, too, the continuation of the Hasmonean wall is delineated in darker stones.

As we continue northward we reach an observation balcony where we can see an excavated section of the first wall to the west. We descend the steps to the base of the wall to observe its impressive height and width (4.5 m — 15 ft). There are signs of a gate which could be the Gate of the Garden mentioned by Josephus.

We return to the observation balcony where we can see sections of two pillars from the Cardo, and below them remains of a plastered cistern used in Ottoman times, as well as additional cellars built on the axis of the Cardo. The wall was breached during the archaeological excavations and the northern entrance to the Cardo was constructed. Visitors coming from Jaffa Gate descend through David Street and may begin the tour of the Cardo and the Jewish Quarter from this point.

We continue north through the Suk el-Bashoura section of the market to David Street. On the left is a cafe in which stands a thick stone pillar without a capital, similar to the pillars in the Cardo, supporting the arches of the cafe's ceiling. This pillar may mark the original intersection of the main streets.

We turn east and then immediately south to Hayehudim Street (Jewish Quarter Street).

12. The Broad Wall We continue southwards along Hayehudim Street to Plugat Hakotel Street. To the east we once more see the arches of the shops in the Cardo and nearby a section of the Broad Wall. We enter Plugat Hakotel Street and come to an open space below street level. In this space we see remains of the wall 7m (23ft) wide and 40m (131ft) long, built with relatively small stones. This wall, to which no written reference has been found, was built in the 8th century BCE by King Hezekiah for the defense of the northern approaches of the city, against the army of the Assyrian King Sennacherib. The wall encompassed the city's western heights

The Cardo —restored section.

The Broad Wall

and united it with the City of David "as a city that is compact together" (Psalms 122:3). This section of the wall has been left exposed as it provides decisive proof of the expansion of Jerusalem beyond its western heights during the First Temple period, a point of contention among archaeologists carrying out excavations in Jerusalem. This area of the Jewish Quarter is apparently the "second quarter" referred to in the Bible as the first settlement in the area. The unusual thickness of the wall raises the conjecture that this is the "broad wall" mentioned in the Book of Nehemiah. (It is not clear why the wall is so thick and why it twists and does not join up with the other exposed sections of the wall from the First Temple period.) On the wall to the east is a map of Jerusalem in the First Temple period showing this wall, and an indicator demonstrating its original height.

In the Rachel Yanait Ben-Zvi Center, on the corner of Shunei Halahot Street is a model of Jerusalem in the First Temple period. Visits are by appointment with the Center at 22, Misgav Ladach Street. The model measures 5 × 7 m (16.5 × 23 ft) and is topographically accurate. It shows the upper and lower parts of the City of David and their walls. Sections lift up to reveal Warren's Shaft and Hezekiah's Tunnel (see Tour No. 1 — The Early Days of Jerusalem).

13. The Israelite Tower Visiting hours: Sun.–Thurs. 9.00 a.m.–5.00 p.m.

We continue along Plugat Hakotel Street and enter No. 10, descend the steps to the cellar, where we can see the remains of walls exposed during archaeological excavations. There are also remains of a tower gate in the First Temple period wall as well as ruins of a Hasmonean tower. Remains of the Israelite tower are especially impressive, rising to a height of 8m (26ft) and width of 4.5m (15ft). This tower may possibly be the "middle gate" referred to in the Book of Jeremiah (39:3). Heaps of ashes, soot and charred wood, as well as iron and bronze arrowheads uncovered on this site provide evidence of a battle — probably the attack by Nebuchadnezzar, who in 586 BCE breached the wall, took Jerusalem and burnt down its houses. Iron arrowheads were used by Jews in this period and bronze arrowheads by the Babylonians. The Hasmonean tower (9 × 9 m — 30 × 30 ft) faced with dressed stone was an integral part of the first wall built by the Hasmonean kings. Reliefs on the wall, showing a tower and battering ram taken from the description of the capture of

The Israelite Tower.

THE JEWISH QUARTER

Lachish by the Assyrian army, demonstrate methods of warfare at that time.

We continue along Plugat Hakotel Street and visit the **Moghrabi Synagogue**, and then retrace our steps to the next site on our route. Plugat Hakotel Street veers to the left and then right and joins up with Hashalshelet Street. At the first turning we reach a courtyard containing a number of buildings. Building No. 15 is the Moghrabi Synagogue (founded by immigrants from North Africa) built in 1860. The door and windows are original and the façade of the three-storey building ends in a gable. During the British Mandate an old people's home for members of this community existed in the compound. During the War of Independence battles raged in the compound but the synagogue remained unscathed and has been renovated; in 1982 the Tsuf Devash Yeshiva was established there.

Immigrants from North Africa began to settle in Jerusalem in the 18th century and one of the most famous was Rabbi Haim Attar who came in 1742. In 1860 the North Africans broke away from the Sephardi community upon the arrival in Jerusalem of their leader David ben Shimon. They maintained their traditions, customs and style of prayer. In 1865 immigrants from

Hamidan Square and adjacent building.

North Africa founded Mahaneh Yisrael, the second Jewish quarter outside the walls. In 1867 members of the community settled in the Muslim Quarter (in Khalidyya Street, now the Torat Cohanim Yeshiva).

We turn onto Shunei Halahot Street and continue to Hamidan Square (also accessible from Hashalshelet Street). This street, actually a lane, was hardly touched during the War of Independence. The paved lane is picturesque, as are the lanes leading off it. Jews settled in this Arab Quarter (Esh-Sharif) after the Ottoman conquest in the 16th century, and most of the inhabitants were members of the Sephardi community from the Balkans and Turkey. The buildings were constructed in

The Western Wall.

typical Old City style — with an inner courtyard. The Sephardi community's religious, educational and welfare institutions were situated in this neighborhood. The Jews abandoned it during the 1936–1939 riots.

14. Western Wall Observation Point
The Western Wall, 485 m (530 yd) long, is the western retaining wall of the Temple Mount, built by Herod. A *Midrash* (homilectic interpretation of the Scriptures) states: "This is the western wall of the Temple which will never be destroyed because the Divine Presence dwells in the west." It is the most sacred place of prayer for Jews. From the time of the Ottoman conquest Jews were permitted to pray at the section of the Western Wall which was not built up. Pilgrims from throughout the Diaspora and Israel come here to pray and to place notes bearing supplications in the cracks between the stones. For centuries the prayer area in front of the Wall was no more than a narrow lane, 3.5 m (11 ft) wide and 28m (92ft) long. Jews were permitted to pray on certain days only, at fixed times. Since June 1967 visitors flock to the Wall at all hours of the day and night, every day of the year. Immediately after the Six Day War the plaza in front of the Wall was expanded and lowered to expose eleven courses of large dressed stone blocks from the Herodian period, and above them are rows of smaller ones (five courses of medium-sized stones were built in the early Arab period. The courses above them were added in the Mameluke and Turkish periods). The prayer section is 60 m long, 28 m wide and 17 m high (65 × 30 × 18 yd). Below ground level are a further 16 courses of blocks 18 m (59 ft) deep. This section has been repaved with stones similar in size to the Herodian ashlars in the Wall. Bar Mitzvah ceremonies and other family celebrations are held here. In a special paved plaza to the west of the prayer section ceremonies to mark national occasions, swearing-in ceremonies for soldiers in the Israel Defense Forces and other events are held. The plaza can be reached by a wide stairway (Maalot Yehuda Halevy) leading down from the Jewish Quarter. An underground passage has been opened from HaGai St. under Hashalshelet Street. During the works carried out to expand this site three entrances have been exposed on the northern side of the plaza leading through passages to the area underneath Wilson's Arch (see Tour No. 3 of the Western Wall excavations, part 1). The Moghrabi Gate in the Wall leads to the Temple Mount and can be reached by a ramp at the southern end of the Wall (see Tour No. 2 — The Temple Mount). The Temple Mount compound lies at the level reached by the medium-size blocks of the Wall which apparently were added during the early Arab period. The uppermost small blocks were added in the 19th century. Near the southern end of the Wall, above the stairs leading to the women's gallery, is an especially long (8m — 26ft) stone block. This block, which served as a lintel of an ancient gate (9m high and 55 m wide — 29 × 60 ft), was discovered in the 19th century by the English explorer G. Barclay. This could be the Coponius Gate mentioned by Josephus.

We continue along Misgav Ladach Street and stop outside No. 11, site of the Laemel School, the first modern school to be established in Palestine. It was founded in 1856 with monies donated by the Jewish community in Vienna and was named for one of its leaders, Shimon Laemel. In 1903 the school was transferred to the Zichron Moshe quarter in the new city.

We continue along Misgav Ladach Street preserved almost completely as it was before the War of Independence.

15. German Hospice (Archaeological Garden) Along the continuation of Misgav Ladach Street near the Yehuda Halevy steps leading to the Western Wall, a complex of Crusader buildings was discovered during the restoration of the quarter. During the second Crusade, in 1128, a group of German knights, the order of St John of the Hospital, was organized to assist pilgrims in the Holy Land and this complex, consisting of a church (Saint Mary of the German Knights), a hospice and a hospital was built by them.

The church has been restored in part, the hostel replaced by apartments, and a public park has been created on the site of the hospital.

The German Hospice.

The Bazaar Many Crusader buildings existed in the Jewish Quarter and their remains have been discovered in the cellars of existing buildings. Arches of Crusader buildings have been found opposite the German hospice during the restoration of the Jewish Quarter. They have been renovated and shops and cafes have been opened there.

Along the continuation of Misgav Ladach Street to the south, are two large buildings: Yeshivat Hakotel (on the right) and Porat Yosef Yeshiva, (on the left). **Yeshivat Hakotel** was founded in 1967 immediately after the Six Day War, by members of the Bnei Akiva movement. The Yeshiva moved to its present quarters in 1980. The **Porat Yosef Yeshiva**, first founded in 1923 (named after the donor Joseph ben Avraham of Calcutta, India), is the largest Sephardi Yeshiva in Israel. The building, which served as an important Jewish defense post during the War of Independence, was captured and razed to the ground by the Jordanian Legion. The new building constructed over the years 1968 to 1985 is larger than the original. Remains of floors, walls and household utensils from the Second Temple period have been uncovered in the cellars of both buildings (see below).

A small building lot in Misgav Ladach Street, behind the Porat Yosef Yeshiva, was the site of the Misgav Ladach Hospital. It was established by the Sephardi congregation and in 1888 took over the former premises of the Rothschild Hospital (which had moved to new quarters). The hospital building was blown up in 1948 by the Jordanian Legion and since then only a deep crater remains on the site.

16. The Burnt House Visiting hours: Sun.–Thurs. 9.00 a.m. to 5.00 p.m. Friday and eve of holidays till 1.00 p.m. Entry fee.

An audiovisual presentation in Hebrew and English of the archaeological discoveries in the Jewish Quarter is on show (commentaries in German and Spanish are available on request).

We mount the stairs opposite the German Hospice, turn right to the doorway leading to the basement of a new building at the end of Tiferet Israel Street. We descend the stairs to a hall and find the remains of the basement floor of a Second Temple-period building consisting of an internal court, four rooms and a *mikveh* (ritual bath). Stone furniture pieces, stone vessels, a stove, weights, a spearhead and the bones of a young woman's hand are on display. The name Bar Katros of a Jewish priestly family mentioned in the Babylonian Talmud, was found carved on one of the stone weights. These finds, and especially the ashes, confirm Josephus'

The Burnt House.

description of the upper city having been captured and put to the torch by the Roman legions on the 8th of Elul, a month after the Temple was burned down in 70 CE. This basement could have served as a workshop for the production of incense and perfume for use in the Temple. Other archaeological excavations exposed ruins of other houses which had been destroyed in a great fire. The basement was thus named the Burnt House.

17. Tiferet Israel Synagogue We continue along Tiferet Israel Street and go up the stairs on the south side of the street or go via the cafe at the top floor of the building, and reach the Tiferet Israel Synagogue. This had been a tall, elegant building constructed between 1864 and 1872 on a plot of land purchased with funds donated by Israel Friedman (in whose honor it is named). The initiative for the synagogue came from Nissan Bak, the leader of the congregation of Hassidim, and thus it was also called the Nissan Bak Synagogue. The dome was built with the assistance of the Austrian Emperor Franz Joseph, who, during a visit to Jerusalem asked where was the synagogue's roof and received the reply: "Even the synagogue is rejoicing at Your Highness' visit and has taken off its hat in your honor." The allusion was understood and the Emperor donated the funds required for the completion of the dome which capped the two-storey building. Rising to a height of 20 m (65 ft), it dominated its surroundings. During the War of Independence the building was destroyed by the Jordanian forces. Only part of its façade remains, with its high central arch framed by arched windows on either side. Sections of walls as well as vestiges of the *mikveh* in the basement also remained. The structure has been reinforced.

18. Karaite Synagogue Visiting hours: Sun.–Thurs. 9.00 a.m.–5.00 p.m. Group visits by appointment — telephone 280657. (Requests to visit the synagogue can be made to the Karaite rabbi who lives on the premises.)

Opposite the facade of the Tiferet Israel Synagogue is one of the first buildings in the Quarter, and its basement serves as the Karaite Synagogue. This building was constructed after members of the sect moved here in the 15th century from their original dwellings south of the Temple Mount. To the left of the gate is an inscription which indicates that this is the Anan ben-David Synagogue of the Karaite community, and that it was founded in the 8th century, reconstructed in (5738) 1978.

The Karaites are a Jewish sect founded in the 8th century by Anan ben-David in Babylon. They believe in the written Scriptures but reject oral tradition and later interpretations of the Bible. The community had centers in Jerusalem, Egypt and in some European countries. After the establishment of the State the majority of the sect immigrated to Israel and set up a number of settlements. Today, there are about 20,000 Karaites in Israel, living mainly in Ramleh.

At No. 6 HaKaraim Street is the Karaite Museum with religious articles, books and photographs on show. There are information leaflets in Hebrew, English and French. The synagogue can be viewed below through a window in the museum. A

The Torah Ark in the Karaite Synagogue.

Torah scroll dating to 1322 is preserved in the synagogue.

19. Herodian residential quarter Visiting hours: Sun.–Thurs. 9.00 a.m. — 5.00 p.m. Fri. and eve of Jewish holidays till 1.00 p.m. Entry fee. Entrance through the basement of Yeshivat Hakotel from HaKaraim Street. Visitors must keep to the marked paths. The 600 sq.m. (1968 sq. ft.) area consists of a mansion built on different levels on the eastern slope of the Jewish Quarter, facing the direction of the Temple Mount. Some of the wings of the building have been uncovered and its walls have been preserved up to a height of 3m (10 ft). On the ground floor are the living and guest rooms and service and storerooms are in the basement. By the entrance are two rooms with colored mosaic floors with geometric designs, and the walls of one of the rooms are covered with decorated stucco. Other such walls can also be seen in the western wing. To the east is a large central enclosure, and below is a *mikveh* (ritual bath) and a small mosaic tiled courtyard. North of the enclosure is a mosaic tiled passage and an additional arch-covered *mikveh*. The exit is from the basement of the Porat Yosef Yeshiva, in the lane leading to the Yehuda Halevy steps. A depiction of a seven-branched candelabrum was found on the walls of one of the rooms. It is considered to be a more accurate rendering of the original candelabrum in the Temple than the candelabrum on the Arch of Titus in Rome, from which it differs slightly, because it was a contemporary drawing.

We continue along Tiferet Israel St. to the Hurva Synagogue Square, passing a park east of the Hurva and Ramban Synagogues, which till 1948 was a built-up area. In the basement of one of the new houses to the south of the square is a Second Temple period cistern which was turned into a ritual bath. In a nearby two-storey building is the Mekubalim Yeshiva and the Bet-El Synagogue, founded in 1737 by the Turkish Kabbalist Gedalia Hayyun. The building has been renovated and today houses the Kohanim Yeshiva.

We cross Hayehudim Street, near the Hurva, climb the steps of a narrow lane above the open section of the Cardo,

(left) The mikveh *mosaic floor. (right) Pottery found in one of the cisterns in the Herodian residential quarter.*

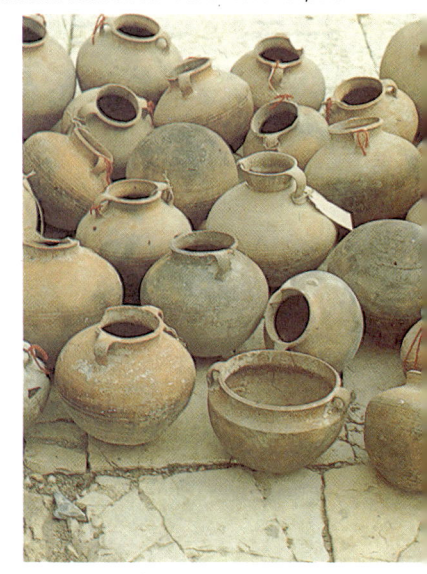

reach Habad Street facing the entrance of the two-storey building housing the Habad Synagogue. Its original name was the Eliyahu Synagogue (as indicated by a marble slab fixed in the wall), in honor of the donor Eliyahu Sassoon of Bombay.

Other sites of interest in Habad Street are the Hessed-El Synagogue, at No. 48, built in 1860 by Shlomo ben Yehezkiel Yehuda, who immigrated from Baghdad; "Hush de" Rabbi Tzadok, at No. 36, a building of apartments constructed by Tzadok Krauz around a courtyard. Four of the first Jewish families to settle in the area inhabited these apartments in the 19th century. Eventually there were 17 apartments in the complex housing 500 persons. There were also two synagogues — Ahavat Zion, founded in 1835 by the Association of Dutch and German immigrants, and Beit Hillel, founded in 1862 by the Khorodna-Grodna community.

We turn into Or Hahayim Street and reach No.6.

20. Old Yishuv Court Museum Visiting hours: Sunday–Thursday 10.00 a.m.–4.00 p.m. Entry fee.

This was the residence of the Weingarten family whose head served as the rabbi of the Jewish Quarter and was taken prisoner by the Jordanians in 1948. It is one of the oldest housing complexes in the area and the Pach (Rosenthal) family has lived there for five generations. Shlomo Pach was the emissary of the community who in 1820 obtained a *firman* (decree) by which the debts of the Ashkenazi families living in Jerusalem were to be cancelled one hundred years later. The Rabbi's daughter, Rivka Weingarten, initiated the establishment of the Old Yishuv Court Museum after 1967. (It was made possible through the support of Isaac Fellen of South Africa and the Jerusalem Fund.) On show are utensils used by the inhabitants of the Jewish Quarter at the end of the 19th century and the beginning of the 20th. In the rooms one may see a scribe, a gold-

"Hush de" Rabbi Tzadok: new lease on life for the courtyards.

smith, a shoemaker, a tailor and other artisans, Ashkenazi and Sephardi style guest-rooms, bedrooms, kitchen, storeroom, washroom, etc. Two synagogues in the courtyard have been restored and included in the museum. The Or Hayim Synagogue (second floor) was founded by Hayim Ben-Attar, who immigrated from Morocco in 1742. He also established a Yeshiva which was taken over by the Ashkenazi community when they moved here from Safed in 1812 and served them until the Menachem Zion Synagogue was completed. The Ari Synagogue (on the first floor) is a typical Sephardi synagogue named after the "Ari" (Yitzhak Lurie Ashkenazi), one of the leaders of the Kabbalah movement. He is said to have been born here in 1534, but lived in Safed till his death in 1572.

21. Bikur Holim Hospital We continue along Or Hahayim Street and turn north to Ararat Street, walk to the end, turn left into a cul-de-sac and come to a two-storey building. Built by the Protestant Missionary Center in the 19th century, it was bought by a group of Jews headed by Moses Montefiore to serve as a Jewish hospital. Founded by an association called Bikur Holim, the hospital functioned here until 1924 when most of its departments moved to a building in the new city. The department for chronic diseases remained here until January 1948 when the building was evacuated. The internal section was destroyed after 1948 and although the restored building now serves as a youth hostel, it is planned to activate the hospital once more to serve the Jewish Quarter.

From here we return to Ararat Street. We can also leave by way of St James Street through the Armenian Patriarchate Rd. north of Jaffa Gate, or south to the parking lot outside Zion Gate.

22. Other sites in the Jewish Quarter
Zibenberg Museum (7, Hagitit Street.) Visiting hours: Sunday–Friday at 12.00 a.m.–1.00 p.m. Group visits by appointment (tel. 282341; 287969). Entry fee. This is the basement of a private house whose remains from the First and Second Temple and Byzantine periods are on show. Two ritual baths, apartments, a cistern, and burial chambers were found here during building operations.

Rachel Yanait Ben-Zvi Center at the corner of Shunei Halahot and Plugat Hakotel Streets, 22, Misgav Ladach Street. An institute for the study of the history of Jerusalem for Israeli and overseas youth.

Sapir Center for the study of the Jewish heritage at Mishmeret Hakehuna Street opposite the Sephardi synagogues.

Shunei Halahot Street.

The old Bikur Holim hospital.

TOUR No. 5

THE MUSLIM QUARTER

Details of tour: The Mameluke buildings are the most interesting aspect of the Muslim Quarter. We shall also visit the covered markets of the Old City which are also in the Muslim Quarter.
Distance covered: approx. 3 km (2 miles)
Time: approx. 4 hours
Transportation: Buses No 1, 3, 13, 19, 20, 41, 80 and 99
Parking lots outside the Gates for private vehicles
Starting point: Jaffa Gate
End of tour: Jaffa or Damascus Gate
The Sites: 1. Khan es-Sultan; 2. Tashtimuryya; 3. Khalidi Library; 4. Tazyya; 5. Turkan Khatun; 6. Tankizyya-Mahkama; 7. Square of the Gate of the Chain; 8. Ashrafyya; 9. Shomrei Hahomot building; 10. Hammam el-Ein; 11. Cotton Market; 12. Iron Gate Street; 13. Ala ed-Din Street; 14. HaGai Street; 15. Harat Sa'adyya; 16. Havatzelet building; 17. Sitt Tunshuk; 18. Takyya; 19. Rasasyya; 20. Hebron Street – El-Khalidyya; 21. Es-Sarayya Street; 22. Es-Sarayya; 23. Kirami Street; 24. The buildings around the markets.

FOREWORD

The north-east section of the Old City of Jerusalem is the Muslim Quarter and is the largest of the Old City. In this area and especially north and west of the walls surrounding the Temple Mount, are to be found many of the Muslim religious institutions and organizations. The Quarter includes residential sections, markets, shops, workshops, cafes, and educational institutions. It extends from the northern city wall to the northern and part of the southern walls of the Temple Mount, and is bounded on the south by the Street of the Chain (Hashalshelet Street). Beit Habad Street and the three markets constitute its western border. The northern section is the residential area, which is the poorest and most crowded of the Old City, housing some 16,000 Muslims (of the 130,000 Muslims living in Jerusalem in 1987).

The majority of the Muslims living in the Quarter are descendants of families that settled in Jerusalem after the Arabs evicted the Crusaders at the end of the 12th century. In the following centuries other Muslims from Egypt, North Africa and Turkey settled here, and after the reunification of the city in 1967 a certain number came from Judea and Samaria.

In this Quarter there are also several Christian religious institutions, mainly in the Via Dolorosa, inhabited by nuns and monks. Jews, too, have returned to the Quarter after the reunification of the city to their family homes and a number of *yeshivot* have been established there.

The central section of the area was first settled at the end of the Second Temple period, when it was enclosed by the Second Wall built by Herod the Great. Later the area was enclosed by the Third Wall built by Herod Agrippa a short time before the destruction of the Second Temple. During the reign of the Roman Emperor Hadrian, a triumphal arch and a forum were built in the eastern section. A number of churches were erected during the Byzantine period. Jews settled here during the early Arab period and fought alongside the Muslims against the Crusaders when they invaded the city: many were killed in battle and the remaining families fled. The Jewish houses were taken over by Christian Jacobites from Syria. After the conquest of Jerusalem by Saladin in 1187, Muslims

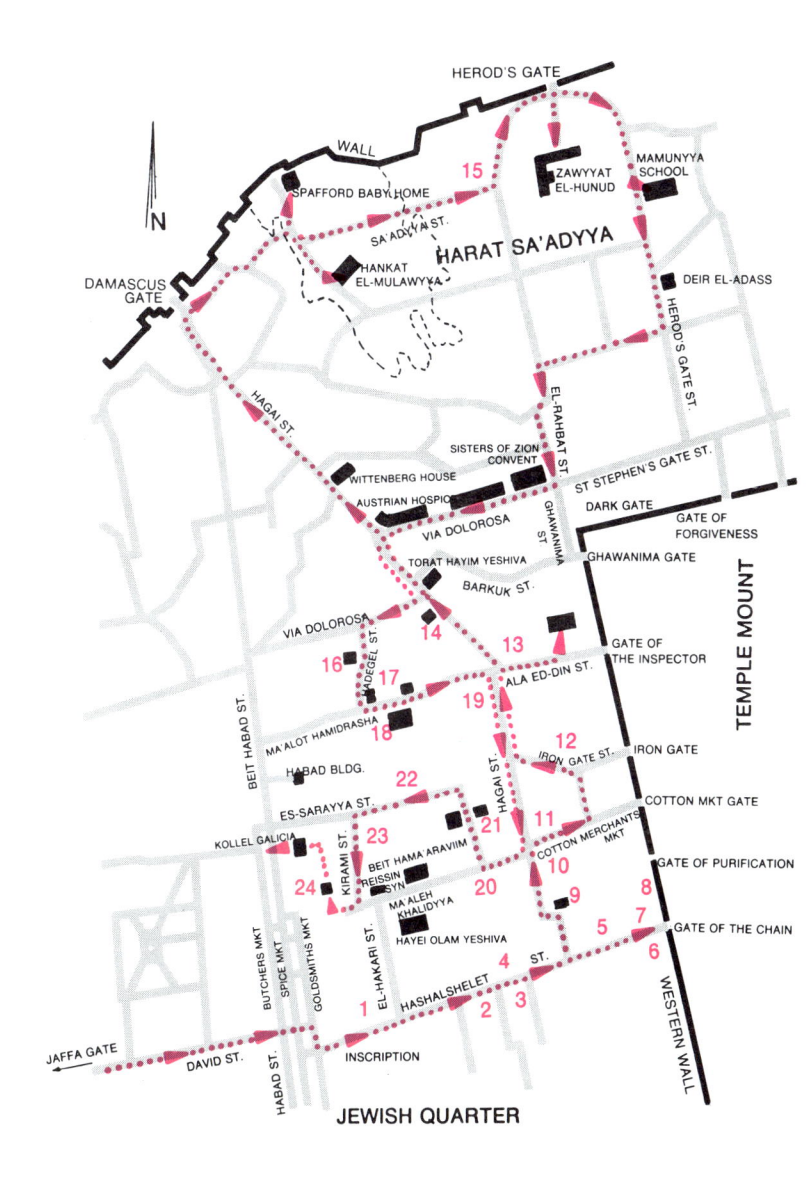

73   THE MUSLIM QUARTER

Map of the tour.

settled in the Quarter once again and during the Mameluke period (1267–1517) public buildings were constructed, many of which still stand today. During the Ottoman period, mainly residential housing was built.

In the middle of the 19th century, Jews from Safed settled north of the Temple Mount (near Bab el-Huta); they built houses and synagogues and lived in the area up to the 1929 riots. Jews also settled in the western section of the Quarter, north of the Street of the Chain, which borders the Jewish Quarter. At the end of the 19th century there were more Jews than Muslims in the Muslim Quarter. During the Arab riots that took place during the British Mandatory rule, Jews left the Muslim Quarter and only returned after the unification of the city in 1967.

THE TOUR

In the course of our tour we will visit Mameluke buildings, Jewish institutions and the Muslim residential sections. We enter the Quarter from Jaffa Gate and go down David Street until we reach Habad Street opposite which is a large hall (built by the Crusaders) in which fruit and vegetables are sold. Behind the vegetable market are three covered markets: the butchers' market, the spices market and the goldsmiths' market. There is evidence that these markets existed under the Crusaders, and may even date back to the early Arab period. They were in existence along the main Roman road (the Cardo) in Roman and Byzantine times. On some of the arches supporting the roofs of the markets the letters carved on the wall show that these shops were the property of church organizations during the Crusader period.

We can visit the markets and then return to David Street, or we can go inside each of them at the end of the tour on our way back to Jaffa Gate. The westernmost of the three is the Butchers' Market (Suq el-Lahamin) in which meat, fish and fowl are sold. The center one is the fragrant Spice Market (Suq el-Atarin) where spices and household utensils are sold. The Crusader Queen Melisende established (or perhaps renovated) this market in 1152. To the east is the Goldsmiths' Market where the craftsmen were mainly Jews and today cloth and clothes are sold here. From the mid-19th century up to the Arab riots in 1929 and 1936, Jews had shops in all these markets. All three are linked on their northern edge to the Beit Habad Market (Suq Khan ez-Zeit), which extends northwards to Damascus Gate.

The Mameluke buildings are situated mainly in the Muslim Quarter. They include mosques, *madrassa* (religious colleges) *khans*, (caravanserai) hospices *(ribbat)*, bathhouses *(hammam)*, fountains *(sabil)*, markets *(suq)*, tombs and cisterns. The majority of these structures are dilapidated but their past beauty and dignity is still apparent; some of them still fulfil the function for which they were built (inscriptions still in place give the name of the founder, the date of construction and the purpose of the building. We shall visit only a few typical structures and will indicate others as we go along.

The Mamelukes ruled Palestine and neighboring countries from 1250 to 1517, and turned Jerusalem into an important Islamic center. Many religious institutions were built in the Temple Mount area (Haram esh-Sharif) as well as buildings for

The Butchers' Market.

secular purposes in the Muslim Quarter. The buildings were designed in the typical Mameluke style brought by architects from the various countries under Mameluke rule. Its main elements are round domes, ornate entrances surmounted by stalactite-decorated half domes (brought from Syria), the use of stone of different colors in various architectural patterns (Byzantine). Other characteristic elements are borrowed from Andalusia in Spain, among which are the U-shaped arches and double windows with a central pillar. Crusader architecture also left its mark: pointed arches, rounded apertures and arches above the windows. Stone benches gracing the entrances to buildings, and inscriptions adorning gateways in beautiful script, are unique to the Mameluke style.

1. Khan es-Sultan As we enter the Street of the Chain, we see a vaulted entrance between the shops leading north (to the left) into a courtyard enclosed by a two-storey building. This was a Mameluke *khan* built in 1386 under the rule of the Sultan Barkuk. At the left of the entrance is an inscription stating the name of the builder and that its income is devoted to the upkeep of Haram esh-Sharif. A further inscription dating to the 18th century, on the northern wall of the courtyard, describes the renovation of the building. Merchandise and cattle were kept in the ground floor rooms, while the guests were accommodated on the second floor. The *khans* have a central courtyard with the storerooms and living accommodation all around. The room facing the street, the largest of all, served as a prayer hall.

Opposite the *khan*, at the corner of Plugat Hakotel Street, is a Mameluke inscription which tells of the construction of shops for the poor by the judge Imam ed-Din in 1312.

2. Tashtimuryya At No. 106 the Street of the Chain (corner of Misgav Ladach Street) is a typical Mameluke *madrassa*. Beside the entrance is a drinking fountain and on both sides stone benches. The inscription indicates that it was built by the Emir Tashtimur in 1382. Beyond the windows one can see a small room in the center of which are the tombs of the Emir Tashtimur

Tashtimuryya.

and his son. The entrance leads to a passage and to the right is the opening to the burial room and further on are openings to other rooms: the central hall (capped by a dome) gives on to four other rooms. In the southern wall there is a prayer niche *(mihrab)* and from the room on the right is an exit to Misgav Ladach Street.

The Street of the Chain.

The tomb of Barakat Khan.

3. Khalidi Library At No. 116 the Street of the Chain is a Mameluke building which was originally built by the Crusaders. It was turned into a mausoleum during the years 1246 to 1279, and was renovated in 1390. A library containing 12000 books and manuscripts was established here at the end of the 19th century by the Khalidi family, but was moved in 1947 as the result of a family quarrel. In one section of the structure was an open courtyard with three tombs, one of which is that of Barakat Khan, head of the Tartar kingdom in the Crimea who died in 1246, and of his two sons. In the front of the building is a window surmounted by an arch adorned with colored stones. Next to it is a small window covered with a grille and a second larger window. On the lintel of the small window is a two-line inscription telling how the structure was built and giving the names of the Emir and the date of his death. On each side of the inscription are identical blazons bearing the Emir's coat of arms — a pair of polo mallets with a ball between them. Above the large square window is an arch and between the windows is a round aperture, below which is a seven-line inscription, quoting passages from the Koran. The building next to it is part of the Strauss building (built in 1912) in which the Idra Bet Hamidrash (Jewish Religious Seminary) was completed in 1986. The entrance is through the southern side, at the end of Hakotel Street.

4. Tazyya On the northern side of the Street of the Chain are more Mameluke buildings:

Madrassa et-Tazyya (No.111) was built by the Emir Taz in 1362. His name is mentioned in the inscription above the low window with a grille. On both sides of the inscription are the Emir's blazon — a goblet, indicating that he had been a court Cupbearer. Above the inscription are interlocking voussoirs of colored stones in clover patterns.

Turba Kilanyya (No.109 of the Street of the Chain) is the mausoleum of the Emir Kilanni (1352). The two-storey imposing structure has three cupolas.

Turba Jalikyya (No.121) is the tomb of the town clerk, the Emir el-Jalek (1307). A two-storey structure at the eastern extremity of which a six-line inscription, partly erased, describes the repair of the aqueduct to Jerusalem due to Mohammed Bey el-Nashashibi in 1469. The aqueduct continues under the Street of the Chain, and it is part of the upper conduit from Solomon's Pools that enters the Temple Mount esplanade through the Gate of the Chain.

5. Turba Turkan Khatun At No.149 of the Street of the Chain is a tomb of a Mongol princess who died on pilgrimage to Mecca in 1352. The façade is ornamented with arabesques in the grey stone.

Nearby, at No.151 of the same street is Turba Saadyya. There are two windows in its façade with two small pillars. The structure has no inscription, but it has been identified by the historian Mujir ed-Din, in his description of Jerusalem in 1492, as the tomb of sheikh Saad ed-Din, Commissioner of Damascus who died in 1311.

6. Madrassa at-Tankizyya also called the **Mahkama** (the Tribunal) because it served as a law court during the Turkish period. This is a two-storey school building at 166 of the Street of the Chain. The structure was built by the Emir Tankiz, governor of Damascus, in 1329. At both ends of the inscription is his blazon — a cup. During the British Mandate this was the residence of the religious and national leader of the Muslims in Palestine, the Mufti Hadj Amin el-Husseini. Under Jordanian rule it served as a religious college. The high inset entrance has a particularly beautiful ornamentation, interlocking voussoirs in different colors and forms, a half-dome with stalactite decorations.

The Mahkama rests on Wilson's Arch and underneath is a blocked up entrance in the western wall of the Temple Mount enclosure identified as the Bet HaMidrash Gate. It is possible that the Chamber of Hewn Stone (where the Sanhedrin met) in the Second Temple period was in this vicinity. In the early Arab period permission was granted to build a synagogue here, used by the Jews who lived in the area north of the Temple Mount.

7. Square of the Gate of the Chain The external square of the Gate of the Chain is encompassed by a number of structures. On the southern side, Madrassa et-Tankizyya; to the east, the Gate of the Chain and the Gate of the Divine Presence; to the west, the Suleiman fountain; and in the northern wall of the square, a passage to the closed Gate of the Divine Presence.

The Gate of the Chain (Bab es-Silsileh) is the southern gate of the square which opens on to the Haram esh-Sharif (Temple

Turba Turkan Khatun.

Mount esplanade) and is considered to be the main entrance to it. The northern (closed) gate was known as the Gate of the Divine Presence *(Shechina)*. Both gates were built by the Crusaders in the style typical of the period: a pair of intertwined pillars and a straight one; on their capitals are carved floral motifs, animals and human figures (the figures have been defaced, but one can still discern a monk wearing a long robe and another which is the Prophet Daniel with a lion on either side). The gates are protected from rain and sun by cupolas. The Crusaders called this double gate the Beautiful Gate and this was the central gateway to the Temple Mount mentioned in the New Testament. The gates were built near a Second Temple period gate, and it is possible that this is the Kasistos Gate mentioned by Josephus (*Wars* 6:3).

On the wall on the western side of the Gate of the Chain, is the Suleiman Fountain. In its upper section is an arch decorated with geometric motifs carved into the stone, and in the center is a Crusader rosette which was transferred here by the builders of the fountain, in 1537. Under-

Square of the Gate of Chain.

neath is a Roman sarcophagus used as a basin by the builders of the fountain whose water was brought from the aqueduct that passed under the street at this spot.

8. Ashrafyya The Madrassa at No.161 of the Street of the Chain is named for the Mameluke Sultan Ashraf Qayt Bey and was built in 1482. The façade and entrance of the two-storey building face the Haram esh-Sharif and we get a view of them by entering the area through the Gate of the Chain (after obtaining permission from the guard). Above the entrance are three pointed arches of back and white interlacing voussoirs. Above the panel over the entrance is an arch adorned with numerous geometrical patterns, typical of 15th century Mameluke art. On either side of the doorway are benches of red stone.

We return to the Street of the Chain and enter HaGai Street which runs the length of the Muslim Quarter up to Damascus Gate. This was part of the valley formed by a tributary of the Kidron River which originated on a hill near the Russian Compound, passed along the Street of the Prophets, through the Damascus Gate (see tour 15), along the Street of the Chain, southwards through the Western Wall plaza, left the Old City through the Dung Gate, and then coursed westwards towards David's City and united with the Kidron River (see tour 1). In Second Temple times the valley was called Tyropoeon (in Greek) and in short — the Valley (in Hebrew *gai*). Under the Romans the road reached the Siloam Pool. In the Byzantine era, a road was built here called Cardo Valensis, lined with columns on both sides. Under Turkish rule houses were built along this street and many of them were either built by Jews or rented to them. The first Jews to reside in this street came from Hebron and thus the street was also called Hebron Street.

9. Shomrei Hahomot (Guardians of the Wall) Building We walk along HaGai Street and mounting the steps to the right, come to the wall of a building in ruins. Above the high windows in the wall are round apertures. This is one of the walls of the building belonging to the Shomrei Hahomot community which lived in this area up till the 1929 riots. It was built from 1862 to 1904, and there was a *yeshiva* (Jewish religious school) on the ground floor, and a synagogue on the second. There is now a Jewish book store in the restored ground floor of the building.

10. Hammam el-Ein We continue along HaGai Street in a northerly direction and pass by a cistern built in the 16th century at the entrance to the Hammam el-Ein bath-

THE MUSLIM QUARTER

The Cotton Merchants' Market.

El-Wad fountain beside Hamman el-Ein.

house. Despite its name (which means spring in Arabic), no spring existed here and the rain water was piped to the spot through the underground drainage system in HaGai Street. The large underground pool extended to the wall of Haram esh-Sharif and also served the Hammam Ashifa situated near the Cotton Merchants' Gate. This pool may possibly be the "upper pool" mentioned three times in the Bible (II Kings 18:17; Isaiah 7:3 and 36:2) which existed at the time of King Hezekiah. The "spring" was believed to have

Walls of the Shomrei Hahomot building.

dried up over the ages and water was carried by donkeys and camels. In 1821 the bathhouse was connected to the aqueduct that passed through the Street of the Chain.

11. Cotton Merchants Market (Suq el-Qattanin) We continue along HaGai Street to the junction with El-Khalidyya Street in a westerly direction. To the right is the entrance to the covered Cotton Merchants Market built by the Emir Tankiz, governor of Damascus in 1336. In the past there were cotton weaving and spinning workshops in this area. The shops along the roofed street were dubbed the "dark shops". The roof is made of pointed arches and there are square windows above the shops.

In the southern wall is an opening which leads to the Khan Tankizyya. A second gateway leads to the Hammam Ashifa. At the eastern extremity of the market is the Cotton Merchants Market Gate (Bab-el-Qattanin) and it is one of the most beautiful of all the gates leading to Haram esh-Sharif. It was built under the rule of the Mameluke Sultan Ibn-Kala'un. Wooden gates open to the marketplace and above them is an inscription giving details of the market's origins.

We return to HaGai Street and go

through an entrance to the right leading to a courtyard surrounded by an apartment building. This compound was set up in the 1890's by the Jewish philanthropist Mendel Rand. The building has three storeys with 30 rooms. There are inner courtyards, water cisterns and four shops.

12. Street of the Iron Gate (Tariq Bab el-Hadid) We continue along HaGai Street to the north and come into the Iron Gate Street (Sha'ar Habarzel) whose houses were built mainly in the 15th century and have retained their original Mameluke character.

We continue to the east, and to the right (No.12) is the two-storey **Madrassa Muzhiryya** building. The entrance is rectangular, and above it is an adorned trefoil arch. We enter the square courtyard and come to a prayer hall. Around the courtyard are rooms which today are used as residential quarters. According to the historian Mujir ed-Din, it was built in 1480 by Ibn-Muzhir, an important official from Egypt who died in Nablus.

The nearby two-storey building (14–16), with its impressive facade, is the **Madrassa el-Arghunyya**. It has a side entrance and a window with a grille looking into a burial chamber. The carved inscription on the entrance mentions the date 1353 and the name of Arghun el-Kamili, who died in exile in Jerusalem when he was about 30. He began his career as Master of the Robes (hence the blazon above the door). In a western room are three tombs in which are buried Ali Jamah, leader of the Muslim League of India (1931); Mussa Khattim Pasha el-Husseini, President of the Supreme Arab Council (1933); Abd el-Kader el-Husseini, the leader of Arab marauder gangs who was killed in 1948.

On the northern side of the road are the following buildings:

Madrassa Jawharyya (No.11) a low structure built in 1440 as a hospice for pilgrims by Jawhar, an Abyssian eunuch (who became superintendant of the Royal Harem in Cairo).

Ribbat Kurd (No.13) built in 1293–1294, a three-storey building north of the Iron Gate which was a hospice for Muslim pilgrims. An entrance in the eastern corner opens on to a courtyard in which a section of the western supporting wall of the Haram esh-Sharif area known as the Small Wall can clearly be seen. This section is 20m (66 ft) long and it is 175m (190 yards) distant from the Western Wall plaza. We enter the low opening to a courtyard. At the northernmost end, adjoining the wall, is a two-storey building reinforced by iron supports because its foundations were weakened as a result of the digging of the tunnel along the Western Wall. In the Small Wall we can discern two courses of Herodian ashlars and places where repairs or later additions of smaller stones were made.

The Iron Gate is a two-storey structure with a rectangular entrance surmounted by an arch. In the upper storey is a rectangular window above which is a decorated arch. (The Iron Gate is mentioned in the New Testament — Acts 12:10 — but its location is unknown). This gate was first built in 1293 during the construction of the western colonnade of the Haram esh-Sharif esplanade. According to Mujir ed-Din, it was rebuilt in 1357.

13. Ala ed-Din Street We return to HaGai Street and walk to the next junction. At the corner we find a fountain — **Sabil el-Haram.** The inscription tells how it was built in 1537 in the time of the Sultan Suleiman. We turn right and enter Ala ed-Din Street. A number of interesting sites in this street are worth inspection:

Ribbat Ala ed-Din el-Basir (No.17), a two storey structure, one of the oldest remaining from the Mameluke period. Above the entrance is an inscription recalling the name of Emir Ala ed-Din, buried here, who dedicated the building to poor pilgrims in 1267. When he became blind he settled in Jerusalem and was appointed inspector of the holy places of Jerusalem and Hebron. His judgment was so respected that he was called el-Basir, the clear-sighted. The entrance leads to a courtyard with a number of rooms around it where Muslims from Africa live; there is also a mosque with a minaret. In Ottoman times the windows were barred and the building served as a prison.

Ribbat Mansuri (No.4). Built for the poor

by the Mameluke Sultan Kala'un in 1282. This building was also turned into a prison in Turkish times and today is inhabited by Muslims from Africa. The deep entranceway is particularly impressive because of its benches and the arch above it. A passage to the right leads to a large courtyard around which are a number of rooms.

Madrassa Hasanyya (No.19), built in 1433 by Emir Hasan el-Kaskili, inspector of the holy sites on Haram esh-Sharif and the Cave of Machpelah in Hebron and later the Sultan's representative in Jerusalem.

Madrassa el-Manjikyya (No.12) a two-storey building adjoining the western colonnade of Haram esh-Sharif, near the Gate of the Inspector (see below). It was built in 1361 in the time of the Emir Manjib, governor of Damascus. A school for boys was run here until the end of World War I, and under the British Mandate the Supreme Muslim Council met here. Today the offices of the Muslim Waqf are situated in the building. The archives of the Council are kept here and academic research is carried out. The **Gate of the Inspector** or Gate of the Prison is a gateway to the

The Gate of the Inspector.

Haram esh-Sharif situated at the end of Ala ed-Din Street, named after the inspector of that name who built the hospice and the gate. The first gate at this spot was apparently built in Crusader times and was called St. Michael's Gate. It was rebuilt in 1203 and later by Ala ed-Din.

The **Fishel Lappin building** was bought in 1862 by a rich Jew who immigrated from Grodno in Russia. He himself lived here and rented out apartments. He also built a synagogue and a *yeshiva*. The complex included among others a workshop for preparing parchment used by scribes. Fishel Hacohen Lappin was one of the leading personalities of the Jewish community of the Old City.

14. HaGai Street Along the continuation of HaGai Street is a two-storey building, Beit Hazon Yehezkiel (House of the Vision of the Prophet Ezekiel) which was the center of the Georgian Jewish community who settled in Jerusalem in the 1860s. There was a synagogue and Talmud Torah here, and its name symbolized the fulfilment of Ezekiel's prophecy of the return to Zion. The building was plundered during the 1929 riots and lay in ruins until after the Six Day War.

Further along the road we come to the **Torat Hayim Yeshiva** (next door the 4th Station on Via Dolorosa). It was built in 1894 by Rabbi Itzhak Winograd who immigrated from Russia. Beyond the two-storey building were a number of buildings in which the 300 students lived. The *yeshiva* continued functioning until the Jews fled during the 1929 riots, but its Arab caretaker and his family looked after the buildings, and in 1967, after the Six Day War, returned the property to its owners, who found everything, including the several-thousand volume library, in perfect order.

Wittenberg House (No.33) is a three-storey building, part of which is built over the street; its two courtyards are surrounded by apartments. It was purchased in 1881 by Moshe Wittenberg, and the apartments rented out to poor Jews. On the upper floor is a synagogue which was burned down in the 1921 riots.

15. Harat Sa'adyya This complex of

apartment buildings built in the Ottoman period in the northern section of the Muslim Quarter houses the majority of Muslim families living in the Old City. We continue along HaGai Street up to Damascus Gate, turn east and come into Sheikh Lulu Street, named after the mosque built in 1385 by Emir Lulu. We continue along the street to the junction, turn left and ascend the steps to a gate opening onto a courtyard where we see a two-storey building adjoining the city's northern wall. This is the **Spafford Baby Home**, run by the American Colony (see Tour 11). We return to the junction of the streets and go down the Ibn Jarah Street and come to the **Hankat el-Mulawyya** Mosque. The building was originally St. Agnes, a Crusader church turned into a Muslim shrine by Saladin in 1187, where the Crusader architecture has been preserved. The apses in the eastern wall are still recognizable beside the *mihrab* which faces south.

We return to the junction, turn right and walk to the end of Sa'adyya Street, enter Hatzariach Ha'adom Street and come to **Herod's Gate** or Flower Gate; or Bab ez-Zahra, a corruption of Sahira, (which means "the place where people stay awake") the name of a hill opposite on which is a cemetery where pilgrims to Mecca are buried. According to Muslim tradition these people will be resurrected at the end of time. This is one of the gates in the north city wall, east of Damascus Gate. Originally it was a wicket which opened into the tower to ease the movement of traffic in the northern section of the town. This area was densely settled in the 19th century. The wicket was in the eastern side of the tower which protruded from the wall and opened into the internal part of the wall facing the city. In 1875 the present gate was opened in the northern wall and the wicket was closed. The pointed arch over the wicket, and the remains of the battlement above it, can be seen on the eastern side of the gate. Above the gate is a guardroom and iron steps lead up to the rampart.

The name Herod's Gate was given by Christian pilgrims who identified the nearby church (Deir el-Adass, below) as the palace of Herod Antipas to whom Jesus was sent by Pontius Pilate (Luke 23:7). The Crusader army of Godefrey de Bouillon was encamped here and entered the Holy City on July 15, 1099 through a breach in the wall east of Herod's Gate.

We continue southward to a large building within which is a mosque. This is **Zawyyat el-Hunud** a hospice built in the Ottoman period for Muslim pilgrims from India. Today it houses a clinic.

We turn right into Herod's Gate Street (Sha'ar Haprachim Street) until we reach the **Mamunyya School**, which was built on the ruins of a Crusader church. We continue along this street to a lane that leads left to the Deir el-Adass (the Monastery of

Herod's Gate.
"Flower" above Herod's Gate.

the Lentils) where according to tradition lentils were distributed to the poor. It is a small Crusader Greek Orthodox church, named after St. Nicodemus. During the Crusader period it was called St. Elie, and according to a tradition popular among pilgrims, this was the dwelling place of Herod Antipas.

We continue along Herod's Gate Street to the junction with St. Stephen's Gate Road. We walk in a westerly direction till we reach the first lane to the left — Ghawanima Street, and walk to the end. To the left the Ghawanima Gate opens on to Haram esh-Sharif.

The lane continues to the west and to our right is **Ez-Zawyya el-Afghanyya**, a hospice for pilgrims from Afghanistan. In the courtyard is a mosque. We continue along Barkuk Street to the west until we reach HaGai Street.

16. The Havatzelet building From HaGai Street we continue west to the Via Dolorosa, and after passing the 5th Station we turn north into HaDegel Street. The three-storey building at No.4 was the home of the Frumkin family from 1865 to 1908. It was from this building that in 1870 Dov Frumkin, together with Michael Cohen, began publishing the Hebrew newspaper "Havatzelet".

We continue along HaDegel Street to the end and turn left in Ma'alot HaMidrasha Street. At the corner of these streets is the **Shmuel Leizer Synagogue**.

17. Sitt Tunshuk At No.31 on Ma'alot Hamidrasha Street is a tomb built by a noble lady, Sitt Tunshuk, in 1392, and in which she was buried six years later.

18. Takyya This is a large structure at Nos.30–32 Ma'alot HaMidrasha Street built by Sitt Tunshuk as a hospice for Muslim dervishes. The building is particularly impressive because of its height, its size and its many embellishments, which are similar to those in Sitt Tunshuk's tomb. Over the centuries the building was used by the Ottoman Sultan as part of the local authority offices, but later served as an orphanage.

19. Rasasyya According to the inscription on the building next door, the structure at No.40 HaMidrasha Street was built as a hospice for pilgrims by the Turkish Emir Biram Jawish in 1540. The name derives from the Arab word for "lead" which was used between the courses of stone. At the top of the entranceway is an arch ornamented with sun rays, and geometric designs on either side.

20. Hebron Street — El-Khalidyya Street At the junction of HaGai Street and the Cotton Merchants Market we go up El-Khalidyya Street — also called Hebron Street because its first inhabitants came from Hebron in the mid-19th century. The street was the center of a Jewish neighborhood (part of which we have already seen on our tour through the Street of the Chain to the end of HaGai Street) and was inhabited by hundreds of Jewish families up to the riots in 1929 and 1936.

The **Moshe Rachtman building** (at No. 52) is a two-storey structure built around a courtyard. Its owners immigrated from Russia in 1885 and set up a sheep's milk cheese factory. There are eight apartments and seven shops.

The Hayei Olam Yeshiva is the large

Entrance to Sitt Tunshuk's tomb.

TOUR NO. 5   84

Entrance to Beit Hamaaravim.

building on the left at the top of the street. We ascend the steps into a wide courtyard surrounded by two-storey structures. In 1913 there were 400 students at the Yeshiva and 25 teachers. After 1967 the building was returned to its owners and to its original purpose, after renovation.

Beit Hamaaraviim is a three-storey building built in 1865 at the initiative of Rabbi David ben-Shimon, who was also instrumental in the construction of the Mahaneh Israel neighborhood in the New City. The first Jews from North Africa (the "Maaraviim") immigrated to Eretz Israel in the 13th century. At the beginning of the 19th century members of this community settled in the Jewish Quarter and families soon began to settle in the Muslim Quarter. In this building a hostel was set up for poor members of the community, as well as a synagogue and a *yeshiva*. After the reunification of the city, the building was renovated, a number of Jewish families returned to live there, and the Torat Cohanim Yeshiva established.

The **Reissin Synagogue** structure included apartments and shops. In the center is a synagogue belonging to the Reissin Hassidim and a Kollel. Jews purchased the building and renovated it in 1853 and named it Kehal Hassidim. After the 1936 riots it was rented out to Arabs and thus remained intact.

Two streets go northwards from El-Khalidyya Street: Es-Sarayya Street and Kirami Street.

21. Es-Sarayya Street A Jewish institution worthy of our attention is situated here. The **Rabbi Diskin building** is surrounded by three-storey buildings built in 1881 by Rabbi Moshe Yehoshua Leib Diskin, one of the leading personalities in Jewish communal life in the Old City. An orphanage functioned here up to 1896, when it moved to its quarters to the New City. Jewish families lived in the building up to the 1929 riots, and after the reunification of the city, Jewish families returned to live in most of the apartments.

22. Es-Sarayya On the continuation of Es-Sarayya Street is a building erected at the beginning of the 16th century on the initiative of Suleiman the Magnificent's wife. This was the site of a soup kitchen for Muslim pilgrims and poor people up to the 1870s when the local government offices were housed here. It served as the residence of the Pasha of Jerusalem and as a civil court. During the British Mandate the Muslim Orphanage moved here.

23 Kirami Street We reach this street from the western end of El-Khalidyya Street or from the south through Es-Sarayya Street. Two Mameluke structures are situated on the eastern side of the street.

The gate of Es-Sarayya.

The **Kirami Tomb** where a Muslim saint, Shams ed-Din Mohammad Kirami, who died in 1386 is buried, as well as his son. In another room there is a mosque.

Badryya — a house of learning established in 1214 by the Kurdish Emir Badr ed-Din el-Hakari for students of the Sunni sect. The Emir was killed in 1218 by Crusaders on Mount Tabor and a plaque to his memory was placed above the entrance.

24. The buildings around the markets

The Hirshenzon house situated at the end of El-Khalidyya Street contains the family's synagogue.

The Kollel Galicia, in a lane at the end of Es-Sarayya Street, was built in 1830 by the Galicia community to accommodate thirty families; it included a synagogue. A number of Jewish families returned to live there in 1967, and a *yeshiva* was established.

The Habad building can be reached from the Beit Habad market.

It is worthwhile ending our tour on the roofs of the covered markets which can be reached through the Kollel Galicia. From here we have a view of the Muslim Quarter to the east, the Christian Quarter to the west and the northern section of the Jewish Quarter to the south. We can also see the Mount of Olives and Mount Scopus on the horizon to the east and the new northern neighborhoods.

Our tour ends here. We can return to Damascus Gate through the Beit Habad market or to Jaffa Gate through David Street.

An alley in the Muslim Quarter.

TOUR No. 6

FROM ST STEPHEN'S GATE TO THE CHURCH OF THE HOLY SEPULCHER

Details of tour: From St Stephen's Gate to the Via Dolorosa. We shall be visiting holy sites — modest dress is required.
Distance covered: approx. 3 km (2 miles)
Time: about 5 hours
Transportation: Buses No 1, 42, 43, 64 (to the corner of St Stephen's Gate Road and from there on foot to the starting point by the gate. Bus No 99 reaches the starting point. Parking lots for private vehicles near Jaffa Gate and St Stephen's Gate.
Starting point: St Stephen's Gate (Lions' Gate)
End of tour: Jaffa Gate
The Sites: 1. St Stephen's Gate; 2. Church of St Anne; 3. Pool of Bethesda compound; 4. Via Dolorosa (including nine stations of the Cross along this street and other sites); 5. Church of the Holy Sepulcher (including the last five stations of the Cross).

THE TOUR

1. St Stephen's Gate Known in Hebrew as the Lions' Gate, it is in the eastern part of the Turkish wall of the Old City. Legend has it that the two pairs of lions engraved on either side of the gate were placed there by the Ottoman sultan Suleiman the Magnificent because he had dreamt that he would be devoured by lions unless he built a wall around the Holy City for the defense of its citizens. The "lions" are in fact panthers and are derived from the heraldic emblem of the Mameluke Sultan Baybars, re-used by Suleiman.

Other names of the gate are Jehoshaphat Gate — the name commonly used in medieval Christian sources since the road from here leads down to the Valley of Jehoshaphat (See Tour No.1: The Early Days of Jerusalem); Bab er-Riha (Jericho Gate) a medieval Arabic name; Sittna Mariam (the Gate of Our Lady Mary) used by Christian Arabs; St Stephen's Gate, used by Christians today, since St Stephen was stoned to death nearby.

The Turkish inscription on the inside of the gate records its construction by Suleiman the Magnificent in 1538. Traces of the original back wall of the gate, creating an L-shaped entry, can still be seen. The western wall of the gate was removed to form the present direct entry to enable vehicles to pass. On the north side of the gate is a guardroom. In addition to the panthers, the gate is adorned with geometrical forms and plant motifs. Over the outer side is a typical 16th century turret. A fragmented Greek inscription from the Second Temple period was found here during excavations, prohibiting gentiles from entering the Temple. The inscription is now on display at the Rockefeller Museum. North-east of the gate, outside the wall, there used to be a small pool called Mary's Pool after the Virgin Mary who is said to be buried nearby.

Going through the gate into the Old City, we immediately see the north wall of the Temple Mount esplanade which meets the city wall south of St Stephen's Gate. Nearby is Bab el-Asbat which opens onto the Temple Mount area. The name is probably a distortion of the Hebrew name of the Gate of the Tribes which stood nearby in the Second Temple period.

Further along St Stephen's Gate Road is a recently built rest area in which paving stones from the Second Temple period were incorporated. South of the area is a car park next to the Temple Mount wall.

87 ST. STEPHEN'S GATE TO THE HOLY SEPULCHER

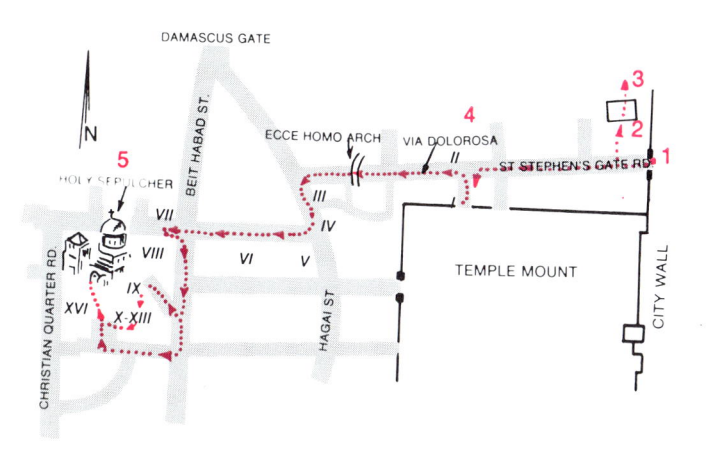

Map of the tour. The Stations of the Cross are indicated by Roman numerals.

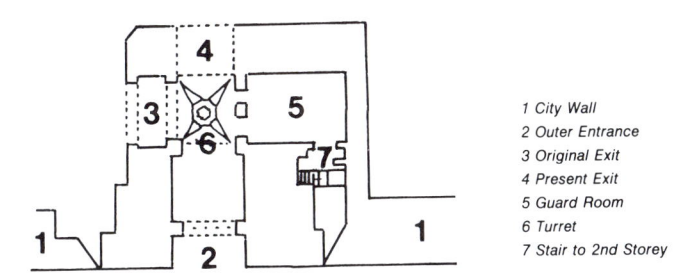

1 City Wall
2 Outer Entrance
3 Original Exit
4 Present Exit
5 Guard Room
6 Turret
7 Stair to 2nd Storey

Plan of St Stephen's Gate.

The pools and churches near St Stephen's Gate.

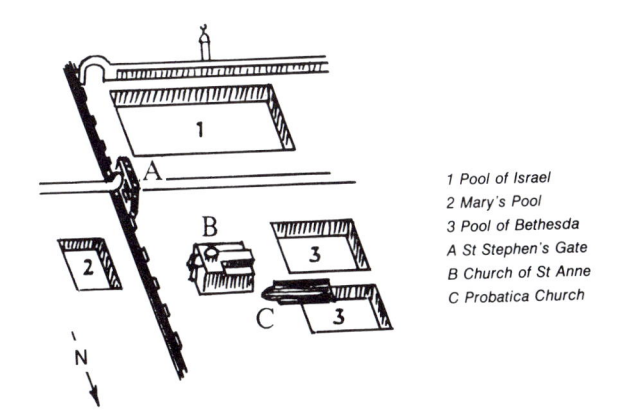

1 Pool of Israel
2 Mary's Pool
3 Pool of Bethesda
A St Stephen's Gate
B Church of St Anne
C Probatica Church

The rainwater pool, the **Pool of Israel**, that was at this site was filled up in 1936 because it constituted a health hazard. It was dug in the Second Temple period to drain the waters of the Bezetha river, a northern tributary of the Kidron. The water flowed through other more northern pools, including the Bethesda Pool, and only pure drinking water reached the Pool of Israel. This may have been the Large Pool mentioned in the First Book of the Maccabees, the largest pool in Jerusalem in the Second Temple Period.

Near number 19 of St Stephen's Gate Road is the Monastery of the White Fathers, built in 1865. In the same year the site was given to Napoleon III by the Sultan Abd el-Majid, in appreciation of French aid to the Turks in the Crimean War. The monastery compound contains the Church of St Anne, the Bethesda Pool and vestiges of other churches (see below). The compound is open every morning and afternoon except Sunday, closing for a midday break.

2. Church of St Anne Open 8.00 a.m.–12.00, 2.30 p.m.–6.00 p.m.; daily except Sunday. A 12th-century Crusader church built on the traditional site of Mary's birthplace, the home of her parents Anne and Joachim. Following his conquest of Jerusalem (1187), Saladin turned the church into a Muslim theological school, named Salahyyah after him; the Arabic inscription is still above the door. Under other Ottoman rulers, the site was abandoned, and was used for worship once more only in 1878, when it was given to the White Fathers.

This solid, heavy church, with its simple lines and almost total lack of adornment, is a characteristic example of Romanesque style. Its plan is that of a cruciform basilica; it is divided into a main hall and two aisles each ending in an apse. The ceiling of the nave is higher than the ceiling of the side aisles. The whole structure leans slightly to one side, a feature that is thought to symbolize Jesus on the Cross. The walls incorporate vestiges of a Byzantine

(top) One of the two pairs of "lions" which flank St Stephen's Gate.
(bottom) St Stephen's Gate, also called the Lions' Gate.

church. In the southern aisle a flight of steps leads down to the crypt, originally a cave hewn out of the rock, which contains an altar dedicated to Mary.

3. Pool of Bethesda West of the Church of St Anne in the monastery compound, the two basins of the original pool were discovered in the excavations undertaken between 1915 and 1958 and identified as the Pool of Bethesda where Jesus cured the blind and the paralytic (John 5:2). From the Second Temple period it is identified with the Sheep Pool or Pool of Probatica which was next to the sheep market (both outside the city wall at that time). The name Bethesda, mentioned in the New Testament only, may have been a symbolic name, or a distortion of the name of the Bezetha suburb, which stood here in the Second Temple period. The pool was built in the time of the Hasmoneans to collect the waters of the Bezetha river. The two sections of the pool measure 50 × 150m and are 15m deep (160ft × 480ft × 48ft). In the Byzantine period a church was built against the wall, between the two parts of the pool, but was destroyed by the Persians in 615. In the Crusader period the Bethesda Church was built on its ruins. The apse of the Crusader church, the Byzantine basilica and part of its supporting pillars are still at the site. In the excavations to the north of the church, small pools and Roman bathing facilities were discovered, thought to be connected with the cult of Aesculapius, the Roman god of healing. Findings from the excavations are on display in the museum at the site.

4. Via Dolorosa — The Way of the Cross The way followed by Jesus bearing his cross on his back to the place of his crucifixion. This is one of the holiest sites in Christendom.

The tradition for pilgrims to walk along the route taken by Jesus began in the Byzantine period (in the 4th to 7th century), with the processions of the faithful from Gethsemane to the Golgotha, via the Kidron Valley, the house of Caiaphas on the slopes of Mount Zion, and northward

(top) Inscription over the door of St. Anne's.
(bottom) Interior of the Church.

Pool of Bethesda, foundations of Byzantine church and remains of Crusader church.

via the Church of St Sophia, which was identified as the site of the Praetorium (today the Fourth Station). From the 8th to the 12th century the procession began from the room of the Last Supper (the Cenacle) on Mount Zion, and proceeded north of Golgotha. The present route of the Way of the Cross was set in the Crusader period, in the 13th century, and was finally fixed in the 19th century. It begins at St Stephen's Gate, and winds its way westward towards the Church of the Holy Sepulcher. This is the route Jesus walked from the place of his trial to the place of his crucifixion. There are fourteen Stations on the Via Dolorosa, nine along the route and five inside the Church of the Holy Sepulcher, to commemorate the very last events of Jesus' life. At these spots churches or shrines have been erected.

The Third, Fourth, Fifth, Sixth and Seventh Stations are open on Friday afternoons during the procession along the Via Dolorosa.

The First Station This station is known as the Praetorium (Court of Law), the place

Beginning of the Via Dolorosa.

where the Roman governor Pontius Pilate condemned Jesus to death by crucifixion. Most scholars believe that the trial was held in the Antonia fortress (they situate the place of judgement in Herod's palace, in today's Armenian Quarter). In the 14th century a Mameluke college was built on the site of the fortress. It housed the Muslim governor's offices and the law court from the 15th century to the mid-19th century. The Muslim El-Omaryya College is now located there. The entire Temple Mount area is visible from the courtyard of the school, the First Station, and vestiges of a Crusader chapel were uncovered here. The site is open to the public at the time of the Friday afternoon procession along the Via Dolorosa. At other times permission must be obtained from the school.

The Second Station is made between the Omaryya College and the Franciscan Compound. To the right of the entrance is the **Chapel of the Flagellation,** built on the ruins of a Crusader church at the site where, according to Christian tradition, Jesus was scourged by Roman soldiers, after he was sentenced. The Franciscans were given the site by the Egyptian ruler Ibrahim Pasha in 1838 and the Italian architect Barluzzi constructed the church in 1927–1929. The church's three stained-glass windows, portray the liberated Barabbas, the flagellation of Jesus, and Pontius Pilate washing his hands. A crown of thorns is depicted in mosaic on the ceiling.

The Church of the Condemnation and Imposition of the Cross is on the left of the compound entrance gate. The structure, which once served as a mosque, was reconstructed in 1903 in the style of the Byzantine church upon the ruins of which it was built. The apses contain large paintings, depicting Jesus condemned to death and John concealing Jesus from his grieving mother. The window motifs depict Pilate washing his hands, the Imposition of the Cross and an angel holding instruments of torture. The chapel was found to be standing on part of a Roman pavement, the Lithostrotos (the other part is in the basement of the Convent of the Sisters of

Zion, as we shall see below). The churches are open to visitors from 8.30 a.m.–12.00 noon and 2.00 p.m.–6.00 p.m., except on Sunday.

The Franciscan School for Biblical Studies (Franciscan Biblicum Studium) was built in 1927 as a research institute for Rome's University Faculty of Theology. It has a rich library and a museum, where archaeological collections from Israel and the Near East are displayed. We shall continue a few meters west along the Via Dolorosa to the Convent of the Sisters of Zion.

Convent of the Sisters of Zion Open daily (except Sundays) 8.30 a.m.–12.30 a.m. and 2.00 p.m.–4.00 p.m. Entry Fee. To the west of the Church of the Condemnation, the convent is a three-storey building, built in 1858 by the French Father Alphonse Ratisbonne — a Jewish convert (who, with his brother Theodore, also built an orphanage-monastery in the New City, and a convent in Ein-Karem, where he is buried). On the ground floor is a small museum, containing archaeological finds, models of the Antonia fortress and of Via Dolorosa, and a map of Jerusalem at the time of Jesus, drawn by the scholar L.H. Vincent. On the top floor is a hostel for pilgrims and tourists, with an open balcony affording an extensive view of the entire Temple Mount area. The nuns act as guides and show vestiges discovered in the 1931–1937 excavations, including a subterranean cistern for collection of rainwater, identified with the Struthion Pool (Ostrich Pool) mentioned by Josephus (*Jewish Wars* 5, 11, 4). The double reservoir is hewn out of the rock and has a row of arches and a vaulted roof. Above are substantial parts of the Lithostrotos, the ancient pavement which until recently was believed to have been the courtyard of the Praetorium. This pavement is now known to have been part of a 2nd-century forum built by the Roman emperor Hadrian. Grooves were etched in the massive blocks of stone to prevent the horses and chariots from skidding on the smooth surface. In the so-called area of the Game of the King, gaming boards incised in the stone of the pavement by the Roman soldiers can also be seen (Matthew 27:27).

West of the Roman pavement is a triple triumphal arch erected by Hadrian. It spans the Via Dolorosa and continues into the Church of the Ecce Homo where the smaller northern section can be seen by entering from No. 15, Via Dolorosa. For centuries it was known as the Arch of Ecce Homo (Behold the Man), because it was thought to be at the spot where Pilate presented Jesus to the crowd (John. 19:5). The Lithostros, Game of the King and Ecce Homo Arch are illustrated overleaf.

The Prison of Christ West of the Convent of the Sisters of Zion on the Via Dolorosa, the Greek Orthodox own a section of pavement and some grottoes. According to Greek Orthodox tradition, Jesus' prison was in one of these grottoes. They also call it the Prison of Barabbas. Archaeological evidence shows that these caves may have once served as a prison.

We shall continue up to the corner of HaGai Street. On our right is the Austrian Hospice, the first hotel in Jerusalem, inaugurated between 1857 and 1863. Among

Facade of the Church of the Flagellation.

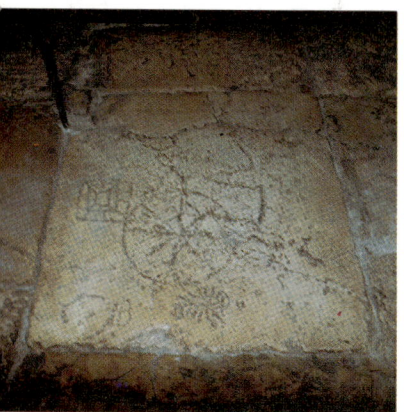

the many pilgrims who stayed there was Austrian Emperor Franz Joseph in 1869. The hospice served as a hospital up to 1985, when it again became a hotel. The Third Station of the Cross is on the corner of the streets opposite the Hospice.

The Third Station commemorates the spot where Jesus fell under the weight of the heavy cross. The site was purchased in 1856 by the Armenian Catholic Church who built a chapel. It was renovated thanks to donations from Polish soldiers and refugees during the Second World War. The church has a small musuem, where findings from the excavations carried out here in the 19th century by the scholar S. Clermont-Ganneau are on display. Most of the exhibits are from the Second Temple period.

The Fourth Station is in the next building, the Stabat Mater Dolorosa, the Armenian Church of Our Lady of the Spasm, built in 1881 on the ruins of the Byzantine St Sophia Church. The mosaic in the crypt depicts the imprint of a pair of slippers, marking the place where Mary stood watching her son pass by. The meeting place of Jesus and his mother is marked by a small chapel. Above the door is a half-bust of Christ and his mother. This church and the Polish church stand on the site of the Hammam es-Sultan, Turkish baths which functioned up to the 18th century. Opposite the two churches, incorporated in the paving of HaGai Street, are large paving stones from the Second Temple period, uncovered 3 m (9 feet) below the level of the present street during the installation of a sewage pipe.

The Fifth Station This Station is where HaGai Street turns west (right), onto the continuation of the Via Dolorosa. The Franciscan chapel on the left corner was built in 1895 and is called after Simon of Cyrene, a pilgrim to Jerusalem, who was compelled by the Roman soldiers to help Jesus carry the cross (Matthew 27:32,

(top) The Lithostrotos.
(center) The "Game of the Kings" incised in the stone by Roman soldiers.
(bottom) Part of Hadrian's three-entrance triumphal arch at the Ecce Homo.

Luke 23:26). On the right of the church gate is a depression in the wall where, according to tradition, Jesus rested the palm of his hand. The next house, over the vaulted passage through which the street passes, is said to be that of the "wicked rich man" (Luke 16:19) and served as a military hospital during the Ottoman period.

The Sixth Station Continuing along the Via Dolorosa, we pass under a series of flying buttresses and soon reach, on the left side of the street, a fragment of pillar embedded in the wall where the 6th station of the procession of the Way of the Cross is made. It marks the place of the house of St Veronica. A Greek Catholic church was built here in 1885 on the ruins of a 6th-century monastery, and was restored by the Italian architect Barluzzi in 1953. Part of the church belongs to the Little Sisters of Jesus and houses a school.

According to tradition, Veronica was one of the women who lined the street along which condemned criminals were led. One of these women is said to have stepped forward to wipe the blood and dirt from Jesus' face, and his image remained on the cloth which she used. Hence her name *Vera Icone*, "true likeness", given to this legendary woman, who is not mentioned in the Gospels.

The Seventh Station We shall continue along the Via Dolorosa up to the Beit Habad Street intersection. Further on, on the left hand side of El-Hanka Street, is a small Coptic church (the locality was acquired by the Franciscans in 1875). A red granite pillar, a vestige of the Byzantine Cardo Maximus, marks the place where Jesus fell for a second time. According to tradition, this was the site of the Gate of Judgement where the names of the accused and their sentence were posted before they went out of the city wall.

The Eighth Station Further up, on a stone on the left, bearing a Latin Cross, and a Greek inscription — NIKA ("Jesus

(top) The Third Station of the Cross.
(center) The Church of Our Lady of the Spasm at the Fourth Station.
(bottom) The Franciscan chapel at the Fifth Station of the Cross.

Christ conquers") is said to be the spot where Jesus met the lamenting women of Jerusalem and to have said to them: "Daughters of Jerusalem, do not weep for me but weep rather for yourselves and for your children" (Luke 23:27).

Going back to the intersection, we shall turn right along Beit Habad Street (Khan ez-Zeit market). A few meters along, in the storeroom of Zalatimo shop, are ancient vestiges of a wall and gate that have not yet been investigated. They are thought to be remains of a temple to Venus, of Constantine's original Church of the Holy Sepulcher, and of the basement of a Crusader monastery. Continuing south in the market, we shall turn onto HaTsaba'im Street, where we will go into the Russian Orthodox **Alexander Nievsky Church**. Open 9.00 a.m.–1.00 p.m.; 3.00–5.00 p.m. daily excepting Sundays. Admission fee.

Impressive archaeological remains were discovered here during the church's construction in 1887, including: a) stone arch from Hadrian's time, which may have been the gate of the Roman forum; b) vestiges of a stone wall, built from hewn stones like those in Herodian buildings which, according to one supposition, were part of the Second Wall in which the Gate of Judgement was set. Another conjecture sees it as a wall of the first Church of the Holy Sepulcher which incorporated Herodian stones in its structure. The holes in the stones indicate that marble tiles may have covered the wall; c) a flight of steps and the facade of the entrance nave of the first Church of the Holy Sepulcher; d) pillars of the Roman Cardo.

Opposite the entrance to the Russian church, Crusader ruins are incorporated in the north wall of the German Church of the Redeemer. The main vestige is the arch that was over the entrance of the Crusader St Marie la Latine Church. Symbols and names of the months are etched in the

(top) The Sixth Station at the site of St Veronica's house.
(center) The Seventh Station.
(bottom) Latin cross with Greek inscription at the Eighth Station.

ST. STEPHEN'S GATE TO THE HOLY SEPULCHER

stone. The engraved figures and inscriptions are blurred. We shall return to the outer wall of the Russian Church on Beit Habad Street and go up the steps at the back of the building. After turning left, then right, we come to the entrance of a **Coptic monastery church**, opposite which is an open courtyard.

The Ninth Station In the courtyard, right of the entrance of the compound, the shaft of a pillar set in the wall of the Coptic Patriarchate marks the Ninth Station. The open courtyard is the eastern part of the Church of the Holy Sepulcher complex and contains the cupola of St Helena's Chapel. In the Crusader period the monastery of the Knights of the Holy Sepulcher stood here. Vestiges of the walls, arches and pillars are still visible. Ethiopian monks have been living here since the 17th century. The olive trees with a cross, on the east side, mark the site where Isaac was to be sacrificed. The compound is known as Deir Es-Sultan (the monastery of King Solomon), who is revered by the Ethiopians. The rooftop is disputed by the Copts and the Ethiopians. From the courtyard we proceed to the several Ethiopian chapels beside it: the Chapel of the Redeemer; the Chapel of the Angels. The Byzantine style images on the walls depict the Queen of Sheba's visit to King Solomon in Jerusalem. Solomon is portrayed with a beard, sideburns and a Star of David at his neck. The Queen's retinue comprises women, and one man bearing two elephant tusks. We shall go down the steps, through St. Michael's Chapel, to the courtyard of the Church of the Holy Sepulcher.

The last five Stations of the Cross are inside the Church of the Holy Sepulcher.

5. Church of the Holy Sepulcher — Open 4.30 a.m.–8.00 p.m. daily (7.00 p.m. in winter). This is the holiest Christian site in Jerusalem. It is a place of prayer and of pilgrimage for Christians throughout the world. Here Jesus was crucified,

(top) Alexander Nievsky Church where Roman remains were found during construction.
(center) Deir Es-Sultan, the Ethiopian compound on the Holy Sepulcher roof.
(bottom) The Ninth Station of the Cross.

entombed and resurrected. The present edifice is a Crusader church, the fourth on this site since Emperor Constantine and his mother Helena built the first church in the 4th century. The church contains a number of chapels, and is maintained mainly by the Greek Orthodox, the Armenian and Roman Catholic Churches. Small areas within the structure are held by the Copts and the Syrian Jacobites, and a small area outside is held by the Ethiopians (see Ninth Station). The keys of the church are held by two families of Muslim notables since the time of Saladin. The church includes under its roof the place called Golgotha, that is, the "place of a skull" in Aramaic (Matthew 27:33, John 19:17) or Calvary, possibly because the cross was placed on a rock which resembled the shape of a skull (*calvaria* in Latin).

originally outside the walls, since in accordance with Jewish tradition (strictly observed in Jesus' time) a place of execution and of burial would have to be outside the city. It seems that not far from the northwestern section of the city wall of those days were two adjacent places — Golgotha, the place of execution, and another hill where Joseph of Arimathea had bought for himself a sepulcher (John 19:41) in a burial site which was a disused quarry where tombs had been cut into the vertical surfaces left by the quarrymen. The tomb was no doubt a burial cave with a rock-cut open antechamber from which an opening led into the burial chamber where niches in the wall were cut into which the deceased were laid.

History of the Church — There is a tradition that the early Christians of Jerusalem

View of the Holy Sepulcher.

Chapel of the Franks, on the right.

According to Byzantine tradition Adam was buried here, and the Chapel of Adam is below the Golgotha. Within the compound are also the Chapel of St. Helena and the Chapel of the Finding of the Cross. The site of the tomb was identified during Queen Helena's visit in 324 (about 250 years after the establishment of the first Christian community in Jerusalem, which knew the location of Jesus' burial place.

The Holy Sepulcher is now in the heart of the Christian Quarter of the Old City, but both the Golgotha and the Sepulcher were

commemorated Jesus' death at least until 66 C.E., and the memory of the site of his burial remained even after Hadrian in 135 had prepared to build a temple to Venus there. At the Ecumenical Council of Chalcedon in 325 it was resolved to locate the tomb of Jesus and build a church at the site. The Emperor Constantine and his mother Helena came to Jerusalem and during her visit she found the remains of the Cross in an underground cistern.

Before construction was undertaken, the area was prepared. Part of the cliff of

Golgotha was cut away in order to isolate the tomb-chamber. Construction of Constantine's church started in 326 and the church was dedicated in 335, before the work on the tomb was quite finished. It comprised five principal structures: an atrium at the head of the steps from the main street; a covered basilica, an open courtyard with the Golgotha in the southeast corner; the tomb. The large basilica encompassed under one roof all three adjacent holy sites — the Sepulcher, Golgotha-Calvary and the Cave of the Finding of the Cross. Remnants of the Constantine basilica have been preserved in various places in the present-day church and surrounding area. Entrance was from the east, via steps, and there were three entrances that can be seen in the basement of the nearby Alexander Nievsky Church. These led to the atrium (open courtyard) that preceded the huge basilica which was divided by four rows of columns into five naves. The basilica was called the Martyrium ("Witness"). Behind the apse was a cloister in the southeast corner of which was the square rock, all that was left of Golgotha. The westernmost part of the edifice was a circular church, the Anastasis ("Resurrection") with the Sepulcher — from around which all the rock was removed — in the center.

Constantine's basilica was destroyed in 614 by the Persians; soon after, it was rebuilt, with very few changes, by the Patriarch Modestus after the victory of the Byzantine Emperor Heraclius in 628, who fought to regain the Holy Cross taken by the Persians. This church remained intact after the Arab conquest, until 1009 when all but the Sepulcher and the structure over the rock of Golgotha was razed by the Fatimid Caliph Hakim.

After reaching an agreement with the Muslim rulers, the Byzantine Emperor Constantine Monomachus rebuilt the church between 1042 and 1048. He restored the rotunda of the Anastasias and built a roof over it in the form of a truncated cone open to the sky. At the east side he added an apse, and in place of its atrium he built an open courtyard, "the Holy Garden". East of the garden were three chapels: the Flagellation, the Thorns and the Sharing of the Raiment. To the north was a fourth chapel.

Monomachus' construction was incorporated in the present structure, erected after the Crusader conquest of Jerusalem (1099), and inaugurated in 1149. The high eastern apse of the rotunda was removed, and in the courtyard to the east, a tall, typically 12th-century, Romanesque-style church, was built. The church has a dome and galleries, which were built on the site of the Holy Garden. On the south side, the adorned facade had a double portal. To its west a belfry was built (the bells were destroyed in 1187 by Saladin). To the east, on the site of Constantine's basilica, a monastery was built for the Augustinian monks who served in the church. The courtyard of the Ethiopians is on the ruins of the cloister of this monastery (on the roof of St. Helena's Chapel). Stone ornaments from the Crusader period remain on the facade of the Church, together with a mosaic in the ceiling of the Chapel of Golgotha, depicting Jesus' ascension to heaven. The sepulcher, refashioned by the Crusaders, forms the basis of the later structure existing today. They built three chapels in the church's semi-circular ambulatory and steps going down to the St. Helena Chapel. The Stone of Unction was set in its present site in the 12th century. The tomb structure was rebuilt in the 19th century. The upper part of the belfry collapsed in an earthquake. In 1808 the Church, and principally the rotunda, was severely damaged by a fire. Repairs were carried out in 1810 and between 1863 and 1869. The stability of the structure was undermined by further earthquakes, and in particular by a severe one in 1927. The condition of the church was examined in 1934, but restoration work was delayed because of disagreements between three major communities (Latin, Greek and Armenian), and commenced only in 1960, lasting for 20 years.

Visit to the Church — We shall start with the entrance and the last five Stations.

The parvis is built over the ceiling of an ancient cistern, that was a quarry in ancient times. Its paving dates from the

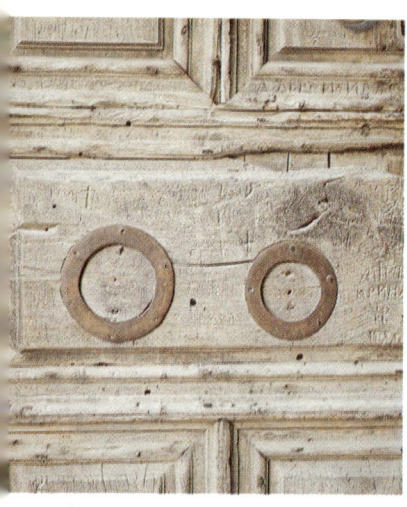

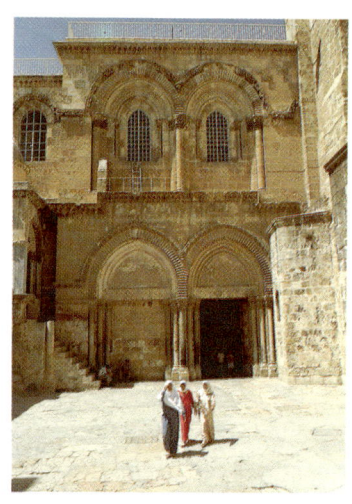

Detail of door at the Holy Sepulcher. The whole facade of the church is shown on the right.

.12th century. Vestiges of the colonnade that closed the parvis at the south are still visible. A number of structures open on to the parvis. In the south is the **Monastery of St Abraham** a 12th-century Greek Orthodox monastery, which was destroyed, and then rebuilt in 1690. A hostel was established here in the 19th century. The Chapel of Abraham inside marks the place of Isaac's sacrifice, according to Byzantine tradition. Beneath the structure is a gigantic, 4th-century cistern. The ceiling is supported by large, solid arches. The Greek Orthodox Custodian of the Church of the Holy Sepulcher lives in this monastery. The center door leads to the Armenian **Chapel of St John**. The north door leads to the **Ethiopian Chapel of the Angel**. Beyond the pavement, south of the parvis, is the Greek Gethsemane Monastery (built on the ruins of the Crusader monastery of St John). To its west we can see the minaret of the Omar Mosque (built in the 15th century) marking the place where the Muslim conqueror of Jerusalem prayed (in 638). West of the parvis are three apses of chapels, two of which belong to the Greek Orthodox Church: the **Chapel of St James**, the bishop of Jerusalem, and the **Chapel of Mary Magdalene**, where Jesus is said to have appeared to Mary Magdalene. The third, the **Chapel of the Forty Martyrs**, which belongs to the Armenians, is dedicated to the soldiers who died here because they refused to apostasize. Above this chapel rises the 12th-century Crusader belfry. In the north-east corner of

Vaults of the 4th-century cistern.

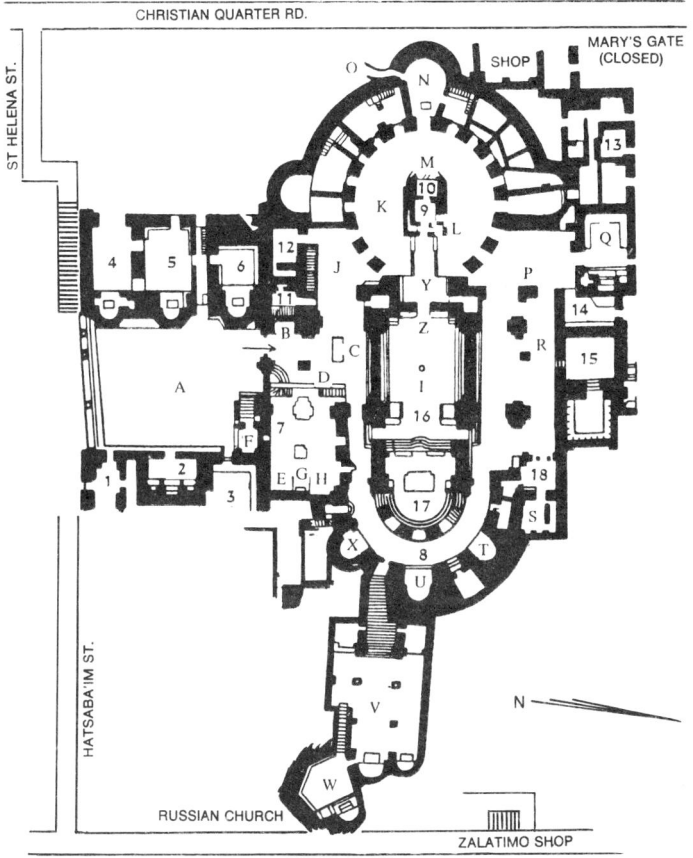

ST. STEPHEN'S GATE TO THE HOLY SEPULCHER

Map of the Church of the Holy Sepulcher.

1 Monastery of St Abraham
2 Chapel of St John
3 Chapel of St Michael
4 Chapel of St James
5 Chapel of Mary Magdalene
6 Chapel of Forty Martyrs
7 Mosaic — Sacrifice of Isaac
8 Ambulatory
9 Chapel of the Angel
10 Holy Sepulcher
11 Copts' Room
12 Armenians' Room
13 Latins' Room
14 Franciscan Sacristy
15 Service Yard

16 Catholicon Altar
17 Catholicon Apse
18 Chapel of the Shackles

A Parvis
B Guard
C Stone of Unction
D Chapel of Adam
E Eleventh Station
F Chapel of the Sorrows (Franks)
G Thirteenth Station
H Twelfth Station
I Catholicon
J Place where the 3 Marys stood
K Rotunda

L Tomb of Jesus
M Chapel of the Copts
N Syrian-Jacobite Chapel
O Tombs of Joseph and Nicodemus
P Altar of Mary Magdalene
Q Chapel of the Apparition
R Arches of the Virgin
S Christ's Prison
T Chapel of St Longinus
U Chapel of Division of the Raiment
V Chapel of St Helena (Armenian)
W Chapel of Finding of the Cross
X Chapel of the Mocking
Y Latin Choir
Z Apse of Monomachus

the parvis, the domed structure against the Church is the Roman Catholic **Chapel of the Sorrows**. Its arches rest on a pair of graduated columns, a typical Crusader style. The arch is adorned with vine and birds, including an eagle and a peacock; and the remains of a Crusader mosaic, with plant motifs. Above the arch are decorations with acanthus leaves and bunches of grapes. In the Crusader period there was direct access from here to Golgotha. Beneath is the **Chapel of Mary the Egyptian** from Alexandria, who visited Jerusalem in the 5th century, and converted to Christianity.

The two-storey façade dates to the Crusaders. The entrance is composed of twin portals, one of which has been blocked since Saladin's time. Each portal is flanked by a group of three marble pillars standing on high-stepped bases. The capitals are decorated with a pattern of acanthus foliage. Above the doorways the gables are surrounded by a double frieze. The rich mosaics that embellished the tympana have disappeared but the lintels with marble reliefs depicting the Last Supper, and the resurrection of Lazarus, remained intact; they are now on display at the Rockefeller Museum. They depict the Last Supper, Jesus entering Jerusalem on a mule, the Raising of Lazarus in Bethany, etc. The lintels were placed on display in the Rockefeller Museum in 1935.

The Atrium In the left corner of the entrance is the tomb of Philip d'Aubigny, tutor of Henry III of England, a Crusader who died here in 1228. Opposite the entrance, by the wall of the northern nave, is a rectangular stone slab on the floor, surrounded by three pairs of huge candelabra (Franciscan, Greek and Armenian). This is the **Stone of Unction**, upon which Jesus' body was prepared for burial. The new pink wall behind the stone shuts off the Catholicon.

On the right of the Stone of Unction is the **Chapel of Adam** where the skull of Adam is buried according to Byzantine tradition. Through the glass covering the rock of Golgotha, we can see the crack in the rock created at the time of Jesus' Crucifixion. The Greek Orthodox identify this spot with the burial site of Melchizedek, king of Salem (Genesis 14:18–24), here. From the writings of Christian pilgrims, we know that the tombs of the Crusader kings of Jerusalem, Godefroy de Bouillon, conqueror of Jerusalem and "Protector of the Holy Sepulcher", and Baldwin, were on the west side of the Chapel. The tombs were destroyed by fire in 1808.

Golgotha (Calvary) The semicircular steps in the eastern corner of the atrium lead up to the rock of Golgotha opposite the sealed entrance to the Church of the Holy Sepulcher (previously, Golgotha was reached through the Chapel of the Franks). We mount the platform of Calvary (about 5 m — 16 ft high) to the hall containing the last four Stations.

The Tenth and Eleventh Stations At the top of the steps we reach Calvary, divided into two chapels, one Greek Orthodox and one Roman Catholic or Latin. The 10th and 11th Stations are made in the Latin chapel, on the right. According to tradition, Jesus

The Stone of Unction.

ST. STEPHEN'S GATE TO THE HOLY SEPULCHER

Eleventh, Twelfth and Thirteenth Stations.

Altar of Greek Orthodox Chapel of Golgotha.

was disrobed at this site before being nailed to the Cross (John 19:23). The mosaics on the wall of the Chapel depict Abraham preparing to sacrifice Isaac and Jesus being nailed to the Cross. On the ceiling is a figure of Jesus, a remnant of a Crusader mosaic. Below the east wall mosaic is a silver-plated Renaissance altar from Florence (donated by Ferdinand di Medici, Grand Duke of Tuscany, in 1609), with six reliefs depicting Jesus' Passion. The 11th Station is made here.

The Twelfth Station A chapel, at the far left of the hall, belonging to the Greek Orthodox, marks the place of death of Jesus. The altar is flanked by two supporting columns with a silver disk beneath the altar table, with a cavity in its center, to mark the place where the Cross stood. The rock of Golgotha can be touched through the opening. Two black disks on each side of the altar mark the place of the crosses of the two thieves crucified with Jesus (Mark 15:27). On the right of the altar, an opening in the marble reveals the fissure caused by an earthquake which followed Jesus' death (Matthew 27:51). The fissure continues down to the Chapel of Adam under Calvary.

The Thirteenth Station Between the 11th and the 12th Station is the Latin Chapel, an altar marking the spot where, after Jesus was taken down from the Cross, Mary received the body of her son.

Above the altar is a glass case containing a 16th-century wooden statue of the Sorrowful Virgin, covered with jewels, presented by Maria of Braganza, Queen of Portugal in 1778.

In repairs carried out in 1937 another part of the Golgotha was discovered beneath.

Descending from Calvary in the northeast corner, we reach the level of the church. We go again past the Stone of Unction and continue west until we reach a round mark on the floor — the spot where the three Marys stood by Jesus. On the wall opposite this spot is a new mosaic executed in 1980 by an Israeli artist, depicting the three Marys (the Virgin, Mary Magdalene and the wife of Cleophas) witnessing the Passion. This area where the Rotunda begins belongs to the Armenians. The chapels have been restored in the last few years. Steps lead up to the Armenian sacristy.

The Fourteenth Station The Chapel containing Jesus' sepulcher is the last Station on the Way of the Cross. This round, domed structure is in the center of the Rotunda. The tomb was originally in a cave hewn in the rock, that remained as an island after it was cut off the surrounding rock, under Constantine. The Rotunda was built over and around it. It is an impressive space surrounded by a huge cupola. In its center is the Holy Sepulcher in the form of a richly decorated edicule. Inside are two small chambers. The first is the **Chapel of the Angel** with a rock bench on which the three women saw an angel who announced "he is risen" (Mark: 16:6), and in the second is the Holy Sepulcher itself, to which one enters through a low door. The room is 2 × 2 m (6½ ft × 6½ ft). Half the area contains the tomb, covered by a smooth marble slab. Over the tomb are three reliefs symbolizing the Resurrection, and 42 lamps which burn day and night (13 each for the Latins, the Greek Orthodox and the Armenians and four for the Copts). Behind the edicule over the Sepulcher is a tiny chapel belonging to the Copts, and behind it, beyond the pillars of the **Rotunda**, is a chapel of the Syrians-Jacobites. From this chapel one can enter an anonymous burial cave in the rock, proving that this area was indeed a Jewish cemetery in the time of Jesus. In front of the Sepulcher, in the very center of the church, is the Greek Orthodox Catholicon chapel, newly remodeled with a lavishly decorated iconostasis. On the floor is a stone goblet which represents the Omphalos, the center of the world.

The Rotunda: the round structure where the Sepulcher stands, with a ceiling resting on columns, preserves Constantine's original structure. It has a large opening to the sky. The tomb is in the center of an area 35 m (112 ft) in diameter, hewn in the rock. In a concentric circle around the Sepulcher are twelve round pillars and four pairs of square columns. The structure has two storeys and three apses: in the south, the west and the north. The external walls have been preserved up to a height of 11m.

The north apse is used as a storeroom and is divided lengthwise between the Latins and the Greek Orthodox. The north and the east of the apse are Latin and contain the **Altar of Mary Magdalene**. Its 12th-century Venetian style marble floor, made of round and square tiles, was discovered and restored in 1960.

The **Chapel of the Apparition** is the new Franciscan church, built on the northern side of the external wall of the Rotunda. It marks the site where Jesus appeared to his mother after the Resurrection. By the altar is the **Pillar of Flagellation** to which Jesus is said to have been tied and scourged by the Roman guards. Another smaller room at the west communicates with the Franciscan monastery, north of the Chapel of the Holy Sepulcher. East of the Church of the Apparition is the **Franciscan Sacristy**, where one can see spurs, a cross and a blade said to be the sword of

Altar of Mary Magdalene.

Chapel of the Apparition.

Godefroy de Bouillon, the first ruler of the Kingdom of Jerusalem.

The Ambulatory is the circular passage east of the Catholicon. South and north of the Catholicon are aisles divided lengthwise by partitions into rooms.

We shall go back to the Altar of Mary Magdalene. The north aisle begins from here and continues eastward. On one side is the north wall of the Catholicon, and on the other two columns of the Crusader structure. On one side of the pillars are seven arches, the **Arches of the Virgin**, belonging to the portico of the Crusader church. Here the "join" between the Crusader and the Byzantine structure is apparent. At the end of the straight section of the gallery is a small room owned by the Greek Orthodox, known as the **Chapel of Christ's Prison** where Jesus was chained to a pillar when the Cross was being prepared. The Ambulatory encircles the Catholicon on the east side, and in this section there are three chapels: the Greek Orthodox **Chapel of St Longinus** after the Roman soldier who pierced Jesus' side with his lance in order to end his suffering (John 19:34; the name Longinus is legendary); the Armenian **Chapel of the Division of the Raiment** marks the place where the garments were taken from Jesus and divided between those who accompanied him. Nearby is the **Chapel of the Mocking**, where the stump of the column on which Jesus sat while the soldiers insulted him is on display inside a glass chest below the altar.

The **Chapel of St Helena** Between the last two chapels, 29 steps lead down to the Armenian Chapel of St Helena. This is the subterranean chamber beneath the courtyard of the Ethiopians (see Ninth Station), where the cupola of the chapel protrudes. The central altar, in the south apse of the chapel, is dedicated to St Helena the Empress who brought to light the places of the Passion. In the north apse is an altar dedicated to St Dismas, the Good Thief who was crucified with Jesus. On the floor of the chapel is a mosaic made in 1950, commemorating the 1915 massacre of the Armenians in Turkey. In the last excavations, in the 1970s, parts of the walls of Constantine's basilica were discovered east of St Helena's Chapel, together with a Roman structure from Hadrian's time and the vestiges of an ancient quarry. On one of the stones in the wall of the basilica is a depiction of a sailing ship and a Latin inscription dating from 330: *Domine Ivimus* (we went with God), probably expressing the joy of the pilgrim arriving at his destination.

Chapel of the Finding of the Cross On the south side of the Chapel of St Helena we go down a flight of steps to the Chapel of the Finding of the Cross. On both sides of the steps we can see cavities hewn in the rock of the cave, showing that an ancient quarry was situated here. Helena is said to have discovered here fragments of Jesus' Cross and fragments of the crosses of the two thieves crucified beside him. (She sent the fragments of the cross to Rome where a special church was built to house them, the Church of Santa Croce in Gerusaleme). There are two altars in the chapel: on the left-hand altar, owned by the Franciscans, is a statue of Helena carrying the Cross. (An inscription on the altar records that the statue was donated by Archduke Maximilian of Austria, later king of Mexico, who was killed in 1864). The right-hand altar is owned by the Greek Orthodox.

Leaving the Church of the Holy Sepulcher, we turn west and take the steps up to St Helena's Passage. We shall turn south on Christian Quarter Road and then west onto David Street, which takes us back to the Jaffa Gate.

Crosses carved on the wall of the chapel by medieval pilgrims.

TOUR No. 7

THE CHRISTIAN QUARTER

Details of tour: The Christian Quarter, not including the sites described in the tour from the Lion's Gate to the Holy Sepulcher.
Distance covered: approx. 3km (2 miles)
Time: approx. 5 hours
Transportation: Buses No 1, 3, 15, 19, 20, 30, 41, 80 and 99
Parking lot below Jaffa Gate for private vehicles
Starting point: New Gate
End of tour: Jaffa Gate
The Sites: 1. New Gate; 2. Monastery of Saint Savior; 3. Latin Patriarchate; 4. Casa Nova; 5. Greek Catholic Patriarchate; 6. Greek Orthodox Patriarchate Museum; 7. Greek Orthodox Patriarchate; 8. Ethiopian Patriarchate; 9. Coptic Patriarchate; 10. Church of the Redeemer; 11. Muristan; 12. Church of St John the Baptist; 13. Coptic Khan; 14. Roman Column.

FOREWORD

The Christian Quarter is in the northwest section of the Old City. Here are concentrated more than 30 Christian religious institutions including monasteries, churches, schools and most of the Christian sects' headquarters. In the center of the quarter is the Holy Sepulcher. A number of hospices built to house Christian pilgrims are situated in the east and southern sections. A few hostels and Christian institutions are also found in the Muslim and Armenian Quarters, the latter being a separate Christian quarter in itself.

During the First Temple period the site was outside the city's walls and was probably uninhabited. It was only at the end of the Second Temple period that it was encompassed by the Third Wall and became part of the Bezetha quarter. In the Roman period, when Jerusalem was known as Aelia Capitolina, the area was mostly desolate. A Roman temple dedicated to Venus was situated in the eastern section, and close by was the market place — the forum. The first Christian structures — the Holy Sepulcher, monasteries and churches — were erected in the Byzantine period, and some of the present structures were built on their remains. During the early Arab period a royal decree stressing the Christian character of the quarter was issued to protect the Christians against persecution by Muslims. Christians settled in all parts of the city under the Crusaders, and many Christian institutions were established, most of them clustered in the vicinity of the Holy Sepulcher. In this period, also, the Armenian Quarter was built. During the following periods (Mameluke and Ottoman), the situation of the Christians deteriorated, and led them to group in one quarter.

In the 19th century the Christians were once again granted permission to build within and outside the Christian Quarter and it was at this time that most of the existing buildings were constructed. The belfry of the Franciscan Monastery, which was built in 1931, is among the most recent in the quarter.

TOUR

1. New Gate First called Bab es-Sultan Abdul Hamid. It was breached in the Turkish wall in 1889 at the request of the European Powers and with the agreement of Sultan Abdul Hamid to facilitate contact between the Christian Quarter and the new Christian buildings constructed outside the Old City during the last quarter of the 19th century.

Simple in style, without portals, its lintels

THE CHRISTIAN QUARTER

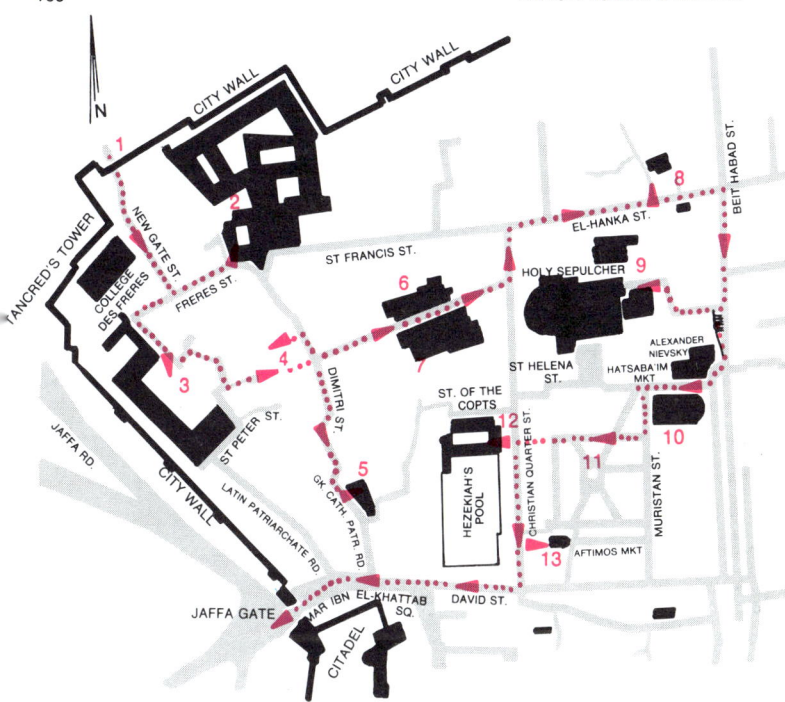

Map of the tour.

The New Gate.

and posts are typical of door and window frames in contemporary Palestine. The gate was blocked in 1948 by the Jordanians, and in 1967 it was opened to pedestrians as well as to cars.

To the west of the New Gate, inside the wall, is the Kamra Mosque, in memory of a Muslim woman (nothing is known of her except her name) whose tomb lies in a small room near the prayer hall.

2. Monastery of St Savior East of New Gate, inside the city wall, the road runs eastward to an iron gate bearing the name Terra Sancta and the emblem of the Franciscans. This is the western entrance to the Franciscan St Savior Monastery which extends over an area of 10 ha (2.5 acres), between the city walls and St. Francis Street.

In 1342, Pope Clement IV entrusted the Franciscans with the custody of the Holy Land, a privilege which is theirs to this day. Their first center in Jerusalem was set up in 1335 on Mount Zion, but the monks were expelled in 1552. In 1560 the Franciscans purchased the present site from the Georgian Christians, who at that time maintained a small nunnery — Deir el Ammud.

Clock tower of St Savior Monastery.

The Latin Patriarchate church.

The new monastery was constructed in stages: the carpentery and metal workshop were built first (in 1600) and then the school, workshops, the printshop, library, the church and finally the clock tower. The monthly magazine "Terra Sancta", which appears in five languages, is printed here, as well as guidebooks for pilgrims.

The monastery can be visited by appointment only. The church is open daily from 7.30 to 11.00 a.m. and can be reached from St Francis Street. From the southern entrance to the monastery, up the stairway at the left we reach the church, which is built in the form of a basilica; 30 m (98 ft) long and 12 m (39 ft) high. Its apse is long and high. The hall is higher than the portico and has windows in its upper section. There are about 200 pews in the hall, and seven chapels. The pillars, floor tiles and altars are all grey-white marble. There are four confessionals on both sides of the church entrance. The church was built at the end of the 19th century and one of the altars was brought here from the original church on Mount Zion. It serves the Roman Catholic community of Jerusalem.

We return to New Gate Street and reach the College des Frères, a boys' high school situated in the large building which almost touches the city wall. The College was founded by the Franciscans in 1876 and enlarged by the "Frères" (Brothers) who established schools throughout the Holy Land. In the lower part of the College are remains of an ancient fortress (it can be visited by permission of the school authorities). This was a 12th-century Crusader fortress known as Tancred's Tower (in honor of one of the knights of the First Crusade who had his camp nearby during the siege of Jerusalem in 1099) and in Arabic Kal'at Jalud (Goliath's Tower). The tower walls are built with Herodian blocks in secondary use. Stones of the Third Wall were found at its base. Archaeologists believe that the Tower of Psephinos, mentioned by Josephus as being in the northwestern corner of the Third Wall, stood here.

To reach the Latin Patriarchate, we turn into Frères Street and go through the Burskaim and St Peter's lanes. (Note: this site can also be visited toward the end of this tour and can be reached north of Omar ibn el-Khattab Square, near Jaffa Gate.)

3. The Latin Patriarchate The seat of the Latin (Roman Catholic) Patriarch, in

Jerusalem, the highest Catholic dignitary for Israel, Jordan and Cyprus. The Roman Catholic community in Israel has some 170 churches and monasteries as well as 180 other religious institutions.

These are 17 Catholic orders in Jerusalem, 9 for monks and 8 for nuns who live in 21 monasteries and convents (2 in the Old City). They run educational, medical and research institutions.

The Latin Patriarchate was established in Jerusalem during the First Crusade in 1099, when the spiritual head was the Bishop of Pisa in Italy. It was first situated near the Holy Sepulcher, but after Saladin conquered the city in 1187 the Patriarchate was moved to Acre. It was returned to Jerusalem in 1847 at the initiative of Pope Pius IX. Inaugurated in 1872, the adjoining church was built in the form of a basilica, in the Italian style popular at that time: a gabled facade below which is a round decorated window with a cross in the center. Above the church entrance is a pointed decorated arch and on both sides are vaulted windows within triangles supported by short pillars. There are also statues of the Patriarchs who are buried in the church.

4. Casa Nova Hospice We can reach the hospice through Frères Street and Casa Nova Street or return to Latin Patriarchate Road, walk to Omar ibn el-Khattab Square near Jaffa Gate and then along the Greek Catholic Patriarchate Road, Dimitri and Cava Nova Streets. A low round stone near the entrance to the hospices served as a stepping stone for pilgrims mounting their donkeys, the main form of transport until not so long ago. Casa Nova (new house) was constructed by the Franciscans in 1866 as a hospice for pilgrims. It was considered to be of a high standard in those days, especially as it had toilets to each of the 16 rooms. Today, the hospice can house 300 guests. Pope Paul VI stayed here when he visited the Holy Land in 1964.

5. The Greek Catholic Patriarchate The seat of the largest Catholic church in Israel. It was established in 1772 in Antioch, Turkey, when it broke away from the Greek Orthodox Church. In 1846 the Pope

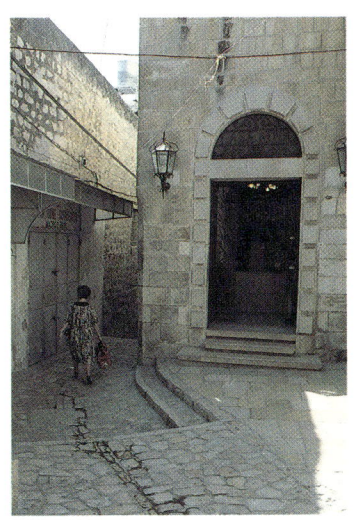

Entrance to Casa Nova Hospice.

appointed a Patriarch to Jerusalem, and in 1848 the construction of the seat of the Patriarchate and the Church of the Gospel was undertaken.

The church is open throughout the day, but cannot be visited during services. It is built in the style of an oriental basilica, and the apse is crowned with a copula, and concealed by a copper partition. The walls are covered with Byzantine-period frescoes depicting scenes from the life of Jesus and the saints, and Jesus with the Twelve Apostles are seen in a painting on the cupola. Among the engravings on the copper partition one can discern images of peacocks (symbol of eternity in Christian tradition) and a two-headed eagle, symbolizing the Russian Empire which supported the Greek Church. Next to the eagle is the symbol of the Russian Provoslavic Church which gave its patronage to the Greek Church.

6. The Greek Orthodox Patriarchate Museum Visiting hours: daily 9.00 a.m.–1.00 p.m., 3.00–5.00 p.m.; Sat. 9.00 a.m.–1.00 p.m. (closed Sunday). Entry fee.

The museum, opened in 1980, is situated within the Greek Patriarchate building. It contains artifacts from the collections of the Patriarchate, as well as archaeological finds. Among these are two limestone sarcophagi, found in the Hasmonean family mausoleum, with exquisite carvings of floral motifs. Also on show are Crusader capitals with carvings of saints found in the St Mary la Grande Church in the Muristan. A wooden door inlaid with mother-of-pearl was salvaged from the Holy Sepulcher when it was gutted by fire in 1808. The original document of surrender submitted by the Byzantine Patriarch Sophronius to the Arab conquerors in 638 is also on show.

7. The Greek Orthodox Patriarchate It is situated between Dimitri Street, the Christian Quarter Street, the Street of the Copts and the Greek Monastery Street. In Christian tradition this was the site of "The Mother of all Churches" from the time of James, Jesus' brother, the first Bishop of Jerusalem. The most ancient buildings date to the 4th century, but the complex took on its present form in the 17th century and was renovated several times during the 20th century. Entrance is from Greek Monastery Street, but it is generally closed to the public. Above the entrance is the Greek Orthodox symbol comprising the two Greek letters T P signifying the word *Taphos* — tomb in Greek — referring to the Holy Sepulcher.

The Greek Patriarchate of Jerusalem is

Entrance to Greek Patriarchate Museum.

the oldest in the city. It was established at the Ecumenical Council in Chalcedon in 451 and was appointed as custodian of the holy sites in the Holy Land. After the Arab conquest of Palestine, in 638, the Patriarchate continued to fulfil this function. Following the Crusader conquest (1099) the Greek Orthodox Patriarchate of Jerusalem moved to Constantinople, and remained there until the conquest of the Holy Land by Saladin in 1187, when the Roman Catholics were evicted and the Greek Orthodox returned to the holy places. In the 14th century the Latins were permitted to return to Jerusalem, but hostility continued between the sects under Ottoman rule. The Roman Catholics were supported by West-European countries, the Greek Orthodox by the Russians.

The peace treaty signed at the end of the Crimean War (1856) included a clause whereby the Great Powers guaranteed the rights of non-Muslim minorities living in the Ottoman empire. From then on, until the First World War, the income of the Greek Orthodox Patriarchate greatly increased from pilgrims from Russia and the Balkan countries. The Patriarchate built many buildings in Jerusalem (among them the Muristan, to be visited on this tour).

After the war this source of income dried up and the Patriarchate was forced to sell the major part of its holdings. The Greek Orthodox Patriarch of Jerusalem was given authority over the holy sites in Palestine and Transjordan.

The Constantine monastery complex, at the center of the Patriarchate, is the residence of the Patriarch and the living quarters of most of the members of the Council, about a hundred. The 15 hectare (3.5 acre) plot is the largest single block in the Christian Quarter. It contains scores of rooms and a large courtyard enclosed by buildings. The roof of the second floor of the eastern building overspans the Christian Quarter Street and reaches the dome of the Rotunda of the Holy Sepulcher. There are chapels on the roof: Saints Tekla, Demetrius and Constantine, and Helena. The convent has a very important library with some 500 manuscripts, bibles, and a copy of the New Testament dating from the Byzantine period. The printing-press prints the periodical "Nova Zion" and sacred literature.

The Greek Orthodox Church has a number of small churches in the Christian Quarter: St. Theodorus, near Casa Nova; St Basiliceus, near the New Gate; St Michael on St Francis Street, in honor of the angel Michael who is believed to have appeared to David beside the threshing-floor of Araunah on Mount Moriah. This church has a cupola, and in the courtyard are rooms for pilgrims and monks; St Catherine, on the lane going north from St Francis Street, inhabited by nuns; St Eptimius on the lane leading off the Via Dolorosa, a convent and church, in honor of one of the first hermits to dwell in the Judean Desert in Byzantine times; St Nicholas, near the Greek Orthodox Patriarchate.

8. The Ethiopian Patriarchate We continue along Christian Quarter Road and turn into El-Hanka Street. At the corner we see the El-Hanka Mosque, a name given to the Dervish hospice, built during the rule of Saladin and hence its name Hanka Salahyya. The present structure was renovated and extended under the Mameluke ruler Mohammed Kala'un in 1341 as evidenced by the inscription above the *mihrab* (prayer niche). The mosque is built in the early Mameluke style, with a dome made of small stones in two colors.

The second lane to the left leads to a two-storey convent and church, the seat of the Ethiopian bishop. The church, which has served the Ethiopian community since 1891, is dedicated to Tekela Haymanot, the saint who established the order in Ethiopia. The walls are decorated with frescoes depicting stories related to the Apostles from the New Testament. An Ethiopian is shown seated in his chariot while Philip the Evangelist baptizes him (Acts 8:26–39).

9. The Coptic Patriarchate The Copts are an early Christian sect founded in Egypt, and according to their tradition, they were baptized by the Apostle Mark in Alexandria. The name Copt is a corruption of the Greek word for Egypt, *Aegyptios*. The Copts settled in Jerusalem in the Byzantine period. Many fought in the ranks of Saladin's army against the Crusaders. Under the Mamelukes they had an archbishop, who was responsible to the Patriarch of Alexandria. They have a chapel behind the Holy Sepulcher, and a hospice (see below).

We return to El-Hanka Street and continue along Beit Habad Street, turn south to the market, up the steps to the right leading to the 9th Station of the Cross and to the Ethiopian compound Deir es-Sultan on the roof of St Helena's Chapel (Church of the Holy Sepulcher). We mount the

(left) Living quarters at the Greek Orthodox Patriarchate. (right) Coptic Patriarchate

stairs and turn right again into a long passage and at the end turn left. Opposite the entrance to Deir es-Sultan is the entrance to the Coptic Patriarchate building, and the Patriarch's residence is reached by the stairs in the internal courtyard. Here is the church of St Antony who was born in Egypt, and built the first Coptic church in the 4th century. The building also houses a hostel for Coptic pilgrims. The church walls are decorated with paintings depicting the life of Jesus, executed by Coptic artists in the 19th century. Below the courtyard is a large cistern, named for St Helena, apparently dating to the Byzantine period.

We return to Beit Habad Street, turn right and reach the Alexander Nievsky Church and continue to the Church of the Holy Sepulcher. Details about these two sites are given in Tour No.6 — From St Stephen's Gate to the Church of the Holy Sepulcher.

10. Church of the Redeemer Open to visitors: Monday 8.00 a.m.–1.00 p.m.; Tuesday–Saturday 9.00 a.m.–1.00 p.m., 2.00–5.00 p.m.; closed Sunday. Opposite the entrance to the Alexander Nievsky Church is the German Lutheran Church of the Redeemer. It was built on the foundations of the Crusader church Sainte Marie la Latine, established in the 11th century from donations made by merchants from the Italian city Amalfi. The land was granted as a gift by the Sultan to the King of Prussia, Friedrich Wilhelm, in 1869. The new church was consecrated in 1898 by the Kaiser, Wilhelm II, during a visit to Jerusalem.

The northern entrance to the Crusader church has been restored and includes an arch decorated with the signs of the zodiac. The cloister has also been restored within the hostel at the side of the church. During building operations remains from the First and Second Temple periods were uncovered below the church floor.

The new church is exquisite in its simplicity. It has an excellent organ used for concerts held here. A panoramic view of the Old City as well as parts of the new city and surroundings can be had from the top of the new church square bell tower, which is reached by climbing several hundred steps (entrance fee).

South of the church is the Lutheran school, and next to it a monument to the Hospitalers hospital and church situated in the Muristan dating from the Crusader period. Inside the school is a pre-World War I collection of stuffed birds belonging to the German Fund for the Exploration of Palestine.

11. The Muristan The area bounded by Muristan Street and Christian Quarter Road and by David and Hatsaba'im Streets is called the Muristan. In Roman times this was the site of the forum.

Muristan means "hospital" in Persian. In 1099 the Warden of St. John's monastery took in a number of Crusader knights wounded in the siege of Jerusalem. Those who stayed to take care of the sick and to protect pilgrims were known as the Knights of St John of the Hospital. They became the military order of the Hospitalers (and later the Knights of Malta). The hospital disappeared in the 16th century.

Church of the Redeemer.

THE CHRISTIAN QUARTER

Fountain in the Muristan.

Christian Quarter Road.

Nearby was the Crusader church Sainte Marie la Latine, and the site also included St John the Baptist Monastery. In 1903 the Greek Orthodox Patriarchate built a marketplace with some seventy shops on part of the area. A baroque fountain was built in the center of the market to mark the 25th anniversary of Sultan Abdul Hamid's rule. The southern section is called the Aftimos Market (after the Greek Patriarch). Some of the shops were owned by Jewish merchants and there used to be a synagogue situated opposite the church of St John the Baptist.

In the northwest corner of the Muristan, on St Helena Street (which leads down to the Church of the Holy Sepulcher) is the Omaryya Mosque, named for Omar ibn el-Khattab, who led the Muslim forces which conquered Jerusalem in 638. The mosque was built under Saladin and was restored under the Sultan Abdul Hamid, after its tower had collapsed in an earthquake.

12. Church of St John the Baptist At the edge of the Aftimos Market in the Muristan is the Greek Orthodox monastery. The entrance to the monastery's courtyard is from Christian Quarter Road, through a small opening, above which is a painting of the head of John the Baptist.

We go down a few steps to the courtyard and reach the church built on the remains of the Crusader church Sainte Mary la Latine. The external walls of the church, restored by the Greeks in 1842, have decorated stones in secondary use. There is a silver icon of St. John on the church wall which contains a relic of what is said to be part of his skull.

In the church's basement are remains of a 5th–6th century Byzantine church with a large central apse and two smaller ones. On the wall is an inscription in English dating to 1926 telling of prayer services held here by English Protestants by permission of the Greeks.

13. Coptic Khan Near the Greek Orthodox Patriarchate is a hostel built by the Coptic church in 1838 for pilgrims from Egypt. We walk along Christian Quarter Road to the Street of the Copts.

The building on the southern side of this courtyard is the Coptic monastery dedicated to the patron saint of the Copts, St George. The street to the south of the nearby Greek Catholic Patriarchate is named after him.

From the roof of the building we can see the Pool of Pillars dating to the Second Temple period. It is also called Hezekiah's Pool due to a belief that this was the upper pool where King Hezekiah met messengers sent by the King of Assyria. Josephus

(above) View of the Christian Quarter. (below) The Roman Column.

refers to it as Amigdalon (almond) which sounds also like the Hebrew *migdal,* meaning "tower", and in Arabic it is known as Birkat Hamman el-Batrak — the Pool of the Patriarch's Bath, because of its proximity to the Greek Catholic Patriarchate.

The open pool was used as a reservoir, served by conduits channeling rain water from the Mamilla Pool in the north of the city and the northern conduit. The western wall was hewn out of the rock and the other walls are built of limestone. The pool is presently dry and is used as a garbage dump.

14. Roman Column We come out at Omar ibn el-Khattab Square, near Jaffa Gate, and enter the lane between Patriarchate Road and Christians' Street. In a circle at the intersection of four covered streets, west of the square, is a lamppost embedded in a column bearing an inscription in Latin in honor of the Roman Prefect of Judea and the Legate of the Tenth Legion who participated in the capture of Jerusalem in 70 CE. The Tenth Legion was based in the city and occupied the area of what has been the Armenian Quarter for 250 years. The column was uncovered in 1885 during construction work.

Our tour of the Christian Quarter ends at Jaffa Gate (details about Omar ibn el-Khattab Square and Jaffa Gate will be found in Tour 9 — From Jaffa Gate to Mount Zion).

TOUR No. 8

THE ARMENIAN QUARTER

Details of tour: The tour includes sites within the Armenian compound, as well as the religious institutions of other Christian communities which are located outside the Armenian compound, in the northern part of the quarter. It is advisable to begin the tour in the morning and to visit first the sites in the northern part of the Armenian quarter (sites 8, 9, 10), then the Armenian compound and its various institutions which are mostly open in the afternoon. (The one exception is the Mardigian Museum which opens daily at 10 am and is closed on Sunday; the Church of the Archangels is open only on Saturday afternoons.)
Distance covered: 2 km (1½ miles)
Time: approx. 3 hours, including visits to the churches and the museum
Transportation: Buses No 1, 3, 19, 20, 30, 41, 80, 99. Parking lot for private vehicles near the Jaffa Gate
Starting point and end of tour: Jaffa Gate
The Sites: 1. The Kishla; 2. Cathedral of St James; 3. Mardigian Museum and Gulbenkian Library; 4. Church of the House of Annas; 5. The Armenian Garden; 6. Church of St Thomas; 7. St Mark's Church and Convent; 8. Watson House; 9. Maronite Church; 10. Christ Church.

FOREWORD

The Armenians number about 2.5 million altogether and most of them live in the Soviet Armenian Republic, although they can be found scattered in many other countries as well. About 3,000 live in Israel, with the majority residing in the Armenian Quarter of Jerusalem. They believe that their native Armenia is the site of the Biblical Ararat. It was St Gregory who, in the 3rd century brought Christianity to that region, hence the Armenian Church is also known as the Gregorian Church. By the 4th century the entire Armenian nation was Christian.

There is also an Armenian Roman Catholic church, which has just a few dozen followers in Jerusalem (see the fourth Station of the Cross, Tour 6). The seat of the supreme spiritual leader of the Armenian Church, the Catholicos, is at Etchmiadzin in Soviet Armenia. In 1915, one and a half million Armenians living in Turkey were exiled or massacred by the Ottoman authorities. This Armenian holocaust has played a very significant role in the history of the Armenian community. As an exiled people their unity is founded on their language and culture, rooted in their church.

The Armenian Quarter is located in the southwestern part of the Old City, and is bordered by the corner of the western and southern city walls. This is the plateau of Jerusalem's western hill, whose elevation is 773 m (2475 ft) above sea level. The wall which enclosed this area to the west and the north was built toward the end of the First Temple period as a continuation of the wall which surrounded the City of David. Remains of this wall can be found in the Citadel area and in the Jewish Quarter. No signs of habitation were found from this period or from the period after the return from Babylonian exile.

During the Second Temple period, this area was the western section of the Upper City, which included public buildings, the High Priest's palace and King Herod's palace. The Roman Tenth Legion, which was stationed in Jerusalem, was encamped here. In the Byzantine period, a paved street from Mount Zion passed through this area, as shown on the Madaba map. The Crusader Kings of Jerusalem built their palace in the western part of the area. A Georgian convent was also built here,

TOUR No. 8
114

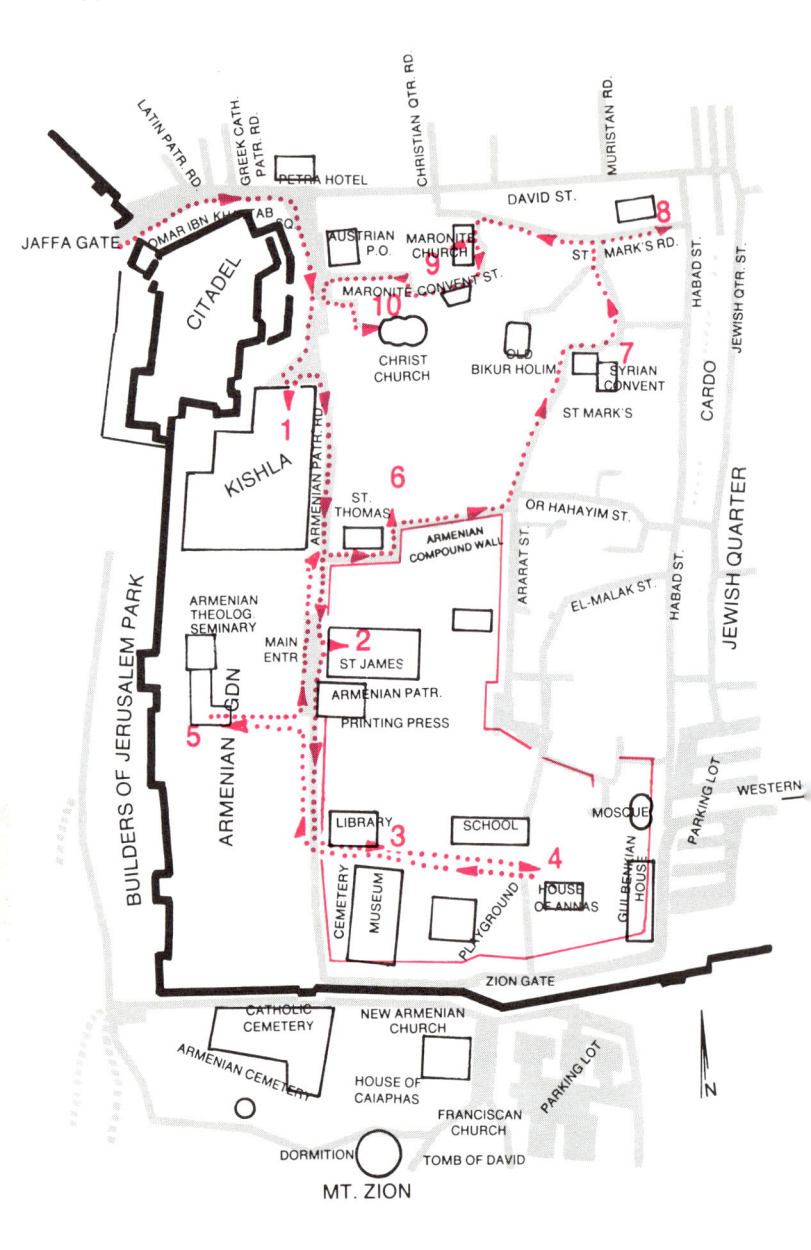

Map of the tour.

but it was taken over by the Armenians early in the 13th century and served as a nucleus around which Armenian families later settled. The convent was surrounded by a wall, and several churches were erected on its grounds. With the passing of time, the area became the Armenian Quarter, like a city in miniature, since it includes residential quarters, schools, a library, and religious and cultural institutions for the community. During the 1870s, the Armenians began to build new education institutions for their community outside the monastery compound, west of the Armenian Patriarchate Road, in the area called the Armenian Garden. In the northern part of the Armenian Quarter (outside the compound) we find a number of churches built by other Christian denominations, which we will visit later on in the tour. The eastern part of the Armenian Quarter (outside the compound) connects with the Jewish Quarter (between Habad Road and Ararat Road).

The Armenians engage in business, crafts, the free professions, jewelry and banking. Their traditional ceramic work is especially famous, and the Armenians who originate from Anatolia have continued this tradition, which developed particularly during the British Mandate period.

THE TOUR

1. The Kishla We enter through the Jaffa Gate and pass through Omar Ibn Khattab Square (details given in Tour No. 9, Jaffa Gate to Mount Zion). We turn right and pass by the gate to the Citadel. Before the turnoff to the Armenian Patriarchate Road, and south of the Citadel, we come to a stone building which houses a police station. This is the Kishla (barracks), built in 1837. It served as barracks, police station and prison. The fortified building was erected around the courtyard with a single entrance. The Turkish garrison, responsible for Jerusalem and the surrounding area, was stationed here. The building contained living quarters for the soldiers, an infirmary, and stables. The British Mandatory Police used the prison cells, and many Jewish underground fighters were held prisoner here. We enter the Armenian Patriarchate Road, pass by the entrance to St James Road (to the east), and continue past the vaulted portion of the street until we reach the main entrance of the Armenian compound on the eastern side of the street. Carved in the stone over the heavy iron gateway is an Arabic inscription from the year 1450, which confirms the recognition by the Mameluke sultan of the Armenian Church and the cancellation of the special tax on the church, and warns potential intruders. The Armenian inscription on the heavy door indicates that the Armenian Patriarch Kerikor built the entrance in the year 1646. Near the guardian's room is a marble drinking fountain on which appears an Armenian inscription from the year 1900, to mark the 25th year of the Turkish sultan Abdul Hamid's reign.

The residence of the Armenian Patriarch and his monks is on the second floor, to the right of the convent.

The Armenian Patriarchate in Jerusalem is the institution of supreme spiritual and religious importance to all Armenians in Israel. It is second in importance only to the Patriarchate in Armenia. In the 7th century there were 70 Armenian monasteries in the Holy Land. The Patriarchate was

Entrance to Armenian Quarter.

established at the end of the 12th century, after the eviction of the Crusaders. During the Mameluke and Ottoman periods, the Patriarchate enjoyed a special status as leader of all the Christian communities in Jerusalem. Among its possessions are St Helena's Chapel and a number of other chapels within the Church of the Holy Sepulcher. The Patriarchate owns many religious and educational institutions in Jerusalem and in Haifa, as well as extensive real estate, including houses.

St James Cathedral courtyard.

2. Cathedral of St James
Visiting hours during services only: Monday through Friday, 3:00–3:30 pm; Saturday and Sunday, 2:30–3:15 pm.

We enter the front courtyard of the church. Hung on the southern wall is a wooden board and a piece of iron which were used to summon worshippers to prayer instead of bells which were prohibited by the Muslims until the year 1840. On the walls surrounding the courtyard are hung stone plaques, known in Armenian as *katchkars*, engraved with crosses and inscriptions, which were brought by pilgrims and put up to commemorate their visit. The oldest dates to 1151.

The Cathedral of St James is the largest and holiest place of worship of the Armenians in Israel. It was built in the 11th century on the remains of a Byzantine church dating to the 6th century, and the style of the ancient basilica has been preserved in the later structure. The church has a large central dome and two small chapels on either side. The Cathedral is named after two different saints, both named James, who were killed and buried at this site, according to two different Armenian traditions. The first is James the brother of Jesus, the first bishop of Jerusalem, while the second is James the Apostle, brother of John the Evangelist, who was beheaded by Herod Agrippa in 44 C.E. (Acts 12:1,2). The Chapel of the Beheading is richly decorated with ceramic tiles and mosaics of rare beauty. The ceramic tiles and interior wooden doors (which are inlaid with mother-of-pearl and precious stones) were

Two katchkars.

imported from Anatolia in the 17th and 18th centuries. The floor of the cathedral is covered with magnificent soft carpets.

In the southern wall of the main hall is a small chapel named after the holy city of Etchmiadzin in Armenia, where Jesus was revealed to St Gregory. Three stones are preserved in this room: one from the River Jordan, one from Mount Tabor, and one from Sinai. The small chapels are dedicated to various saints (St Macarius, St Menas, St Stephen), and to St James the Great. The tradition that St James is buried here dates to the Byzantine period.

3. Mardigian and Gulbenkian Library
We leave the church and continue southward along the Armenian Patriarchate Road for about 50m (155 ft), until we reach the gateway to a courtyard on the eastern side of the street. The museum is on the right. The library is opposite the museum, on the left.

The museum is open to visitors daily (except Sundays) from 10:00 am. until 4:30 pm. There is an entry fee. The two-storey structure served as an Armenian theological seminary until 1979. The museum contains the following: an Archaeological Section containing parts of Armenian mosaic floors which were found in Jerusalem (on Mount Zion, on the Mount of Olives, and near the Damascus Gate), and artifacts found in the Armenian Garden, including sections of frescoes from the Herodian period; various items from Armenian monasteries in the Judean Desert, dating from the 4th century onwards are displayed in the historical section, along with treasures from the Armenian church and manuscripts dating from the 7th century; the art and folklore section includes Armenian ceramic vessels, wood carvings, illuminated manuscripts, ceremonial objects, headdresses, priestly vestment, etc.; the printing and photography section exhibits the original presses from the Armenian printing press, which was the first in Jerusalem, as well as books and pamphlets which were printed at the Armenian press. Also on display are rare books and manuscripts, and photographs taken in the 1860s by the Armenian Patriarch, who was one of the first photographers in the Holy Land.

The library: visiting hours are from 4:00 pm to 6:00 pm, daily except Sunday. The library is in the two-storey structure opposite the museum, and is named after its Armenian benefactor, Gulbenkian. It was built in 1929, and contains over 30,000 volumes as well as a collection of rare manuscripts. The reading room contains newspapers from all over the world.

4. Church of the House of Annas (Convent of the Olive Tree; Convent of the Archangels) Visiting hours: Saturdays only, between 3:00 pm and 4:00 pm. The

Armenian manuscript dating to 1265.

Church of the House of Annas.

church, which is located in the southeastern corner of the Armenian compound, was built in about 1300 in the style of a Byzantine basilica, on the remains of a 6th century church. According to tradition, this was the site of the house of Annas, the father-in-law of the High Priest Caiaphas, before whom Jesus was brought by the Romans (John 18:13). The olive tree near the wall is said to be the tree to which Jesus was bound during the scourging, and for this reason the convent here is called Deir ez-Zeituneh, in Arabic, Convent of the Olive Tree. The church is dedicated to the Angels who, according to tradition, covered their faces to avoid seeing the persecution of Jesus. Adjacent to the church is the room of Jesus' imprisonment, the room of the scourging of Jesus (which contains a cistern), a foyer, and a side room whose wooden door is artistically carved with an ornamented cross and Armenian inscriptions. Here also, embellished *katchkars* decorate the walls.

5. The Armenian Garden This is the name of the area opposite the Armenian compound, to the west of the Armenian Patriarchate Road. The new buildings of the Armenian Theological Seminary were inaugurated in 1979. The seminary was previously located in what is now the museum. The remains of two different palaces were unearthed here in archaeological excavations carried out in 1970 and 1971 — the foundations of Herod's palace, and the basements of the Crusader Kings' palace. (Note: the area is not open to the public.)

Thus Josephus, the Roman historian, describes in great detail the magnificence of Herod's palace. Herod raised the ground level and created a broad, elevated platform on which the palace was built (just as he built an enormous platform to serve as the foundation for the Temple). The platform stretched from the Citadel to the present line of the Turkish walls on the west and south. The buildings standing along the eastern border of the palace platform prevent excavations. The platform was built by constructing multiple retaining walls and filling the space between them with earth. The remains of four walls were discovered, 3.5 m (11½ ft) high and 2.25 m (7 ft) wide, which probably served as the foundation of the palace. The investigators believe that this was the residence of the Roman procurator when he visited Jerusalem, and that here was the Praetorium where Jesus was sentenced, not at its traditional site on the Via Dolorosa. The ancient course of the "Way of the Cross" leads from Caiaphas' house on Mount Zion to here, and from here to the Sepulcher.

The Crusader Kings' Palace was built here because of its proximity to the Citadel (for this same reason, Herod's palace was built here). At first, the Crusader Kings of Jerusalem ruled from the El-Aksa Mosque. The foundations of the Crusader palace reach the bedrock, obliterating the remains of any earlier structures that might have existed. The ground floor of the southern wing of the Crusader palace was uncovered. In it were found two 17m (57 ft) long halls which apparently served as storerooms for food. Two rock-hewn plastered basins were probably wine vats. Large water cisterns were carved in the rock beneath the two halls. In the wall of one of the halls appears a bas-relief carving of a cross.

6. Church of St Thomas We return to the Armenian Patriarchate Road and turn right (eastward) onto St James Road. To our left is the southern wall of a 12th-century Crusader church dedicated to St Thomas. The entrance has been sealed up. Opposite the church of St Thomas stands the wall of the Armenian compound. We continue walking along St James Road until we reach Ararat Street, turn left, and follow it until we turn into Deir es-Siryan (the Syrian Convent) Road. The Convent and Church of St Mark are on the corner.

7. St Mark's Church and Convent Visiting hours: every day 9:00 a.m.–12:00 noon, 3:30–6:00 p.m.; closed Sundays. This is the center of the Syrian Orthodox Christians, who are also called Jacobites (after the 6th century founder of the sect, Jacobus Baradaeus). This is a Monophysite sect, which owns sections of a number of churches (Mary's Tomb, and the Church of the Ascension) and a chapel in the Church of the Holy Sepulcher. In Jerusalem, the sect numbers about 80 people, all of whom live in the vicinity of the convent. The convent and church were built in the 12th century on the foundations of a Byzantine church. An ancient Aramaic

Entrance to St Mark's Church.

inscription was discovered here, which identifies the site as the house of Mary, mother of Mark, to which Peter went when an angel released him from prison (Acts 12:12). The tryptich above the entrance is a description of the events associated by tradition with the church which is believed by the faithful to be the world's first church. It was built over the remains of a 4th-century church. The door, the vaults and the gilded apse are of the 12th century. In the southern wall is an ancient gate through which Peter is said to have passed. According to the Syrian tradition, this is also the "upper chamber" in which the Last Supper took place and in which the holy spirit descended upon the Apostles. An ancient painting on the southern wall of the Virgin Mary is attributed to St Luke. The site is also identified as the place of Mary's baptism, and a small baptistry marks the spot where this event took place.

8. Watson House: Lutheran Hostel We turn onto Deir es-Siryan (the Syrian Convent) Road, which leads to the Jewish Quarter. The apartment house at No. 2 was once the Jewish Hospital of the London Missionary Society. The hospital was founded by Dr. MacGowan in 1842, and was the very first hospital in Jerusalem. In 1897, the hospital was moved to a new building on the Street of the Prophets (see tour No. 15).

We return to Ararat Street and continue to the right (north) until we reach St Mark's Road. Across the street from us is the arched entrance to the Lutheran Youth Hostel. Above the gate is an Arabic inscription which reads "Dar Watson Basha" (the Pasha Watson House). The British General Charles Watson was active in the Palestine Exploration Society, and received the Turkish honorific title *Pasha*. A hospice bearing his name was established in 1856 for pilgrims. The site was the center for English missionaries. Today, the hostel is owned by the German Lutheran church.

Carved in the stone at the base of the wall opposite Watson's House is a symbol placed there in 1864 by C. Wilson, one of the Palestine Exploration Fund's investigators, in order to measure the elevation above sea level for a map of Jerusalem. Similar symbols can be found in various other places in the Old City.

Interior of the Maronite Church.

9. Maronite Church We turn left (west) on St Mark's Road, and then turn off to the left on the stairs which form Maronite Convent Road. At house number 25 there is an iron door above which is a large cross with the inscription "Mar Maron". Visits are permitted all day. The two-storey structure encloses an inner courtyard. The second floor houses the church of the Maronite Christians. The sect was founded in the 5th century and now has its stronghold in Lebanon and a Patriarchal Vicar in Jerusalem since 1895. During the Crusader period, in the 12th century, a number of Maronite monks came to Jerusalem. In 1895, this building was purchased by the Maronite bishop from its previous owners, the German Order of Deaconess Sisters, who had moved to new quarters. The Deaconess Sisters ran a hospital and hospice for pilgrims from 1851. In the same building was a school for girls, and an orphanage. On the two floors of the building, we see the dormitories, dining halls, and classrooms, which are used today for pilgrims and tourists. The Maronites preserved the simple form of the church when they converted it from the original Protestant church, whose ceiling has Gothic arches. On the third floor, built over the west side of the building only, are the living quarters of the Maronite priests.

From the church, we step out onto an open balcony, where we can appreciate the view which includes the nearby Christian Quarter, other parts of the Old City, the Mount of Olives, and Mount Scopus to the east. The square belltower, is reminiscent of the tower of the German Lutheran Church of the Redeemer.

We continue westward on the Maronite Convent Road, passing by a mosque without a minaret, between two residential buildings. This is the Yakubieh Mosque, which still preserves the name of its original dedication in the Middle Ages to St James the Cut-up of Persia who was martyred by being cut up in small pieces, also called St James Intercisus. The structure is Crusader, and was probably built on Byzantine foundations. The street also bears his name. We continue along the street until we go out onto Omar Ibn Khattab Square. We turn left and walk until we reach an iron gate, which marks the entrance to the courtyard of Christ Church.

10. Christ Church Open every day, all day long. Explanatory brochures are available in various languages. The entrance to the courtyard, which is surrounded by buildings, is opposite the eastern entrance of the Citadel. The land was purchased in 1838 by the London Society for Promoting Christianity Amongst the Jews. Building was carried out between the years 1841 and 1849. The London Society built a

Christ Church courtyard.

Interior of Christ Church.

church and living quarters for the bishops of the Protestant church, which was jointly owned by the Anglican and Lutheran Churches.

Christ Church was the first Anglican church to be built in the Ottoman Empire. The tall building has Gothic arched windows and is built in the Victorian, neo-Gothic architectural style, popular in England at the time of its construction. The stones are chiseled out in a unique, smooth fashion, and were dressed and laid in place by masons brought specially from Malta. The building is laid out in the shape of a cross. The inner hall has Gothic arches. Above the entrance and in the eastern wall there are stained-glass windows. The buildings adjacent to the church today serve as living quarters for the staff and guest rooms for pilgrims.

We now return to Omar Ibn Khattab Square, beside the Jaffa Gate.

Our tour ends here.

TOUR No. 9

FROM JAFFA GATE TO MOUNT ZION

Details of tour: The tour includes Jaffa Gate, the Citadel, the garden along the western wall of the Old City, and several sites on Mount Zion. The tour may be split into two parts by devoting one entire tour to the Citadel alone.
Distance covered: approx. 3 km (2 miles)
Time: approx. 5 hours, including visiting the museum and viewing the slide show
Transportation: Buses No 1, 2, 13, 16, 19, 20, and 23
Parking lots for private vehicles at Jaffa and Zion Gates
Starting point: Jaffa Gate
End of tour: Zion Gate or Yemin Moshe
The Sites: 1. Jaffa Gate; 2. The Citadel; 3. Along the ramparts; 4. House of Caiaphas; 5. Dormition Abbey; 6. The Cenacle; 7. Tomb of David; 8. Holocaust Chamber; 9. Palombo Museum; 10. Church of St Peter in Gallicantu; 11. Franciscan Convent; 12. Greek Orthodox Monastery; 13. Gobat School.

THE TOUR

1. Jaffa Gate Jaffa Gate is the only gate on the western side of the walls surrounding the Old City. It was built by the Ottoman Sultan Suleiman the Magnificent, on the site of a former Crusader gate. Its name derives from the fact that the main road leading to the port of Jaffa begins here. In the Byzantine and Crusader periods this gate was called "Porte David" (The Gate of David) because the Tower of David in the Citadel is adjacent to it. In the early Muslim period the Arabic name of the gate was Bab Mihrab David (Gate of David's Prayer Niche) because of the mosque located in the nearby Citadel. The modern name of the gate is Bab el-Khalil (Hebron Gate). The Arabic word means literally "the Friend", denoting the connection of the Patriarch Abraham with Hebron, for the road south of the gate leads to that city.

The gate stands on the watershed between the Valley of the Citadel and the Transversal Valley, along which David Street runs eastward. Near the outer approach to the gate there is an open pit, surrounded by a railing, in which a section of the Byzantine city wall was discovered in 1983 when work was undertaken to lay a telephone cable. On the facade of the gateway there is an Arabic inscription indicating that Sultan Suleiman the Magnificent built the gate in 1538. Under it is a more recent inscription in Hebrew and Arabic, indicating the completion of repairs to the wall in 1970. The inscription reads: "The walls of Jerusalem were made up" (Nehemiah 4:7).

The gate has a heavy wooden door faced with iron, in which is a smaller door. Above the gate are narrow apertures through which was lowered the portcullis, which protected the gate from the battering rams of attacking armies. As additional defenses, a barbican, or defensive tower, was built above the outer approach to the gate, and embrasures, through which arrows could be shot, were built in the walls, as well as machicolations for pouring boiling oil and tar on the intruders. Access to the barbican is via the roof of the gatehouse, which can be reached by way of a staircase behind the inner opening of the gate. Outside the barbican is an Arabic inscription praising God and Abraham, His servant.

We enter the gatehouse. It is built so that attackers attempting to penetrate the city are forced to make a ninety-degree turn to the left, thus making access difficult for soldiers holding weapons in their right hand. The inner opening of the gate leads to Omar Ibn Khattab Square, which is named after the Caliph who led the Muslim

TOUR No. 9   122

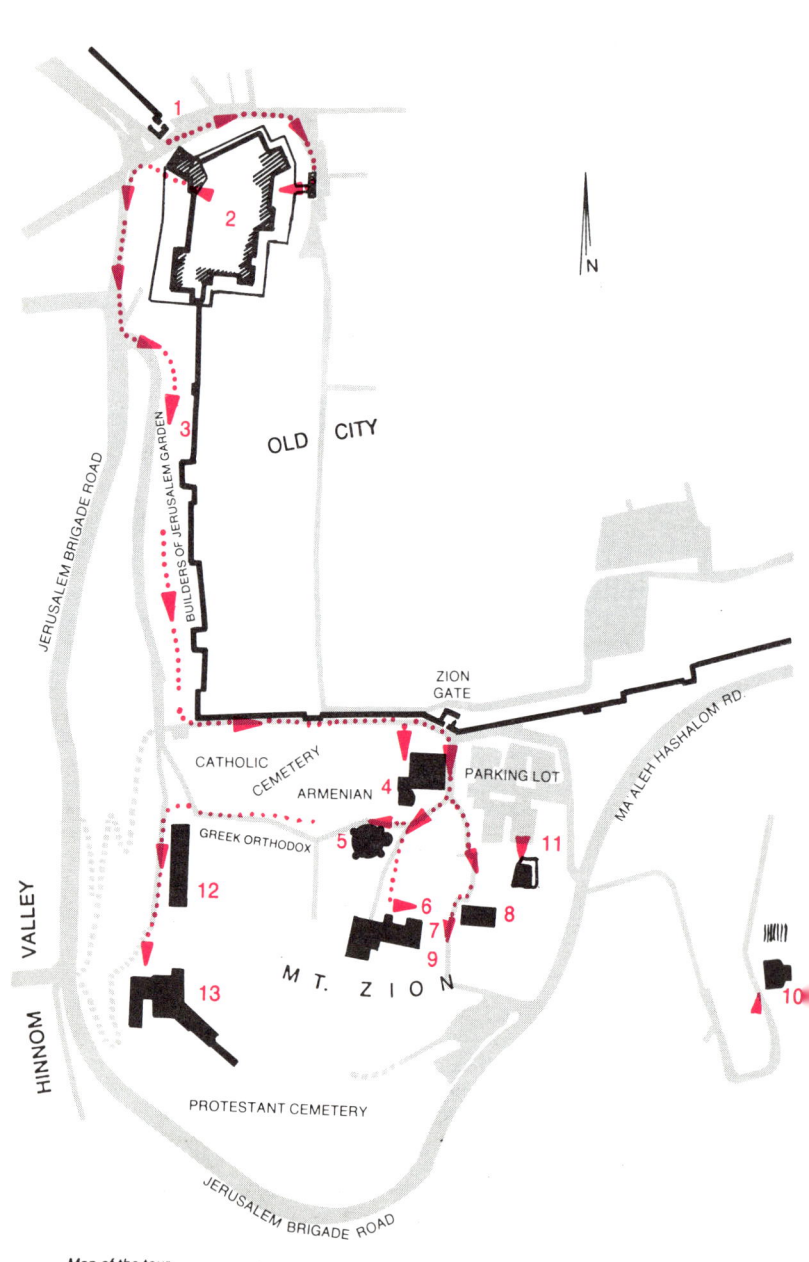

Map of the tour.

JAFFA GATE TO MOUNT ZION

conquerors in 638. Just beyond the gate, on the left side of the street, are two tombs whose ornamentation indicates that they belong to Turkish notables. Local legend tells us that these are the graves of the two engineers charged with building the city walls, who were executed by order of the Sultan for leaving Mount Zion and the tomb of King David, outside the walls. Until 1898 there was a wall between the Jaffa Gate and the Citadel. On the occasion of a visit of the German Kaiser Wilhelm II, this wall was demolished, part of the moat was filled in, and a paved road was built across it along the line of the present-day road. In 1917, the British General Allenby entered the city on foot, via the Jaffa Gate, at the head of the British troops.

The gate was locked in 1948, and a defensive wall was built next to it. In 1967, with the reunification of the city, the gate was reopened, and it was refurbished with donations from South African Jews, as recorded on the plaque beside the inner opening of the gate.

Omar Ibn Khattab Square abuts the Citadel on the north and east. Around it are souvenir shops for tourists, cafés, taxi stands and hotels. At the end of the 19th century, this was the central business district of the Old City. Banks, travel agencies, shops, post-offices, consular and government offices were all found here. The business area also extended to the plaza outside the gate. The Grand New Hotel was built in 1889 by the Greek Orthodox Church. What is today called the Petra Hotel was once the famed Amdursky Hotel, built in the 19th century by the wealthy Jew, Amdursky. The building, which now serves as an information bureau for Christian pilgrims, was originally Jerusalem's first modern hotel. It also housed the Austrian post-office, as indicated by the (newly) affixed sign on its facade. The "Posta Austriaca" was the first of several foreign post-offices for subjects of the major European Powers, under the special rights granted them under the terms of the Capitulations treaty with the Ottoman Empire. Mail was sent by sea from Europe to the port of Jaffa, and from Jaffa to Jerusalem by means of a special coach service. The foreign postal services operated until 1914.

(top) Jaffa Gate from inside the Old City.
(bottom) Suleiman's inscription at Jaffa Gate.

The two Turkish tombs at Jaffa Gate.

2. The Citadel Visiting hours: every day during daylight hours. Admission charge.

The encircled numbers in the text correspond to the numbers on the signs at the site at present. Please note that with the opening of the Museum of the History of Jerusalem the numbering is likely to be changed.

Jerusalem's Citadel, known as the Tower of David, is one of the most famous sites in the city. The walls and towers which were built in the Middle Ages with additions in the Ottoman period still exist. Along the sign-posted walkway, in the archaeological garden in the courtyard and in the moat are archaeological remains spanning the Citadel's three-thousand year history. Some of these remains have been reconstructed and explanatory signs have been provided. From the towers of the Citadel the breathtaking view encompasses the Old City, the New City and the surrounding hills in all directions. Inside the Citadel is a model of Jerusalem, a display of ethnological dioramas representing the various communities of the city and a Museum of the History of Jerusalem to be completed in 1988, where archaeological finds will be exhibited. An audio-visual presentation and a film bring to life the history of Jerusalem.

The apellation "Tower of David" was given to the Herodian tower ⑧ during the Byzantine period (as a result of an incorrect interpretation of the writings of Josephus Flavius, the Second Temple period historian). The nearby gate is also named after King David. Later, the Muslims and Crusaders used the same name. In the 19th century this name was transferred to the minaret of the Citadel's mosque, which was built in the 17th century. In a rather perverse manner, the minaret, mistakenly called the Tower of David, became a Jewish symbol and appears on dishes, prayer

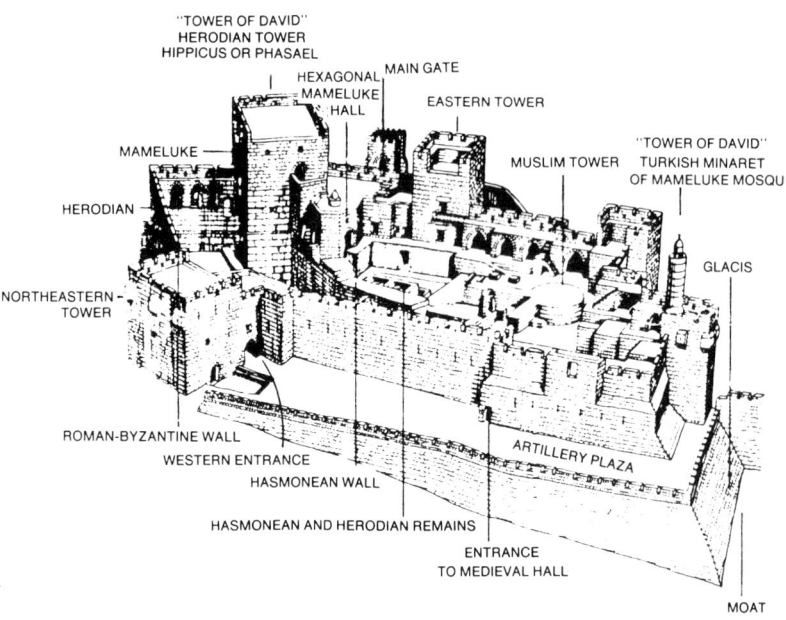

The Citadel today.

books, and all kinds of objects. With the establishment of the State of Israel, the symbol of the minaret became the symbol of Jerusalem.

The elevation of the Citadel is 780 m (2560 ft) above sea level, on the summit of the western hill of Jerusalem. Its natural defenses on its north and west consist of the Valley of the Citadel, which runs into the Valley of Hinnom. The wall which was built here before the construction of the first citadel included towers for the defense of the northwest section of the city.

The earliest remains found on the site, resting on the bedrock, are from the **First Temple period.** At a depth of 11 m (36 ft), were found remains of buildings, a seal with ancient Hebrew writing, and other finds testifying to the expansion of the city to the western hill in the First Temple period. Excavations in the eastern moat of the Citadel uncovered a section of a broad wall, perhaps the continuation of a similar wall from the First Temple period which was uncovered in the excavations in the Jewish Quarter. The large, unhewn stones in the center of the courtyard have also been attributed to the same wall, which is presumed to have been built by King Hezekiah and destroyed by the army of the Babylonian King Nebuchadnezzar in the year 586 BCE. In the center of the courtyard there are also remnants of a wall and two towers dating from the Hasmonean period. The building style of this period is characterized by its small ashlars with carved margins and bosses. The central tower is attributed to the Hasmonean ruler Simeon, who began its construction, and to Johanan, his brother, who completed it, and fought the Seleucid, Alexander Sidetes. This battle is described in the Book of the Maccabees and is illustrated by the arrows and catapult stones which were found here. The already mentioned Hasmonean wall is part of the so-called First Wall of Jerusalem, as described by Josephus Flavius. Other sections of the First Wall were found in the City of David, the Jewish Quarter, and along the western city wall. The southern tower ⑨ is ascribed to Alexander Yannai. The northern tower ⑧ was also first built by the Hasmonean kings.

In the **Herodian period**, a new tower was built on the foundations of the northern tower ⑧. The new tower was thick, wide, high and solid, and the enormous ashlars seen in its lower courses are similar to those used in the Western Wall. Some identify this as the Tower of Phasael (named after Herod's brother) while others identify it as the Tower of Hippicus (named

Herodian tower (Phasael or Hippicus).

Remnants from the Hasmonean period.

after Herod's friend). Herod erected a third tower and named it after Mariamne, his wife. Of the three towers described by Josephus, only one is intact today. The position of the other two towers is not certain. Excavations uncovered two Hasmonean towers, faced with typical Herodian stones. Some researchers believe these to be the two missing towers.

The three towers were built in order to strengthen the defenses of Herod's palace, which lay to the south of the Citadel. The palace was destroyed, and only a few remains in the area of the Citadel can be attributed to it: a colored fresco on the southern wall (which is now covered with protective glass), the base of an enormous pillar, and monumental steps in the southern part of the moat. During Titus' siege of Jerusalem in 70 CE, the soldiers of Agrippa's army, and later the Zealots, took refuge in the towers. After the destruction of the Second Temple by Titus, the Roman Tenth Legion was based around the towers. Sections of clay pipes and roof tiles, bearing the stamp of the Tenth Legion, were found.

In the **Byzantine period**, the fortifications were restored, and to the north of the northern tower a wall was built, above which can be seen a medieval structure. In addition, a cistern was also dug ㉓. The Herodian tower ⑥ which has since been called the Tower of David, is indicated on the Madaba map (details in Tour No.4 — The Jewish Quarter). In the early **Muslim period**, the city's citadel was first erected. Its western wall was east of the Valley of the Citadel, and included the earlier fortifications (the three towers and sections of the First Wall). A round corner tower ㉙ was built on the south side, and from it a wall connected to the northern tower. There are indications of two additional round towers at the other corner of the square citadel, which was surrounded by a wall. The fourth tower of the Muslim citadel was the north-eastern Herodian tower ⑥.

There are no explicit references to the Citadel from the Crusader period. Only the name Tower of David is mentioned, and nearby stood the fortified royal palace, which was apparently east of the Muslim citadel. There were found remains of Crusader arches and of a much later wall.

The present-day Citadel was built in the Middle Ages, to the west of the early Muslim citadel, and modeled after a European castle, surrounded by a moat. The northern and western walls were then built on the floor of the Valley of the Citadel, part of which also served as a moat. The northern Herodian tower ⑥ was integrated in the eastern wall of the Citadel, to which were

Outer gate of the Citadel.

"Tower of David" — the minaret.

added two towers. More towers were also added to the western wall (㊹ and ㊳). All of the remaining earlier fortifications were left in the courtyard of the Citadel, and in the excavations only their remains were found. In the 14th century, the Mamelukes expanded the southwestern tower ㊳ and under it they built the prayer hall of the mosque. They also added the hexagonal room ⑲.

In the **Ottoman period**, Suleiman the Magnificent, the builder of the city walls, gave the Citadel its final form. At that time the eastern gate, the bridge over the moat, the eastern entryway, the open mosque ⑦, the artillery plaza on the western side and the glacis were also built. The Mameluke mosque was restored. In 1635 Mohammed Pasha built the minaret ㊾ near the mosque, which today is known as the Tower of David.

During the British Mandate period the Citadel was restored and it no longer served as a military encampment. In one part of the structure a museum was established for folklore and traditional local dress, as well as for antiquities. In 1934 the first archaeological excavations were carried out in the courtyard of the Citadel by C. Johns.

In the period of Jordanian rule the Citadel was used again as a military encampment. After the reunification of the city in 1967, the Citadel ceased to be a military outpost. A number of archaeological explorations were carried out at the site, and the Citadel was restored and adapted as an archaeological site open to visitors. Exhibitions were set up in the rooms of the Citadel, and a sound-and-light show was prepared.

Visit to the Citadel: There are three separate routes marked in different colors. The archaeology route starts in the hexagonal hall and continues to the signposted sites in the courtyard. The museum route begins on the upper storey of the eastern tower where the audio-visual presentation takes place and leads through the exhibition halls, each representing a different historical period. The third route starts on the roof of the northern tower and continues via the eastern tower to the observation points from which there are fine views of the Old and New City.

Our tour begins at the eastern entrance. We ascend the steps to the entry plaza ①. On the 9th of December, 1917, it was in this plaza that General Allenby received the letter of surrender from the Turkish military governor and declared the beginning of British rule in Palestine. We enter the outer gateway ② above which is a Turkish inscription indicating that the gate was built in 1531 by the Sultan Suleiman the Magnificent, who built the walls of Jerusalem. We cross the wooden bridge over the moat. From the bridge we have a clear view of the glacis, which slopes down from the Citadel to the moat ③. We now reach the guard area ⑤, which was built over part of the moat. The entrance to the open mosque ⑥ is to the south. Above the entrance is an inscription commemorating the repair of the mosque in the 18th century. A circular inscription on the *mihrab* (prayer niche) ⑦ praises the deeds of Suleiman the Magnificent. We return to the plaza. The base of the wall to the north consists of 13 courses of large Herodian stones. These are the remains of a tower ⑧, either the Hippicus of Phasael Tower, which was built by Herod to defend his palace. The upper courses of the tower are Mameluke. At the foot, we can see the remains of a wall from the Byzantine period ⑨. The end of the new wooden walkway, which leads to the exhibition halls in the northwestern tower ㊽, connects to the plaza. Steps descend from the plaza to the moat.

We continue up and across to the stone entry bridge ⑩, which is supported by two arches resting on a column set in the moat. On the outside of the guardrail of the bridge is a circular inscription, mentioning once again Suleiman the Magnificent. Above the main entrance ⑪ is an empty niche, which once held a Mameluke inscription, commemorating the restoration of the entrance in the year 1312. The entrance was originally built in the Crusader period. The entrance area opens into the guardroom ⑫, which has stone benches along the walls. The nearby gate ⑬ has iron-clad wooden doors, which

TOUR No. 9   128

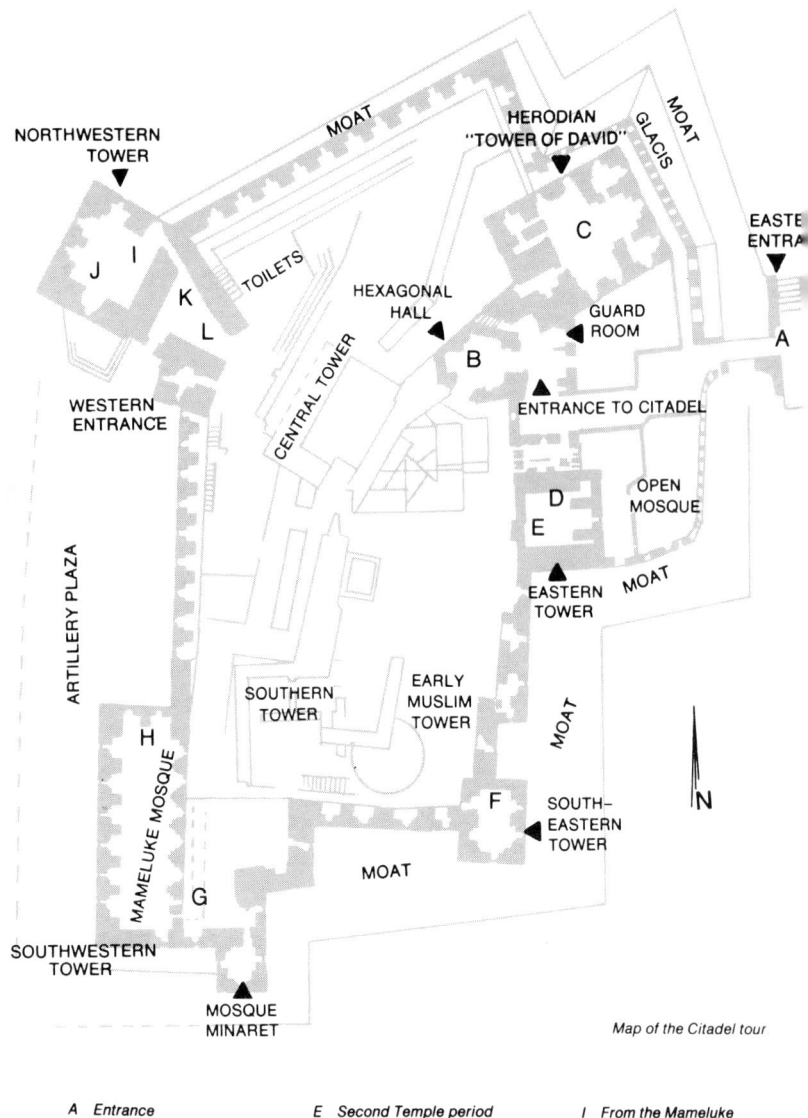

Map of the Citadel tour

- A Entrance
- B Beginning of tour
- C Introductory film
- D Canaanite and First
     Temple periods
     (upper storey)
- E Second Temple period
- F Roman-Byzantine period
- G Various periods
- H From the Early Arab
     period to the
     Ayyubid period
- I From the Mameluke
     period to the British
     Mandate period
- J Audio-visual presentation
- K–L Temporary exhibitions
       and museum shop

apparently date to the Ottoman period. On either side of the gate are grooves through which the drawbridge, which protected the entrance, was lowered.

We enter the vestibule, which today serves as a souvenir shop. The north wall of this room is part of the Herodian tower ⑤. From here we turn left to the hexagonal hall ⑩ which was built in the Mameluke period. In this hall are displayed plans of the Citadel at different periods, and a topographical map of the Old City. We ascend the steps on the right which lead to the roof of the hall. As we go up we can see a section of the wall of the Herodian tower. In the center of the hexagonal roof there is a small, pointed stone dome with windows. The upper Citadel walkway begins from the roof, and we will return here when we come down from the observation roof. We ascend a flight of stone steps which lead to the Mameluke hall at the top of the Herodian tower. This room houses an exhibition of wooden figurines depicting the various traditional costumes worn by Jerusalemites. From this hall we go up a winding iron staircase to the roof of the tower from which we have a panoramic view of the Holy City.

From the observation roof we return to the roof of the hexagonal hall and proceed from there to the upper walkway, via the interior hall of the eastern tower ⑮. This is planned to house the Museum of Jerusalem, which will include exhibits from the Canaanite period to the end of the Second Temple period. We continue on the wooden walkway, and view from here the remains of Second Temple buildings ⑧ and the base of a Crusader pillar ⑰. The Citadel wall ⑲ and its round tower ⑳ are from the early Arab period. We ascend a flight of stone steps to the southeastern tower ㉒ which will house a display from the Byzantine-Roman period. It is also possible to go up to the tower roof, from which we can look out to the south of the New City and the hills on the horizon. We continue on the walkway past the minaret ㊵ which is today called the Tower of David, and was built by Mohammed Pasha in the year 1635. We go up to the observation point on the roof of the southwestern tower, and from there down to the mosque. Above the entrance ㊶ is an inscription which mentions the restoration of the mosque by Abdul Hamid II in the year 1897. In the mosque artifacts from the early Arab period to the Ayyubid period are displayed. On the eastern wall is an inscription which commemorates the construction of the mosque in the 13th century. Another inscription dating to the 14th century appears above the *minbar* (preacher's pulpit).

From the mosque we descend to the southeastern section of the Citadel courtyard, and we visit the various sites which are identified by explanatory signs. We begin with the round tower ㉓ of the early Muslim citadel. Its walls ⑲ are built over a Second Temple tower ㉒ upon which is an arch ㉓ from an undated structure (apparently Mameluke). We see Herodian reinforcements made to the First Wall ㉔, near which is a Roman-Byzantine cistern ㉕ and a complex of Second Temple period walls ㉖. These are generally identified as part of the foundation on which Herod's palace was built, to the south of the Citadel. We pass by a section of the First Wall ㉗, next to which is the Hasmonean tower ㉝ and its Herodian reinforcement ㉞. We continue through a narrow, dark corridor ㊹ to the medieval defense system, in which we see machicolations. We ascend to the observation roof on the northwestern tower.

We descend from the roof to the Citadel courtyard and continue via an underground passageway, to the fortifications ㊳ and the second Hasmonean tower ㊱, which is preserved to a significant height. Above it is a corner of the Herodian tower ㉝ on which can be seen a colored fresco, behind protective glass. We descend through a medieval tunnel ㊻, and reach a subterranean Mameluke chamber ㊼, above which the mosque is built. Crusader remains and a part of the Hasmonean tower ⓪ can be seen within the chamber. A tunnel leads from this underground chamber to the moat. Another exit leads to the artillery plaza outside the walls of the Citadel, to the west. We walk towards the western exit of the Citadel, and follow the sign and descend to the basement where a model of Jerusalem is displayed. The model, which is made of zinc, depicts Jerusalem as it was in 1873. The model was built by Stefan Eilas, a Hungarian Catholic artist who lived in Jerusalem, by order of the Turkish ruler of the city who commissioned the model for an exhibition in Vienna. It was stored in Basel, Switzerland, until it was transferred to the Citadel Museum in 1985. The model is complemented by slides of various sites shown in the model, which are projected onto a screen while the corresponding section of the model is illuminated.

A sound-and-light show is presented in the Citadel courtyard on summer evenings, Saturday through Thursday in Hebrew and in English, and in other languages upon request in advance. The times of presentation are available at the site. It is advisable to dress warmly for the one-hour show.

3. Along the ramparts We leave the Citadel through the western exit, and go down to the foot of the glacis which is below the artillery plaza ⓑ. From here, at the foot of the minaret, we can appreciate the size of the glacis and the southern moat of the Citadel. We walk downhill along Jerusalem Brigade Road, and turn into the Builders of Jerusalem Park, which runs along the foot of the ramparts. We walk through the park up to the southwestern corner of the city wall. From 1973 to 1978, excavations were carried out along the entire length of the wall. A layer of earth and rubble 2 to 5 m (7 to 16 ft) deep was removed, revealing the remains of ancient walls at the base of the Ottoman rampart. These remains have been partially reconstructed, identifying signs have been posted, gardens have been planted, and the area has been opened to visitors. The paved path is for pedestrians only.

The remains of 120 m (394 ft) of the Hasmonean First Wall have been exposed here. This is the continuation of the wall that we saw in the Citadel courtyard. The 5.5 m (18 ft) thick wall rests on bedrock above the quarry from which the stones were hewn. The ashlars are smoothly dressed, and have margins and protruding bosses like those we saw in the Citadel courtyard. The remains of four towers can be seen on the wall. One of these has been integrated into the Ottoman wall, and we can make out the threshold and doorjambs of the entrance to the tower.

The face of the Hasmonean wall was found to contain the remains of a 2.5 to 3.5 m (8 to 11 ft) thick wall from the Herodian period, intended to strengthen the Hasmonean wall, up to a total thickness of 8 m (26 ft). It seems that only the foundations of the Hasmonean wall were reinforced, to form a sort of forward wall which served as a glacis. Herod's palace was built on an elevated platform within the present-day city wall in what is today the Armenian garden. It is possible that the aforementioned reinforcements to the Hasmonean wall were necessary for the building of this elevated platform.

A few remnants were found of the Ayyubid wall, which was destroyed by Malek el-Mu'azzam in 1219, so that it would never be used again by the Crusaders. The tower at the corner of the wall was in ruins, and has been reconstructed by archaeologists. Underneath the Ottoman wall, near the Citadel, we can see three openings in the rock which have been closed with iron bars. These are rock-cut burial caves from the First Temple period. The first tower of the Ottoman wall is to the north of the burial caves. Near the second tower in the Ottoman city wall are remains of the Hasmonean wall, the Herodian reinforcement wall and the remains of a Herodian tower. Above the Herodian tower are the ruins of a medieval tower, above which is the Ottoman tower.

Further on, we come upon the remains of a six-room structure from the First Temple period, which was apparently used for industrial purposes. Nearby is the entrance to a Second Temple period gateway, which includes a stairway with walls on either side. Adjacent to the gateway is the third tower in the Ottoman wall. The fourth tower is in the southwestern corner of the city wall. Just before it is a medieval tower which was destroyed in 1219 and reconstructed by archaeologists in 1980.

South of the wall and opposite the Ayyubid tower is a plaza which contains a

JAFFA GATE TO MOUNT ZION

commemorative plaque about the Garden of the Builders of Jerusalem. From the plaza there is a fine view of the Hinnom Valley, the neighborhoods on its western slope (Mishkenot Sha'ananim, Yemin Moshe and Abu Tor). From the plaza, we ascend the steps to the cobblestone path which passes between the ramparts and the wall opposite them, which encloses several cemeteries. The first gate in the wall on the right is of a Catholic cemetery, one of the first to be established on Mount Zion, where C. Costigan, the first European to sail in a boat from the Sea of Galilee to the Dead Sea is buried. Adjoining the Catholic cemetery is an Armenian cemetery. Affixed to the wall are *katchkars* (plaques left by pilgrims). In the courtyard a new Armenian church is being built and a monument commemorating the Armenian holocaust of 1915, during which the Turks murdered 1½ million Armenians living in Turkey. Permission to enter must be obtained from the guard.

Mount Zion extends to the south of the western hill of Jerusalem, outside the southern city wall. Its steep slopes descend to the Hinnom Valley on the west and south, and to the Tyropoeon Valley on the east. The elevation of the summit is 765m (2510 ft) above sea level. The area along the southern city wall is a flat saddle and Mount Zion can be regarded as the southern extension of the western hill.

The name "Mount Zion" was first applied in the Bible to the Temple Mount (Mount Moriah). With the passing of time, "Zion" became a poetic name for Jerusalem and for the entire Holy Land. By the Second Temple period the name was given, for unknown reasons, to the present Mount Zion, and the tradition that the tomb of King David was on this mountain was born. This tradition sanctified the mount in the eyes of the Jews and, later, of the Christians and of the Muslims as well.

According to the Bible, various important events occurred on Mount Zion.

Above the tomb of King David is the Cenacle or Room of the Last Supper. East of the Cenacle is the Holocaust Chamber, and to the west is the Dormition Abbey. To the north of King David's tomb is the House of Caiaphas, and on the eastern slope of the hill is the church of St Peter in Gallicantu.

Mount Zion was first settled toward the end of the First Temple period, in the 7th century BCE, as is shown by the remains of buildings and utensils which were unearthed near the Armenian cemetery. During the Second Temple period, this was a wealthy residential neighborhood and part of the Upper City which was surrounded by the First Wall. In the Byzantine period, the Church of Mount Zion, one of the four earliest churches of the Holy Land, was erected here by Emperor Constantine. It appears on the Madaba map. This church is also referred to as the "mother of all churches". The whole area was then called Zion Quarter. Remains of the Church of Mount Zion were found below the Dormition Abbey and the Cenacle. The Pilgrim of Bordeaux who visited Jerusalem in 333 relates in his journal that there were seven synagogues on Mount Zion. We also know from the Madaba map that during this period there was a paved road running northwards from the Church in the direction of the Armenian garden in the Old City of today. It is possible that this road already existed in the Herodian period and led to the royal palace in what is now the Armenian garden. The Church of Mount Zion was destroyed by the Persians

Mount Zion from the west.

TOUR No. 9

in 614. In the Crusader period a new church complex, Our Lady of Mount Zion, was built over the ruins of the Byzantine church, as shown by excavations at the Dormition Abbey. The church complex was surrounded by a wall and included a monastery housing the Room of the Last Supper. Later, the structure was included in a Mameluke building erected on the ruins of the church, which was destroyed by the Ayyubid ruler Malek el-Mu'azzam in 1219.

The Jewish community in Jerusalem was revived by the Ramban (Nachmanides) on Mount Zion in 1267 when a synagogue was built. The Jewish tradition of pilgrimage to King David's tomb began in the 12th century. In the 15th century, the Christians claimed possession of the building containing the Cenacle, but they were expelled from Mount Zion and the building was turned over to the Muslims. The new cemeteries and churches on Mount Zion were built in the 19th and early 20th century.

In 1964, Pope Paul VI visited Mount Zion. In honor of his visit, a new road was paved up the mountain, and was called the Pope's Road. Today, the road is the part of the Jerusalem Brigade Road which climbs Mount Zion.

The House of Caiaphas.

4. House of Caiaphas After obtaining permission from the guard, we go through the iron gate opposite the Zion Gate into the courtyard where the new Armenian church is being built. Before the construction was begun, archaeological excavations were carried out, in 1971. They revealed the remains of buildings from both the First and Second Temple periods, as well as the paving stones of a street from the Byzantine period which led northwards from Mount Zion to the site of the Armenian garden. South of the spot where the new church is being built is another Armenian church and behind it is the House of Caiaphas. According to an Armenian tradition this is the site of the house of the High Priest where Jesus was imprisoned after his arrest (Matthew 26:57). These two structures were built in 1145 on the ruins of Roman and Byzantine buildings. The courtyard of the church contains the tombs of the Armenian Patriarchs from the 12th century to 1948. The altar of the church is made from a fragment of a stone which once sealed the entrance of a Roman burial cave. The area is abandoned and neglected and the old church is kept locked. The Armenian cemetery begins to the west of the church. We leave by the same gate through which we entered and pass by the Zion Gate. We turn right (south) on a path until we reach a fork. We go to the right, between the wall which surrounds the courtyard of the Armenian church and the circular wall of the Dormition Abbey. Passing the entrance to the church courtyard, we turn left, and come to a doorway whose doorposts are of the Crusader period. We go back along the path to the entrance of the church courtyard. The remains of the Byzantine Church of Mount Zion were recently found here.

5. Dormition Church and Abbey A relatively modern church and monastery built between 1906 and 1910. The church is built on a plot of land which was given by Sultan Abdul Hamid II as a gift to the German Kaiser Wilhelm II during his visit to Jerusalem in 1898. In the same year, the Kaiser laid the cornerstone for the church, and handed over the land to the Union of

German Catholics of the Holy Land. Monks of the Benedictine Order live in the monastery and run the church, built on the site where, according to tradition, Mary "fell asleep", hence the full name of the church: Dormitio Beatae Mariae Virginis.

Visiting hours are 7.00 a.m. to 12.30 p.m. and 2.00 to 7.00 p.m. daily.

The octagonal church building on the summit of Mount Zion is easily recognizable from afar due to its conical grey dome and the four smaller towers surrounding it. We enter the door to the corridor leading to the right, to the coffee shop, in which a model of the monastery and church is displayed. Opposite the door of the church is a room where books and souvenirs are sold, and through it, we enter the prayer hall with an open balcony. The hall is circular and is adorned with colorful mosaics depicting events from the Bible, Christian and Benedictine history. The mosaic floor shows the signs of the zodiac arranged in a circle, with three interlocking rings representing the Holy Trinity at its center. The outer circle of the mosaic floor has depictions of the Prophets and the Twelve Apostles. There are six chapels around the church.

From the church, we descend the stairs to the crypt. In the center is a life-size

Dormition Church and Abbey.

The Cenacle (Room of the Last Supper).

statue of the sleeping Mary made of cherry wood and ivory. The dome above the statue is adorned with a mosaic picture of Jesus in the center, surrounded by famous Biblical women. Six chapels surround the crypt, three of them dedicated to Austria, Hungary and the Ivory Coast who donated funds to the church.

We return from the church along the path and turn right until we reach the entrance to the building on the left. To the right of the entrance is a round stone column built of several sections. This is a remnant of the Byzantine church which was integrated into the current structure, which also includes a Crusader hall. Above the entrance is an arch adorned with pillow decorations and an Arabic inscription mentioning the 15th century Mameluke Sultan during whose rule the building was erected. We go through the entrance to the courtyard and ascend the steps on the left.

6. Cenacle (Room of the Last Supper)
Visiting hours: 8.30 a.m. to sundown.

The upper floor of this building, in whose lower floor is the Tomb of King David is, by tradition identified with the "upper room" where Jesus and his disciples held the Passover feast — the Last Supper, before he was taken away to be tried (Matthew 26:17–29; Mark 14:12–25). It was here also that Jesus appeared after the Resurrection, and tne miracle of the Pentecost took place, when the Holy Spirit descended on the disciples and made them speak in many languages (Acts 2:1–4).

The hall is part of the 12th century Crusader Church of Our Lady of Mount Zion. It received its present form from the Franciscans, who purchased it in 1335. The architectural style is Gothic, typical of the late 11th century. The vaulted ceiling is supported by three piers within the hall and eight other columns along the walls. Drawn on the column to the right of the entrance is a Crusader shield bearing the name of the German city of Regensburg. The pillars in the entrance to the hall are older than the Crusader structure and, in view of their Corinthian capitals, could be the remains of the Byzantine Church of Mount Zion. Above the landing at the top of the stairs are marble columns supporting a small domed, arched structure. One of the columns has a capital with three sculptured pelicans, the two on the sides plucking at the breast of the one in the middle -- a motif used in Christian symbolism to typify the atonement. This capital is one of the best examples of Crusader art found in Jerusalem.

In the beginning of the 15th century, Jews attempted to purchase the building, which contains King David's tomb on the ground floor. This resulted in a dispute between the Jews and the Christians, one of the consequences of which was the expulsion of the Franciscans from Mount Zion. The building became the property of the Muslims, who turned it into a mosque and built a *mihrab*, (prayer niche), in the southern wall. Nearby are two Arabic inscriptions, one dedicated to King David, the other to Sultan Suleiman. In the southeastern corner of the room steps lead to a small room which serves as a passageway to yet another room beyond, where the Muslims set up a tomb, allegedly of King David, towards which the Jews used to turn to pray during the holiday of Shavuot (Pentecost).

7. Tomb of David We go back down the stairs and cross the internal courtyard which contains classrooms and dormitory rooms of the Diaspora Yeshiva. We enter the passage which has to its left the Holocaust Chamber, and to its right steps which lead up to a closed courtyard, south of the southern wall of the Cenacle. The lower courses of the wall are built of large Roman-Byzantine ashlars, similar to those in the room containing King David's tomb.

Tomb of David.

From the courtyard we enter the ground floor of the building into a room which now serves as a synagogue. The vaulted ceiling is supported by two square pillars. We enter the right-hand doorway into the prayer room. In the southern wall is a *mihrab* covered with ceramic tiles, built in the Mameluke period. In the next room is the cenotaph which marks the spot of King David's tomb. The first to refer to it was the Muslim Jerusalemite historian al-Muqadassi in 985. It was mentioned by the Crusader historian Raymond d'Aguillers in 1100, and by the famous Jewish traveller Benjamin of Tudela in 1165. Since then it has become entrenched in Jewish, Muslim and Christian belief and the focus of Jewish pilgrimage.

The tombstone is covered with a velvet cloth, and over it are Torah crowns from the synagogues of Jewish communities which were destroyed in the Holocaust. On the tombstone itself, under the cloth, is a carving from the Crusader period of a lily flower surrounded by acanthus leaves in the Gothic style. In the northern wall behind the monument is a niche facing in the direction of the Temple Mount. Remains of a colored mosaic, characteristic of the late Roman or Byzantine period, were found below the level of the present floor in excavations carried out in 1949. The archaeologist J. Pinkerfield theorized that a synagogue stood here, perhaps one of the seven synagogues mentioned by the Pilgrim of Bordeaux, or the meeting place of the first Christian community in Jerusalem. Under the shrine is the entrance to a cave discovered by E. Pierotti in 1859. This seems to be the origin of the legend that King David's tomb is in a cave.

Steps on the west side lead to the Temple Mount Observatory on the roof of the building (follow the signs). On the roof is the minaret of a mosque and a dome built over King David's tomb, both of the 16th century.

8. Holocaust Chamber Visiting hours: Sunday through Thursday, all day.

Opposite the entrance to the chamber is a square stone memorial column, on which epitaphs in several languages are engraved. On Israel's Memorial Day, ceremonies are held here for communities which were obliterated during the Holocaust. In the first room is a display of Torah scrolls, sacred books and prayer shawls which were burned or damaged in Germany on *Kristallnacht* (the night of November 9, 1938, when many synagogues were burned). The room to the right is dedicated to the fighters of the Warsaw Ghetto uprising. In the central room is a monument bearing the names of all the concentration camps, with an eternal light burning above it. In the room on the left is a jar containing the ashes of the martyrs engraved with the names of the places from which the ashes were brought, and a piece of soap made from human fat, which is stamped with the letters "RJF" (*Reine Jüden Fette*, "pure Jewish fat").

9. Palombo Museum Visiting hours: Sunday through Thursday, all day. Fridays and eves of holidays, mornings only.

David Palombo was a Jerusalem-born sculptor who specialized in wrought-iron ornaments. Among his works are the gates of the Hall of Remembrance at Yad Vashem and the gate of the Knesset courtyard. He lived near the Tomb of King David and died in a tragic accident nearby. His works are displayed in a museum in the ground floor of a building adjacent to the Tomb of King David.

To reach the church of St. Peter in Gallicantu we turn onto the road which leads eastward.

10. Church of St Peter in Gallicantu The church is named after the episode of Peter's triple denial of Jesus and his repentance (Matthew 26:34) and taken from the words of Jesus (Luke 22:61): ". . . before the cock crow thou shalt deny me thrice" (*Gallicantu*, in Latin "cock-crow"). We reach the church from the plaza near the Palombo Museum by way of the Ma'aleh Hashalom road, from which we follow either a side road or the ancient stone steps. Visiting hours: 8.30–11.45 a.m.; 2.00–5.30 p.m. (closed Sunday).

The neo-Byzantine structure has four protruding walls, each of which is topped by an arch and colored mosaics. The church was built over the ruins of Byzantine and Crusader churches, on a site identified by the Assumptionist Fathers who

Entrance to the Holocaust Chamber.

Church of St Peter in Gallicantu.

own it as the house of the High Priest Caiaphas — an alternative to the Armenian site on the summit of Mount Zion. The church was built in 1931.

Before entering the church, it is worthwhile to look eastwards from the balcony towards the Central (Tyropoeon) Valley, the village of Silwan, the City of David, the Temple Mount, the Kidron Valley and the Mount of Olives. The ancient stone steps in the courtyard to the north of the building descend to the valley. They are the remnants of a Byzantine stepped street which lead to the Pool of Silwan. In the courtyard are the remains of several ancient structures: olive presses, a bath house, caves and a section of the low-level Herodian aqueduct.

From inside the church we can reach several rockcut caves, one of which, according to tradition, was used to imprison Jesus.

The remains of the Byzantine church seen here were uncovered in archaeological excavations in 1888. A number of column capitals and a section of mosaic floor are all that remain of the Crusader church which was built on top of the Byzantine one. According to investigators, the older remains are houses from a wealthy, Second Temple period residential quarter. The results of the excavation are on display here.

On the slope of Mount Zion, south of the church, is the Jewish Sambursky cemetery, which was in use for hundreds of years, until 1921. Poor Sephardic Jews were buried here (see tour No.13 of the Hinnom Valley). From here, we return to the parking lot and go up to the gate of the nearby Franciscan convent.

11. Franciscan convent South of the parking area stands a wall surrounding the new Franciscan convent. The Franciscans were permitted to return to Mount Zion only during the British Mandate period. The convent was built in 1936 and improved in 1962 and 1980. The Franciscans first settled on Mount Zion in the 14th century, on a plot purchased for them by the King of Sicily. They began to rebuild sites holy to Christianity and tended them. The convent building has three stories,

and was designed by the Italian architect Barluzzi (who designed many other buildings and churches in Jerusalem and throughout Israel). The building includes residential quarters and a small but unique chapel, the only part of the building open to visitors (daily, 8.30 a.m.–12.00 noon and 3.00–6.00 p.m.). The church is dedicated to St. Francis and faces westward towards the Cenacle, in contrast to other churches where the direction of prayer is usually towards the east. Especially noteworthy are the bronze sculptures and a replica of Da Vinci's painting of "The Last Supper". Polish monks live here today.

12. Greek Orthodox Monastery We continue once again along the path leading to the Dormition Abbey, and walk straight ahead until the end of the path. To the right is the Armenian cemetery, and to the left is the American Protestant cemetery which was used only in the beginning of the 19th century. Behind it is the Greek Orthodox cemetery and Mount Zion Monastery, which also includes a theological seminary. We turn right onto the road which

The Franciscan convent and Dormition roof.

Gobat School courtyard.

The Protestant cemetery.

leads to the memorial to the Builders of Jerusalem and the southwestern corner of the city wall. From here, we descend along Araunah the Jebusite Road. To our left is a disused Greek-Catholic cemetery. At the end of the road is a gate, to the left of which are several courses of Hasmonean masonry from the First Wall along with its Herodian reinforcement. These stones were taken from a section of the wall which was discovered by the archaeologist Bliss near the Gobat School in 1894. These stones were also used to build a retaining wall for the cemetery above the school. To the right and below the level of the road is another entrance to the school. Near it can be seen the upper entrance of the tunnel which was dug during the War of Independence to connect the neighborhood of Yemin Moshe to Mount Zion.

13. Gobat School Visiting hours: Monday through Saturday, all day.

The American Institute for Holyland Research is housed in the building encompassed by a stone wall at the end of Araunah the Jebusite Road. The following inscription is carved on a stone by the gate: "Bishop Gobat School. Founded in the year 1853. G.M.S. 1977". This was the first building to be erected outside the walls of the Old City on Mount Zion in the 19th century. It was named after the second Protestant bishop in Jerusalem, Samuel Gobat. It was a vocational missionary school where Arab youths were taught.

Additional remains of the First Wall are integrated into the interior walls of the building. In the courtyard behind the building, more remains can be seen, including parts of towers. The wall continued southwards and turned eastwards at the edge of the cemetery

The Protestant Cemetery Entry is permitted only by prior arrangement with St George Cathedral, telephone number 02-718628. The cemetery is south of the courtyard of the American Institute. The Protestant community in Jerusalem buried its dead here from 1896 until the end of the British Mandate. Among those buried here are German, Swiss and English Protestants. Some of the most well-known people buried here are: the first two Protestant bishops; the British archaeologist Petrie; Conrad Schick, architect and Jerusalem scholar (see Tour No.15 of the Street of the Prophets); the Spaffords, founders of the American Colony in Jerusalem; the archaeologists Drake and Starkey; German soldiers killed in the First World War; and British officers and policemen. Excavations carried out after 1970 revealed the remains of a gate in the First Wall to the south of the cemetery. This is perhaps the Gate of the Essenes mentioned by Josephus.

We end our tour at the Zion Gate or at Yemin Moshe. A path called "Benny's Ascent" leads us down to the Jerusalem Brigade Road across from Yemin Moshe, where our walk ends.

TOUR No. 10

RAMPARTS WALK

Details of tour: The tour is around the walls of the Old City. A paved walkway with guard rails atop the city walls is reached by stairways. We will see views of the Old and New City against the background of the Judean hills. There are five entry/exit points: at Zion Gate, the Citadel, Jaffa Gate, Damascus Gate, and St Stephen's Gate, and three exit points only at Dung Gate, New Gate, and Herod's Gate. Admission fee. Tickets are sold at five stations of access and are valid for two days from the time stamped and for four entries.

Visiting hours: Every day from 9:00 am to 5:00 pm; Fridays and eves of holidays until 3 pm. For Saturdays and holidays tickets must be purchased in advance or at a nearby store. The section between the Citadel and Zion Gate is illuminated after dark and is open until 9.30 pm.

Distance covered: 4 km (2½ miles)

Time: 3 hours

Transportation: Buses No 3, 13, 19, 20, 30, 80 and 99
Parking lots near Jaffa Gate for private vehicles

The Sites: 1. From Jaffa Gate to Damascus Gate (about 1000 m– 1090 yd); 2. From Damascus Gate to St Stephen's Gate (about 1150 m–1250 yd); 3 From the Citadel to Zion Gate (about 550 m–600 yd); 4. From Zion Gate to Dung Gate (about 750 m–820 yd); 5. The Dung Gate; 6. The Zion Park (Beit Shalom Park).

Remarks: This tour should be made after the tours of the Old City. Sections 1 and 2 of the Ramparts Walk can be done consecutively, as can sections 3 and 4. Please note that the Ramparts Walk does not connect the Dung and St Stephen's Gates.

It is advised to make this tour with a group. Visitors can divide the tour into two or more separate visits, taking into account the limitations of the tickets.

FOREWORD

The walls of the Old City were built by the Ottoman Sultan Suleiman the Magnificent, during the years 1535–1542. Most of the walls' course follows roughly the line of earlier walls, where there were old foundations, or wall fragments. This is one of the world's most beautiful and complete 16th-century walls.

The city wall is about 4.5 km (3 mi) long, between 5 and 15 m (16–50 ft) high, and about 3m (10 ft) thick at its base. At the height of the battlements the wall is about 1.6 m (5 ft) thick. At the top of the walls are a series of paved paths reached by steps. The walls' battlements include 35 square towers and crenelations along the entire length. They have 15 machicolations (overhanging parapets for the defense of gates and other strategic points along the wall), 16 inscriptions praising the Sultan, and numerous geometric and floral decorations.

The wall was intended to provide security for the residents of the city, and to defend the places holy to Islam. The Sultan was also concerned about a possible recurrence of the Crusades. The architect was Suleiman — court architect. In order to speed the construction, the foundations of earlier walls were utilized.

The towers in the wall protrude outward, and their openings face the city. Steps ascend to the towers from the city side of the wall. The embrasures in the towers face three directions. In some of the towers there are embrasures on each storey. Each large tower was essentially a fortress in which guards were permanently stationed. The southern and eastern walls

RAMPARTS WALK

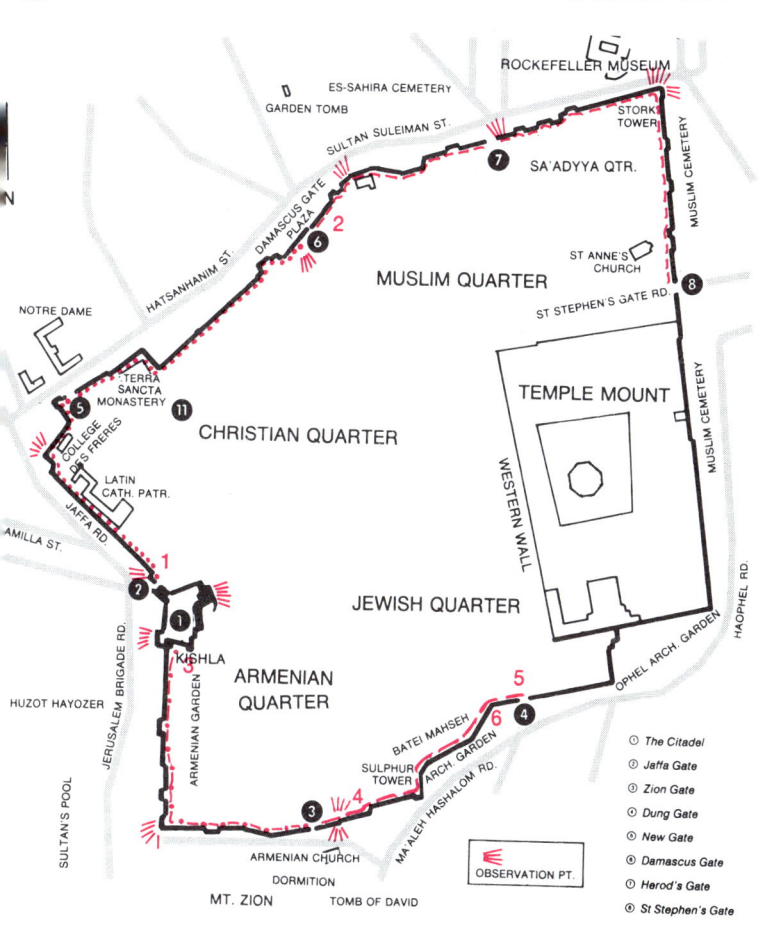

Map of the tour.

have 6 towers each, while the western city wall has 8 towers. The northern wall, which faces a section of ground higher than within the city, has 15 towers, as well as a moat.

Above the gateways, and on some of the towers, are protruding battlements with machicolations, and along the crenelations of the walls are loopholes for discharging missiles. These openings are narrow slits (up to 15 cm–6 in wide, and 1.8 m–2 yd long). There are over 350 embrasures in the wall.

THE TOUR
1. From Jaffa Gate to Damascus Gate

Before ascending to the rampart walkway it is advisable to read about the Jaffa Gate (Tour No. 9). We ascend the stone steps behind Jaffa Gate, as directed by the sign above the gate. Tickets are sold at the entrance to the parapet. We note the side parapets, north of the gate (double-domed indentations set one upon the other), in which are found embrasures. The parapet is walled on three sides, and is open on the side facing the city. In the wall is set an

TOUR No. 10   140

The Old City walls at Jaffa Gate.  *The city wall and spire of St Savior.*

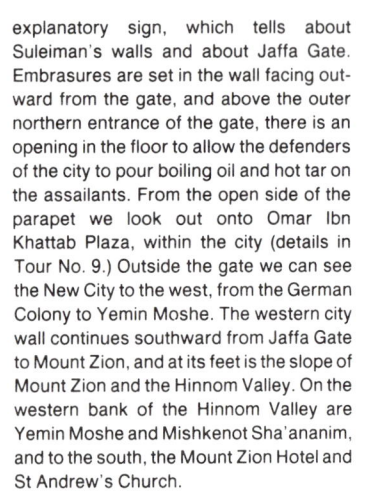

explanatory sign, which tells about Suleiman's walls and about Jaffa Gate. Embrasures are set in the wall facing outward from the gate, and above the outer northern entrance of the gate, there is an opening in the floor to allow the defenders of the city to pour boiling oil and hot tar on the assailants. From the open side of the parapet we look out onto Omar Ibn Khattab Plaza, within the city (details in Tour No. 9.) Outside the gate we can see the New City to the west, from the German Colony to Yemin Moshe. The western city wall continues southward from Jaffa Gate to Mount Zion, and at its feet is the slope of Mount Zion and the Hinnom Valley. On the western bank of the Hinnom Valley are Yemin Moshe and Mishkenot Sha'ananim, and to the south, the Mount Zion Hotel and St Andrew's Church.

We ascend the iron steps to the path at the top of the wall, and walk beside the crenelations. The path ascends via steps to the top of the towers which protrude from the city walls. Through the crenels we can see, to the southwest, the Mamilla area, and above that the buildings of the Hebrew Union College, the Pontifical Institute, and the French Consulate (for details see Tour No. 14 — The Beginnings of the New City). We can also see the King David and King Solomon Hotels. On the horizon, to the south, we see the hills of Gilo, the neighborhood of Talpiot and Armon Hanatziv (the High Commissioner's palace). This is described in the explanatory sign on the tower. Our path runs beside the Christian Quarter of the Old City. Nearby is the red-tiled roof of the Latin Patriarchate building. Behind it, in the distance, we can see the dark bell tower of the Franciscan Monastery with its clock. We continue past the buildings of the Collège des Frères, whose buildings are taller than the city wall (details in Tour No. 7 — The Christian Quarter). Here the western city wall comes to an end. This wall apparently followed the course of the Third Wall from the Jaffa Gate northward and was built on the foundations of later walls, along the same line. Here the city wall turns to the east and then again north. Below and outside the city wall is a rectangular trench carved in the rock and a grassy area which extends to the street. In the trench we see the remains of Tancred's Tower. Until the War of Independence, the old Post Office stood here. Across Tsahal (I.D.F.) Square we see the Jerusalem Municipality building and the French Hospital. The street which runs between the wall and the French Hospital was blocked off by a concrete wall in the years 1948–1967. We can view the entire length of Hatsanhanim (Paratroopers) Road, which descends to Damascus Gate. Near the point where the wall turns eastward, the dome of the Kamra Mosque rises above the Old City. We continue to the New Gate, where we have the choice of descending to the street by way of the iron steps, or continuing to the Damascus Gate (details about the Mosque and the New Gate can be found in Tour No. 7 — The Christian Quarter).

The Ottoman Wall, extending from the New Gate to the Damascus Gate, was built over the remains of earlier walls from the Byzantine, early Muslim, and Crusader periods, and the Middle Ages. Remains from walls of earlier periods were not found here. The path runs next to the wall of the St Savior's Monastery (details in Tour No. 7). We pass its northwestern entrance, above which is the inscription "Terra Sancta". Outside the city, across from us, are the buildings of Notre Dame. On the horizon we see Mount Scopus and the Mount of Olives. An explanatory plaque is affixed at the observation point in the wall detailing the view. In the Crusader period, the gate of St Lazarus was located here. We continue along the path which passes very close to the windows of residential buildings in the Christian Quarter, above a school playground, and near the dome of a small Greek church. We are now approaching Damascus Gate. We can see its unique ornamentation at the top of the wall above the gate.

We ascend to the roof of the Damascus Gate. To the south is a breathtaking vista of the Old City. In the center, below us, is the Central Valley. The golden Dome of the Rock stands out above the Temple Mount to the south. To the west, on our right, are the buildings of the Christian Quarter, including the towers of the Franciscan, Latin, and Lutheran churches, and the domes of the Church of the Holy Sepulcher. Continuing to the south, we see the slopes of the Jewish Quarter, and its northernmost buildings. To the east, on our left, we can see part of the Muslim Quarter, the Austrian Hospice, the Convent of the Sisters of Zion, and the minaret in the northwest corner of the Temple Mount. Below the wall is the area which contained the "Plaza of the Pillar" during the Roman period. Here stood a pillar supporting a statue of the Emperor Hadrian, and from here, also, extended colonnaded streets across the city (the Cardo Maximus and the Cardo Valensis). The road from Damascus Gate splits into HaGai (El Wad) Street to the left, and Khan ez-Zeit (Oil Market) to the right. Outside the city wall, to the north, we can view the recently rebuilt plaza in front of the Damascus Gate. Three streets begin here: the Street of the Prophets, which runs to the northwest, Nablus Road, which runs northward, and Suleiman Street, which runs parallel to the wall. In the distance are the buildings of the Italian Hospital, which today houses the Ministry of Education, and the neighborhood of Morasha (Musrara). To the west we see the facade of the Notre Dame building with its statue. From the Damascus Gate we may choose to descend and leave the Ramparts Walk via an exit-only iron turnstile, or to descend via the gatehouse by way of steps which lead to the reconstructed guardhouse below the present-day gate.

2. From the Damascus Gate to St Stephen's Gate If we begin the tour here, we ascend to the path along the top of the wall via the steps leading from the guardhouse in the eastern Roman tower (details of the reconstructed Roman gate and of Damascus Gate itself can be found in Tour No. 11 — From the Tomb of the Kings to Zedekiah's Cave). At the top of the Gate we tarry a while to appreciate the beautiful view to the south, into the Old City (details in section 1). We go up the steps to the east

The Old City from atop Damascus Gate.

The new plaza outside Damascus Gate.

to the tower in the wall, and pass by the Spafford Children's Home. The playground of the Home can be seen from the wall. The wall at this point is only 4 m (13 feet) high, but it is built at the top of a stone escarpment which is 6 m (20 feet) high. The escarpment started out as a quarry in the First and Second Temple periods. The Crusaders turned the quarry into a moat which ran the length of the city wall, through which Suleiman Street runs today. The entrance to Zedekiah's Cave lies below us. The cave, which was also an ancient quarry, is hewn in the rock to the south of the entrance, and continues under a portion of the Muslim Quarter (for details see Tour No. 11). To the north, beyond the corner of Nablus Road, is the German Monastery of St Paul. To the east of the monastery is the parking lot for East Jerusalem's central bus station, which abuts a cliff. The caves in the cliff give it the appearance of a skull when viewed from a distance. The Protestants identify this site as Jesus' burial place. At the base of this cliff is the traditional location of the so-called court of the guard, where Jeremiah was imprisoned. Above the cliff, at the top of the hill, is a Muslim cemetery called Es-Sahira (those who are vigilant), which is mentioned in the Koran as the site of the Resurrection of the Dead at the end of days. The nearby gate (Herod's Gate) into the Old City was called Zahira (flowers) Gate, based on a corruption of the name of the cemetery. On the eastern horizon we can see Mount Scopus and the Mount of Olives, and the buildings along the ridge. Three towers stand out above the other buildings: those of the Russian Church of the Ascension, Augusta Victoria Hospital and the Hebrew University. Prominent on the slope of the Mount of Olives is the arched Mormon university. Proceeding along our path on the wall, we reach Herod's Gate (see Tour No. 5 — The Muslim Quarter). To the south, within the Old City, we see spread out before us the Muslim Quarter. Several streets originate at the Gate and lead into the Muslim Quarter: to the right, the Red Minaret Street; in the center, the road leading to the Indian Hospice; and to the left, the road leading to the Mamunyya building and to the Deir el-Adass (Convent of the Lentils), whose unique dome can be seen opposite Herod's Gate (details in Tour No. 5). Outside the Old City, to the north, we see Salah ed-Din Street and the post office. To the east of the post office is the Rashedyya High School, and the Rockefeller Museum, with its prominent octagonal tower built of white stone. From the tower of Herod's Gate, we descend the iron steps to the continuation of the path along the top of the wall. Behind us, we can see the original opening on the eastern side of the gate, which was sealed and then reopened. We

Looking east from atop Herod's Gate

may also discern the inscription and the rosette carved in the stone. A bit farther along the path, a plaque marks the spot where the Crusader armies, led by Godfrey de Bouillon, succeeded in breaching the walls of the city on July 15, 1099. We soon reach the Stork Tower, at the northeastern corner of the wall, which has an explanatory sign.

Here, the eastern city wall turns south, perhaps following the course of the Second Temple period Third Wall, to St Stephen's Gate. Alongside the wall, to our left, is a Muslim cemetery. Inside the wall, we can see the Old City bereft of buildings. This area was enclosed by a separate wall during the Crusader period, and had its own postern. The next section of the walkway is called the Path of the Storks, and leads to St Stephen's Gate. From the tower near the gate there is an excellent view to the east of the Kidron Valley, the Mount of Olives and its churches. The path leads down to the cobblestoned roof of the gatehouse. From here, we can clearly see the area of the Church of St Anne (for details see Tour No. 6 — From St Stephen's Gate to the Church of the Holy Sepulcher). The walkway ends at St Stephen's Gate.

3. From the Citadel to the Zion Gate

The ascent to the walkway is outside the Citadel, on the south side. We walk to the far, southern end of the Garden of David Plaza which is to the west of the Citadel, and then turn left. We descend steps through the arched entrance to the room where tickets are sold, and from there we leave the Citadel. The southern walls of the Citadel tower above us to a height of 18 m (59 ft). The minaret of the mosque (which is incorrectly called the Tower of David) rises above the corner of the wall. There are three machicolations, or overhanging turrets, in the corner of the wall. On the wall is a rectangular frame which was intended to enclose an inscription. Crusader stones from elsewhere have been incorporated into the Ottoman wall. On the exposed bedrock are signs of quarrying from the Roman-Byzantine period (4th century CE). We can even see a rectangular block of stone still partially attached to the bedrock.

On the south side are rock-hewn steps leading to a ritual bath dating to the Second Temple period.

We ascend to the top of the wall by way of a spiral iron staircase, alongside the wall of the Kishla (the Ottoman police fortress; see Tour No. 8) and reach the paved path, from which we take in the magnificent view in all directions: to the south, nearby, we see the courtyard of the Kishla and the buildings around it, and behind them, part of the Armenian Quarter. Outside the city wall, Jaffa Road climbs from the Jaffa Gate to Tsahal (I.D.F.) Square and the municipality buildings. We can also see the Convent of St Vincent de Paul in the Mamilla Mall, and behind it, the towers of Zion Square and the Clal building. We see the newly paved HaEmek (Valley) Street and beyond it, the Jerusalem and Eilon towers. We can look down on the bullet-scarred facade of the Tanus building which stood opposite what used to be no-man's-land until 1967 at the foot of the city wall. To the left of this are the Mitchell Garden and the buildings of the Artists' Quarter. Further along we see the neighborhoods of Yemin Moshe and Mishkenot Sha'ananim. Behind them are the Hebrew Union College, the Sheraton-Plaza Hotel, the French Consulate, the building of the Chief Rabbinate, the King David Hotel, one of the domes of the YMCA building, a residential building with arches, and the tower of the

The view towards Yemin Moshe.

King Solomon Hotel. To the southwest, the German Colony and St Andrew's Church (with the Scottish flag flying above it) are visible. Above the dome of the church rise the Gilo ridge and the houses of the neighborhood of Gilo, as well as the Talpiot ridge with its houses among the trees. To the south, the High Commissioner's Palace (Armon Hanatziv) is visible through the grove of trees, with the neighborhood of Abu Tor below it.

We follow the path along the battlements at the top of the wall, and ascend the tower in the wall. The western wall has eight towers, which are built at vulnerable points in the wall. The tower we have just climbed was built on the site of an earlier tower. Looking into the Old City, we see the Armenian Theological Seminary which was built between 1970 and 1978. Archaeological excavations were carried out on the former location of King Herod's palace, and later, the palace of the Crusader kings (see Tour No. 8).

We go down from the tower back to the walkway atop the wall. Opposite the next tower is a vacant area of the Old City which has not yet been excavated. We can tell from the elevation of this area that it was part of the raised platform upon which Herod built his palace. We continue to the next tower, which is the southwest tower of the city wall, and bears an inscription indicating that this tower stands on the remains of a medieval corner tower which

Section of the Ramparts Walk.

was destroyed by the Ayyubid Sultan Malek el-Mu'azzam in the year 1219.

At this point the wall turns eastward. We are now walking on the southern wall, on the section which crosses Mount Zion. On Mount Zion, outside the wall, is the Catholic cemetery. Here is buried Costigan, the first European to sail the entire length of the Jordan, from the Sea of Galilee to the Dead Sea, in 1935. We can also see the buildings of the Greek-Orthodox Seminary, and behind them, the hills of Abu Tor, Talpiot, and the High Commissioner's palace (Armon Hanatziv). Several other buildings can be seen on Mount Zion, among which the Dormition Abbey, with its black conical dome; the new Armenian Church; and several others. Within the city can be seen the buildings in the Armenian compound (the museum, the library and the school). Behind them, to the north, are the so-called Tower of David, the clock tower of the Franciscan Monastery, and the edge of the square white tower of the Lutheran Church. On the southern wall there are six towers. From the top of the second tower we see, to the east, the buildings at the southwestern edge of the Jewish Quarter. On the horizon are Mount Scopus, the Mount of Olives and the Hill of Offense, which are above the village of Silwan (details in Tour No. 12 — The Mount of Olives).

From the roof of the tower above Zion Gate we see the dome of the El-Aksa Mosque and the shining, golden cupola of the Dome of the Rock. Between them, in the distance, we discern the gilded, onion-shaped domes of the Russian Orthodox Church of Mary Magdalene on the slopes of the Mount of Olives. From here we descend the steps to the gatehouse of the Zion Gate and to the plaza in front of it (details in Tour No. 4) or we can continue to the next section of this tour.

4. From Zion Gate to the Dung Gate In this segment of the wall we are walking the length of the southern boundary of the Jewish Quarter. From atop the wall we can see the various buildings of the quarter: Yeshivat Imrei Binah (the Warsaw Kollel), conspicuous by the stone arch atop its roof; the domes of the four Sephardi syna-

The Dung Gate.

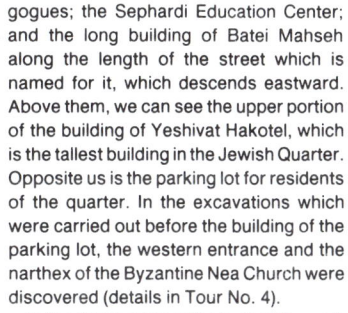

Zion Gate from inside the walls.

gogues; the Sephardi Education Center; and the long building of Batei Mahseh along the length of the street which is named for it, which descends eastward. Above them, we can see the upper portion of the building of Yeshivat Hakotel, which is the tallest building in the Jewish Quarter. Opposite us is the parking lot for residents of the quarter. In the excavations which were carried out before the building of the parking lot, the western entrance and the narthex of the Byzantine Nea Church were discovered (details in Tour No. 4).

In the depression at the foot of the wall, archaeological excavations were carried out and remains of the buildings that were brought to light were partially reconstructed, and an archaeological park was built. Below us is a square stone structure, the remains of the gate that was here in the Ayyubid period (the 13th century). In the center were found the remains of a Crusader church. At the eastern edge of the area were found the water cisterns of the Nea Church and an inscription of the time of the Emperor Justinian (details in Tour No. 4).

We continue eastward until the corner tower of the wall known as Burj Kibrit (the Sulpher Tower). To the south, outside the wall, we can see the lower slopes of Mount Zion. Most prominent is the large dome of the Church of St Peter in Gallicantu (details in Tour No. 9), surrounded by a grove of pine trees. To the east we see the Hill of Offense, on whose slopes spreads the village of Silwan.

We turn and cross near stepped gardens (which were originally intended to be an amphitheater). Beneath them were found the cisterns of the Nea Church. We continue on the wall along the slope of Batei Mahseh Street, and reach the end of the walkway.

5. The Dung Gate This is the lowest of all the gates in the wall. It faces the village of Silwan and thus its Arabic name — Bab Silwan, which has been used since the Middle Ages. During the Mameluke and Ottoman periods, the gate was called Bab Almaghraba, named for the Moghrabi (Moors) neighborhood which was where, today, stands the Western Wall plaza. The Dung Gate is the name of a gate in the Jerusalem wall which was near the Siloam Pool in the days of the Second Temple. The name was transferred to this gate in the 19th century. At first, the gate was a small rectangular postern in the tower of the wall. Above it, in the wall, is an arch built from "pillows" of stone, and over it is a rosette. There is a Star of David in the center of the row of stones between the lintel of the postern and the arch. This decorative motif was common during the Mameluke and Ottoman periods. More recently, renovations were carried out and the gate was made wider.

6. Zion Park (Beit Shalom Park) After the Six Day War, archaeological excavations were carried out outside the southern wall and at its base, between the Dung Gate and Zion Gate. These excavations were sponsored by a group of Swedish Christians, known by the name "Beit Shalom" (House of Peace). The archaeological park is open to visitors and explanatory signs are affixed. Near the Dung Gate the tower of a Crusader gate juts out, the partially reconstructed Gate of the Tanners. Near it was discovered the pavement of a colonnaded Byzantine street (the Cardo Valensis) which crossed from the Damascus Gate plaza, near the beginning of the Cardo Maximus, through the Central Valley southward, and across to the Siloam Pool. On the sides of the pavement are several column bases. We pass near several cisterns and ritual baths which were in the basements of buildings of the Second Temple period. Some of the baths are quite well preserved, and we can discern the steps and the water store, and the pipe for the passage of the rain water from it to the bathing basin. Continuing westward, we can see a corner built of large stones at the foot of the Sulphur Tower. This is, apparently, the corner of the Byzantine Nea Church. Below the Sulphur Tower we also find the remains of the lower aqueduct from the Second Temple period, which brought water from Solomon's Pools to the Temple Mount. We also see a section of the clay pipe protected by a stone structure. The exposed pipe is also seen on the slope of the road from Mount Zion to the Hinnom Valley in several places where the aqueduct is destroyed, and in Mishkenot Shaananim. Our tour ends here.

Remains of gate and pavement at Zion Park.

TOUR No. 11

FROM THE TOMBS OF THE KINGS TO ZEDEKIAH'S CAVE

Details of tour: The tour passes through the area north of the Old City walls, which constituted the western section of the city's municipal border during the period that Jerusalem was divided (1948–1967); a period detailed in the Tourjeman Post Museum. At the end of the Second Temple period, a neighborhood called Bezetha existed in this area, and it was encompassed by the Third Wall. In the same area the so-called Tombs of the Kings were excavated. In the 19th century residences were built here; the American Colony was established; churches were erected, and the Garden Tomb discovered. The tour ends with a visit to two sites in the Old City walls — the Damascus Gate and Zedekiah's Cave.

Distance covered: approx. 3 km (2 miles)

Time: approx. 5 hours (including 2 hours devoted to a visit to the Tourjeman Post Museum

Transportation: Buses to Damascus Gate No 27, 12, 99; to Central Command Square No 1, 11, 12, 27, 99

Parking lot opposite Damascus Gate for private vehicles

Starting point: Central Command Square

End of tour: Damascus Gate

The Sites: 1. Kikar Pikud Merkaz (Central Command Square); 2. American Colony; 3. Tombs of the Kings; 4. St George Cathedral; 5. The Third Wall; 6. St Etienne; 7. Garden Tomb; 8. Hospice of St Paul; 9. Damascus Gate; 10. Zedekiah's Cave.

THE TOUR

1. Kikar Pikud Merkaz (Central Command Square) The square is at the junction of Shmuel Hanavi and Shivtei Yisrael Streets and St George and Pikud Merkaz Streets. This was the site of the Mandelbaum Gate (after the owners of the building at the road junction) which served as a checkpoint between the two parts of the city, manned by Israeli and Jordanian police. Mandelbaum House was and still is under United Nations jurisdiction. Another Israeli building at this junction is the municipal Tourjeman Post Museum devoted to one particular aspect of life in Jerusalem during the 19 years the city was divided (1948–1967), through photographs, maps, documents and audiovisual presentations. The museum is open Sundays through Thursdays from 9.00 am to 4.00 pm. Entry fee. Group visits and guided tours have to be arranged in advance. Tel: (02)-281278.

2. American Colony We walk along St George Street to the American Colony

The Tourjeman Post.

TOUR No. 11   148

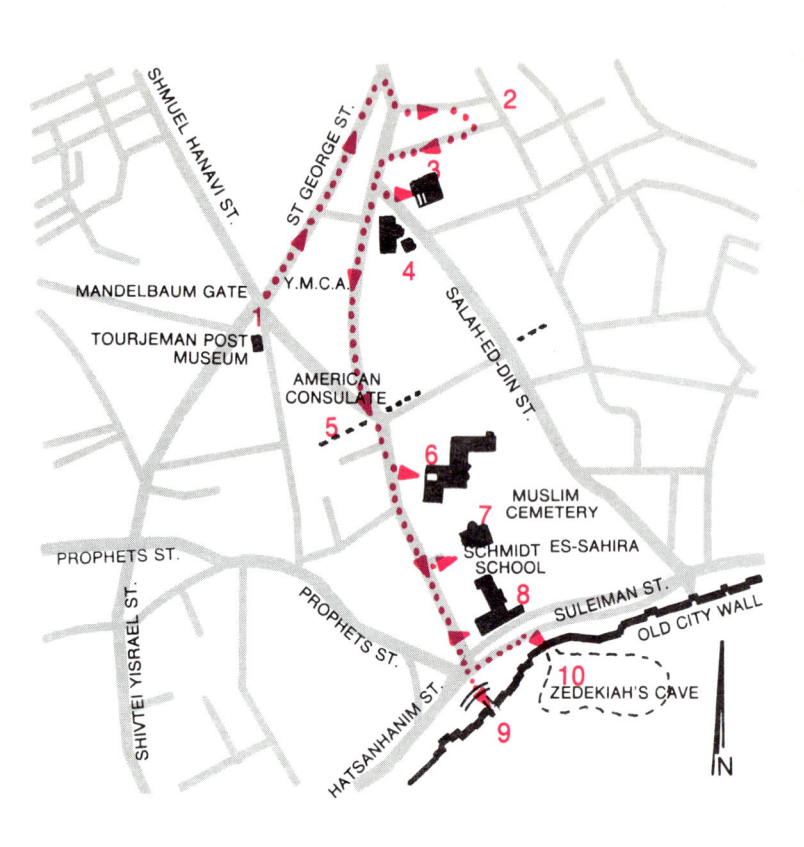

Map of the tour.

Hotel. This was originally the villa of a wealthy Arab dignitary. It was purchased by an American couple, a Chicago lawyer Horatio Spafford and his wife Anna, who in 1881 decided to engage in public activity in Jerusalem (see details of the Spafford Baby Home in Tour No. 5 of the Muslim Quarter) following the tragic death of their four daughters who were drowned on a cruise. A group of Swedish farmers also decided at this time to make their homes in Jerusalem and joined up with the Americans. The story of this colony has been told by the Swedish author Selma Lagerlof, winner of the 1909 Nobel Prize for literature, in her book *Jerusalem*. The members of the colony lived as a commune; some of them worked in the nearby fields, while others dealt in commerce and in the production of souvenirs for tourists, including photographs of places throughout the Holy Land. The colony disbanded during the First World War but some of its members remained in Jerusalem.

3. Tombs of the Kings At the end of Salah ed-Din Street, at the corner of

The American Colony Hotel.

Entrance to the Tombs of the Kings.

Nablus Road we reach a gate in the stone wall with a sign put up by the French: "Tombs of the Kings" (alluding to the kings of Judah). The site is open during daylight hours. Entry fee.

The wall encompasses a series of Second Temple period tombs hewn in the rock, similar to the tombs found in the Kidron Valley. They were built by Helena Queen of Adiabene (now in northern Iraq). In the 1st century CE Queen Helena converted to Judaism, together with her two sons Izates and Monbaz and their families. She made a pilgrimage to Jerusalem and arriving during a famine (mentioned in the New Testament) she had food imported from Cyprus and Egypt. They built magnificent palaces in the lower city (the site of David's City) which were razed to the ground by the Romans in 70 CE and a magnificent burial complex where Helena was buried in 50 CE. Josephus (in *The Antiquities of the Jews* 24; and *Jewish Wars* 5:2b) describes the opulent royal necropolis. According to Jewish tradition this was the tomb of Kalba Savua (in Aramaic the sated dog), the nickname of Rabbi Akiva's wealthy and righteous father-in-law of the Second Temple period who used to provide the poor with rich meals, "for anyone who entered his house hungry as a dog left it sated". This description of riches also fitted Queen Helena, who brought large amounts of food to Jerusalem during a period when its inhabitants were starving. Jews used to come here to pray in times of drought.

In 1847 the Turkish governor ordered the area to be searched for a treasure, but as none was found, the workers plundered and damaged the buildings, leaving them covered in dirt and ashes. The first archaeological dig in Jerusalem was carried out at this site by the French explorer De Saulcy. He uncovered a number of stone sarcophagi (now in the Louvre Museum in Paris). The tombs were erroneously said to be those of the kings of Judah and are still known today as "The Tombs of the Kings." In 1847 the site was purchased by the Pereyre family who gave it to the French Government in 1886.

We enter a large courtyard hewn in the rock and descend 23 steps (each 9 m — 29 ft wide). To the right of the stairs a gutter was dug to direct rainwater into cisterns at the bottom of the stairs which were used for purification. At the bottom of the court we reach a vaulted opening, 8 m (26 ft) high, and through it we enter an internal court 26 × 27 m (28½ × 29½ yd), and see the remains of two Doric pillars found between two pilasters. The architrave is ornamented with a wreath; the frieze has a projecting tablet. In the center of a frieze are a carved bunch of grapes and acanthus leaves. Josephus Flavius describes three stone pyramids above the center of the facade, but today there is no sign of them.

TOUR No. 11

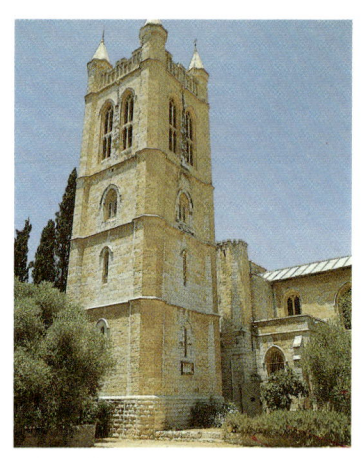

St George Cathedral belltower.

The passageway leads to an open antechamber. At its southern end, at ground level, is an opening closed off by a rolling stone leading to a burial chamber. There are a number of grooves in the floor of the passageway, for moving the large stone closing the entrance.

We descend the stairs below the opening and come to a passage leading to a central hall with openings to eight burial chambers at various levels with burial niches and vaults. Narrow, low passages connect the chambers, which can be gained only by stooping.

4. St George We continue along Nablus Road and come to a wide gate on the northern side of the road, near the corner, which leads to an inner courtyard, surrounded by a number of buildings. This is the St George Cathedral — center of the Anglican Church in Israel. To the left is the Bishop's residence and to the right a highschool for boys. At the end of the courtyard stands a square belltower with four pointed turrets in each of its corners, a replica of the belltower in a church in Oxford. The belltower is named for King Edward VII, who contributed towards its construction. All the buildings were planned by the British architect, Jeffrey, in the neo-Gothic style popular in England at the end of the 19th century.

In 1887 the Anglican Bishop Blyth was sent to Jerusalem to head the Jerusalem and Oriental Mission after the English Protestants broke away from the Germans (see Tour No. 8 of the Armenian Quarter). The first buildings in the St George complex were workshops, orphanages, a school for girls and one for boys. The building was completed on the eve of World War I. During the war the complex served as headquarters of the Turkish General Jamal Pasha. After the British conquest of Palestine, the buildings were returned to their owners. A youth hostel has been opened here; organ concerts are held in the church hall. Apart from the belltower, the complex is open to visitors and both written and oral information is supplied free of charge.

5. The Third Wall We continue along Nablus Road to the south, pass the YMCA building and the Palestine Pottery Company which manufactures Armenian pottery, to the corner of the American Consulate building. Large dressed stones were found in the vicinity during archaeological excavations, and others were uncovered near the site where the Paz gas station stands today and near the memorial to the paratroopers who fell in the Six Day War. In excavations carried out here in 1972 large dressed stones (2.5–5 m — 8–16 ft) were uncovered, as well as the base of a tower (9 m —29½ ft). These two sections, added to a section 75 m (82 yd) long, constitute the Third Wall. In 1940 Profs. E. Sukenik and L.A. Mayer of the Hebrew University, discovered sections of the wall 1200 m (1312 yd) long (from Shivtei Yisrael Street up to the courtyard of the Albright American School of Archaeology in Salah ed-Din Street). The first remains of this wall were discovered in 1838 by Edward Robinson and further sections in 1961 to 1967 by Kathleen Kenyon.

According to Josephus, the Third Wall of Jerusalem was begun by King Agrippa I in 44 CE, but work was stopped under pressure of the Romans. It was finally completed just before the outbreak of the Jewish revolt in 66, but did not reach the planned height, and in a number of places it was never completed. There were 90 towers in the entire wall and a space between each tower of 100 m (109 yd). It covered an area double that of the previous (Second) city wall and the entire area was called the Bezetha suburb. The remains discovered were of the northern section of the wall. The eastern section probably ran along the Jehoshaphat Valley (the upper section of the Kidron Valley); the western section began at the Hippicus Tower, in the vicinity of the Citadel, and continued northwards, apparently in the direction of the Russian Compound.

6. St Etienne (St Stephen) The complex, named for St Stephen (in French St Etienne) is to be found at No. 9 Nablus Road. It consists of a new basilica built in 1900, the Ecole Biblique et Archéologique Française founded in 1890 by the French Dominicans as the first graduate school for biblical and archaeological studies in the Holy Land, a library and a museum. Stephen was the first Christian martyr; he was stoned to death by order of the Sanhedrin (Acts 6:8; 7:58-60). According to Christian tradition the stoning took place near Damascus Gate, which in Crusader times was called St Stephen's Gate (according to another tradition the stoning took place near the Lions' Gate). St Stephen is said to be buried at this site where the Byzantine Empress Eudokia built a church in 460, to receive his relics, and she herself is buried there. The church was destroyed by the Persians in 614, and rebuilt by the Crusaders. Excavations carried out here in 1882 revealed remains of the Byzantine church and its mosaic floor. In 1884 the Dominicans purchased the site and put up a stone fence around it. In the course of archaeological excavations in the courtyard, burial chambers from the First Temple period were revealed.

The church is open to visitors daily 7:30 am-1:00 pm and 3:00-6:00 pm.

We enter through a gate and walk up to a portico lining a square courtyard. The church's gabled facade rises on the eastern side of the high portico (26 m — 85 ft). The church is built as a Byzantine basilica, and Gothic arches support the roof. The ornamented walls are coated with marble of various types and there are carved arches above the entrances. The remains of the Byzantine mosaic floor are protected by a carpet. The Ecole Biblique et Archéologique Française (which publishes the quarterly "Revue Biblique") is built in Gothic style. The belltower is north of the basilica, and behind it is the monastery. The archaeology collection in the entrance hall of the École includes 13th-century BCE Egyptian exhibits; remains of the Byzantine and Crusader churches; sections of Second Temple period sarcophagi and artifacts discovered in the excavations undertaken by the Dominicans in the area.

We move southwards and descend to a basement leading to burial chambers. Names of well-known members of the

Cave with burial niches.

Stone headrest on a burial bench.

Dominican order buried here appear on plaques on the wall. There are ledges on three sides of the burial chamber and above them hewn into the rock are niches where skulls are kept, and below them are other recesses where the bones of the dead are placed. These tombs date to the First Temple period and apparently wealthy or noble persons were interred here.

7. Garden Tomb Opening hours: 8:00 am–12:00 noon; 2:30–5:00 pm daily (closed Sunday). We continue southwards along Nablus Road and into the first turning on the left to Conrad Schick Street. We enter a hall in which souvenirs are sold, and go out to a courtyard surrounded by a beautiful landscaped garden.

It lies beneath a hill resembling a human skull, which was identified as the site of Golgotha (the skull) by the British General Charles Gordon in 1883. For this reason the place is also known as Gordon's Calvary. The area had been dug several years before and a rock-cut tomb discovered; later an ancient cistern was cleared nearby, proving that the place had been a garden in antiquity. The shape of the hill, the burial cave, and the garden seemed to fit the New Testament descriptions (Matthew 27:60; Luke 24:1–4; John 19:41, 20:5). The place was purchased by the newly founded Garden Tomb Association which to this day keeps it open for visitors and maintains guided tours (free of charge) on the site. In the southern slope of the hill above the burial cave are other caves, and above them is a Muslim cemetery. The caves were inhabited by hermits in the Byzantine and Crusader periods.

We ascend the path eastwards to the end of the garden and walk along Nablus Road to the south.

8. Hospice of St Paul Today this is a German hostel opposite Damascus Gate, and next to it the Schmidt Catholic School for Girls (a German monk who purchased the plot of land in 1899 and was the first principal of the school). During the excavations tombs were found here as well as remains of a small Byzantine church. The hostel was designed by an architect from Cologne, Germany. The building has three stories, spacious halls, rooms to accommodate pilgrims, service rooms and storerooms. Completed in 1910, it looks like a German castle with oriental vaulted windows and balconies, and little stone domes on the roof.

A zoological museum in the basement has unique specimens, including a collection of stuffed animals indigenous to the Holy Land, some of which are rare, while others are extinct. These animals were captured and stuffed by Father Schmitz, who was sent to Jerusalem in 1908 to manage the German Catholic institutions in Palestine.

The Garden Tomb.

"Gordon's Calvary".

TOMBS OF THE KINGS TO ZEDEKIAH'S CAVE

Damascus Gate and the causeway built to span the excavations below.

The museum also has an archaeology section with a model of the Second Temple desgined by Conrad Schick. The building can be visited daily, except Sundays and the museum may be visited by appointment (Tel: 02-282032).

9. Damascus Gate This is the central gate in the northern wall of the Old City, the largest and most impressive gate in the Ottoman walls. The Gate is called Sha'ar Shechem in Hebrew — after the city of Shechem (Nablus), the road to which begins here; the road also leads to Damascus, hence its name in English. (In Byzantine times the gate at this site was called St Stephen's Gate). The Arabic name, Bab el-Amud, refers to the column *(amud)* that stood in the gate square in Roman times (see below). From this column distances were measured from Jerusalem to other places throughout the country which were marked with milestones along the Roman roads. The gate is known for its exquisite ornamentation; the entrance is protected by a high tower on each side. Above the entrance is a decorated arch. The Arabic inscription over the gate recalls the name of Suleiman the Magnificent by whose orders the gate was built during the years 1536 to 1538. Above the arch is an ornamented window, and on both sides are turrets. The inside of the gate has a double angle to prevent the inrush of a sudden attack; two guardrooms have been turned into shops. There were three pairs of double wooden gates covered in iron, but only one pair remains. The causeway leading to the gate was built in the 19th century, and the steps to the square were built in 1980.

We descend to the foundations of the gate to look at the remains of ancient structures. To the west of the causeway are ruins of a Crusader church, and to the east are the remains of the Crusader wall which passed about 20 m (22 yd) north of the Ottoman wall. Steps descending to a paved square lead to the arch of an ancient gate. All these remains were uncovered in archaeological excavations and are open to visitors every day of the week in daylight hours. Entry fee.

We enter the ancient gate on whose lintel are the vestiges of a Roman inscription. This is part of a Roman triumphal arch,

Damascus Gate and the Roman gate.

built by the Emperor Hadrian, perhaps with stone blocks from the Herodian gate that existed here previously. The triumphal arch, that stood without any supporting wall, consisted of a main central gate and two smaller lower gates; the gate we see today is the one to the east.

We turn left inside the gate into the tower and we can identify the stones from the Herodian period, in secondary use, in the wine press installations and in the guardrooms. From here we ascend a stairway (part of which is the original) to the roof of the present gate. We return to the entrance of the gate and go into the Roman forum. Part of the original pavement was uncovered in excavations and we actually tread on it during our visit. (The original column which appears in the Madaba map has not been found.) On the spot where it is presumed to have stood is a hologram showing the column with the sculptured figure of the Roman emperor upon it. An exhibition of ancient maps and photographs of Damascus Gate and its environs throughout its history is on show here. We continue along Suleiman Road to the east.

10. Zedekiah's Cave Below the city wall to the east is an opening to a cave known as Zedekiah's Cave. It takes its name from the tradition that the last king of Judah, Zedekiah, used it as an escape route to Jericho, when he attempted to flee from the army of the Babylonian king Nebuchadnezzar at the time of the conquest of Jerusalem and the destruction of the First Temple. The place was described as a quarry by the 10th-century Muslim historian El-Muqadassi. The cave was blocked when the Ottoman wall was built in order to prevent a possible enemy from penetrating the city from the direction of Jericho. The entrance was discovered accidently in 1854 by the English explorer Barclay. The pillars supporting the roof, placed there when it was used as a quarry, are still visible.

The Freemasons used to hold special ceremonies here as they believed these were the Quarries of Solomon (considered to have been the first Freemason), and their carved symbols appear on the wall. The cave was sealed under Jordanian rule and was reopened in 1968 and renovated in 1985. It is open to visitors daily from 9:00 am to 5:00 pm. Entry fee.

In the wall opposite the cave entrance is another cave traditionally known as the Court of the Prison, recalling the pit into which Jeremiah was let down with ropes, as related in the Book of Jeremiah (38:6–13).

Our tour ends here.

The entrance to Zedekiah's Cave.

TOUR No. 12

THE MOUNT OF OLIVES

Details of tour: The tour includes several Christian holy sites, observation points. Most of the churches are open from 9.00 a.m. to 12.00 a.m., from 2.00 p.m. to 4.00 p.m. It is recommended to do this tour on Tuesday or Wednesday (on Sunday the Pater Noster Church is closed, and the Church of Mary Magdalene is open on Tuesday and Wednesday only). Appropriate dress is desirable.
Distance covered: approx. 3 km (2 miles)
Time: approx. 4 hours
Transportation: Bus No 27 to Damascus Gate, change to No 75 or 99
Private vehicles: parking lot on the Mount of Olives
Starting point: A-Tur Street (on the summit of the Mount of Olives)
End of tour: Jericho Road (the Valley of Jehoshaphat)
Sites: 1. Viri Galilaei; 2. Russian Church of the Ascension; 3. Church of the Ascension; 4. Pelagia Cave; 5. Eleona Church (Pater Noster); 6. Moriah Observation Point; 7. Jewish cemetery; 8. Tombs of the Prophets; 9. War Monument; 10. Dominius Flevit Church; 11. Church of Mary Magdalene; 12. Gethsemane and Church of the Agony; 13. Grotto of Gethsemane; 14. Church of the Assumption; 15. Tomb of Mujir ed-Din; 16. Church of St. Stephen; 17. Paratroopers' Memorial.

FOREWORD

The Mount of Olives is the name given to the central section of the mountain ridge running north to south, to the east of the Kidron Valley. On its summit, 815m (2675 ft) high, is the Arab village of A-Tur; on its western slope are the Jewish cemetery and a number of churches. On its peak is the pointed tower of the Russian Church of the Ascension and the Intercontinental Hotel. The mountain is named for the olive trees that grew on its slopes in the past, only a few of which remain.

The entire mountain ridge is approximately 3.5 km (2 miles) long and approximately 2 km (1½ miles) wide. It is divided into three sections. The southern section is identified as the Mount of Offense (its peak stands 747 m — 2450 ft high) in connection with the pagan altars built by King Solomon for his foreign wives (II Kings). At the top of the mountain is a pine grove where stands a Dominican monastery. On its slopes is the village of Silwan and burial caves dating to the First Temple period. The northern section — Mount Scopus (829 m — 2720 ft high), is mentioned in the Mishna, the Talmud and in the works of Josephus. Here are the buildings of the Hebrew University and the Hadassah Hospital. The central section of the mountain ridge is the Mount of Olives proper.

The Mount of Olives is first mentioned in the Bible in the description of King David's flight from his son Absalom (II Samuel 15:30, 32). It is also mentioned in Zechariah's prophecy (Zechariah 14:3,4). Ezekiel refers to it as the Mount of the East (Ezekiel 11:23).

In the Second Temple period fires were lit on the summit to announce the new moon. The sacrifice of the Red Heifer was performed on the Mount of Olives (*Mishnah*, tractate "Para"). During the siege of Jerusalem by the Romans in 70 CE, the Tenth Legion camped on Mount Scopus. The rampart built by Titus to complete the siege was built from olive trees, and passed along the slopes of the Mount.

After the destruction of the Temple, Jews believed the Divine Presence still remained there and they would climb to the top. During the Middle Ages, Jewish pilgrims came there to celebrate the Festival

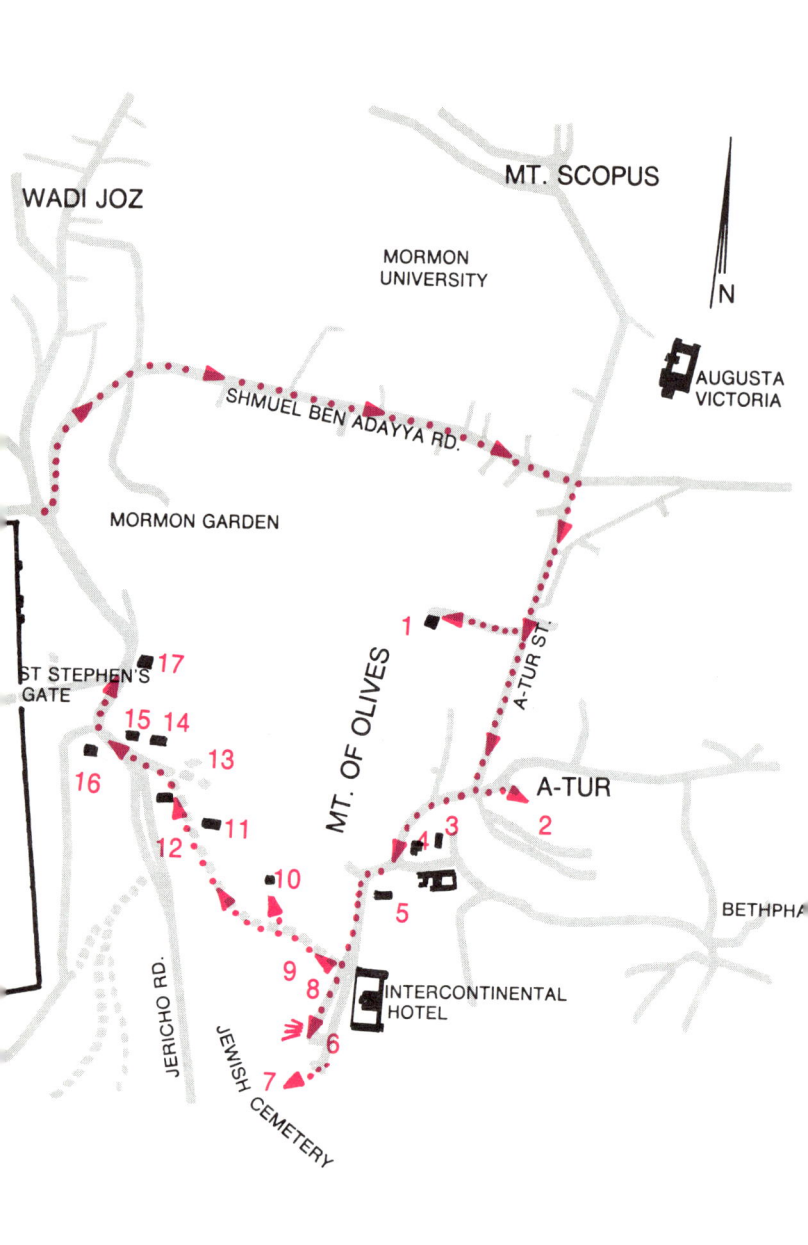

TOUR No. 12

Map of the tour.

The Mount of Olives with the Intercontinental Hotel at the top.

of Hoshana Rabba. From the end of the 15th century, Jews began to bury their dead on the slopes of the Mount of Olives.

In the Christian tradition the Mount of Olives, or Olivet as it is called in the New Testament, is connected with the last days of the life of Jesus. When in the area, Jesus stayed with his friends at Bethany (Luke 10:38; Mark 11:11) and each day he walked to the city and returned at nightfall, passing through the Mount of Olives. Here he spoke to his disciples and prophesied the destruction of Jerusalem and wept at his fate (Mark 13:3; Luke 19:37, 41), and was arrested a few days later in the Garden of Gethsemane (Mark 14:26–52). According to Luke (Acts 1:6–12) the Ascension of Christ took place on the Mount of Olives. These and other events are commemorated by many churches built in the Byzantine and Crusader periods.

The view from the Mount of Olives to the west, of both the Old and New City of Jerusalem, is breathtaking, especially in the morning. On the slopes to the south, above Ben Adayya Road leading up to it, the Mormon sect planted a garden in 1979 to mark the "prophecy of the Mount of Olives" by their prophet Orson Hyde in 1841, in which he envisioned the redemption of the Jewish people. It was here that the Mormons began building their university in 1980. It can be reached by way of a special road leading down from the Hebrew University campus on Mount Scopus, or alternatively, by taking a side road leading from Ben Adayya Road.

THE TOUR

1. Viri Galilaei Visits by arrangement with the Greek Orthodox Patriarchate. The steep Shmuel Ben Adayya Road to the Mount of Olives reaches the crossroads at the top of the ridge, where our tour begins. To the left (to the north) we can see the pointed square tower of the Augusta Victoria hospital, with its grey slate roof. The building is named after the wife of Kaiser Wilhelm II of Germany, who built it in 1898 as a hospice for German pilgrims. During World War I it served as headquarters of General Pasha, the Ottoman military governor, and after the British conquest of Jerusalem it became the residence of the British High Commissioner from 1920 to 1925, and as a British military

Shrine of the Ascension at Viri Galilaei.

Augusta Victoria Hospital.

hospital during World War II. In 1949 the building served as an UNRWA hospital. Today it accommodates an Arab hospital supported by the World Lutheran organization.

From the crossroads we turn right (to the south) along A-Tur Road. Some 250m (275 yd) further along we reach an iron gate with the Greek Orthodox Church emblem above it. Verses from the New Testament in Greek are carved into the gate posts, and the stone wall encompasses an area of approximately 250 ha (100 acres). The Arabic name for the area means "the hunter's vineyard." An inside path leads from the gate for about 100 m (100 yd) to stone buildings constructed by the Greek Orthodox church from 1894.

The name Viri Galilaei (in Latin "men of Galilee") is a reference to the description of Jesus' ascension to heaven as related in the Acts of the Apostles (1:11–12). In the Middle Ages, the site was shown to pilgrims as the place where the eleven disciples worshipped him as told in Matthew (28:16–20), and where they accepted their mission to spread his teachings throughout the world.

In the courtyard tombs dating from the Second Temple period have been found with sarcophagi bearing inscriptions in Hebrew. In 1889 a Byzantine mosaic was uncovered with an inscription in Greek: "Jesus, remember your handmaiden Susana", over which a church has been erected.

At the end of the internal road is another iron gate, which opens on to a courtyard in which there are a number of buildings. To the left of the entrance is a square bell tower and further along is a structure within which there is a lighted oil lamp marking the spot of Jesus' ascension. To the right of the entrance, stairs lead to a stone-paved courtyard. On the right is the Palm Chapel, and on the left the summer residence of the Greek Orthodox Patriarch. The chapel marks the spot where, according to legend, Mary was told of her imminent death by the Angel Gabriel, who handed her a palm branch — symbol of her entrance to heaven. The Orthodox Patriarch of Constantinople, Athenagoras, received Pope Paul VI in the residence of the Patriarch during his visit to the Holy Land in 1964.

2. Russian Church of the Ascension
Visit by arrangement with the Alexander Nievsky Church in the Old City. The church was built between 1870 and 1887 by the Russian monk Antonin Kapustin who is buried there. Today it belongs to the White Russians (the royalists who opposed the Provoslavic church in the USSR). The site is identified as the place where Jesus ascended to heaven, and the spot is marked by a round stone placed in the courtyard surrounded by an iron railing with a cross at the top. In this church, too, is the spot where the head of John the Baptist is said to have been discovered in a niche in the mosaic floor.

The belfry is six stories high and is reached by 214 steps. The view from the top is superb, encompassing the Mediterranean Sea to the west up to the Dead Sea to the east. In the courtyard are two mosaic floors — one depicts a lamb, birds, fishes and a bunch of grapes, and bears an inscription indicating that "the blessed Susana" is buried here. The second mosaic floor has 35 round and square medallions with animals (birds and bears), fruit and leaves. Nearby in a burial cave there are three burial niches with the names of the deceased. The mosaics and burial chambers are apparently from the 6th and 7th centuries.

3. Church of the Ascension Entry fee.

We continue along A-Tur Street to the corner. A gateway in the stone wall opens on to a courtyard in the center of which is a sanctuary. The site is identified in Christian tradition as the spot where Jesus ascended to heaven. Here now stands a mosque, but the various Christian denominations are permitted to celebrate the Feast of the Ascension to mark Jesus' ascent to heaven 40 days after Easter. They have allocated spaces in the court-

The Russian Church of the Ascension.

Ascension Stone with Jesus' footprint.

yard, where they set up altars. Above these, in the wall surrounding the compound, are hooks to which ribbons and flags are tied during the celebration.

The first church on this site was built in the Byzantine period, at the end of the 4th century. In the 7th century a pilgrim describes it as having two rows of pillars bearing arches, with a rotunda, and open to the sky. There is also mention of the footprint of Jesus. The church was destroyed, apparently by the Persians (614), then restored by the Patriarch Modestos (628) and it continued to exist up to the 10th century. In the 12th century the Crusaders built a church whose pillars, arches and bases of the corner posts are still extant. Following the Muslim victory led by Saladin (1187) the church was converted into a mosque. The openings between the pillars and arches were blocked up, thus forming continuous walls. A *mihrab* (Muslim prayer niche) was added and the cupola closed. The Ascension Stone with the footprint was moved from the center to the southern end beyond the *mihrab*.

The courtyard is octagonal, and in its corners are remains of pillars. The mosque in the center is also octagonal and above it is a round drum supporting a dome surmounted by a short rod. It consists of a single hall. On the right side of the floor is a rectangular-shaped stone frame containing the form of Jesus' footprint. On the southern side of the hall is the *mihrab*.

The Crusader capitals have been preserved and their decorative motifs are clear: acanthus leaves, palmettes, griffins, floral designs.

4. Pelagia Cave To the south of the Church of the Ascension are steps leading to a paved square. To the right is the Pelagia Cave, known to the Jews as the tomb of Hulda the Prophetess (II Kings, 22:20) and to the Christians as that of Pelagia the Ascetic of Antioch (5th century). In Muslim tradition this is the tomb of Rabi'a al-Addawyya (8th century). During the Middle Ages, Jews made a pilgrimage to this spot. The site has been maintained by the Muslims and is not generally open to the public.

5. Eleona Church (Pater Noster) Visiting hours: 8.30 a.m. to 11.45 a.m., 3.00 to 4.45 p.m. daily, except Sundays.

The road descending from the Church of the Ascension to the south crosses A-Sheikh Road. An iron gate in the stone fence opens on to the site we are about to visit. On the right a sign reads *Pater Noster Eleona*, and another on the left, in Hebrew, *Path for the Cohanim*. This is the road to Jericho that circumvents the Jewish cemetery. It passes by Bethphage on the Mount of Olives, referred to in the New Testament, where Jesus sent two of his disciples to fetch an ass for him to ride upon in order to make his entrance into Jerusalem amid waving palms (Matthew 21:1–16, Mark 11:1–11). It is from the church built on this spot that the procession starts out on Palm Sunday, following the path which was taken by Jesus.

We descend the steps to a stone-paved yard from which the steps ascend to the left (to the east) to a platform upon which is an altar with a palm tree behind it. In 1920 the French government (owner of the site) began to build the Church of the Sacred Heart over the grotto in which Jesus assembled his disciples and taught them the Pater Noster prayer — the Lord's Prayer (Luke 11:1–4). The building was not completed because of a lack of sufficient funds. Beneath are two grottoes: one where Jesus "revealed to his disciples inscrutable mysteries," and another called the Grotto of the Credo. To the left of the entrance is inscribed the Lord's Prayer in Hebrew and Aramaic (the language used in the Holy Land in the time of Jesus). Here was the crypt of the splendid Church of Eleona (Greek for "olives") erected in the 4th century by Emperor Constantine. It was one of the three churches Constantine ordered to be built in the Holy Land (the Church of the Nativity in Bethlehem, the Church of the Holy Sepulcher and the Eleona Church in Jerusalem).

Restoration of the remains have produced a 30 m (95 ft) long basilica with an atrium, a magnificent entrance gate and an ornate portico. The church was destroyed by the Persians in 614. The crypt was restored in 1927. In the Grotto of the Credo a burial cave was found containing niches

Eleona (Pater Noster) Church. (right) The Lord's Prayer in 82 languages on the walls of the cloister.

THE MOUNT OF OLIVES

View from the Moriah Observation Point with the Temple Mount Esplanade in the center.

in which nine priests were buried between the 8th and 10th century. The magnificent burial place referred to in 4th-century Christian sources has not yet been discovered.

The Crusaders built a small chapel at the site of the Constantine basilica, but it was destroyed by Saladin. In 1868 the land was purchased by the French Princesse de la Tour d'Auvergne who had the present church built, as well as the nearby Carmelite Convent. She herself lived on the site for eight years in a chalet brought from France.

A staircase leads us to the cloister whose high ceiling consists of crossed arches resting on pilasters engaged in the walls. The structure is modeled on a monastery in Pisa, Italy. The Lord's Prayer is inscribed on mosaic tiles in 82 languages (including Braille on metal) on the walls. In the corner is a marble sarcophagus with the sculpted figure of the Princess. She died in Italy but requested to be buried at the Pater Noster, and her remains were brought here in 1957. The Carmelite Convent houses 20 nuns and includes the church and the belfry tower; it is closed to visitors.

6. Moriah Observation Point We continue south on the main road to the square below the Intercontinental Hotel, built on the southern peak of the Mount of Olives and recognizable by its colonnaded facade. It was constructed during the years of Jordanian rule and belongs to the Pan American company in the USA. The Jewish cemetery borders the hotel grounds to the south and west.

The summit of the Mount of Olives is connected with a legend that the Divine Presence hovered over this spot ever since the Temple was destroyed.

From the square at the top of the cemetery there is a panoramic view of the Temple Mount esplanade and of the Old and the New City. To the right, on the slope of the Mount of Olives, is the Dominus Flevit Church and below it are the golden onion domes of the Church of Mary Magadalene. At the bottom of the hill to the left is the Monument of Absalom. In front of us is the western side of the Temple Mount whose slopes reach the Kidron valley. We can see the entire extent of the eastern city wall and in the center the golden Dome of the Rock. At the eastern extremity of the Temple Mount is the black dome of the El Aksa

Mosque. The double Gate of Mercy stands out in the eastern wall, and at the corner where it joins the southern wall it rises to 24 m (79 ft). We can also see the archaeological excavations that have been carried out below the southern wall, with its Second Temple period steps. At the left, to the south, are the slopes of the hill on which is David's City. We can discern part of Area G excavations. Ha-Ophel Road, which leads into Hashalom Road, leads up to Mount Zion and for part of the way runs parallel to the southern city wall. Within the Old City we can make out the domes of the Church of the Holy Sepulcher, the buildings of the restored Jewish Quarter and the arch of the Hurva Synagogue. In the Christian Quarter we can see the square tower of the Lutheran Church, to the north of the clock tower of the Franciscan Monastery, and to the south the Latin Patriarchate tower. The Tower of David — the minaret of the mosque in the Citadel — can be seen to the south.

In the New City we can make out the Rockefeller Museum to the north of the city wall, with its white stone octagonal tower. To the west is the Notre Dame de France hostel, with its twin round turrets. Continuing to look in a westerly direction, we see the black dome of the Ethiopian Church, the green domes of the cathedral in the Russian Compound, and the Schneller Compound clock tower. On the horizon to the south, the dome of Heichal Shlomo Synagogue, the Y.M.C.A. tower and the tower of the Dormition Abbey on Mount Zion can be seen. The new high-rise buildings stand out on the Jerusalem skyline: the Hilton Hotel, the City Tower, the Clal Center, the Plaza Hotel. The crests of the Jerusalem hills can be seen to the west. On the southern horizon are Talpiot, Gilo and East Talpiot; to the east, the inclines of the Judean Desert, the Dead Sea and the mountains of Moab.

7. The Jewish Cemetery The large Jewish cemetery, which extends over the entire southern expanse of the western

(top) The Jewish Cemetery.
(center) Restored tombstones.
(bottom) Entrance to Tombs of the Prophets.

slope of the Mount of Olives, began to fulfill this function from the 15th century. The area was found suitable for this purpose because of a number of factors: the steep slope is unsuitable for building purposes and the land was relatively inexpensive. In addition, the soft rock is easily dug.

The Mount of Olives has been sanctified by popular tradition according to which the resurrection of the dead will begin here. Jews brought soil from the Mount of Olives to the Diaspora and poured it into the graves of their dead to symbolize their proximity to Jerusalem when the time comes for their resurrection with the coming of the Messiah.

Today, there are some seventy thousand graves of Jerusalemites, and of Jews who came to live in the city in their old age with the express purpose of being buried in Jerusalem. During the 19 years of Jordanian rule (1948–1967) the Jerusalem-Jericho road was built over the graves. Gravestones were smashed, many were unprooted, and others were used for building. After 1967 Jews were buried there once again, the section of the Jericho Road was closed and the graves below it were transferred elsewhere.

We enter the cemetery from the square. To the right is the sign of the Jerusalem Hevra Kadisha (Burial Society). We go down a path, turn right down steps along a paved path till we reach a high square monument. The inscription details the desecration of the graves by the Jordanians in 1948, the restoration of the cemetery, the gathering of the scattered remains and their reburial in a common grave in 1967.

To the west the path leads to a lower section in which are graves from the British Mandatory period up to the establishment of the State in 1948. On the western fence is a large plaque with the Hebrew date 5708 (1948), a *menorah* and the Star of David, which marks the section where the first victims in Jerusalem of the War of Independence were buried. The lowest sections reaching to Jericho Road are quite ancient.

We return along the main road and descend the steps into the valley and turn left into a courtyard.

8. Tombs of the Prophets We enter through a gate under a sign "Tombs of the Prophets — Haggai and Zechariah". In the courtyard is the house of the custodian who has the keys to the tomb (torches can be hired from him). The tomb is open to visitors on weekdays, during daylight hours. We descend the stone steps to the burial chamber where burial niches were cut in the rock in the Byzantine period (4th–5th centuries). Three other burial chambers date to the Second Temple period. A Jewish tradition from the Middle Ages holds this to be the burial places of the prophets Haggai, Zechariah and Malachi.

We go down more steps to a round chamber, into which light filters from an opening in the roof. Three openings lead to passages ending in a semicircular tunnel with six burial niches. Four further passages lead to a similar tunnel, with twenty burial niches hewn out of the rock. We go down steps to three Second-Temple-period chambers, purported to be the tombs of the prophets Haggai and Zechariah. Inscriptions in Greek found in the burial niches bear witness to the fact that rich pilgrims were buried here, and list the names of many of them.

9. War Monument A sign at the side of the main road points to the steps leading down to a wide path below the Tombs of the Prophets. Here are buried in a common grave the soldiers and civilians who were killed in the Old City during the War of Independence in 1948. This is a fenced-off military burial site surrounded by cedar trees opened to visitors on Memorial Day only. The names of the fallen are inscribed on the tombstone.

10. Dominius Flevit Church Visiting hours 8.00–11.00 a.m. and 3.00–5.00 p.m. daily. We continue down the path along which, according to tradition, Jesus descended from the Mount of Olives. On the left is the Jewish cemetery and on the right a fence enclosing the area. An iron gate opens onto a garden with olive, pine and cypress trees. Excavations were carried out here from 1953 to 1955 by the Franciscans, who uncovered some 20 burial chambers dated to the Second Temple period, and 38 pit graves of the Byzantine period. A grave dating to the Canaanite period was found to the southwest of the church. A large number of ossuaries, and 7 sarcophagi were uncovered, some decorated with floral and vine motifs. The inscriptions are in Aramaic, Hebrew and Greek, including many familiar names as well as less well-known names. The inscription led the archaeologists to conclude that this was a Jewish-Christian burial site.

We continue to the church building, a striking landmark, recognizable from afar by its tear-shaped dome, recalling how Jesus contemplated the beautiful city from this spot and wept and lamented its future destruction (Luke 19:41–44). The dome is divided into four sections by two intersecting white stripes. The four walls are vaulted and at the tip of the dome a turret with windows is topped by a cross. There are four pillars at the corners of the church and an arched apse extends from each wall, the four apses forming a cross. The church was built in 1954 by the Italian architect Antonio Barluzzi who built many church institutions throughout the Holy Land. The Franciscans built the modern church on the ruins of a Byzantine church. The apses in both churches — the ancient and the modern — face towards the west in the direction of the Temple area. Over the altar is an ornamented window,

Dominus Flevit Church.

through which can be seen the Old City and the Temple area. At the entrance to the church are the remains of the mosaic floor of the Byzantine church discovered in 1954. In the floor is a rhombus shape with intersecting circles; drawings of fruit, leaves, flowers and a fish divided into two decorate the floor, and a Greek inscription. To the south and east of the mosaic floor, the foundations of the Byzantine monastery can be seen, as well as restored columns, a cistern, a wine press and other artefacts. The Muslim conquerors turned the Byzantine Church into the Al-Mansuryya Mosque (The Mosque of the Victorious), which was destroyed (perhaps by the Crusaders) and its remain disappeared until the Franciscans bought the land and built the small church. During the construction work a small pond with a mosaic including a cross and other decorations were discovered near the Byzantine monastery. The mosaic was transferred to the Museum of the Flagellation on the Via Dolorosa. In 1900 the heart of a Scottish nobleman, the Marquis of Bute, was buried near the small monastery as requested in his last will and testament.

11. Church of Mary Magdalene We continue to descend the steep path along the stone fence until we reach on the right the entrance to the grounds of the Russian convent and church named after Mary Magdalene. It is open to visitors on Tuesday and Wednesday, 9.00 a.m. to 12.00 a.m., and 2.00 to 4.00 p.m. Entry fee.

The church's seven golden onion domes are one of the most impressive views Jerusalem offers. Each golden dome is surmounted by a cross ending in arrow-like points, and a diagonal bar, which symbolizes the Resurrection.

In the beautifully landscaped monastery garden, are three interesting spots: the remains of an ancient flight of steps, perhaps the 537 steps that led down from the Mount of Olives to the Kidron Valley, described in 9th-century Latin documents; the rock upon which the belt of the garment worn by the Virgin Mary fell before she ascended to heaven, and the rock from which Mary Magadalene saw Stephen being stoned in the Kidron Valley.

The church was built in the Russian Muscovite architectural style of the 17th century by Czar Alexander III in 1885, in memory of his mother Maria Alexandrova and dedicated to Mary Magdalene, the name-saint of the Czar's mother. The Duke Sergei and his wife (sister of Alexander III) Elizabeth Feodorova were present at the dedication ceremony. She met with a violent death during the Russian revolution in 1917. Her remains were smuggled out of Russia through China in 1921 and buried in the church's crypt.

The interior of the church is decorated with paintings by famous 19th-century Russian artists, such as Alexander Ivanoff, whose "Valley of Jehoshaphat" can be seen here.

A few nuns belonging to the White Russian church live in the nearby convent.

12. Gethsemane — Church of the Agony Visiting hours 8.00 a.m.–12.00 a.m. and 2.30–6.00 p.m. daily (winter 2.30–5.00 p.m. only). At the foot of the Russian Compound rises the Church of the Agony, known also as the Church of All Nations, among the trees of the Garden of Gethsemane. In ancient times this was the site of an oil press for the olives grown nearby, as its Hebrew name — *Gat Shemanim*, meaning oil press — indicates. Some of the olive trees here may be 400 years old. Here Jesus was wont to sit with his disciples. It was here that he came with them to pray after his last supper on the night of Passover, and here he received Judas' "kiss of betrayal" and was then led to prison by the Roman guards (Matthew 26:47ff; Luke 22:39ff; Mark 14:32ff).

Church of Mary Magdalene.

The so-called pillar of Judas' kiss.

The site was first consecrated by the early Byzantine Christians and traces of a 5th-century church can still be seen. It was destroyed and a second one was built on the site by the Crusaders in the 12th century, only to be destroyed by the Muslim conquerors. The present church was built in 1919 and owes its designation to the fact that men of all nations contributed to its construction. Its design is that of the Byzantine basilica over which it was built. In the center is the Rock of Agony, on which Jesus prayed, fenced off by a railing shaped like a thorn crown donated by the Catholic community of Australia. The brown and purple stained-windows and the walls and ceiling painted in dark blue create a melancholy atmosphere in the church. Sections of mosaic from the Byzantine church have been incorporated in the mosaic floor. The modern mosaics on

The Church of the Agony.

View of Gethsemane.

the walls depict Jesus' last moments before and after his betrayal. One of these is due to contributions from Ireland. The roof consists of a dozen cupolas decorated with the emblems of the Catholic churches which contributed to the cost of the building: Germany, USA, Argentina, Brazil, Chile, Mexico, Italy, France, Spain, England, Belgium and Canada.

We leave the church and turn west to have a good view of the church facade: four pillars supporting three arches, surmounted by a brilliant mosaic depicting Jesus as the link between Man and his Creator, with the whole of humanity raising their eyes to him in hope. Above his head appear the Greek letters Alpha and Omega as it is said in Revelation 1:8: "I am Alpha and Omega, the beginning and the ending, saith the Lord." On each pillar stands the statue of one of the Evangelists, each holding an open book in his hands.

13. Grotto of Gethsemane Open to visitors 8.30–12.00 a.m. and 2.30–5.00 p.m.; Sun. and Thur. 2.30–3.30 p.m. From the junction on Jericho Road, north of the Church of the Agony, we go down a paved path to a gate above which is a Franciscan cross and the name Gethsemane surmounted by a sign with the word "Crypta" and the Latin inscription: "Then cometh Jesus with them unto a place called Gethsemane, and saith unto the disciples, Sit ye here, while I go and pray yonder." (Matthew 26:36.) We enter a burial cave, hewn out of the rock in the Byzantine period and also used for burial in Crusader times, now converted into a chapel.

The grotto has been the property of the Franciscans since 1392. The grotto underwent repairs in 1955, and during the excavations ancient sections of the burial cave were uncovered. To the right of the present entrance an ancient opening to the burial cave was found which joined it to what is said to be Mary's tomb. At the eastern end is a square area above which the new central altar has been placed. The central altar is dedicated to Jesus' prayer, the southern one to the kiss of betrayal and the northern one to Mary's assumption to heaven. To its right is an alcove within which are the remains of an ancient wine press. To the left are remains of a fresco and a Crusader inscription. To right of the entrance is a cistern which served as an ancient tomb. At the southern end is a small cave used as a prayer corner for visitors.

14. Church of the Assumption The church is partly below the level of the road in the lowest part of the Kidron valley, known as the Valley of Jehoshaphat. We descend the steps north of Jericho Road, or walk along the path from Gethsemane. The church is from Crusader times and is built in the Romanesque style. The façade is to the north of a paved courtyard which can be reached by steps descending from the southeast. In the southwestern corner of the square is a rainwater conduit flowing into the Kidron valley. Below the courtyard is a giant cistern built in the Crusader period, and its ceiling constitutes the floor of the square, supported by 143 pillars.

We reach the entrance of the church by mounting a few steps which are a later addition and were built to prevent flood water running into the church. Above the entrance are a number of pointed arches surmounted by a large arch. Pillars support the arches on both sides of the entrance. We descend 48 steps in a dark, vaulted passageway inside the church. To the right we see the blocked entrance of a passage leading to the Gethsemane Grotto. About half-way down, also on the right, is a niche with a small chapel dedicated to the Virgin's parents, Joachim and Anne. In this niche the Crusader queen Melisende was buried in 1661. On the left is another niche with a chapel dedicated to St. Joseph. At the bottom of the steps is a wide hall. The original church on this site was built in the time of the Byzantine Emperor Theodosius I, in the 4th century, on the spot where Mary is believed to have been buried. It was destroyed and rebuilt a number of times during the Byzantine Crusader periods. According to Christian tradition, Mary is believed to have been buried here, after her remains had been brought from Mount Zion, and was assumed to Heaven from her burial place. To the left is an apse with a Coptic altar and to the right stands the most important structure in the church — a shrine allegedly housing the tomb of Mary. The shrine is richly decorated with icons, candlesticks and flowers while the interior of the tomb is quite bare, and the ceiling above is open to the sky; there is a stone bench on which Mary's body was laid. Next to the shrine is an altar shared by the Armenians and the Syrians.

The architectural design of the church closely resembles that of the Holy Sepulcher. The present church is only part of the original magnificent Crusader basilica described by pilgrims from that period. In the wall to the south of the tomb is a *mihrab* where Muslims pray.

15. Tomb of Mujir ed-Din South of the Church of Assumption Square and above it at the side of the road is a stone structure enclosed by an iron fence. The structure has pillars in its four corners supporting decorated arches, capped by a shell-like cupola atop an octagonal turret with a crescent. This marks the grave of Mujir ed-Din el-Hanbali, a 15th-century Jerusalem jurist renowned for his scholarly works on Jerusalem and Hebron. The tomb was erected by Jordanian government in the 1950s.

16. Church of St Stephen To the west of Jericho Road at the corner of HaOphel Road, is the new Greek Orthodox Church dedicated to St Stephen, the first Christian martyr who, according to one tradition, was stoned outside the walls of Jerusalem (Acts 7:59) beside the Kidron valley. This tradition places the stoning near the Church of St Etienne in Nablus Road (see tour No.11: From the Tombs of the Kings to the Cave of Zechariah).

17. Paratroopers' Memorial On the eastern sidewalk of Jericho Road is an iron sculpture in the form of an eagle's wings, one raised in flight and the other broken. The monument was erected after the Six Day War as a memorial to five men of a patrol who were killed on the bridge over the Kidron valley on 7th June 1967, when the Paratroopers' Brigade was preparing to attack Augusta Victoria on the Mount of Olives.

Facade of the Church of the Assumption.

Bells of the church and Tomb of Mujir ed-Din.

TOUR No. 13

THE HINNOM VALLEY

Details of tour: The subject of this tour is the two southern sections of the Hinnom Valley: the portion which passes through the New City, and the final portion of the valley which contains ancient tombs. This part of the walk is along a path above the cliffs bordering the valley.
Distance covered: approx. 2 km (1½ miles)
Time: approx. 4 hours (including about two hours visiting artists' studios and the Cinematheque)
Transportation: Buses No 3, 13, 19, 20, 30, 80, and 99 to the Jaffa Gate; No 76 from En Rogel to Givat Hananya and No 5, 6, 7, 8, and 21 from Derech Hevron (Hebron Road). Parking lots near the Jaffa Gate for private vehicles
Starting point: Mamilla Mall
End of tour: Monastery of St. Onuphrius
The Sites: 1. Mamilla Mall; 2. Huzot Hayozer (Artisans' Quarter); 3. Sultan's Pool; 4. Cinematheque; 5. Ancient tombs; 6. The Karaite cemetery; 7. Later tombs; 8. Monastery of St. Onuphrius.

FOREWORD

The 3-kilometer long (2 mi) Hinnom Valley is one of the main offshoots of the Kidron Valley. The valley begins near the Mahaneh Yehuda neighborhood in the New City and continues its descent along Jaffa Road via the Nahalat Shiva neighborhood, the Mamilla Pool and the Sultan's Pool. From the Sultan's Pool, the last section of the valley curves eastward and drops sharply, forming a deep ravine which drains into the Kidron Valley near En Rogel. This last section of the Hinnom Valley delimits the western hill of the Old City and Mount Zion.

The first reference to the "Valley of the Son of Hinnom" in the Bible is in the Book of Joshua (15:8; 18:16), where it is mentioned as part of the border of the territories of the tribes of Judah and Benjamin. The origin of the name of the valley is uncertain. It seems to be a reasonable hypothesis that the name is derived from the name of the Canaanite owner of the land. In the days of the Kingdom of Judah, the Valley of Hinnom is described as being the place of worship of the Canaanite god Moloch. Altars for the sacrifice of children — "the altars of Tophet" — were built in the valley, and it was called "the vale of slaughter" by the prophet Jeremiah (7:31). The use of the name "Gehenna" (Ge-Hinnom, Valley of Hinnom) as referring to the abode of the wicked appeared in the Second Temple period, and has been adopted by all European languages and by Arabic as synonymous with hell.

The Valley of Hinnom is cited in the Book of Jeremiah as being the location of "the graves of the common people" (Jer. 26:23). Jeremiah's prophecy about the Vale of Slaughter is mentioned in the New Testament (Matthew 27:9), which identifies the valley as being the location of "the field of blood" (or the potter's field) where Judas Iscariot was buried (Matthew 27:1–9). Elsewhere in the New Testament, the place is called "Acel dama which is the field of blood" (Acts 1:19). The "field of blood" however, is traditionally located at the lower end of the Hinnom Valley, the site of a Christian cemetery which was in use from the Byzantine period until the 19th century.

THE TOUR

1. Mamilla Mall Mamilla Street runs along the bottom of the Hinnom Valley. After the new Rehov HaEmek (Valley

THE HINNOM VALLEY

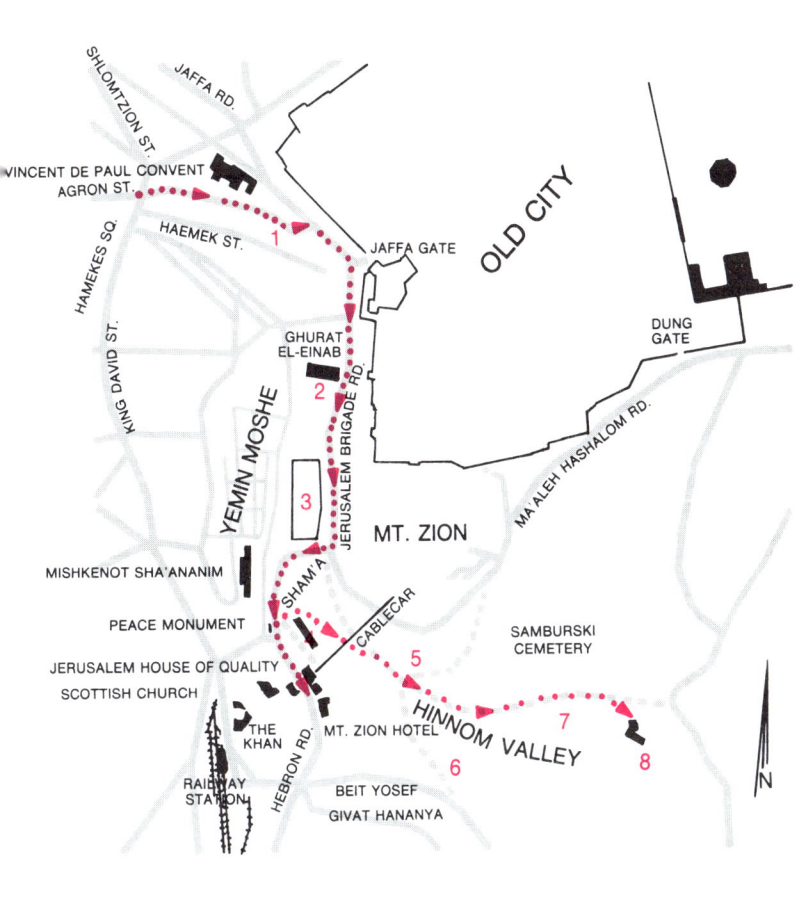

Map of the tour.

Street) is paved for vehicles, the existing Mamilla Street will be turned into a pedestrian mall, and some of the old buildings in the area will be preserved.

The remains of a Herodian aqueduct, which brought water from what is now the Mamilla Pool to the Pool of the Towers in the Old City, were uncovered in the 19th century along the northern side of the Mall. The Pool of the Towers, in the Christian Quarter, is now mistakenly known as Hezekiah's Pool.

Most of the older buildings along the street were built in the 19th century by wealthy Arabs as residences, offices and stores. By the end of the 19th century and during the British Mandate period, Mamilla street was a business district. The two-storey building at number 18 was the home of the Stern family. The structure was built as a family residence and store by the head of a family, who emigrated here from Germany in the 1890s. It was here that Theodore Herzl stayed during his visit to Jerusalem in 1898 and the room where he slept has been preserved as it was then.

The large building on the north side of the street is the Convent of Saint Vincent

Herzl's room in the Stern house.

Convent of St Vincent de Paul.

de Paul. This was the very first building on the street, erected in the year 1886. It is named after the 17th-century French priest who founded the Order of the Daughters of Charity and of the Lazarists. The building contains an orphanage, an old-age home, and a shelter for the handicapped, the mentally ill and the blind. The facade of the convent faces the mall. The neo-classical architectural style of the convent and church was popular in France in the 19th century. In front of the convent, facing the mall, is a row of shops owned by the convent. The eastern end of the street is close to the Jaffa Gate. From here, we descend to the Mitchell Garden, which was, before 1967, a no-man's-land of bombed-out buildings and barbed wire.

2. Huzot Hayozer (Artisans' Quarter) The stepped stone buildings in the Mitchell Garden at the bottom of the Hinnom Valley serve as artists' and craftsmen's studios and galleries. The houses, which were destroyed in the 1948 War of Independence, have been reconstructed, and in 1971 they were turned into an artists' colony which is open to the public on weekdays. In the studios, we can see the artists at work. Every summer an Arts Festival is held here. On the flat roof of the highest building, there is a cafe which commands a magnificent view of the entire area.

These buildings are the remains of a neighborhood, built in the year 1892 by Jews from the Old City. It had about 50 houses and a synagogue. It extended southward and contained two flour mills. The inhabitants fled during the War of Independence, the houses were destroyed, and the area was included in the no-man's-land between Israel and Jordan according to the terms of the 1948 ceasefire agreement.

3. Sultan's Pool The valley between the neighborhood of Yemin Moshe and Hebron Road and the Jerusalem Brigade Road formed a pool for the collection of runoff from winter rains, until the 1967 Six-Day War. Hebron Road passes over a dam which was built across the valley. It is believed that this pool is actually the Snake Pool from the days of the Second Temple, which is mentioned by Josephus. The Herodian low level aqueduct, which carried water from Solomon's Pools, surrounds the pool on its west, north and east sides. Sections of this aqueduct can still be seen in the area. In the Crusader period, the pool was called Lacus Germani (the Pool of Germanus). Later, Christian pilgrims called it the Pool of Bathsheba, where supposedly King David saw Bathsheba bathing. The pool as it presently exists was built by the Mameluke Sultan Barkuk, at the end of the 14th century, although the Arabic name of the pool, Birket es-Sultan, refers to Suleiman the

Magnificent, builder of the walls of Jerusalem, who renovated the pool and built a *sabil* (fountain) on the dam across the valley, above which he placed an inscription bearing his name and the year (which corresponds to 1536).

The pool is 170 m (558 ft) long, 67 m (220 ft) wide, and up to 12 m (39 ft) deep, and the height of the dam is 15 m (49 ft). Until the end of the British Mandate, a cattle market was held in the northern end of the pool, which was dry most of the year. Several tombs from the First Temple period are cut in the rock on the eastern side of Jerusalem Brigade Road, to the east of the pool. The tombs are now sealed up.

After the reunification of Jerusalem in 1967, the conversion of the pool into an amphitheater for outdoor performances was initiated by the Jerusalem Foundation. Grass was planted for audiences to sit on, and a stone stage was built, upon which an acoustic shell is set up during concerts. The spotlit Old City walls serve as a natural backdrop to the stage.

Details on the adjacent neighborhoods, Mishkenot Sha'ananim and Yemin Moshe, can be found in Tour 14.

4. Cinematheque Before the War of Independence of 1948, a small neighborhood — Sha'arei Zion (the Gates of Zion) — stood to the south of the dam of the Sultan's Pool, in the continuation of the valley. The neighborhood was founded in 1900 by a group of Jewish craftsmen who had lived in the Old City. In the 1920s the settlement numbered 85 families. During the War of Independence, the neighborhood was finally abandoned, and many of the houses were destroyed.

Several buildings from the ruined neighborhood have been reconstructed as cultural and artistic institutions. In 1979, the **Youth Music Center** of Jerusalem was established in several houses on the northern slope of the valley. This institution, funded by the trumpet player Herb Alpert, includes practice rooms and concert halls for rehearsals and performances. The Cinematheque and the Israeli Film Archives were established in reconstructed houses on the southern slope of the valley in 1981. We descend by

The Sultan's Pool.

a step path from Hebron Road to the cafe balcony which overlooks the valley. The Cinematheque houses the largest film archives in Israel, a library and 2 cinemas in several interconnected buildings.

We descend from the Cinematheque to the Wolfsohn Gardens below, and from there ascend a path on the southern slope of the valley. Looking up, we can see, suspended in the air above us, a cable to which a small trolley is attached. This is the manually-operated cablecar, which was run by pulleys. During the War of Independence the cablecar was used to carry equipment, supplies and ammunition to Mount Zion, and wounded soldiers were sent back in return. The cablecar was operated only under the cover of darkness to hide it from the eyes of the Jordanian Legion soldiers stationed on outposts on the walls of the Old City. The cablecar connected St John's Ophthalmic Hospital with the courtyard of the Gobat Institute on Mount Zion.

We can visit the buildings on both sides of Hebron Road above the Cinematheque. The **St John's Ophthalmic Hospital** is now the Mount Zion Hotel, perched on the edge of the valley. The hospital was built in 1882 with the assistance of the Duke of York, who was a knight of the Order of St. John of Jerusalem, a British order which sees itself as descended from the Crusader Hospitaller Knights. The hospital played

The cablecar from Mount Zion.

an important role in curing eye diseases which were prevalent in the Holy Land by providing care free of charge.

During the War of Independence, the main building was abandoned and the hospital moved to temporary quarters in the Old City. Since 1960, the hospital has been operating from its new permanent location in Sheikh Jarrah.

Some additional sections of the low level aqueduct can be seen near the Cinematheque and the southern building of the hospital.

5. Ancient tombs The path which rises along the southern cliffs of the Hinnom Valley passes beside the openings of rock-cut burial caves. Hewn steps lead to most of the tomb entrances. The tombs were studied by many of the 19th-century investigators of Jerusalem, who found in them inscriptions and drawings. These have disappeared almost entirely, partly due to natural wear and tear, but mostly due to the quarrying of stones for building by the residents of nearby Abu Tor.

The burial caves along Jerusalem Brigade Road, on the slopes of the Hinnom Valley, and at the foot of the Scottish Church are all part of a First Temple period burial area which lay to the south and west of the city. Others are to be found to the east (in Silwan) and to the north (along Nablus Road). The burial caves can easily be explored. Most of the caves visible in this area were reused during the Byzantine period. On some of the caves we can see the remains of Greek inscriptions which were made by monks from the Hagia Zion Monastery on Mount Zion.

6. The Karaite cemetery Continuing along the path, we reach an iron gate. Steps then lead us to abandoned graves with inscriptions in Hebrew on the flat slabs. All the graves are from the 19th century. Occasionally a short prayer is engraved in the stone below the name of the deceased as well as the dates of his birth and death. This was the burial ground of the Karaite community in Jerusalem.

From here we can see the remains of another Jewish burial ground, the Samburski cemetery, on the southern slope of Mount Zion, above the cliffs on the north side of the Hinnom Valley. According to the official records, the cemetery was first used in 1842.

Above the Karaite cemetery we can see a few houses on the edge of Abu Tor. These one-storey structures with tile roofs were part of a Jewish neighborhood called Beit Yosef, founded in 1888 by a group of craftsmen who had lived in the Old City. The neighborhood had about a dozen houses in which about seventy people lived. The houses were sold to Arabs and the area was abandoned in the beginning of the 20th century.

7. Later tombs We continue along the path on the edge of the cliff. Along the way, we encounter several rock-cut burial caves, most of them from the Second Temple period. They were in secondary use during the Byzantine period, as witnessed by the fragmentary Greek inscriptions that can be seen in some of the caves. The rooms are interconnected in typical Second Temple period fashion, each room containing "shelves" on which bodies were laid out. To the north of the Monastary of St Onuphrius is a magnificent burial site called Furadis a-Rūm (the Roman Paradise). According to tradition, this cave contains the tomb of the Egyptian hermit St Onuphrius, after whom the monastery is named (see section 8 below).

Southwards, on the cliff above the monastery, are the remains of a domed subterranean structure, built in the Crusader period as a place for the mass burial of poor pilgrims. In Arabic the building is known as *sharnien*, a corruption of the French word *charnier* (charnel house). About 70 additional burial caves lie to the west, east and south of the Monastery of St. Onuphrius. These are Second Temple period tombs which were reused during the Byzantine period and later. The caves contain burial niches, shelves for laying out bodies, and, in some of them, fragments of ossuaries were discovered. The stone façades of the caves were once decorated in bas-relief, and in one place, a large round stone used for sealing the cave entrance was found. Some of the Greek inscriptions from the Byzantine period indicate a connection to the Hagia Zion Church on Mount Zion. Crosses are carved on the walls of the burial rooms. Some of the caves have been given names, such as the Cave of the Apostles, but this is a tradition which began only in the 16th century. Monks used some of the caves as dwellings.

8. Monastery of St Onuphrius We descend from the upper path to the road running through the bottom of the Hinnom Valley, which begins to the east of the *sabil* (fountain) on the bridge across the Sultan's Pool. This road connects to Siloam Road, which runs northwards to the village of Silwan, and southwards to the Abu Tor neighborhood. The Hinnom Valley joins the Kidron Valley east of the intersection.

A part of the road leads to an opening in the wall surrounding the monastery. The first buildings were constructed in 1892 by the Greek Orthodox Church. The monastery is named after the Egyptian hermit Onuphrius, who was one of the leaders of the Christian monastic movement in Sinai in the 4th century and was famous for his long beard which, it is told, constituted his sole garment. According to Christian tradition, this is the location of Aceldama (*Akeldama*, in Aramaic: "the field of blood") which was purchased by the Temple priests with the money that Judas Iscariot donated to the Temple. Because this was "blood money" earned from Judas' betrayal, it could not be used for the Temple, so the priests used the money to buy the field from a potter (Matthew 27:6–8). The monastery was built on a Second Temple period burial cave. It is believed that the niches in the burial caves contain the remains of monks killed in the year 614 during the Persian conquest of Jerusalem from the Byzantine Empire. Visits to the monastery are permitted by prior arrangement with the Greek Orthodox Patriarchate.

The face of Onuphrius, with his long beard, is carved on the lintel of the doorway leading to the church. The church is built in a magnificent Second Temple period burial cave. The stone border of the cave is decorated with carved floral designs with a cluster of grapes in the center.

Bus number 76 runs along the Siloam Road, and can take us either to Abu Tor, or to the Damascus Gate via Ophel Road and the Jerusalem-Jericho Road.

Monastery of St. Onuphrius.

Ancient burial caves in Hinnom Valley.

TOUR No. 14

THE BEGINNINGS OF THE NEW CITY

Details of tour: We will visit the first neighborhoods built outside the city walls. We begin with the first neighborhood, Mishkenot Sha'ananim, built in 1860, and end at the Russian Compound constructed in the same year. On the way we will visit other neighborhoods, among them Mahaneh Israel and Nahalat Shiva and other sites in between.
Distance covered: approx. 4 km (2½ miles)
Time: approx. 4 hours
Transportation: Buses No 5, 6, 7, 8, 18, 21
Parking lots at the windmill and the Russian Compound for private vehicles
Starting Point: The Montefiore windmill
End of Tour: Russian Compound.
The Sites: 1.Montefiore Windmill; 2.Mishkenot Sha'ananim; 3.Yemin Moshe; 4.Herod family tomb; 5.Pontifical Biblical Institute; 6.Hebrew Union College; 7.Mahaneh Israel; 8.Agron Street; 9.Mamilla Cemetery; 10.Nahalat Shiva; 11.Buildings in Jaffa Road; 12.Russian Compound.

THE TOUR

1. Montefiore windmill To the east of the junction between King David and Keren Hayesod Streets the sails of a windmill can be seen. We enter a short promenade which passes through a broad and expansive park (named after Bernard and Louis Bloomfield of Canada) and we reach a parking lot. When work was being carried out on this park in 1972, a section of the upper aqueduct which brought water from Solomon's Pools to Jerusalem was uncovered. The aqueduct was built by the Tenth Roman Legion (in the 1st Century C.E.). We go down a path and a few steps south of the parking lot and reach a hewn-out rockface. The section of the aqueduct can be seen behind an iron railing. We return to the parking lot, where a detailed map of the Mishkenot Sha'ananim and Yemin Moshe neighborhoods can be seen. To the right of the square, steps lead to an observation platform from where we can see the Hinnom Valley to the east, Mount Zion and the Old City wall to the north, and to the south Abu Tor. We can also see Hebron Road which crosses the Hinnom Valley, and its continuation — Khativat Yerushalayim (Jerusalem Brigade) Road, leading up to Jaffa Road. Immediately below is the windmill.

We go down to the windmill and turn right to a structure built to house a replica of Sir Moses Montefiore's carriage (the original was destroyed by fire in 1987). To the left of the structure is a ceramic plaque and a bench in memory of the renowned Spanish cellist Pablo Casals who visited Jerusalem on many occasions.

The windmill was constructed in 1857 by Sir Moses Montefiore and began functioning in 1860 to provide work for the needy of

Montefiore windmill.

BEGINNINGS OF THE NEW CITY

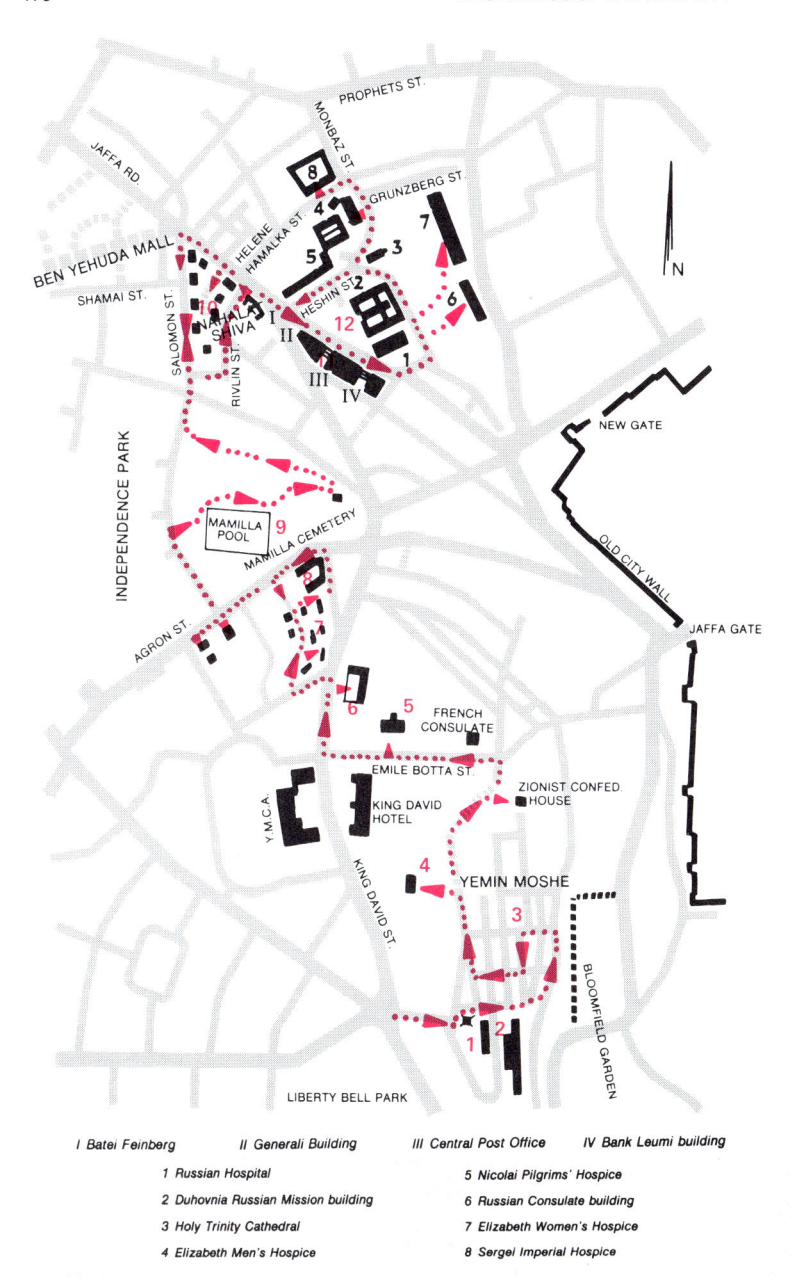

| I Batei Feinberg | II Generali Building | III Central Post Office | IV Bank Leumi building |

1. Russian Hospital
2. Duhovnia Russian Mission building
3. Holy Trinity Cathedral
4. Elizabeth Men's Hospice
5. Nicolai Pilgrims' Hospice
6. Russian Consulate building
7. Elizabeth Women's Hospice
8. Sergei Imperial Hospice

Map of the tour.

Jerusalem and to reduce the price of flour. Its working parts were sent from London to Jaffa by sea and then brought on mules and camels to Jerusalem. The windmill was operated by millers from England over a period of 25 years. This was the most advanced of the seven windmills operating in Jerusalem at that time. A stamp showing the windmill was issued in Israel in 1980 to mark its centenary. The Municipality has renovated the windmill and has set up an exhibition of photographs and documents reflecting Montefiore's lifework. It is open every day from 9.00 a.m. to 4.00 p.m., excepting Fridays when it closes at 1.00 p.m.

Moses Montefiore (1784–1885) was an English philanthropist. He made his fortune in London in banking, business and on the stock market. At the age of 40, Montefiore retired from business and devoted himself to the welfare of the Jews in England and throughout the world, and the settlement of Jews in Palestine. He visited Palestine seven times, was instrumental in the purchase of land, and the establishment of medical and educational services for the Jews. During his last visit he set up the Montefiore Welfare Fund for the construction of six neighborhoods which were named after him: Yemin Moshe, Bnei Moshe, Mazkeret Moshe, Ohel Moshe, Zikhron Moshe and Kiryat Moshe.

2. Mishkenot Sha'ananim During his fourth visit to Palestine in 1855, Montefiore came to Jerusalem bringing with him a permit from Sultan Abdul Hamid to purchase land upon which he planned to build a hospital for the poor of Jerusalem. The monies for this project were from the estate of Judah Touro, an American Jew from New Orleans who left considerable sums to be used for the welfare of the poor of Jerusalem. Montefiore was named executor of this fund. The 40,000 sq m (10 acre) area was on the hill opposite Mount Zion, above the Sultan's Pool, and was called "The vineyard of Moses and Judith as a legacy of the late Judah Touro".

Two rows of apartments called Mishkenot Sha'ananim were erected at the southern extremity of the area. This was the first neighborhood to be built outside the city walls and it was completed in 1860. The name was taken from the verse in Isaiah: "And my people shall abide in a peaceful habitation, and in secure dwellings, and in quiet resting places" (32:18).

We descend the steps in Yemin Moshe Street and turn right to the upper building which today houses the Music Center. At first the building had two synagogues, a bakery and workshops. After the nearby neighborhood of Yemin Moshe was built in 1894, the building was used to accommodate families. In 1970 the buildings were renovated by the Jerusalem Foundation and music workshops with internationally famous musicians are held here.

We continue down Yemin Moshe Street to the Mishkenot Sha'ananim restaurant (built in 1970), turn right along the path outside the new fence enclosing the lower long building (on the way we pass by a stone bench bearing a plaque in memory of Avraham Kirshenbaum, who was born in the neighborhood and fell in the War of Independence). The single-storey elongated building faces east and at the end of the flat roof there is a serrated railing similar in structure to the city wall opposite.

In the top center of the facade is a plaque detailing Judah Touro's contribution and the date, 1860, the neighborhood was built; it is also known as the Touro Housing Estate. The buildings were planned and constructed by the architect Smith,

Mishkenot Sha'ananim.

brought by Montefiore from London. He was replaced halfway through the construction by a Jewish contractor, Itzhak Rosenthal. The building consists of 28 two-room apartments and a small plot of land was allocated to each family for growing vegetables. It was most difficult to find Jews willing to live outside the city wall, despite the attractive conditions which included a high stone fence, a strong iron gate and a guard on duty at the entrance. The book of regulations drawn up by the residents reflects their concern for cleanliness of the neighborhood, for its water sources, for its security and for good neighborly relations. The building was renovated by the Jerusalem Foundation and it now serves to accommodate guests of the Jerusalem Municipality, among whom are famous artists, musicians and writers. There are 10 well-appointed, spacious apartments.

We go through the gateway in the stone fence, turn left and walk on to the balcony. Beyond the fence is an aqueduct covered with stone slabs. This is a section of the lower aqueduct built in the Herodian era through which water flowed from Solomon's Pools. It was in use up to Ottoman times, until the Turks replaced it with earthernware pipes.

We descend from the closed-in balcony, which is the roof of a cistern, to the entrance-way below. This is the opening of a tunnel dug during the War of Independence under Hebron Road, along the Hinnom Valley and up the slopes of Mount Zion. The Israeli soldiers made their way through this tunnel to bring food and ammunition to the beleaguered Jewish Quarter of the Old City. The continuation can be seen on the other side of the bridge and it ends at the Gobat School (see Tour No. 9 from Jaffa Gate to Mount Zion). From here, too, you can see the cable which stretched from the British Ophthalmic Hospital (today the Mount Zion Hotel) to the above school on Mount Zion. At night a wagon suspended from this cable brought supplies and reinforcements to the defense forces in the Jewish Quarter.

The Sultan's Pool is on the site presumed to have been the "Eye of the Crocodile Pool" (also known as the "Snake's Eye Pool") from the Second Temple period. In Crusader times it was called the Geramnus Pool. The bridge supporting the road over the Hinnom Valley was built as a dam in the 14th century by the Mameluke Sultan Barkuk. It was named for the Ottoman Sultan Suleiman, the builder of the city walls, who in 1536 built a pool for the use of travellers, which received water from the aqueduct mentioned above. The Sultan's Pool has been turned into an amphitheater where concerts are given (see Tour No. 13 of the Hinnom Valley).

3. Yemin Moshe We enter the Yemin Moshe quarter through an iron gate facing the Sultan's Pool.

On the area called "Kerem Moshe Viyehudit" (the Moses and Judith Vineyard), the Montefiore Welfare Fund built the Yemin Moshe quarter in 1892 to mark the seventh anniversary of Montefiore's death. The name was chosen from verses in the Book of Isaiah (63:11–12): "Then he remembered the days of old, Moses, and his people. . . that led them by the right hand of Moses with his glorious arm. . . to make himself an everlasting name."

One hundred and thirty houses were built with the aid of loans made available by the Montefiore Welfare Fund. Synagogues and public ovens were built, water cisterns were hewn out of the rock and trees planted. At the end of the 19th century, there were 600 residents in the

Inscription on wall at Mishkenot Sha'ananim.

neighborhood and 900 in the 1920s. The neighborhood suffered from attacks by Arabs during the 1920 riots, and during the War of Independence in 1948 it became a frontier defense post. Some of the residents left the area which seemed dangerous to them, and after the ceasefire agreement was signed with Jordan in 1949, new immigrants, mainly from Turkey, settled in the neighborhood.

After the Six Day War in 1967, the neighborhood became more attractive and was requisitioned by the Municipality and the Ministry of Housing; the residents were given alternative accommodation in other sections of Jerusalem and the East Jerusalem Development Corporation sold the houses to artists and other individuals with the proviso that when they renovated them the original character of the neighborhood be maintained.

We walk through the streets and lanes, visit the artists' galleries, the Sephardi Synagogue (in Malki Street) and the Ashkenazi Synagogue (in Pele Yo'etz Street). We end our visit of the neighborhood by going up Habrecha Street (Pool Street), pass through the iron gates to the Bloomfield Garden, walk along the stone pathway to the north to our next site.

4. Herod family tomb South of the King David Hotel (at the end of Sikra Street) within the bounds of the Bloomfield Garden, we can see a layer of dressed stones that served as the basis of a large stone structure, apparently a monument to those buried in the nearby cave which was uncovered in 1892. A large circular rolling stone is seen at the entrance of the cave, and inside, four burial chambers lead off the central chamber. Stone sarcophagi adorned with floral designs have been found here. Josephus Flavius refers to Herod's Monuments "near the pool called the Eye of the Crocodile" (*Jewish Wars*, 5:12,2). The burial cave and the area surrounding it is now the property of the Greek Orthodox Patriarchate, and one of the sarcophagi found here is on show at the Greek Orthodox Museum in the Christian Quarter. The burial cave is not open to visitors.

We continue along the path in a northeasterly direction, until we reach the Zionist Confederation Cultural Center. In this two-storey building, renovated in 1984, lectures, concerts and workshops are held, and from its cafeteria one has a beautiful view of Mount Zion, the city wall and the citadel. In Byzantine times a convent and church dedicated to St George were built on this site, and reference is found to "a monastery surrounded by vines" in Crusader times. In the 19th century, the Greek el-Hadre Church stood here and was sold to the Abdullah family who named it Abdullah House. The building served as an Arab defense post during the War of Independence in 1948. Remains of an ancient structure are seen here and the visitor can rest on a bench while taking in the breathtaking view.

We turn left to Emile Botta Street (19th-century French consul and archaeologist) and we come to the building next door to the French consulate.

Corner in Yemin Moshe.

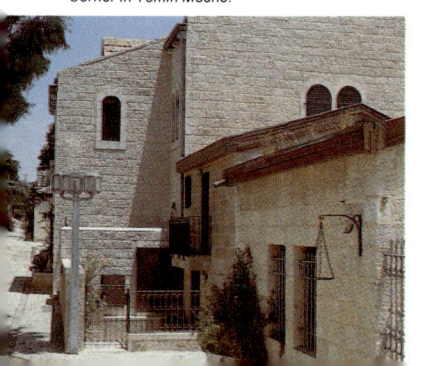

Herod family tomb.

BEGINNINGS OF THE NEW CITY

5. Pontifical Biblical Institute This three-storey rectangular building is easily recognized by the towers in the corners of its flat roof. The only Jesuit monastery in Israel, it was the first modern building in the area when it was built in 1927. Open to visitors on Mondays, Wednesdays and Fridays between 9.00 a.m. and 12.00 a.m.

The Pontifical Biblical Institute with its well-stocked library and museum is situated in this monastery. There are exhibitions of archaeological finds from digs carried out by the Institute in Palestine and Egypt, mummies and stuffed indigenous birds. The church is named after the Spanish-born founder of the Society of Jesus, Ignatius Loyola, who visited Jerusalem in the 16th century, a statue of whom is to be seen in the church.

We leave the Institute and continue along the street and turn into King David Street.

6. Hebrew Union College On the right-hand side of King David Street is the Hebrew Union College complex which houses the offices of the World Union of Progressive Judaism and the Nelson Glueck School of Biblical Archaeology which was built in 1963. The Jewish Institute of Religion was added in 1972. The complex, including the library and the Skirball Museum of Biblical Archaeology is open to visitors free of charge.

7. Mahaneh Israel Across the road from the Hebrew Union College is the Mahaneh Israel neighborhood (between Moshe Hess, David Ben-Shimon, Zamenhoff and Agron Streets). This was the second Jewish neighborhood to be built outside the Old City wall, and the first to be built at the initiative of the Jews of Jerusalem. The majority of the plots were purchased in 1864, and building continued until it was completed in 1918. The founders were Jews who immigrated from North Africa with the encouragement of the community's rabbi, David Ben-Shimon, and the buildings were funded by the residents without any assistance from outside donors. The construction of the houses is similar to that of the Old City; internal courtyards surrounded by one or two-storey houses with arched doorways and windows. The lanes are narrow and the iron gates at the entrance to the neighborhood were locked at night. In the courtyard of No.13 on Hama'aravim Lane are a synagogue and *yeshiva*, and archives of the Moghrabi community have been opened here. Some of the buildings have been renovated by individuals and institutions who have purchased these centrally-situated houses.

8. Palace Hotel Building — Agron Street At the corner of Agron and David Ben-Shimon Streets is a four-storey building, striking for its architectural style and many adornments. It was built on land owned by the Waqf (Muslim Religious Endowment) during 1927–1929, and with monies provided by the Supreme Arab Council, headed by Hadj Amin Husseini. The building was erected as a hotel (the Palace Hotel) for Muslim visitors. The construction work was carried out by hundreds of Arab and Jewish laborers, under

Pontifical Biblical Institute.

Mahaneh Israel.

TOUR No. 14

The Palace Hotel building.

the watchful eye of a Christian Arab and two Jewish contractors; the architect was Turkish. At the front corner is a wide entrance, surmounted by wide balconies. At the top of the facade is an inscription in Arabic which refers to the Supreme Arab Council and the year the hotel was built —1929. The building served as a hotel and offices, and as the venue of Royal British Commissions (the Peel Commission in 1936 — the first to propose the partition of Palestine between Jews and Arabs). The offices of the Ministry of Commerce and Industry have been housed here since the establishment of the State of Israel.

We walk up Agron Street to a building on the southern side enclosed by a stone fence. This is the French Lazarist Convent known as Isaiah House. The facade of the building is capped by a gable in which is a clock, and underneath it a statue of St Vincent de Paul stands in a niche. Designed by Conrad Schick, it was built in 1866 as a home for lepers by Protestant Germans with funds provided by a German nobleman. After the construction of a new Leper Home north of the German Colony (see Tour no. 27), this building became a boarding-house, and in 1904 was sold to the Lazarists after which a third floor and additional wing were added.

At 16–18 Agron Street is the United States Consulate, with its high stone wall surrounding the spacious grounds of the consulate building built by the German Lutheran missionary P. Vester as a private dwelling in 1868. The U.S. government bought the building after the First World War, added a third storey and moved its consular offices from the Street of the Prophets.

9. Mamilla Cemetery On the northern side of Agron Street, within the confines of Independence Park is the Mamilla Muslim cemetery. It was apparently named after a Christian saint buried here in the Byzantine period, but has served as a Muslim cemetery from the 13th century until 1927. In the Middle Ages governors, jurists and Muslim religious functionaries were buried here. In the northern section of the cemetery is the tomb of the Mameluke Emir Aidugdai, the governor of Safed (who built the gate to the bathhouse on Haram esh-Sharif; see the Temple Mount tour). The tomb has a rounded dome supported by a drum. Above the apertures and entrance are adorned arches and the inscription above the entrance recalls the governor's name and date of his death — 1289. To the west of the Mamilla Pool is a similar tomb which is Crusader, and it is presumed that additional Crusader graves existed in the area.

The **Mamilla Pool** is a water reservoir dug in Herodian times on the slope of the Hinnom Valley to provide water for the pools inside the city through a pottery conduit which was in use up to Mandatory times (see Tour No. 7 of the Christian Quarter). This pool is 97m (318 ft) long, 65m (213 ft) wide, 6.6m (21½ ft) deep, with a capacity of 37,000 cu m (145,000 cu ft). The pool has been renovated a number of times, the last during the British Mandate. It provided vital water reserves for the Jewish residents of Jerusalem during the War of Independence. After the establishment of the State, the Jerusalem Municipality developed Independence Park into the main park in central Jerusalem with its lawns and play areas, planted with shrubs and pine, cypress, olive, carob, cedar and other trees.

In the western section of the park, near the Plaza Hotel, a cave dating to the Middle Ages, called the **Lion's Cave**, has been found. In 614 many Christians were killed by the Persians and, says the legend, their bodies were dragged here by a kind lion who guarded the entrance.

We leave the park and cross over Hillel Street to Salomon Street, the main street of Nahalat Shiva.

10. Nahalat Shiva This was the third neighborhood to be established outside the city walls between Jaffa Road, Hillel and Rivlin Streets — opposite the Russian Compound (see section 12 below). The land was purchased in 1869 by seven Jewish residents of the Old City. The land, extending over an area of 15 dunams (3½ acres) was divided into long equal strips between Jaffa Road to the north and the Mamilla cemetery to the south. Each of the seven paid an additional amount towards the cost of constructing the first house which was allocated by lottery. Joseph Rivlin won it, and his was the only family to live in the area between 1869 and 1872. After they completed their houses in 1872, the founders sold the remainder of the 42 plots, and dwellings, synagogues, shops and cafes were built. The neighborhood quickly developed, until on the eve of World War I there were about 100 houses with 860 residents. Three wide lanes and many narrow ones were laid down between the houses. External stairways were built, wells dug in the courtyards and vegetable gardens laid out.

We walk through the lanes, look at the old houses and the recently-opened shops and coffee shops that have sprung up throughout the neighborhood. At the corner of Rivlin Street and Jaffa Road is Beit Yoel, a modern building, and on its outer wall a copper plaque recalls the memory of the seven founders of the neighborhood.

11. Jaffa Road We continue along Jaffa Road to the east and visit four buildings in the section opposite the Russian Compound. **Batei Feingold** — An elongated two-storey building opposite Beit Yoel. It was built in 1895 by David Feingold, who also built a hotel in Jaffa Road. Shops, workshops, offices and various institutions operated in the building — including the Hebrew newspaper "Doar Hayom", the first cinema in Jerusalem, the Hamashbir cooperative store, the Histadrut loan fund, the labor exchange, the workers' restaurant and a cultural hall. The building has a tiled roof, protruding window frames and arched entrances; its facade faces Jaffa Road and its western wing Rivlin Street. There are two entrances from Jaffa Road opening onto courtyards between its three wings.

The Generali Building Situated on the corner of Jaffa Road and Queen Shlomtzion Street is a five-storey building on whose roof is a sculpture of a winged lion and in large letters the name of the Italian insurance company for whom it was

House in Nahalat Shiva.

The Generali Building.

constructed in 1934. The building incorporates modern and neo-classical styles. The winged lion, the symbol of the insurance company, is also the symbol of the town of Venice. During the last years of the British Mandate the building was part of the British security zone. Since the establishment of the State, it has housed the regional offices of the Ministries of Interior and Finance, and the Ministry of Transport's meteorological station.

The Central Post Office — Next door to the Generali building, the Central Post Office was built between the years 1923 and 1937 according to the plans of the British architect Harrison (who also planned the Rockefeller Museum, the High Commissioner's residence and the Government Printing Center). This is a simple-style four-storey bulding with a central section, two wings and two main entrances from Jaffa Road. The rear of the building on Koresh Street is the workers' entrance as well as the entrance to the parcel section. The mural inside is the work of the Israeli artist A. Ofek in 1972 on the theme "From Exile to Redemption".

Bank Leumi building The Bank Leumi (formerly the Anglo-Palestine Bank) building next to the Post Office was constructed between the years 1936 to 1939 according to plans drawn up by the Jewish architect Mendelsohn. Both the building and the windows are rectangular with round windows in the corners. The entrance is from Jaffa Road.

We continue along Yohanan Migush Halav Street (which joins Jaffa Road) opposite Bank Leumi. At the junction of these streets is a stone fence along the length of the street and at its end is a gateway. At both sides of the entrance are stone pillars with capitals in the form of a pyramid, on each of which was a lamp. This section of the fence and its southern gateway are the remains of a wall that surrounded the Russian Compound. We enter the gateway, continue along Heshin Street (after the first Israeli Supreme Court Judge) to the first building on the left (the Russian hospital — below).

12. The Russian Compound The Russian Compound (about 75000 sq m — 19 acres) between Jaffa Road, Helene Hamalka, Shivtei Yisrael and Yohanan Migush Halav Streets, was built on a flat hill top (800 m — 290 ft above sea-level), some 300m (330 yds) north-west of the corner of the city wall. During the Second Temple period the Third Wall probably passed through this site and a quarry was excavated nearby. The Second Roman division encamped on this spot during Titus' siege of Jerusalem. During the first Crusade Tancred arrayed his forces here in preparation for the attack on the corner of the tower of the city wall. In Ottoman times it served as a parade ground and as a race course for military horses. Part of the land was purchased by the Russian consul in 1853 and another part was presented as a gift by the Sultan to the Czar. The Russian Orthodox Palestine Society erected a number of buildings for Russian pilgrims, the local clergy and the Russian consulate between 1859 and 1864 according to plans drawn up by the Russian

Holy Trinity Cathedral.

architect. An additional building was constructed in 1889.

The Russian Compound included a hospital; the Duhovnia Russian Mission building; the Holy Trinity Cathedral; the Elizabeth Mens' Hospice; the Nicolai Pilgrim's Hospice; the Russian consulate building; the Elizabeth Womens' Hospice; the Sergei Imperial Hospice.

During the Mandatory times, the buildings were rented out to the British authorities. In 1948 the buildings were taken over by the Israel government and used as offices, courts, prison, police headquarters and by the Hebrew University. In the 1950s the Israel government purchased most of the buildings from the USSR government, but the Cathedral and southern wing of the Mission building remained Russian property.

The Duhovnia Russian Mission building The two-storey building nearby (No. 6, Heshin Street) was built in 1863. In its southern section (not open to the public) are the offices and residence of the Muscovite Patriarchate. In its northern wing are the supreme court (on the top floor) and the magistrates court, which can be visited on weekdays during working hours. The square building has an internal courtyard in the center of which is a private chapel. In the southern section of the building is a library. Under the British Mandate, government offices occupied the section now serving as court rooms.

Christian churches in Jerusalem). Golden Provoslavic crosses are fixed on the domes. Its architectural style is similar to the Cathedral of the Kremlin in Moscow. The windows in the main hall are late Renaissance, and the capitals on the pillars inside the hall are neo-classic in style. The structure is typical of Provoslavic churches: an eastern basilica in the form of a cross with the transept in the center; a large dome surrounded by four smaller cupolas. The apse is closed off to visitors by a screen. The dome and walls have paintings depicting scenes from the life of Jesus and the saints.

Between the Cathedral and the building to the north, a cracked 12m long (38 ft) pillar lies on the ground called the "finger of Og" (the giant King of the Bashan). The pillar was uncovered during the building operations and has been dated to Herodian times. Its dimensions are similar to those of the pillars from the Temple as recorded by Josephus Flavius (a similar

Symbol of the Provoslavic Russian Mission.

Herodian column ("the Finger of Og").

The Holy Trinity Cathedral Visiting hours: daily between 9.00 a.m. 1.00 p.m.

The Cathedral is in the center of the Russian Compound. It is particularly impressive because of its height, its white stone facade and its 18 graceful green domes. On both ends of its gabled facade are octagonal bell towers. The bells were brought from Russia in 1856 and were the first in Jerusalem (prior to this, Ottoman rulers did not allow bells to be rung in

pillar has been found in the Mahaneh Yehuda area (see Tour No. 20 from Beit Yaakov to the Laemel school).

Hall of Heroism What was originally the Elizabeth Women's Hospice is now the Hall of Heroism (Hechal Hagevurah). Visiting hours Sundays through Thursdays: 10.00 a.m. to 4.00 p.m., Fridays to 1.00 p.m. Entrance fee.

The building extends to the northeast end of the compound, and from here

Tombstones made by Jewish political prisoners when the Hall of Heroism (right) was used as a prison during the British Mandate period.

Grunzberg Street leads to the northern gate of the Russian Compound, to the junction of Heshin, Helene Hamalka and Monbaz Streets. We walk to the corner building outside the compound.

The Sergei Imperial Hospice A two-storey building enclosing a square courtyard, it has a tower with a Renaissance-style round turret above the second storey. It was built during the years 1886 to 1889 on a plot of land 35,000 sq m (9 acres) in area. The hospice was named for Prince Sergei Romanov (son of the Czar Alexander II) who was President of the Provoslavic Palestine Association. The original facade faces Monbaz Street and at its center is a triangular gable. The building originally served pilgrims.

Sergei Imperial Hospice.

We go in through a wide entrance facing Helene Hamalka Street. In the courtyard we see two round towers which can be entered from both stories. The second storey can be reached by mounting the stairs at the left of the entrance, or by other stairways in the wings. The low building which closes off the courtyard to the north has served as stables, storerooms, chicken houses and a laundry. To the east is a large well. The building was constructed in the style of 19th-century buildings in St Petersburg, with its large dining-hall, kitchen, service rooms, accommodation for the administrative staff, storerooms and a chapel.

During the British Mandate the building was used for the offices of the Public Works Department, the Forestry Department and the Immigration Office. The Russian Mission used the eastern wing until 1967, but since then it has remained empty. Today, offices of the Ministry of Agriculture are situated in the rest of the building. In the courtyard there is an exhibition of agricultural implements used in the 19th century.

The low building to the north of the courtyard houses the Nature Preservation Society. The building can be visited during office hours.

We return to the Russian Compound and walk along Heshin Street to Jaffa Road and we can visit the Nicolai Pilgrims' Hospice on the way.

Our tour ends here.

TOUR No. 15

THE STREET OF THE PROPHETS AND ITS VICINITY

Details of tour: The tour of this street highlights life in Jerusalem at the time the center of the New City began to develop. The buildings, on the whole, have remained as they were at the beginning of the 20th century, and reflect the variegated European style of construction during this period.
Distance covered: approx. 2 km (1¼ miles)
Time: approx. 4 hours (including 2 hours visiting museums and churches)
Transportation: Buses No 7, 8, 10, 12, 13, 18, 20, 21, 26, 61
Parking lots for private vehicles in the Street of the Prophets, corner of Rabbi Kook Street and in Monbaz Street
Starting point: Herut (Liberty) Square
End of Tour: Damascus Gate
The Sites: 1. Herut (Liberty) Square — the Davidka; 2. English Hospital; 3. Kamenitz Hotel; 4. The Pasha's house; 5. Joseph Navon Bey house; 6. Evangelical Church; 7. Bikur Holim Hospital; 8. Israel Medical Association building; 9. German Hospital; 10. St Joseph Convent; 11. William Holman Hunt's residence; 12. Thabor House; 13. Ethiopia Street; 14. Ethiopian Church; 15. B'nai B'rith building; 16. Yad Sarah; 17. Ticho House; 18. Beit David neighborhood; 19. Rothschild Hospital; 20. German Evangelical School; 21. O.R.T. School — Probst Building; 22. Ethiopian Consulate; 23. Italian Hospital; 24. Mahanaim House; 25. Armenian Mosaic; 26. Nissan Bak neighborhood.

FOREWORD

The development of the Street of the Prophets (Neviim) constituted an important phase in the building of the New City of Jerusalem. Private houses, hospitals, religious and educational institutions, consulates and residential quarters were built in the latter part of the 19th century along the road that leads to Damascus Gate. Today there are no consuls residing there, and just a few public buildings remain.

The area was desolate, apart from the Muslim Nebi Ukasha complex (a 13th century Mameluke period tomb with a minaret). It was described in detail in the memoirs of the English artist William Holman Hunt who first visited Palestine in 1845. "It was a bleak hill, from which there was a spectacular view of the Old City, its walls, Haram es-Sharif and the Holy Sepulcher. Outside the walls were the tops of many windmills." In 1869 Hunt built his own house there. Both to the south and to the north of the street were Jewish neighborhoods: to the south — six along Jaffa Road, and Mea She'arim and the new neighborhoods which began to spring up in the vicinity, to the north.

Two neighborhoods were set up by Jewish pioneers on either side of the Street of the Prophets: Beit David and Kirya Ne'emana.

Christian activity appeared with the establishment of German educational institutions, and the erection of the Ethiopian Church. The first hospital outside the walls was the Rothschild Hospital which moved here in 1887 from the Jewish Quarter in the Old City. It became well known as a modern medical institution and received patients from outside the city. In the wake of this success, the Anglican Mission set up its own hospital here. Later a German hospital, a French convent and German

TOUR No. 15   186

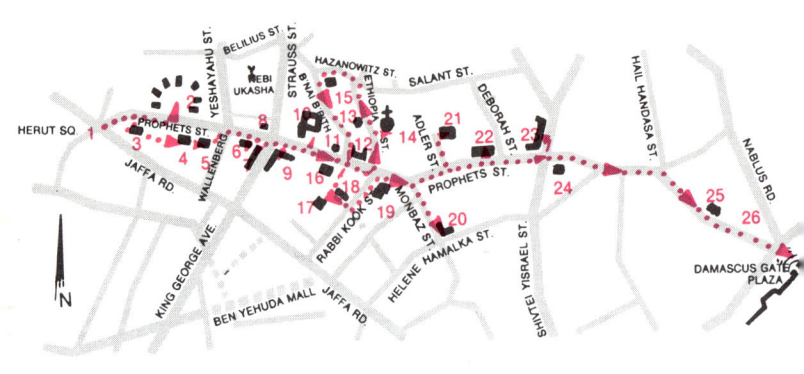

Map of the tour.

religious and educational institutions were built. The Arab Nashashibi family built several houses for rental near the Ethiopian Church. Leading Jewish men of letters and scholars resided in these houses, such as Eliezer Ben-Yehuda and the Yellin family. Near here, too, the B'nai B'rith library was built, and some of the first modern Jewish educational institutions in the New City.

The Street of the Prophets was given its name by the British Governor of Jerusalem Sir Ronald Storrs, who was impressed by the tombs of the Prophets situated in the Nebi Ukasha courtyard. Despite changes in the composition of the population and the institutions in the street, it has maintained its character to this day.

The Davidka.

THE TOUR

1. Herut (Liberty) Square — the Davidka This is the square at the junction of Jaffa Road and the Street of the Prophets. In the center is a memorial to the defenders of Jerusalem in the War of Independence, composed of four dressed courses of stones, culminating in rounded rocks which look like "stocking caps" (worn by the fighters in 1948). The memorial bears the biblical verse: "For I will defend this city to save it for my own sake and for my servant David's sake" (II Kings 19:34, Isaiah 37:35). In front of the memorial is the so-called Davidka, a home-made mortar which produced little damage but was the most terrifying weapon that the Israelis possessed for their defense in 1948. The tremendous noise made by the explosion created fear and confusion among the Arabs. It was used most effectively during the War of Independence in the conquest of Katamon, Mount Zion, the Allenby Barracks and other places and served to encourage the fighters and residents in their stand against the attacks of the Arab Legion.

2. English Hospital North of the square, behind some shops, is the high Central Hotel building erected in 1966 on the grounds of a sanatorium built in 1862 by the London Society for Promoting Christianity among the Jews as a summer resort for its members. Under the British Mandate the building was used as a hostel for British policemen. During the War of Independence, it was the headquarters of the Israel Military Police. The building within the fenced courtyard (No. 82) is now the Anglican School and is attended by children of diplomats and the United Nations staff. It was built in 1896 as the hospital of the Anglican mission which moved here from the Old City. The architect was the German Templar, Sandel, who planned other buildings throughout the city.

Around the courtyard, with its pine and carob trees, is a single-storey stone building in the form of a horseshoe. The entrance to the hospital is through an archway; in the center is a two-storey section which housed the clinics.

The English Hospital was set up in competition to the Rothschild Hospital. When it was dedicated, the leadership of the Jewish community began a desperate struggle to prevent Jews from using its services. Jews who died in this hospital were not buried by the Jewish burial societies. Despite this, many Jews chose to be hospitalized there because of its high medical standards. Jews ceased to go there only after Sha'arei Zedek Hospital was set up. It continued to function up to the War of Independence.

3. Kamenitz Hotel Opposite the English Hospital, behind an elongated building is a delapidated two-storey structure with a tiled roof. At the end of the 19th century this was a magnificent building, surrounded by a garden, trees and a driveway for carriages. The main entrance faced Jaffa Road. It was built by the apostate Bergheim (a well-known Jerusalem merchant banker) and was bought by a wealthy Jew, Jacob Fichtenholtz who gave it to the Wolhin Kollel, who in turn rented it to Kamenitz.

The Kamenitz Hotel was one of the most magnificent hotels in Jerusalem, and the first modern one to be included in all the guide books of the period. Today, a few families live in the run-down building.

(top) The English Hospital.
(center) Kamenitz Hotel.
(bottom) Joseph Navon Bey house.

4. The Pasha's house East of the Kamenitz Hotel is a two-storey house with a tiled roof; the ground floor has rounded arches and the doors and windows pointed arches. The building was erected by the Greek Church in the 1890's and was the official residence of the Turkish pasha (governor). The house had beautiful grounds, and military bands played here on official occasions. After the First World War the building was purchased by Banin, a wealthy Jewish merchant from Aden. It now is an office building with a parking lot.

5. Joseph Navon Bey house The facade of this two-storey building, east of the Pasha's house, has a gable with a round window, and small, pointed turrets in the corners of the roof. Its style is a mixture of oriental and western architecture. The building was erected during the 1880s by the banker Frutiger for his Jewish partner Joseph Navon (who added the Turkish title of a nobleman *Bey* to his name), one of the founders of several Jewish neighborhoods and the holder of the concession for the Jaffa-Jerusalem railway line. The Navon family resided in the building up to 1917. Navon's splendid carriage stood inside the magnificent gateway and there were stables for the horses behind the house. It had electricity run by a generator in the basement, a novelty in Jerusalem in those days. This building, too, was bought by the merchant Banin, and changed hands many times.

6. Evangelical Church East of the Navon House is Raoul Wallenberg Street linking the Street of the Prophets to Jaffa Road. The street was paved in 1984 on a plot of land formerly part of the German Consulate building, and named for the Swedish diplomat who was instrumental in saving a great number of Hungarian Jews during the Second World War.

Building No. 55 which houses the International Evangelical Church was built next door to the German Consulate during the British Mandate. The stone building is unique in its modern, simple style. It is open to visitors.

7. Bikur Holim Hospital At the corner of the Street of the Prophets and Strauss Street is the new building of Bikur Holim

Hospital built between the years 1910 to 1925 to which the hospital moved from the Jewish Quarter where it was founded in 1857.

After the establishment of the State, a third storey was added to the building and the former German Hospital across the street was attached to it. In the facade of the building facing Strauss Street is a triple doorway, and each of its sections is covered in beaten copper, designed by Ze'ev Raban, decorated with the symbols of the Tribes of Israel and verses from the Book of Isaiah.

8. The Israel Medical Association building This building on the northwestern corner of the junction of Strauss and the Prophets Streets houses the Medical Academy in Jerusalem, founded in 1913, as well as offices, a library, meeting rooms and the Meir Segaless Auditorium.

On the northeastern corner of the junction is the four-storey former San Remo Hotel built in 1927. The small rounded balconies are of the Art Nouveau style popular in Europe at the end of the 19th century.

9. German Hospital The building on the south-east corner of the junction was erected between 1892 and 1894 as the new hospital building of the German nursing sisters — the Diakonissen Kaiserwerthes Schwestern — which moved here from the Old City, where it was founded in 1851. It was designed by Conrad Schick and built by Sandel in the style of the church buildings common in Germany at the end of the 19th century.

The facade of the two-storey building has a rounded balcony with decorated openings supported by pillars and topped by broad capitals. At the top of the building is a chapel and a spire. Above the main entrance a verse from Exodus is carved in German and Hebrew: "I am the Lord that healeth thee" (15:26). The figure of Jonah, the emblem of the Diakonissen sisters, adorns the entrances and some of the window sills. After the War of Independence, some services of Hadassah Hospital were moved here, and it became the Ziv Hospital.

10. St Joseph Convent and School (66, Street of the Prophets) A high fence with an iron gate surrounds a courtyard in which a three-storey building stands. It was built in stages between the years 1887 and 1893 by the French nuns of the St Joseph Order.

In the courtyard is a statue of the founder of the order, St Emilie de Violar. The main building is built in French Renaissance style — pilasters with capitals in the facade of the building, and pillars on both sides of the entrance. The window arches are built from sculptured stones on plinths. Above the entrance appears the order's emblem.

On the ground floor are the nuns' dormitories and a small chapel. A separate entrance leads to the church hall, with its vaulted ceiling with interlocking arches, pillars with Corinthian capitals on both sides of the hall, and an apse at the end. On the floors above are rooms for visiting nuns.

Visits to the church can be arranged with the Convent. Of late, permission has been granted for visits on Saturday evenings during the prayer service.

(top left) The Evangelical Church.
(center left) The German Hospital.
(bottom left) Bikur Holim Hospital.
(right) St Joseph Convent.

11. Hunt residence (64, Street of the Prophets) The tall building near the courtyard of St Joseph was the house of the English artist William Holman Hunt (1827-1910), built in 1869 and surrounded by a lush garden. The living quarters were on the ground floor and his studio upstairs, surrounded by balconies with a panoramic view of the Old and New City and the hills beyond. Hunt became famous in England for his landscape paintings of Jerusalem, the Judean hills and characters from the Scriptures. His best known work "The Scapegoat" was painted near the Mar Elias Monastery on the road to Bethlehem. His widow set up a stone bench in the vicinity in his memory after his death in 1902.

Dr. Helena Kagan, one of the pioneering pediatricians in this country lived here until her death in 1978.

The poetess Rachel lived in the house at the eastern end of the courtyard in 1925.

12. Thabor House (58, Street of the Prophets) We walk in an easterly direction, cross over B'nai B'rith Street and come to a high stone wall. Two closed balconies are to be seen on the front of the building; on one is carved the name "Thabor", and underneath Psalm 89:13 and 1882, the year the building was constructed; on the other balcony the letters C and F appear — the initials of Conrad and Frederica (Schick) owners of the building and the date 1889 when the building was completed. The house is open to visitors every day except Sunday before noon. It was once the residence of Conrad Schick (1826-1902), a Protestant missionary, born in Germany and sent to Jerusalem in 1846. He soon abandoned his calling for various activities: carpentry, archaeological digs, research on Jerusalem, and architecture — planning many buildings and neighborhoods in the holy city, and introducing new techniques of construction and design.

He named his house Thabor to express his wonderment at the works of God, as reflected in Psalm 89:12: "The north and the south, thou hast created them: Tabor and Hermon shall rejoice in thy name".

A stone wall encloses the grounds. The gate and the balcony over it are built in the

Thabor House.

style prominent in the Middle Ages. Above the second balcony is a circular window in a recessed arch in oriental style. The top of the wall, stepped on either side of the keystone, has palm leaves and the Greek letters Alpha and Omega carved on it.

After obtaining permission we enter through the gateway into a well-kept courtyard and go into a two-storey structure built in a mixture of European and oriental styles. The building is embellished with ancient and modern stone ornaments — arches, gables, palm trees and stones in the form of the "horns of the altar" in the corners of the roofs.

The building has passed through many hands since Schick's death, and today it is occupied by the Swedish Theological Institute.

13. Ethiopia Street We enter Ethiopia Street, bounded on either side by high stone walls enclosing courtyards and buildings built for rental by the Nashashibi family at the end of the 19th century. The two-storey luxurious buildings with their tiled roofs were typical of the style popular with Muslims at this time. Each building is surrounded by a large garden with trees, bushes and flowers. This was a prestigious neighborhood whose inhabitants were consuls, scholars from overseas, and other personalities. Eliezer Ben Yehuda, the "father" of modern Hebrew lived at No. 11 for several years.

STREET OF THE PROPHETS

14. Ethiopian Church Located at No. 9 of the street, and from which Ethiopia Street takes its name. Visiting hours: every day during daylight hours. In the center of the gate's lintel is a cross, a crown and inscriptions in Ethiopian script, and at each end is an engraved crowned lion bearing a cross — the symbol of the Ethiopian royal house. The church is situated in the courtyard surrounded by a number of buildings. The roof is covered with a black dome, and at its apex an Ethiopian cross — a cross within a circle, with seven arrow-like points. The church is called "Bond of Mercy" in Geez. The entire complex is called "The Hill of Paradise". The building was begun by the Ethiopian Emperor Johannes IV and was completed by his heir Menelik II between the years 1882 and 1893. The monks' quarters are to the left of the gate and behind them is a building for receptions, and a belltower. To the right of the gate and east of the church are buildings for rental to provide an income for the monks. They were built with contributions from the Ethiopian royal court and noble personalities, and they are called after them. Additional houses were built for rental in the vicinity between 1895 and 1935.

The Ethiopians were introduced to Christianity in the Byzantine period by the Copts of Egypt; the head of the church was a Coptic bishop. The Ethiopian Church gained independence in 1948 and an Ethiopian bishop was sent to Jerusalem in 1953; he resides in the Ethiopian Monastery in the Christian Quarter in the Old City. The sacred language of the Ethiopians is called "Geez", and is written in a script similar to ancient Hebrew; the Bible, and other holy scripts have been translated into this language. There has been an Ethiopian community in Jerusalem continuously since the 7th century in the Christian Quarter in the Old City.

The church building we are about to visit is round and its dome is supported by a drum. Only one of the three entrances to the church is open and before entering we must take off our shoes. Inside there are two passageways that go around the central circular structure. Between the passages are square pilasters supporting arches. The central structure is the "holy of holies"; the altar is built according to the description of the incense altar in the Second Temple. Details regarding the construction of the church are inscribed in four languages (Amharic, Italian, Arabic and French). The walls are decorated with icons.

We leave the Ethiopian Church and continue our tour of the neighborhood until we reach Beit Hanna, where the Tachkemoni School was founded and the Hebrew Teachers College first functioned. We come to Hazanowitz Street and then turn left into B'nai B'rith Street where we see

The Ethiopian Church.

The Danish Consulate in B'nai B'rith Street.

buildings housing the offices of HaPoel Hamizrahi religious political party and the clinics of Kupat Holim (the Sick Fund of the Histadrut — General Federation of Labor) which were built in the 1930s.

15. B'nai B'rith House (18, B'nai B'rith Street) This two-storey building was erected in 1902 by B'nai B'rith, the world Jewish association for Jewish communal services founded in 1843 in the USA. The building was planned by the German architect Palmer in a neo-classic style, but only part of the plan was carried out.

A library of Hebrew books established in 1892 in memory of Isaac Abarbanel (to mark the 400th anniversary of the expulsion from Spain of the community he headed) was brought to this building by B'nai B'rith, but in 1920 it was handed over to the World Zionist Organization and served as a basis for the National Library. In the 1930s the books were transferred to the Hebrew University on Mount Scopus (and in 1958 they were brought to the National and University Library building at Givat Ram). Between 1930 and 1948 a public library for children and youth existed in the B'nai B'rith building, and after the establishment of the State the books were moved to the municipal library. The building was renovated in 1978 by the Jerusalem Foundation. A library devoted to the study of the Holy Land was opened on the second floor of this building, with a reading room for youth.

House No. 16 B'nai B'rith Street stood in the Tachkemoni School grounds and No. 10 is the Danish Consulate.

16. Yad Sarah (43, Street of the Prophets) Next to the German Hospital a disused railway carriage can be seen with a sign "Yad Sarah" above the doorway. The two-storey building next to it was built at the end of the 19th century as a hospice for Russian women and the symbol of the Russian Church can still be seen above the gateway. The building is the national headquarters of Yad Sarah, a voluntary organization founded in 1980 for the loan of medical equipment and the rehabilitation of the sick and the aged. One of the supporters of the organization is Avraham Hava, who established the Hava Museum of Micrographics to exhibit his unique works of miniature writing. The museum is open daily before noon. Entry fee.

17. Ticho House At the end of Ticho Lane, we enter a courtyard in which an isolated house stands in a lush garden. This is now the Ticho Museum which belongs to the Israel Museum, open to the public on weekdays from 10.00 am. On show are works by the artist Anna Ticho and a collection of Hannuka lamps gathered by Dr.

B'nai B'rith House.

Ticho House.

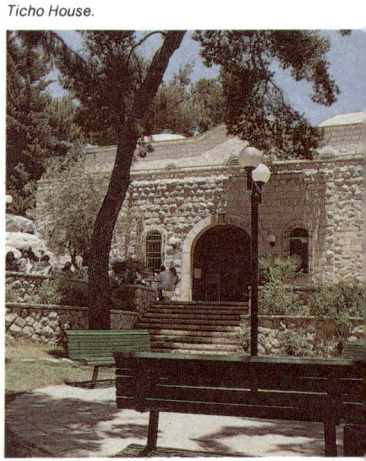

Ticho, her husband as well as a library with books on Jerusalem, art and literature. There is also a small shop and a garden café. The building was erected in 1868 by a wealthy Muslim, Hajj Rashid, the first house in this area. In 1871 it was purchased by Moses Shapira, an antique dealer who was exposed as a forger of ancient artifacts, and it was acquired by the Tichos in 1924.

Dr. Avraham Ticho was an eminent eye doctor who came to Jerusalem in 1912 from Vienna with his wife Anna, a qualified nurse and artist. They ran an eye clinic here which became famous throughout the Middle East and operated until the doctor's death in 1960.

After visiting the Ticho Museum we return to Ticho Lane and on the stone gateway of the first building see a plaque "Beit Harav" (the Rabbi's House) with a list of names of donors. The second floor of this house was the residence of the Chief Ashkenazi Rabbi of Palestine (1865–1936), Abraham Isaac Hacohen Kook and his *yeshiva*. He was a renowned rabbinical scholar and one of the greatest Jewish spiritual leaders of modern times. The building has been renovated and the *yeshiva* reopened. Rabbi Kook's room has been preserved intact and is open to visitors.

18. Beit David The two-storey house at the corner of Rabbi Kook Street (No. 7) is named for David Reiss, a philanthropist who built it in 1873 and designated it for the poor. On the second floor are the offices of the Central Committee of Knesset Israel which distributes money gathered from Jews abroad to various communities. The Rabbi Meir Baal Haness Fund is also administered from here.

We pass by the parking lot at the corner of Rabbi Kook and the Prophets Streets. This was the site of the Patt pastry shop and café, which also served as Haganah headquarters in Jerusalem. It was taken over by the Evelina de Rothschild school when it moved outside the city walls.

19. Rothschild Hospital (37, Street of the Prophets) The inscription on the lintel above the front entrance is in Hebrew, Arabic and French. A later sign in Hebrew and English states: "The first Hadassah hospital in Eretz Israel established under the auspices of the Hadassah Women's Zionist Organization of America." The red-tile roofed three-storey building has decorated gables above its windows and was built with funds provided by Baron Jacob de Rothschild and the Alliance Israelite Universelle.

The hospital, originally established in the Jewish Quarter of the Old City in 1835, moved here in 1888. It was closed down during World War I and reopened in 1918 by the Hadassah Women's Organization. It had 120 beds, clinics and modern medical equipment. In 1939 the hospital moved to the medical center built on Mount Scopus, but when the hospital was cut off from the main city in 1948, the departments were scattered among other hospitals until the new Hadassah medical complex was built in Ein Karem. After the Six Day War, the Hadassah medical center on Mount Scopus was reopened. (See Tour No. 28.)

The Rothschild Hospital building and its newer wing serve now as the Hadassah Community College and its technical college.

20. German Evangelical School In the single-storey houses between Monbaz and Queen Helene Streets, a German

Rabbi Kook's house.

Mosaic depicting the Lion of Judah on the facade of the former Ethiopian Consulate.

Evangelical School for Boys was opened in 1873. In 1905 the children of the Templar families who settled in the German Colony also came to study here. In 1910 the school, run jointly by the German Protestant and Templar Communities, moved to the German Probst building (now the Ort Technical School). The Anglican Protestant community was situated in houses 25–29, Street of the Prophets (now a kindergarten).

21. O.R.T. School — Probst Building (Corner Adler and Street of the Prophets) The first building on this site, erected in 1910, was the German Probst house. The plot of land was granted to the Germans by the Sultan after the visit to Jerusalem of Kaiser Wilhelm II in 1898. A large camp of tents was set up for the emperor and his entourage, and it was here that Theodor Herzl, founder of the World Zionist Organization, had his famous meeting with the German Kaiser. The two-storey, tiled roof structure was planned by the architect Palmer, in the neo-classic style popular in Germany at the end of the 11th century. On the wall facing Adler Street is an inscription in German from Psalm 122:6. On the ground floor was a chapel and a dining hall. At the end of Adler Street are three structures that were built for the German Evangelical Society's school and kindergarten; today they house the Municipality's public health services and the WIZO day creche.

After the First World War the Probst building became the residence of the first governor of Jerusalem, Sir Ronald Storrs. During the last years of the British Mandate the buildings served as a school for Arab boys and from 1948 to 1951 some of the departments of the Hadassah Hospital were housed here. In 1952 the Ort Technical school opened on this site.

22. Ethiopian Consulate (38–40, Street of the Prophets) We walk downhill to the corner of the Prophetess Deborah Street. On the facade of the three-storey building is a colored mosaic depicting the Lion of Judah, the heraldic symbol of the Ethiopian royal house. An inscription in Geez states: "The Lion of the tribe of Judah has conquered." According to Ethiopian tradition, their first king was the son of the Queen of Sheba, who visited Jerusalem and King Solomon. The modern-style building, erected in 1925–1928, has about 90 rooms. It was built by the Empress Zaudito and housed the Ethiopian Consulate. Some of the rooms were rented out and further buildings in the vicinity were constructed for rental.

23. Italian Hospital At the corner of the Prophets and Shivtei Yisrael Streets is one of the most imposing buildings in the New City. Its square belltower and octagonal church can be seen from afar. It was built in 16th century Italian Renaissance Style. The religious symbols, the knights' blazons and the insignia of towns in Italy have

The Italian Hospital.

almost all been removed over the years. The building was designed by the Italian architect Barluzzi and was built between 1912 and 1919. After the First World War it served as a hospital. The nurses were Italian nuns. In the Second World War it was requisitioned by the British authorities; it served as a military hospital and also as the RAF regional headquarters.

During the War of Independence, the building served as a forward command post for the Israeli forces, and it was badly hit by Jordanian artillery. After the establishment of the State, it was returned to its owners and was used to house Italian nurses. In 1963 it was sold to the Israeli government and is part of the Ministry of Education. The church was renovated with funds provided by the Rothschild family and the hall is used for lectures and conferences. It can be visited by permission of the Ministry of Education maintenance division.

We continue our tour, and on the pavement at the northwestern corner we can see a large stone covered in concrete, and follow its continuation on the other side of the fence. This is part of the Second Temple period Third Wall of Jerusalem.

24. Mahanaim House (34, Shivtei Yisrael Street) A stone fence encloses a three-storey tile-roofed building covered with climbing plants. Above the door is the name Mahanaim given it by its first owner, Jacob Johan Frutiger from the verse in Genesis 32:2 –" And he [Jacob] called the name of that place Mahanaim". The building, designed by Conrad Schick, has over 40 rooms and a basement. In the grounds was a house for the gardener and stables for the owner's carriage horses. There are round windows on the top floor and many ornamentations. A second gateway for carriages opens on to the Street of the Prophets.

The Swiss banker Jacob Johan Frutiger came to Jerusalem in 1862 to manage the branch of the bank of the Chrichona Mis-

(top) Mahanaim House.
(center) The Rumanian Orthodox Patriarchate in Shivtei Yisrael Street.
(bottom) Detail of the Armenian Mosaic.

sion. Later he set up the Frutiger and Co. Bank which acted as the Jerusalem branch of the Imperial Ottoman Bank. Frutiger founded a company to purchase land and construct housing neighborhoods together with his Jewish partners Joseph Navon Bey and Shalom Konstrum. They were instrumental in the building of Mahaneh Yehuda, Succat Shalom, Beit Yosef and other neighborhoods. In 1896 the company went bankrupt and they were forced to sell Frutiger's house.

The building housed the Evelina de Rothschild School for Jewish girls. It was expanded, and a gymnasium set up in the basement. Since 1951 it has served as the offices of the Israel Ministry of Education.

25. Armenian Mosaic The so-called Bird Mosaic is at 16, Street of the Prophets. Visiting hours: during daylight.

We continue downhill towards the Old City and enter the building, turn right into a hall where an ancient mosaic has been perfectly preserved. A chapel existed here in the 6th century, built above a burial cave carved out of the rock. The mosaic was discovered in 1894 when the foundations were being laid for the present building, the Chapel of St Polyeuctus. The Armenian inscription in a frame at the edge of the floor reads: "In memory and to the success of all Armenians. Our Lord knows their names". According to tradition, Armenians slaughtered by Muslims were buried in the chamber below the floor.

The mosaic is made up of medallions containing baskets of fruit, plants and many species of birds, as well as a bird in a cage and a magnificent amphora.

26. Nissan Bak neighborhood The house in which the Armenian Mosaic floor is situated and the buildings next to it were erected between 1875 and 1895 by the Wolhin Hassidic community in the Old City. This was the Kirya Ne'emana neighborhood, also called the Nissan Bak neighborhood after the leader of this community.

Our tour ends here. There is a taxi stand near Damascus Gate and bus stops in Nablus Road.

TOUR No. 16

FROM GAN DANIEL TO MEA SHE'ARIM

Details of tour: This is the continuation of the tour of the Street of the Prophets (Tour No. 15). We shall commence in the area developed by the French in the late 19th century, and proceed to Mea She'arim which opened the northwest axis (Damascus Gate — Kerem Avraham — Schneller) in the development of the New City.
Time: approx. 3 hours.
Distance covered: approx. 3 km (2 miles)
Transportation: Buses No 1, 5, 6, 18, 20, 21 to Shelomzion HaMalka Street. From Mea She'arim: No 11 and 29.
Parking lot at the Russian Compound for private vehicles.
Starting point: Gan Daniel
End of tour: Mea She'arim
  In Mea She'arim modest attire is required (women must wear dresses).
The Sites: 1. Gan Daniel; 2. The Armenian buildings; 3. Former French Consulate; 4. Bergheim Houses; 5. Bible Society building; 6. Town Hall; 7. Feil Hotel building; 8. Tsahal Square; 9. St. Louis (French) Hospital; 10. Notre Dame; 11. Morasha Quarter (Musrara); 12. Church of St. Paul; 13. Mea She'arim.

THE TOUR

1. Gan Daniel (Daniel Park) The small municipal garden opposite 19, Jaffa Road, is named after Daniel Auster, the first mayor of Jerusalem of the State of Israel. Yohanan Migush Halav Street, which today passes behind the park, was within the original park created by the Ottoman authorities in the 1890s. This was the first public park in Palestine and the Turkish army band gave concerts here. The park has an entrance on each of the three streets which encircle it, and contains a modern mosaic map of Jerusalem and a board displaying photographs and statistics relative to the different communities in Jerusalem from 1840 to 1977.

2. The Armenian buildings Opposite Gan Daniel, on the other side of Jaffa Road, are two long three-storey buildings (Nos 17 and 19), containing shops and offices. The stones used in the construction are smooth, and the arches of the windows and the doors are ornamented. The symbol of the Armenian Church is carved over the doorways and the shops. The buildings were erected by the Armenian Patriarchate at the end of the 19th century.

Behind Gan Daniel, on **Yohanan Migush Halav Street**, there are a number of historical buildings (see below).

3. Former French Consulate (No. 3). The first French consulate building outside the city walls was constructed here in 1893, behind the municipal garden (a French consulate was opened in the Old City in 1843). From the roof of the house we shall see spreading before us a panoramic view of the Old City, the New City and the hills around, as far as Bethlehem and Herodion in the south. The consulate was located here until 1930, when it moved to Paul Emile Botta Street (see: Tour No. 14).

Under the British Mandate, the building housed offices of the Jerusalem District, and since 1948 the Hebrew University Zoological Department is housed here.

The early 20th-century style of the building does not fail to impress with arches in the facade, the courtyard and the garden behind, and the high-ceilinged, spacious rooms. The doorkeeper's authorization is required to visit the building.

4. Bergheim Houses (No. 5 and 7). Melville Peter Bergheim was an apostate Jew, born in Posen, Germany. In 1851, he created a private bank and a large busi-

TOUR No. 16 198

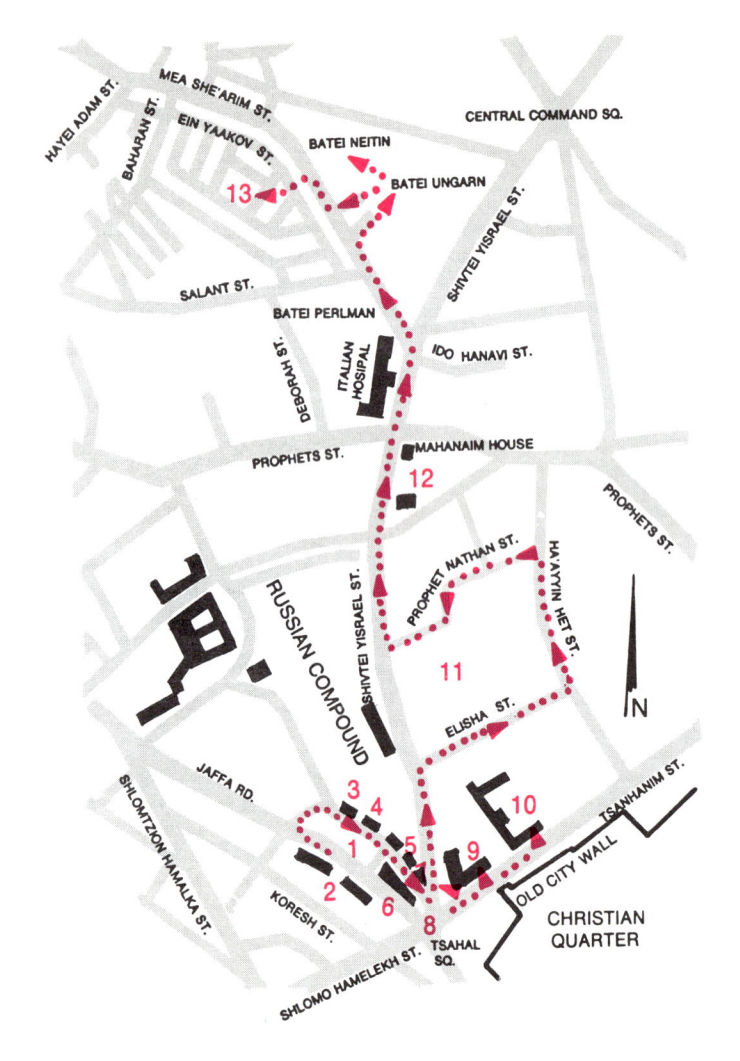

Map of the tour.

ness and dealt in real estate. In 1877, north of the Damascus Gate, he built the first steam-powered mill in Palestine. Bergheim's offices were located at No. 5 Jaffa Road. Under the British Mandate the house was enlarged and converted into a government hospital. Following the creation of the State of Israel, the Hebrew University Zoology Department moved into the premises. No. 7 was the Bergheim family residence. On the facade is a sign, indicating that Henrietta Szold's first office was located here.

5. The Bible Society (No. 9) is the modern building planned by an English architect and constructed in 1930. The entrance is arched and at the top of the facade are triangular openings. Over the entrance is the inscription "Connaught House".

6. The Town Hall is at 22, Jaffa Road with its facade facing Gan Daniel. An inscription indicates the year that the cornerstone was laid by the British Government Secretary Spencer (1930).

The Municipal Council hall, in the basement of the building, can be visited by permission of the guard. The stained-glass windows were designed by Avigdor Arikha. On the other floors are the offices including that of the Mayor. Appointments to visit the building during working hours may be made through the Municipal Information Center, across the street at No. 17 Jaffa Road.

(top) Emblem of Jerusalem Municipality.
(bottom) The Town Hall.

Today's Town Hall is constructed on the site of an Ottoman citadel, which guarded the way to Jaffa. Barclay's Bank financed its construction, and in return received the eastern ground floor for its use. The building has been the seat of the Municipality since its completion in 1932.

7. The Feil Hotel building The corner building next to the Town Hall, with its facade facing Tsahal Square, was the first building in this area. Built in 1875, it was recommended to tourists because of its modern rooms on the second floor. The windows offered a magnificent view, beyond the Old City, of the Judean hills and the Moab mountains. This simple trapezoid building faces Yohanan Migush Halav and Shivtei Yisrael Streets. In its center is a small open courtyard, with steps leading up to the second floor. It is occupied today by small shops, stores and apartments.

8. Tsahal Square (I.D.F. Square) between Jaffa Road, Tsanhanim (Paratroopers) Street, Shlomo Hamelekh (King Solomon) Street and Shivtei Yisrael Street.

Tancred's Tower During preparation of the area for the garden next to Tsahal Square, vestiges of Crusader buildings were uncovered in the corner of the Ottoman city wall. In the archaeological excavations carried out on the site in 1971/72, the remains of a Crusader wall, a corner tower and its moat were revealed. These are the continuation of the foundations of the Crusader Tancred's Tower, other parts of which were found during the construction of the French Collège des Frères (inside the walls) in 1896 (see Tour 7). An aqueduct which brought rainwater from the Russian Compound area was also uncovered. It passed under the city wall and apparently reached the Pool of the Tower (Hezekiah's Pool) inside the Old City. The tower is named after the Crusader commander Tancred, who camped here during the conquest of Jerusalem in 1099. It is built from Herodian stones in secondary use. The Psephinus Tower (mentioned by Josephus Flavius) may have been located here, in the northwest corner of the Third Wall. The Crusader tower was destroyed by the Mameluke

The Feil Hotel building.

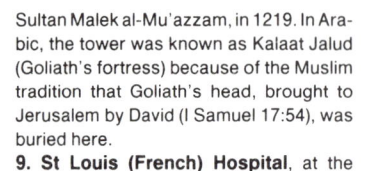

Vestiges of Tancred's Tower, Tsahal Square.

Sultan Malek al-Mu'azzam, in 1219. In Arabic, the tower was known as Kalaat Jalud (Goliath's fortress) because of the Muslim tradition that Goliath's head, brought to Jerusalem by David (I Samuel 17:54), was buried here.

9. St Louis (French) Hospital, at the corner of Tsanhanim Street (Paratroopers Street) and Shivtei Yisrael Street, is a three-storey building. The hospital is called after the French King Louis IX, known as St Louis, who participated in the Twelth Crusade in 1270. It was founded in 1851 in the Christian Quarter. The present building was inaugurated in 1881. The chiselled stone decorations are in the late French Renaissance and Baroque styles. The hospital cared for the sick and wounded from all the religious communities. Since the creation of the State of Israel it serves as a hospital for the incurably ill. The nurses are nuns of the order of St Joseph. The hospital can be visited by permission of the hospital administration.

10. Notre Dame The impressive building east of the French Hospital, opposite the New Gate, was originally the Notre Dame de France Hospice, known by all as Notre Dame. With the guard's permission we shall go into the courtyard on Tsanhanim Street. The building has four storeys and is built as a straight U, with the facade facing east. It has a round tower on each side and a statue of the Virgin and Child on the rooftop. The building was badly damaged in 1948. It has been repaired and renovated. It includes 410 rooms and a chapel and is now a hotel.

The land for the building was purchased in 1884, with the contributions of a thousand pilgrims who came from France. The building was completed in 1904. It was built by the French Assumptionist Fathers and served as a monastery and hospice for pilgrims.

It can be visited by permission of the management. In the basement is a small museum where archaeological finds of the monks are exhibited. The chapel is on the third floor. The observation point on the roof of the building offers a magnificent view, encompassing the Old City, most of the New City and the hills surrounding Jerusalem. Within the Notre Dame complex the Vatican has created a Christian community center, a papal cultural center, and a vocational center for Christian youth. Following construction of the French Hospital and of Notre Dame, close to the northwest corner of the city wall, the New Gate was opened in 1889, in order to facilitate communication between the Christian Quarter and the new buildings.

11. Morasha Quarter (Musrara) Returning to Tsahal Square, we shall turn onto Shivtei Yisrael Street and continue northward. The houses on the east side of the street were part of the Arab Musrara

St Louis Hospital.

Notre Dame.

quarter built between 1889 and 1925 by affluent families. Most of the houses have two storeys, tiled roofs and elaborate entrances with carved stone ornaments.

The neighborhood suffered severe damage during the War of Independence and was abandoned by the residents. New immigrants later settled there. Between the houses, 4-storey and 5-storey buildings were constructed in the 1950s.

Passing through the narrow alleys, we go down to Nathan HaNavi (Nathan the Prophet) Street, and turn north onto Ha'Ayyin Het Street. From here we go up Helene HaMalka Street and return to Shivtei Yisrael Street. On Ha'Ayyin Het Street we shall see the building of the Salesian Nuns (No. 18). The so-called house of the windows (No. 16) has many windows in the back wall, creating an interesting pattern.

On another corner of Shivtei Yisrael and Helene HaMalka streets are two buildings erected by the Ethiopian imperial house, and one of them, built in 1903, still bears its heraldic emblem and an inscription in Amharic. It has housed the Israel radio broadcasting studios since the time of the British Mandate.

12. Church of St Paul at 24, Shivtei Yisrael Street, was constructed in 1874, and was the first building in the entire area. It is built in the style of late 19th-century rural churches in England.

After the War of Independence it fell into disuse and was transferred to the care of

A street in Morasha Quarter.

Church of St Paul.

TOUR No. 16

the Finnish Messianic Center, located across the street. The church can be visited by appointment.

Mahanaim House (34, Shivtei Yisrael Street), built by the Swiss Johann Frutiger, in 1885; today it houses the Ministry of Education and Culture.

The Italian Hospital On the corner of Prophets Street and Shivtei Yisrael Street. Further details on these two buildings in Tour No. 15.

Perlman Houses We shall continue down Shivtei Yisrael Street and turn right onto Mea She'arim Street. On the left side of the street is a row of shops on the ground floor of two-storey houses. These were built in 1887 by Frutiger and his partner, Shalom Konstrum. Additional rows of houses were built behind the first row by Rabbi Elimelech Perlman and the quarter is separated from Mea She'arim by Salant Street.

Batei Ungarn This is the neighborhood on the east side of Mea She'arim Street, opposite the Perlman houses, founded by the Kollel Shomrei HaHomot, whose members came from Austria, Hungary and Bohemia. The neighborhood was founded for the longstanding members of the *kollel* (community) who lived in the Old City. Construction commenced in 1891 and in 1901 about 120 apartments in oblong two-storey houses were inaugurated. The apartments were given free for three years, and the tenants then changed.

Batei Neitin A small quarter built north of the Batei Ungarn by the Jewish philanthropist Menahem Neitin, comprising four rows of about 60 apartments altogether, was constructed between 1903 and 1910.

These neighborhoods, and others in the vicinity, were built after Mea She'arim which opened a new settlement axis northwest of the Old City.

Ohel Simcha adjoining Batei Ungarn, was founded in 1892 and named for Rabbi Simcha Bunem, grandson of the Hatam Sofer, the famous Rabbi of Hungarian Jewry during the years 1762–1839.

Even Yehoshua, west of Mea She'arim, fronting on Even Yehoshua Street, was founded in 1897 with funds provided by the philanthropist Yehoshua Helpman.

Batei Wittenberg (Sha'arei Moshe) West of Mea She'arim, this neighborhood was founded in 1885 by the philanthropist Moshe Wittenberg who helped to finance the erection of buildings in the Moslem Quarter of the Old City.

Batei Werner (Ohalei Moshe), north of Mea She'arim, was founded in 1902 by Moshe Mendel Werner.

Batei Warsaw (Nahalat Ya'akov), north of Mea She'arim, was founded in 1894 by Ya'akov Tonwertzel for the Warsaw *kollel*.

13. Mea She'arim was the 5th Jewish quarter to be established outside the Old City in 1874. It is located between Mea She'arim Street, Baharan Street, Slonim

Courtyard in Batei Ungarn.

A street near Mea She'arim.

One of the gateways of Mea She'arim.

Street and Salant Street. Its founders were families mainly from Poland and Lithuania, who lived in the Old City and founded a building society called Mea She'arim, a name derived from the Bible passage read in the week that the society was founded: "Then Isaac sowed in that land, and received in the same year an hundredfold [*mea she'arim*]: and the Lord blessed him" (Genesis 26:12).

The land was purchased from the village of Lifta. Because of its isolation, the inhabitants had to protect themselves from marauders who plagued the area at that time. The quarter was planned by Conrad Schick (see Tour No. 15) as a rectangle made up of oblong houses built in an unbroken line, their outer walls forming a kind of protective rampart. At night the quarter was closed by six iron gates, Jerusalem Gate: the eastern gate, on Mea She'arim Street; Beit David Gate: the southeast gate, on Salant Street; the Center Gate (Rabbi Yaakov Sofer Gate) between Salant Street and Slonim Street; Rehayim Gate: the southwest gate called after a nearby windmill; Lifta Gate: the western gate (also called Shlomo Shuster Gate); Middle Gate: the northern gate, which faces Baharan Street. There is a market in the center of the quarter.

The construction of apartment houses continued until 1882; 140 units were built and distributed by lottery. A book of regulations to organize communal life in the quarter was written by an elected committee whose function was to ensure the welfare of the residents, peace among them, and mutual aid. The quarter was active and kept up with the times —fairs were held introducing European novelties. It was even dubbed the "Paris of the Orient".

From the 1880s the conservative atmosphere grew in the quarter. The religious extremist tendency increased continually until 1935 when a rift divided the Agudat Yisrael movement, and the Neturei Karta group ("Guardians of the City", in Aramaic) was created. This group is opposed to Zionism and considered the creation of a

Views in Mea She'arim. Note the sign urging women to dress modestly.

Jewish secular state to be heretical and sacrilegious. Its members do not recognize the State of Israel and its laws. They see themselves as guardians of the purity of the Holy City. The neighborhood contains all the necessary public institutions.

Life in the quarter revolves around the many synagogues and *yeshivot* (religious seminaries). The most outstanding of these religious institutions is Beit Avraham, in the heart of the quarter which housed a *yeshiva* and Talmud Torah (religious schools), a free soup kitchen, and a synagogue, the largest of the quarter. Today the building houses also a school for young boys. Another institution, the Hassidic Toldot Aharon *yeshiva*, is notable both for the extreme strictness of its religious observance and for the unusual dress of its students who wear striped robes and white *kipot* (scullcaps).

Visitors to Mea She'arim, particularly women, are advised to dress modestly. Placards in Hebrew, Yiddish and English warn visitors, requesting them to comport themselves with due decency within the quarter. The special atmosphere of the streets is enhanced by the fact that the residents dress in the style of their forefathers in the ghettos of Eastern Europe. They make no concessions to the temptations of modern society, and conduct life according to the letter of Jewish Law whose study is their real joy.

TOUR No. 17

FROM NAHALAT ZVI TO THE BUKHARAN QUARTER

Details of tour: This tour includes the neighborhoods of the northern part of Jerusalem built at the end of the 19th and the beginning of the 20th century. They were founded by immigrants of different Jewish communities, who maintained their lifestyles and built their houses in the style of their countries of origin.
Distance covered: approx. 3 km (2 miles)
Time: approx. 4 hours (including visits to synagogues)
Transportation: Buses No 4, 9
Parking along Yoel Street and streets in the vicinity for private vehicles
Starting point: at the corner of Mea She'arim and Yoel Streets
End of tour: at the corner of Yehezkiel and Ezra Streets
The Sites: 1. Nahalat Zvi; 2. Sha'ar Hapinah; 3. Beit Yisrael; 4. New Beit Yisrael; 5. Bukharan Quarter.
The best time for this tour is during prayer services; please dress appropriately.

THE TOUR

1. Nahalat Zvi At the corner of Mea She'arim and Habakkuk Streets is a group of small two-storey houses. This neighborhood was built by Yemenite Jews in 1889 with funds provided by Baron Morris de Hirsch and named for him (*Hirsch* in German means "deer" which is Zvi in Hebrew). The residents themselves, who had been trained as builders at the Alliance Israelite Universelle School, built their own houses, 75 altogether. Contributions were made to the Eretz Teiman Kollel (Yemenite Community Fund) for a Talmud Torah, a cistern and synagogues. The houses are small and closely-built.

We go down steps from Habakkuk Street to Zechariah Harofeh Street. The Shabazi Synagogue, named for the renowned Yemenite poet, is on the ground floor of the first building to the right. On the second floor is the Arbelim Synagogue of the Iraqi community, and the Adoneinu Yehezkiel Hanavi Yeshiva.

2. Sha'ar Hapinah This neighborhood, also founded by immigrants from the Yemen in 1889, was initiated by a company which built 40 houses. The first residents were from Aden.

We descend the steps from Habakkuk Street to Yehia Kapah Street and we come to a square surrounded by small houses. The gateway *(sha'ar)* in the corner *(pinah)* is the origin of the name given the neighborhood. Its narrow lanes are named after famous Jewish Yemenite personalities.

3. Beit Yisrael We descend Kapah Street in an easterly direction and walk through one of the streets until we reach the Beit Ya'akov Synagogue Square at the center of Beit Yisrael neighborhood founded in 1886 by the same company that built Sha'ar Hapinah. It was first called the New Mea She'arim, and was inhabited by families who could not afford the cost of apartments in nearby Mea She'arim itself.

The main street is named for Itzhak Zvi Dayan, who purchased the land. Originally this was a low-lying plot of land into which rainwater flowed and waste from the nearby soap factory drained.

The name Beit Yisrael comes from the verse in Ezekiel: "And I will multiply men upon you, all the house of Israel, even all of it: and the cities shall be inhabited, and the wastes shall be builded." (36:10)

In the center of the neighborhood is the Mahaneh Yisrael Yeshiva in whose west-

TOUR No. 17

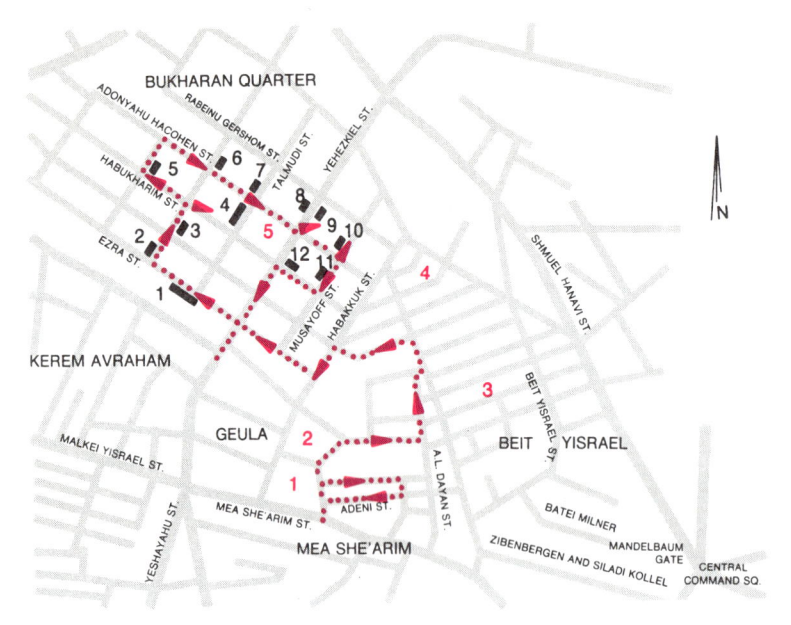

Map of the tour.

ern wing is the Beit Ya'akov Synagogue. The two-storey houses are built along both sides of the streets; behind each house is a courtyard and every two houses share a cistern. In 1900 there were 60 houses and 2 synagogues.

4. New Beit Yisrael neighborhood Situated to the north of Beit Yisrael, and extending up to Shmuel Hanavi Street, the New Beit Yisrael neighborhood was founded in 1922 by the Shevet Ahim Company and built by members of the Gedud

A house in Beit Yisrael.

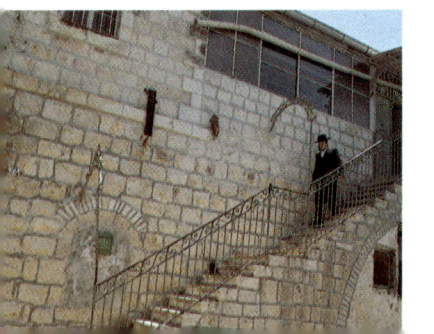

Ha'avoda who set up a camp and a tree nursery on this site.

Two other neighborhoods are situated to the east and the north:

Batei Milner, founded in 1892 by Shlomo Milner, a wealthy miller from Rumania. The relatively small quarter has one or two-storey houses and a flour mill. It was badly hit during the 1936 riots and again in the War of Independence. The mill was destroyed and abandoned.

The Zibenbergen and Siladi Kollel was founded in 1911 to the east of Batei Milner on the way to the Tomb of Simon the Just and not far from the Tombs of the Kings. The neighborhood was founded by the leaders of the Kollel (community), some of whom came from Hungary. This too, was badly damaged during the riots and the War of Independence. The Mandelbaum Gate, which served as the checkpost between the Old and New City from 1949 to 1967 was within its confines.

We cross over Yehezkiel Street, the main street of the Bukharan Quarter, and come to Ezra Street.

5. Bukharan Quarter The Quarter was founded by Jews from Bukhara (Central Asia, now in the USSR) who named it "Rehovot", according to the verse in Genesis: "And he called the name of it Rehoboth; and he said: For now the Lord hath made room for us, and we shall be fruitful in the land," (26:22).

The first immigrants from Bukhara arrived in Jerusalem in the 1870s and 1880s. In 1889 they founded the Hovevei Zion Association of the Jewish community of Bukhara, Samarkand and Tashkent. The land was purchased in 1891 on a hill to the north-west of Beit Yisrael. Planned by Conrad Schick, the quarter first consisted of 40 houses. This was a new style of building with streets three times the width of the broadest thoroughfares of the city at the time, and large courtyards which were sometimes divided. The houses had two stories and generally radiated affluence. The second floor was reached by an external stairway up to a balcony. The synagogues were in the center of the quarter and construction continued by stages during the British Mandate period and even after the establishment of the State of Israel until finally there were 200 houses and 1500 residents.

During the First World War the Turkish army requisitioned a number of buildings and cut down all the trees in the area. With the outbreak of the Russian Revolution the residents were cut off from their families who had been running their businesses at home and sending the funds to support them. Their assets in Bukhara were confiscated. Consequently they were forced to find other sources of income, so many houses were rented to new immigrants. After the war the quarter enjoyed a short period of activity: teachers, writers, officials, Labor activists and Zionist leaders took up residence there. Among the most famous were Itzhak Ben-Zvi (to become second President of the State), his wife Rachel Yanait, Moshe Sharett (Israel's first Foreign Minister and later Prime Minister), the renowned historian Joseph Klausner and many others. Towards the 1920s the center of activity moved to the new garden suburbs of Rehavia, Beit Hakerem and Talpiot, and the population of the Bukharan Quarter began to dwindle. In several of the larger buildings religious and educational institutions were set up (the Blumenthal Orphanage, the Hannah Spitzer Talmud Torah for girls, etc.). Since the establishment of the State, the Quarter has undergone radical changes in its social composition.

Some of the buildings were erected by wealthy residents in Italian Renaissance style, while others reflect Turkish neo-Moorish influence. They are adorned with Jewish motifs, including Hebrew lettering, which can still be seen despite the dilapidated state of the buildings.

Our tour will take us to some of the most interesting buildings in the Bukharan Quarter. The encircled numbers refer to the numbers printed in black on the map of the tour.

We begin our tour at **Beit Yehudayoff-Hefetz** ①, known as The Palace (19, Ezra Street) which is considered to be the most luxurious house in the quarter. It is a two-

A courtyard in the Bukharan Quarter.

Beit Yehudayoff-Hefetz.

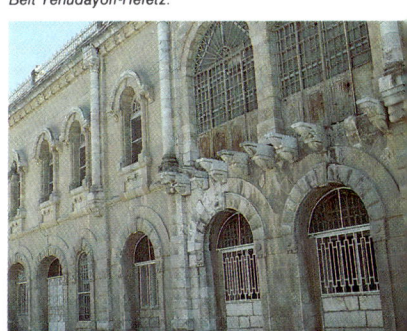

storey building with a flat roof surrounded by a stylized wrought-iron railing, interspersed with stone pillars. The front of the building is 55 m (60 yds) long, the doors and windows embellished with cornices and stone arches, pilasters and reliefs of Corinthian-style marble pillars. Stars of David adorn the iron grille doors on the second floor, the cornices on the ground floor and the arched grilles of the twin windows on the top floor. A *sukka* (booth) on the top floor has a sloping glass roof which slides on iron rails, thus converting the room into an open *sukka*.

The facade is in neo-Renaissance style and recalls the 17th century Capitolina Museum in Rome. Two winding stairways lead up to the entrance on the second floor. Traces of the magnificent rooms can still be seen as well as the frescoes on the walls of the passageway. The synagogue, on the top floor, has four pillars with Corinthian capitals, supporting a pointed arch in the center and a pair of horseshoe arches on both sides (in neo-Moorish style). The walls are marble-faced.

The building, erected in 1907 by the Yehudayoff and Hefetz families, wealthy merchants from Bukhara, is known as the "Messiah's palace", where the Messiah would be greeted upon his arrival. At first the building served as the Zion Orphanage, but during the First World War it was requisitioned by the Turkish army for its headquarters. After the British conquered Jerusalem a reception was given here in honor of General Allenby by the Jewish community and the World Zionist Organization. Today the building houses the Beit Hanna and Beit Ya'akov religious schools for girls.

The **Bukharan Old People's Home** ② (in Ezra Street, entrance from the corner of Fishel Street) is a one-storey building surrounding a paved courtyard. Originally planned as a tenement house, it was purchased by leaders of the community after the First World War to serve as a home for elderly members of the community.

Beit Simhayoff ③ (Yissa Bracha Street, corner No. 6, Fishel Street). The facade of this corner building is of special interest because of the covered balconies on its two floors: on the ground floor the balconies are decorated with engraved stone arches; on the second floor the roof is composed of triangular wooden beams supported by pillars and a stylized wrought iron railing. The **Rubinoff house** in the same courtyard is similar in style.

Beit Davidoff ④ (10, Habukharim Street, corner Talmudi Street). The double tiled roof of this building rises above high walls. It is in the style of building popular in the Tuscany province in Italy. The doors and windows are supported by pilasters with Corinthian capitals. Above the windows are round skylights, and below the gable a Star of David engraved on stone.

The building has a large central hall, and

One of the windows of Beit Davidoff.

One of many dedication plaques in the quarter.

a covered balcony facing north. Planned by an Italian architect, it was erected on the eve of the First World War by Joseph Davidoff. From 1915 to 1925 the Hebrew Gymnasium high school was housed here. The Amal Vocational School was situated here from 1952 to 1983, but has since moved and the building is awaiting its next tenant.

At 14, Habukharim Street there is a branch of the Harry Fischel Institute for Talmudic Studies. The elongated building was erected in 1928 by Yehezkiel ben Yaakov Halevy, as attested by the plaque at the entrance.

The **Mosheyoff House** ⑤ (18, Habukharim Street, corner David Hazan Street). The two-storey building encloses four inner courtyards; note the arcaded pillars on the ground floor and the upstairs gallery balcony. The arches have stone carvings and on one is inscribed the year of construction.

Entrance to the building is through 13-15, David Hazan Street; the gateway has two pillars supporting a stone arch. A rounded stone cornice runs along the building between the two storeys. The building was erected by Simha Mosheyoff, who had been president of the Jewish community of Turkestan. It was the outermost building of the quarter up to the First World War, when it was used as a Turkish prison. After the war it was populated by immigrants of the Second and Third Aliya (waves of immigration) who became leaders of the Jewish community and held official positions in the administration of the country. The building is no longer residential, but has a number of small workshops.

At the northeastern extremity of the Bukharan Quarter a few buildings have been erected by members of a community of Jews from Mashad, Iran who, in 1839, were forced to convert to Islam, but continued to practice Judaism secretly. A few score families immigrated to Jerusalem together with the Bukharan community and set up a group of houses called Givat Shaul, after the head of the Shauloff family who built the first house in the neighborhood.

We will visit two of these complexes:
Beit Hajji Yehezkiel ⑥ (corner of Adonyahu HaCohen and Fishel Streets). The building which encloses a paved courtyard with a cistern was built by Muhammad Ismael, the first member of this community of converts from Mashad to immigrate to Jerusalem, who changed his name to Yehezkiel Halevy. It has 21 rooms and a synagogue. Its windows have ornamented stone frames; a Hebrew dedication is engraved on the 18 window sills.
Beit Hajji Adoniya ⑦ (16, Adonyahu HaCohen Street). The courtyard is surrounded by a two-storey building. The outside stairway leads to a balcony on the second floor, where the synagogue is situ-

Mosheyoff House.

A house in Geula (see overleaf).

ated. The entranceway is decorated with pillars and Corinthian-style capitals. The Star of David is a decorative motif repeated many times on the facade. In the synagogue hall is a *bimah* of white marble and the floor is covered with Persian carpets.

The **Beit Menahem Synagogue** ⑧ (35, Yehezkiel Street). A cupola protrudes above the roof of the synagogue on the second floor of the building. A large eucalyptus tree next to the building is a remnant of a row of trees planted along the streets of the quarter. Most of the trees were chopped down by the Turks during the First World War.

The **Hamam** (Turkish bath) ⑨ (36, Yehezkiel Street). On the ground floor is the steam tank room from which pipes run under the floor of the two steam rooms on the floor above. The Hamam was turned into a laundry in 1987.

Beit Zofayoff ⑩ (13, Musayoff Street). At the entrance is an inscription attesting to the fact that it was built by David and Shlomo Zofayoff Katz in 5664 (1904), a father and son who were wealthy silk merchants in Turkestan. The house had its own synagogue on the top floor.

The **Hekdesh building** ⑪ (11, Musayoff Street). This is a large complex extending between Musayoff, Habukharim, Yehezkiel and Adonyahu HaCohen Streets. It includes one and two-storey houses, four synagogues, 25 apartments, and 12 shops. Above the main entrance is a new sign stating that this is the Mishmarot Kehuna Yeshiva. In the yard are a cistern, a pine tree, and eucalyptus and citrus trees. It was built in phases up till 1914 for destitute members of the Bukharan community.

The **Baba Tama Synagogue** ⑫ (4, Habukharim Street, corner Yehezkiel Street) was built in 1894 with funds provided by a Bukharan Jew of that name. The Holy Ark at the southern wall is covered with a mantle embroidered with silver thread in typical Bukharan style. The women's gallery is separated from the main hall by a lattice-work partition.

We return to Yehezkiel Street, the main street of the quarter and walk down to the Geula Quarter.

The **Geula Quarter** was built from 1924 to 1926 on the southern slope of the hill below the Bukharan Quarter northwest of Mea She'arim. Its streets are named for the Prophets as they are also in nearby Kerem Avraham. It was first inhabited by Orthodox as well as non-Orthodox Jews, but over the years it has become entirely ultra-Orthodox. Famous *yeshivot*, orphanages and other public and religious institutions have been set up here.

We will roam through the streets in order to gain an impression of its inhabitants and the buildings in the area. Our tour ends in Yehezkiel Street where many bus routes have stops.

TOUR No. 18

FROM SANHEDRIA TO THE TOMB OF SIMON THE JUST

Details of tour: We begin the tour at the Second Temple period complex of tombs of Sanhedria, pass through the Ramot Eshkol neighborhood, visit Ammunition Hill, continue through the Sheikh Jarrah neighborhood and end at the Tomb of Simon the Just.
Distance covered: approx. 3 km (2 miles)
Time: approx. 3 hours
Transportation: Buses No 2, 4, 9, 28, 31, 35, 37, 40
Parking lots along the route for private vehicles
Starting point: at the corner of Shmuel Hanavi and Hativat Harel Streets
End of tour: St George Street
The Sites: 1. Tombs of Sanhedria; 2. Eshkolot Cave; 3. Givat HaTahmoshet (Ammunition Hill); 4. Tomb of Simon the Just.

THE TOUR

1. Tombs of Sanhedria At the junction of Shmuel Hanavi (the Prophet Samuel) and Hativat Harel (Harel Brigade) Streets, near the traffic lights, is the Sanhedria cemetery. It was opened in 1948 when access to the cemetery on the Mount of Olives was no longer possible. The neighborhood on the other side of Shmuel Hanavi Street is called Sanhedria. We continue along Shmuel Hanavi Street to the north, turn right to Sanhedria Street, and enter a garden at the edge of which we see burial caves of the Second Temple period hewn out of the rock, known as the Sanhedria Tombs because of the 71 burial niches the cave can accommodate — corresponding to the number of the members of the Sanhedrin (the Supreme religious body in the Hasmonean period until 425 CE). Archeological evidence has shown this to be the mausoleum of a noble Jewish family, and about 100 skeletons have been found there. We descend the stone steps to a square courtyard, with stone benches along three sides. On the facade is a carved gable, ornamented with acanthus leaves, intertwined with pomegranates and other fruit motifs. The entrance is closed off by an iron grille, but through it can be seen the passageway and a central chamber which leads to other chambers. In one of the chambers there are two rows of burial niches one above the other.

The Sanhedria Tombs.

Many pilgrims who have visited Jerusalem since the 13th century have described these burial caves. They were also called the "Judges' Tombs" and were first excavated in 1869 by the French explorer De Saulcy. He found an ossuary with the name Isaac carved in Hebrew. The Jerusalem scholar M. Luncz expressed his concern for the fate of the burial caves, and

TOUR No. 18   212

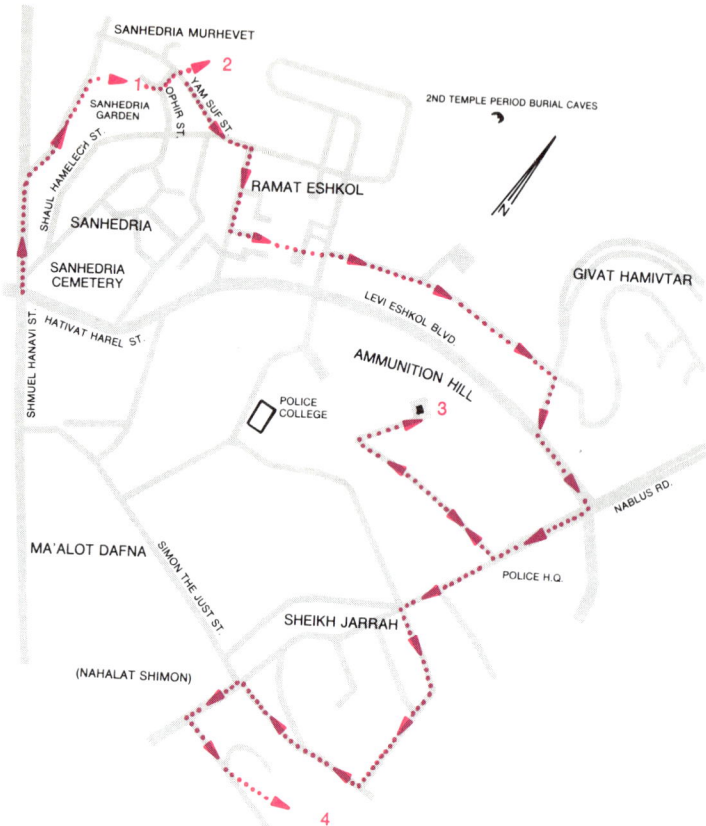

Map of the tour.

advocated that a Jewish neighborhood be set up around it. Thus in 1926, the Sanhedria neighborhood was established in the vicinity.

We ascend the stairs to the left of the burial cave, and see a rock wall with openings to additional burial niches. We turn left to Ophira Street into Shaul Hamelech Street (King Saul Street) which goes down into Yam Suf Street (Red Sea Street). We have now entered the Ramat Eshkol neighborhood, whose streets are named after sites in the Sinai Peninsula. This was the first neighborhood to be built in Jerusalem after 1967. The cease-fire line between Jordan and Israel passed along the border of Sanhedria and the remains of fortifications can still be seen today.

2. Eshkolot Cave We go down a path between houses No. 8 and 10 on Yam Suf Street and we come to the gabled entrance of another burial cave. The ornamentation of bunches (*eshkolot* in Hebrew) of grapes intertwined with vine tendrils has given the name to this burial cave. It was discovered in 1897 and was cleaned out between 1974 and 1976 by the Israel Department of Antiquities and Museums. The cave was the burial site of a prosperous Jerusalem family in the 1st century. It was plundered in ancient times and in the Byzantine period monks lived there; it probably served the same purpose during the Mameluke and Ottoman periods. In the entrance chamber there are adorned corner pillars. To the left is an opening to a chamber with burial niches, and another opening leading to a further central chamber, which in turn leads to six more chambers, with nine burial niches in each.

There were many more burial caves in the vicinity; they are part of a large necropolis that surrounded Jerusalem in the Second Temple period.

We return to Yam Suf Street and continue along Paran Street to Givat HaMivtar reaching Eshkol Boulevard, or alternately we can go straight up through Eshkol Boulevard to Ammunition Hill (see Givat HaTahmoshet, below).

Givat HaMivtar is bisected by the Jerusalem–Ramallah road. On the hill were Jordanian fortifications captured by the Israeli forces on 5th June 1967. In 1968 and when the area was being developed, between 1970 and 1973, a number of Second Temple period burial caves were discovered. In one of them an ossuary was found with the name in Aramaic of "Simon the Temple builder". It is assumed that this was the tomb of one of the craftsmen employed in work on the Temple during its reconstruction by Herod. The cave contained also the remains of a man who had been crucified, as evidenced by the nail hole in his heel bone.

The **Abba burial cave** is also of particular interest, consisting of a courtyard and central burial chamber with a place for laying out the dead and niches for the bones. A seven-line inscription in Aramaic was found on one of the walls; it states that Abba of the priestly family of Aharon, born in Jerusalem and exiled to Babylon, brought back the remains of Mattityahu son of Judah and buried them here. It is presumed that this is the burial place of Mattityahu Antigonus, son of Aristobulus, the first Hasmonean king. He reigned three years in Jerusalem, and was taken as a prisoner to Antioch in northern Syria where he was put to death in 37 CE. Abba was also of the Hasmonean family and had been exiled to Babylon as a youth. The site is closed to visitors.

(top) Gable over entrance to Eshkolot Cave.
(bottom) Eshkolot Cave.

3. Givat HaTahmoshet (Ammunition Hill)

This was the site of the fiercest battle in Jerusalem, in June 1967. There is now a public park and museum dedicated to the fallen of the Six Day War. The Jordanian trenches and fortifications have been left as they were. The park is open at all times. The museum is open Sunday to Thursday from 9.00 am to 4.00 pm (to 7.00 pm in July and August); Fridays and eve of holidays to 1.00 pm. Admission fee.

The site can be reached by the path from Eshkol Boulevard; by car, from Nablus

Givat HaTahmoshet (Ammunition Hill).

TOUR No. 18

Husseini family house in Sheikh Jarrah.

Memorial to the Hadassah convoy victims.

Road, opposite the Police headquarters. There is a parking lot, a grove of pine trees and a picnic site.

We go down Nablus Road to the south (to the right of the Police headquarters) and pass the new building of the English Eye Hospital which moved here from the other side of the city below Mount Zion in 1948. The road turns left to **Sheikh Jarrah**, a Muslim neighborhood built in 1925 around the summer villas of leading Arab families, named for the Sheikh whose tomb is situated at the bottom of the hill. There are a number of hotels in the area as well as consulates.

We continue down the road to the junction where the road to the right used to be the main road to the Hadassah Hospital and the Hebrew University on Mount Scopus. A plaque in memory of the 78 doctors, university scholars and students, victims of the Arab attack on the convoy on its way to Mount Scopus on 13th April 1948, is seen here.

4. Tomb of Simon the Just We go down the road to the junction and turn left to the upper section of the Kidron Valley. The **tomb of Sheikh Jarrah**, who served in Saladin's army, can be seen, surmounted by a minaret, at the right of the entrance to the Kidron Valley. The mosque was built in 1895 and repaired at the beginning of the 20th century. Nearby is the tall new building of the Islamic Council which moved here from the Old City.

On the left bank of the river valley is a burial cave from the late Roman period, belonging, according to a 14th-century tradition, to Simon the Just, a high priest of the 4th century CE, who said: "By three things is the world sustained: by the Law, by divine service and by charity." (*Ethics of the Fathers* 1:2). There are several chambers with burial niches in the cave, in which it is presumed that Simon the Just's four sons were buried. In the past, when natural disasters struck the city, Jews used to come and pray at Simon's tomb. Today the festival of Lag BaOmer is celebrated here.

The tomb, in fact, is that of the Roman matron Julia Sabine, as an inscription proves. The site is open Sundays to Thursdays from 8.30 am to 4.00 pm and to 1.00 pm on Fridays. We return to St George Street where our tour ends.

Tomb of Simon the Just.

Map of the tour. ▶

TOUR No. 19

UPPER JAFFA ROAD TO MAHANEH YEHUDA

Details of tour: Through the Jewish neighborhoods established along the Jaffa Road axis from the 1870s to the 1890s
Distance covered: approx. 2 km (1¼ miles)
Time: approx. 3 hours
Transportation: Bus lines to city center
Parking at Clal Center for private vehicles
Starting point: Jaffa Road–King George Avenue intersection
End of tour: Clal Center
The Sites: 1. Jaffa Road–King George V Avenue intersection; 2. Ezrat Yisrael; 3. Even Yisrael; 4. Sephardi Orphanage; 5. Sukkat Shalom; 6. Mishkenot Yisrael; 7. Mazkeret Moshe; 8. Ohel Moshe; 9. Mahaneh Yehuda Market; 10. Etz-Hayim Yeshiva; 11. Sundial Building; 12. District Health Office; 13. Mahaneh Yehuda Police Station; 14. Alliance Israelite Universelle; 15. Clal Center.

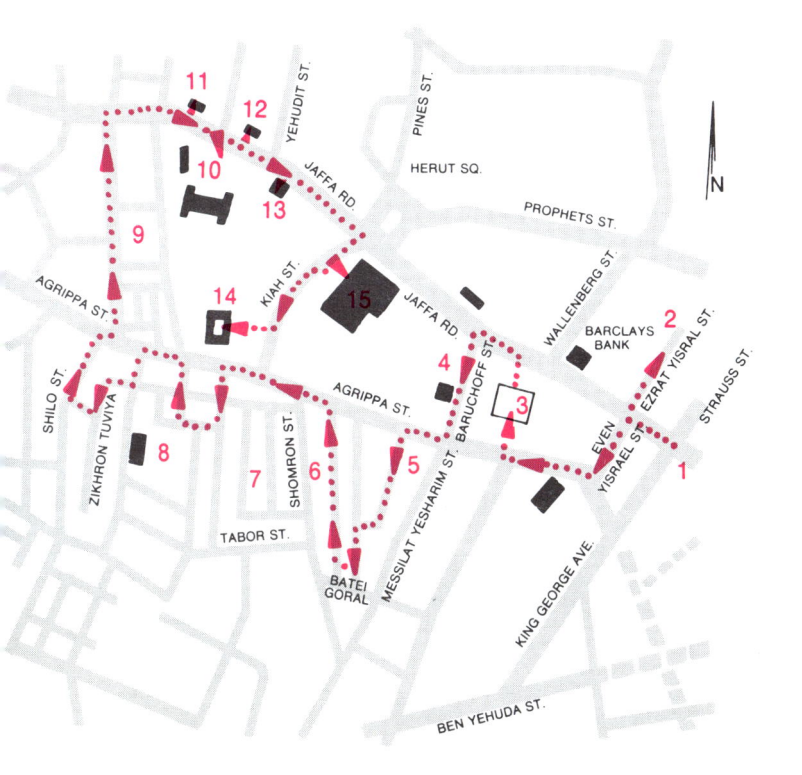

THE TOUR

1. Jaffa Road–King George V Avenue intersection One of the angles of the triangle formed by Jaffa Road, King George Avenue and Ben Yehuda Street, which today constitutes the city center. At the corners are one-storey commercial buildings, which have remained unchanged since the 1930s. A marble slab in the wall of the building on the corner of King George Avenue (No. 2) bears an inscription in Hebrew, English and Arabic, attesting to the dedication of the street on 9 December 1924, by the British High Commissioner Sir Herbert Samuel. The first buildings in this area were the German Hospital built in 1892–1894, and the Bikur Holim Hospital built between 1910 and 1925 (see Tour 15) on the corner of Strauss Street and the Street of the Prophets. We shall go west up Jaffa Road until the first street to the north (right).

2. Ezrat Yisrael This neighborhood on both sides of Ezrat Yisrael Street was constructed in 1892, mainly by the Sephardi Chief Rabbi Yaakov Meir and Rabbi Yosef Rivlin. The symbolical name of the neighborhood is taken from verses in Psalms (20:7; 121:2) which are quoted in the foundation deed. The writer Yehuda Burla, who lived in the neighborhood as a child, describes vividly daily life there in his short stories. The printing shop of the scholar A.M. Luncz was here. Among the residents of the quarter in 1910 were Yizhak Ben Zvi, Rahel Yanait, Yaakov Zerubabel, David Ben Gurion and Yisrael Shohet, who edited and printed the Poalei Zion weekly publication, "Ahdut."

Mashiah Baruchoff's house 64, Jaffa Road, now the Barclay's Bank building, west of the Ezrat Yisrael neighborhood, is famous for the stone lions on both sides of the entrance. It was built by Mashiah Baruchoff as his residence. The balcony in the facade of this sumptuous building has columns with Corinthian capitals over which are arches supporting the ceiling. The owner of the house came from one of the wealthy Bukharan families who founded the Sephardi Orphanage.

3. Even Yisrael Opposite Ezrat Yisrael Street between Jaffa Road and Agrippa Street. This neighborhood was founded in 1875 (together with the Mishkenot Yisrael neighborhood; see below) by the company of this name. Fifty-three apartments were constructed (the letters of the Hebrew word *Even*, "stone", have the numerical value of 53; the name also alludes to the verse in Genesis ". . . by the hands of the mighty God of Jacob; from thence is the shepherd, the stone of Israel" (49:24). Among the founders were Rabbi Yosef Rivlin, Yehoshua Yellin, Y.N. Pines and A.M. Luncz. On the hill to the south was the Talithakumi German Protestant girls' school (today the site of the Rejwan Building, at 16, King George). The residential houses were built around a square courtyard with two entrances, from the north on Jaffa Road and to the south on Agrippa Street. We shall view the mouth of the cistern in the center of the courtyard, the

Freemasons' hall in Ezrat Yisrael, built 1971.

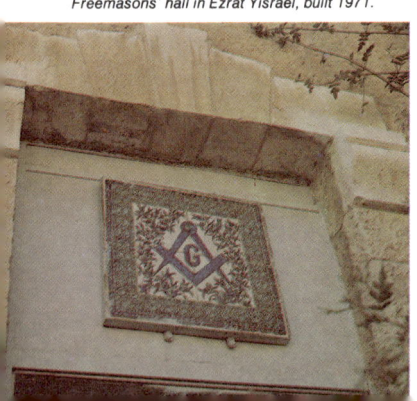

Mashiah Baruchoff's house.

neighborhood oven and the cellars of the houses (where coal, wine and oil were stored). East of the residential courtyard, another courtyard was built, around which were shops and workshops that still exist today. Opposite the neighborhood, north of Jaffa Road, were parks, close to the home of Yosef Navon and the house of the Pasha (see Tour No. 15).

4. Sephardi Orphanage The entrance is on Mashiah Baruchoff Street, No. 4. The two-storey building was erected in 1903 and was financed by the Baruchoff and Issacharoff families and Rabbi Yaakov Meir. The entrance and the windows are elaborately decorated and the construction is of exceptional quality. During the Frist World War the Turkish army occupied the locality. Three synagogues were created in its northern wing.

Opposite, on the other side of Jaffa Road, are shops. Beit Ha'am was on the second floor of this building, and behind it was the Kamenitz Hotel. (See Tour No. 15). We shall go back along Baruchoff Street to Agrippa Street.

5. Sukkat Shalom The neighborhood opposite the Sephardi Orphanage, between Agrippa Street and Messilat Yesharim Street. Construction of the neighborhood was commenced in 1888 by the Swiss banker Frutiger and his partners Yosef Navon and Shalom Konstrum. The neighborhood was called after the latter and after a verse of Psalms (76:2): "In Salem [Jerusalem] also is his tabernacle *[sukka]*, and his dwelling place in Zion".

6. Mishkenot Yisrael The company which constructed this neighborhood in 1875 was headed by Rabbi Yosef Rivlin, Yoel Moshe Salomon and others. Its name was taken from the verse: "How goodly are your tents, O Jacob, and your tabernacles, O Israel" (Numbers 24:5). The land was acquired with the savings of 140 settlers who competed against Christian Churches for its purchase. Until the 44 houses were built, the settlers grew wheat on the lot which they harvested in a festive ceremony. The long apartment houses were built round a courtyard, which contains a ritual bath, an oven, a cistern and a synagogue.

In the south part of the neighborhood the **Batei Goral** houses of Jews from Yemen were built in 1884. The houses were assigned to families by lottery, hence their name (*goral* — "lottery" in Hebrew). The synagogue on the second floor of one of the houses is furnished in the style of a village synagogue in the Yemen. On the sign at the entrance are the names of the donors and the names of the poet Shalom Shabazi and of the Kabbalist Shalom Sharabi, after whom the Yeshiva in the synagogue is called.

7. Mazkeret Moshe The neighborhood between Agrippa Street, Shomron Street, Tabor Street, and Ohel Moshe Street, was built between 1883 and 1885, with the help of the Mazkeret Moshe Fund (established in 1874 in memory of Sir Moses (Moshe) Montefiore). The Fund granted long-term, interest-free loans, and assisted the Mishkenot Yisrael Company on whose land the neighborhood was constructed. The neighborhood was built around a large courtyard, and the number of apartments reached 130 in 1897. The first settlers came from the Old City, and the neighborhood was quite prestigious. The back part of the houses faced outwards and formed a kind of wall around the courtyard.

8. Ohel Moshe The neighborhood is adjacent to Mazkeret Moshe, and its twin as to structure and the period of its construction.

The two-storey building in the center of the neighborhood was built in 1935. It houses the Ohel Sarah synagogue of the

Courtyard of the Sephardi Orphanage.

community of Jews from Yanina in Greece. On the walls of the synagogue is a thin layer of copper.

We shall continue along Zikhron Tuviya Street, west of the Ohel Moshe neighborhood. On both sides of the street are the houses of the **Zikhron Tuviya** neighborhood, built in 1890. Among its founders was Rabbi Yosef Rivlin, and this was the 11th neighborhood that he founded, hence his Yiddish nickname "Yosef the neighborhood builder". The name of the neighborhood, taken from a verse in Psalms 145:7 is an expression of gratitude to him.

We shall continue up to Shilo Street and return to Agrippa Street and to the market.

South of the market is **Zikhron Yosef,** a neighborhood founded in 1931 and named after Yosef Levi who owned the land on which it was built. Its first residents were immigrants from Kurdistan.

9. Mahaneh Yehuda Market The largest market in the New City, between Agrippa Street, Mahaneh Yehuda Street, Jaffa Road and Etz-Hayim Yeshiva. It has shops and open stalls for vegetables, fruit, meat, fish, pastries, household items, etc. The market was established in 1928 and was named after the nearby neighborhood (see Tour No. 20). It has about 120 shops and its streets bear the names of fruit: Agas, Afarsek, Tapuah, Shezif, etc. (pear, peach, apple, plum in Hebrew).

10. Etz-Hayim Yeshiva (115, Jaffa Road). Over the gate is a sign in Hebrew and in English: "Etz-Hayim — The Main Center General T.T. School and Grand Yeshiva and Soup Kitchen." This was an educational institution founded in the Old City in 1862 by Rabbi Samuel Salant, who was the Ashkenazi Chief Rabbi of Jerusalem and the leader of the Old Yishuv. The Center in the Jewish Quarter created branches in various neighborhoods, and this branch became the main center after the Jewish Quarter fell in 1948.

The land was purchased in 1908. In 1910 shops were built on both sides of the courtyard and their revenue serves to maintain the *yeshiva*, which moved to its present locality in 1936. In the courtyard is the large central building containing the Great Yeshiva, which has about 100 students (most of them married), some of whom have their homes within the complex of buildings in the courtyard. The building at the back contains Talmud Tora classrooms, where about 150 boys study. The main building was erected in 1938, and beside it the first soup kitchen. The new soup kitchen is on the east side of the courtyard.

11. Sundial Building (92, Jaffa Road) is a four-storey house with a large sundial on the south wall of the upper storey. The building was constructed in the years

Mazkeret Moshe.

Entrance to Ohel Moshe.

The Sundial Building.

Mahaneh Yehuda Market.

1905–1908 as a hostel by Samuel Levy, an American immigrant. The building originally had five storeys and the turret at the top was the highest in the city. It housed the Zoharei Hama Synagogue. The sundial was built in 1918 by Rabbi Moshe Shapira, a native of Mea She'arim. The upper clock on the right is a regular clock, and the one on the left shows the time according to the reckoning used by the Arabs (6.00 in the morning, when the day begins, corresponds to the first hour in conventional clocks). The building was damaged in 1927 in an earthquake, and the 5th floor with the turret was destroyed. In 1940 the synagogue on the 4th floor was damaged by fire, and was moved to the ground floor. The facade of the building was restored and repaired in 1980. The new brass plaques on the facade give details of the renovation.

12. District Health Office The Mustashfa Building at 86, Jaffa Road has a large courtyard surrounded by a stone wall, between Jaffa Road, Yosef Ben Matityahu Street and Yehudit Street. The gatehouse, facing Jaffa Road, bears at the top the symbol of the Ottoman empire. Steps on both sides lead up to the top of the gatehouse.

Construction of the building as a residence was commenced in 1882 but was not completed. It was abandoned for about 10 years because of a rumor that the house was haunted. It had been built by a rich Christian Arab family for their only son and his bride. The day before the wedding the groom died, but the parents demanded that the wedding ceremony be carried out with the dead groom present. From the time of this macabre ceremony, the house was thought to be cursed. In 1891 the Turkish authorities expanded the building and turned it into a municipal hospital (Mustashfa) containing about 30 beds. Since the Mandate period it has housed the District Health Office.

13. Mahaneh Yehuda Police Station (83, Jaffa Road). The building was originally erected as a Turkish fortress on the Jaffa-Jerusalem highway in the early 19th century, and served as such until the end of the 1860s. The building was renovated and enlarged in 1863. The house served as the residence of the British Consul until the end of the First World War. The structure has thick walls and vaulted ceilings. There were stables at the back, and a large garden with fruit trees. The pair of lions at the entrance were sculpted by the famous 19th century Jerusalem artist Rabbi Simcha Shlomo Yaniwer Diskin. The building served later as a police station and is today a civil guard station. Its courtyard adjoins that of the Etz Hayim Yeshiva.

We shall go down Jaffa Road and turn right onto Alliance Israelite Street.

14. Alliance Israelite Universelle A

The Police Station with the lions at the gate.

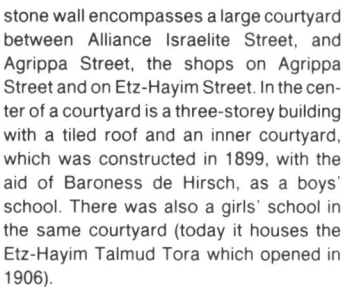

The Alliance Israelite building.

stone wall encompasses a large courtyard between Alliance Israelite Street, and Agrippa Street, the shops on Agrippa Street and on Etz-Hayim Street. In the center of a courtyard is a three-storey building with a tiled roof and an inner courtyard, which was constructed in 1899, with the aid of Baroness de Hirsch, as a boys' school. There was also a girls' school in the same courtyard (today it houses the Etz-Hayim Talmud Tora which opened in 1906).

These educational institutions and the vocational school were established by the Alliance Israelite Universelle, an international Jewish organization, the first of its kind, founded in Paris in 1860, for the defense of the civil rights of the Jews. The Alliance founded a network of Jewish educational institutions in the Balkan regions, the Middle East, and in North Africa. It created the first agricultural school in Palestine in 1870, and schools in Jerusalem, Haifa, Jaffa, Safed and Tiberias. The Alliance institutions in Palestine were the first where general studies were conducted in Hebrew. The boys' school existed in this building until 1967, and today it houses the Experimental School.

15. Clal Center building A new, fourteen-storey high building with three basement stories stands on the corner of Jaffa Road, Alliance Israelite Street, and Agrippa Street. It contains a commercial center with shops, offices, banks, a cinema and coffee shops. It is built around an inner courtyard, with a gallery on each floor looking down onto the courtyard. The building was constructed between 1970 and 1977 by the Clal Company. Alliance Israelite Universelle educational institutions originally occupied this site. Among these was a vocational school whose gate was moved some 60 meters to the east and was kept as a memorial of the school. Our tour ends here.

The Clal Center.

TOUR No. 20

FROM BEIT YA'AKOV TO THE LAEMEL SCHOOL

Details of tour: The tour goes through the neighborhoods built at the end of the 19th century and the beginning of the 20th in western Jerusalem, between Jaffa and Mea She'arim Roads.
Distance covered: approx. 3 km (2 miles)
Time: approx. 3 hours
Transportation: any bus to the center of the city which passes through Mahaneh Yehuda. Buses No 4, 4A and 9 pass by the Laemel School
Parking in the side streets in Mahaneh Yehuda area and in the Clal Building car park for private vehicles.
Starting point: Mahaneh Yehuda market, at 120, Jaffa Road
End of tour: Yeshayahu Street, at corner of the Street of the Prophets
The Sites: 1. Beit Ya'akov; 2. Mahaneh Yehuda neighborhood; 3. Sha'arei Zedek, Ohel Shlomo and Sha'arei Yerushalayim; 4. Batei Sayidoff; 5. Sha'arei Zedek building; 6. Mekor Baruch; 7. Ohalei Simha; 8. Kerem; 9. Schneller; 10. Kerem Avraham; 11. Yegia Kapayim; 12. Ahva; 13. Zikhron Moshe; 14. The Laemel School.

THE TOUR

1. Beit Ya'akov The tour begins at 120, Jaffa Road beside the Mahaneh Yehuda market. The neighborhood was established in 1877 and was the last of 9 neighborhoods to be set up outside the Old City. The founders planned the erection of 70 houses and thus the derivation of its name from the verse in Genesis (46:27): ". . .all the souls of the house of Jacob, which came into Egypt, were threescore and ten." Only 15 families settled at first; the remaining houses were built after the First World War. Because of their isolated location the residents were incessantly attacked by marauders.

An ancient quarry was discovered on the slope of the hill upon which the neighborhood was built and a pillar dating from the Second Temple period, similar to that found in the Russian Compound (see Tour No. 14). The long back wall of the neighborhood faces Jaffa Road, while the anterior section faces Hadekel Street. The sign over the synagogue lists the names of the English Jews with whose donations it was constructed.

2. Mahaneh Yehuda neighborhood, opposite the marketplace, north of Jaffa Road, was built in 1887 by the Swiss banker Frutiger and his Jewish partners Shalom Konstrum and Joseph Navon (after whose brother Yehuda Navon the neighborhood was called). One hundred and sixty houses were built over a period of two years and were inhabited by persons of means.

3. Sha'arei Zedek, Ohel Shlomo and Sha'arei Yerushalayim The Sha'arei Zedek neighborhood consisting of 30 one-storey houses surrounding a central courtyard, lies to the north of the bus station parking lot (bounded by Navon Street) and was built in 1899 on land purchased by the Frutiger Company. Its name was taken from Psalm 118:19: "Open to me the gates of righteousness" *(Sha'arei Zedek)*.

Ohel Shlomo, the neighborhood to the southwest of Sha'arei Zedek, has a series of shops facing Jaffa Road and borders on Haturim Street as well. It was built in 1891, and named after Shlomo Mizrahi who purchased the land.

Sha'arei Yerushalayim, the neighbor-

TOUR No. 20   222

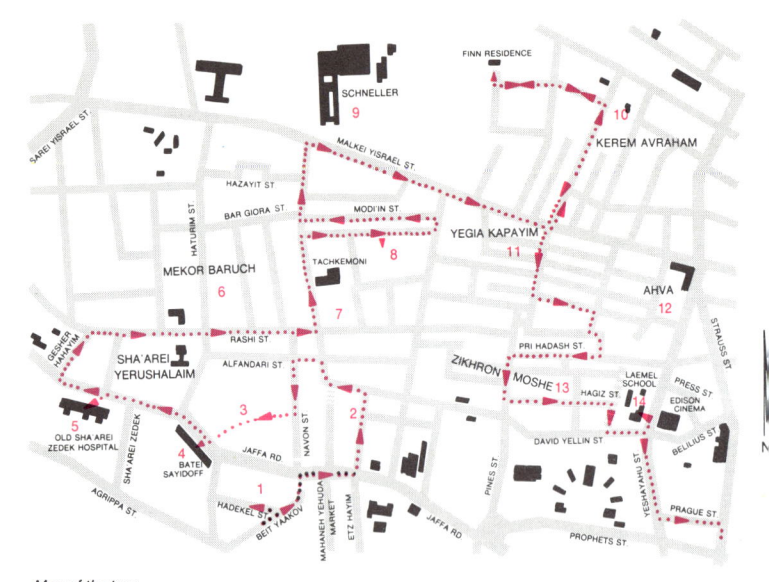

Map of the tour.

hood to the west of Ohel Shlomo, was built in 1891. Some of the 40 single-storey apartments have been turned into workshops and classrooms for *yeshivot*.

4. Batei Sayidoff are a row of two-storey houses opposite the Ohel Shlomo neighborhood. They were built in 1911 by a Bukharan Jew after whom they were named. Shops and workshops are situated on the Jaffa Road side of the neighborhood. The front of the buildings face south, onto a long courtyard enclosed by

View of Beit Ya'akov.

houses to the east and west. The apartments were considered at the time to be luxurious. The facade was renovated by the Jerusalem Municipality in 1983.

5. Sha'arei Zedek building The two-storey building that formerly housed the Sha'arei Zedek Hospital is situated on a large plot of land surrounded by a stone wall. It was built by Dr. Moshe Wallach who was sent to Jerusalem from Cologne, Germany in 1890, by the Jewish Council of Frankfurt. The hospital has moved to modern premises and the building has remained unoccupied.

6. Mekor Baruch Gesher Hahayim Street opposite the Sha'arei Zedek Hospital passes along the border of the Sha'arei Yerushalayim neighborhood and reaches Rashi Street, the southern edge of the Mekor Baruch neighborhood. It was established in 1926. The name was based on the verse from Proverbs 5:18: "Let thy fountain be blessed. . ." (*mekor baruch* in Hebrew). The houses are typical of the buildings erected at the time of the British Mandate. The residents were middle-class families, merchants, tradesmen and offi-

Batei Sayidoff.

The former Sha'arei Zedek building.

cials. Over the years educational and religious institutions were established in the neighborhood.

Rashi Road continues to the east to the **Ruhama** neighborhood. The first building erected in 1924 was the Ruhama School for girls in Yehudit Street which has since moved across the street.

We continue along Rashi Street and turn left into Tachkemoni Street, named after a boys' school (today Beit Avraham Metivta) which was one of the few religious schools that taught both secular and religious subjects with the emphasis on Zionist principles and Hebrew as a spoken language.

7. Ohalei Simha — Plitei Russia The 18 one-storey houses constituting this small neighborhood were built in 1894 for immigrants from Russia with monies raised by *Hassidim* who named it after Rabbi Simha of Pressburg.

On the other side of Rashi Street is the Horodna housing estate — 34 apartments and a synagogue built in 1892.

Another housing estate — Batei Vilna — two rows of houses with 32 apartments, was built in 1891.

8. Kerem A neighborhood built on land previously covered with vineyards (*kerem* in Hebrew), during the years 1885–1890, east of the Tachkemoni school.

All the above neighborhoods are today integrated into a single large Orthodox area and it is difficult to discern the borders of each housing estate.

9. Schneller A high Gothic clock tower can be seen from afar on Malkei Yisrael Street, on one of the buildings in a large fenced-off area of the Syrian Orphanage (in German: Syrisches Waisenhaus) called for short Schneller, after its founder, a German Lutheran missionary, Ludwig

Rashi Street in Mekor Baruch.

Tachkemoni School courtyard.

Schneller. The land was bought in 1855 with contributions made by the German Protestants. The complex was built between 1856 and 1900. It comprised an orphanage for orphans from the massacre of Christians in Syria, and workshops where the orphans were taught a trade. The number of pupils grew, until by the end of the century 130 boys and girls, including blind children, were receiving their education there. In addition to the workshops, laundry and windmill, Schneller rented agricultural land for growing crops. A teachers' training college as well as a factory for the manufacture of roof tiles were added.

During the First World War, the site was turned into an army camp. Today it is used by the Israel Defense Forces.

A number of houses were built in Shivtei Yisrael Street in the 19th century for the staff of the Schneller institutions, and they were named for towns in Germany from which donations were received for their construction. In 1948 families evacuated from the Nahalat Shimon neighborhood near Sheikh Jarrah were settled in these houses.

The area can be visited by permission of the military authorities, but the main building can be viewed from the entrance. The name of the institution appears in Arabic and German on the facade of the three-storey tiled-roof building. Above the inscription is a lamb carrying a cross and a verse from the Gospel of Luke appears in Gothic letters.

The bell tower consists of three tiers: at the lower level are the bells, in the center a clock and the upper level, an observation post. On the onion-like dome is a rod which originally ended in a cross. The building is in the style typical of the Baroque period in southern Germany.

10. Kerem Avraham The streets of this neighborhood founded east of Schneller in 1933 are named after the Prophets. Its history began in 1852 when Elizabeth Finn, wife of the British Consul, bought the plot of land (called in Arabic the "vineyard of el-Khalil" — the beloved, an appellation referring to the Patriarch Abraham). In 1855 the Finns had a house built here, and a garden with fruit trees and vegetables. Cisterns, an olive press, a wine press, and a soap factory were built. The name "Abraham's vineyard, 1852" was inscribed on the gate in English and Hebrew.

Consul Finn and his wife were devoted friends of the Jews, and lovers of Jerusalem. They established a fund in London for the support of Jews and launched a development project to provide work for Jews, believing that the return of the Jews to the Holy Land would be the first step to the Redemption. The English contractor who built the house believed that the English were the descendants of the Ten Lost Tribes and that his own family was descended from the tribe of Dan. After the consul died, Elizabeth Finn continued to live in their house in Kerem Avraham and wrote books on the customs and events in Jerusalem.

We enter Amos Street and turn left to Ovadia Street and find the Finns' residence at No. 24. The two-storey building,

The Schneller clock tower.

with its tiled roof and arched windows now houses a girls' school.

11. Yegia Kapayim This neighborhood on Shivtei Yisrael Street opposite Kerem Avraham was founded in 1909 by an association of artisans. Its streets are named after sages mentioned in rabbinical sources as having been craftsmen.

12. Ahva A large neighborhood built in 1908 by the Ahva Association supported by Bnai Brith. The buildings enclosed a broad courtyard in which there was a synagogue. The 75 buildings contain 250 apartments and shops facing Yeshayahu Street.

13. Zikhron Moshe This was the largest and most modern neighborhood when it was built in 1906, and was the center of Jerusalem's intellectual life at the time. Built on the crest of a hill, with monies provided by the fund set up by Moses (Moshe) Montefiore, it was named after him. The two-family houses are spacious, each with its own garden and the streets were particularly wide for the time, with broad pavements lined with trees. Between Yeshayahu and Strauss Streets a series of large well-appointed two-storey houses were built for distinguished residents of the neighborhood.

We walk along Pri Hadash Street between Ahva and Zikhron Moshe to Pines Street and reach house No. 2 in Moshe Hagiz Street where we find the building that housed the first Hebrew nursery school founded in 1903. No. 5 was the first building of the Hebrew Gymnasium high school founded in 1909. We enter David Yellin Street and continue to the corner of Yeshayahu Street.

14. Laemel School The large two-storey building surrounded by a high stone wall, opposite the Edison Cinema, was at first a solitary structure on the top of a hill between the Street of the Prophets and Mea She'arim Road. The land was purchased in 1901 by Ezra, a welfare association for the Jews of Germany — 48 years after the school was established by Dr L.A.

(top) The former Finn residence.
(center) Street in Yegia Kapayim.
(bottom) Gate in the Ahva neighborhood.

Street in Zikhron Moshe.

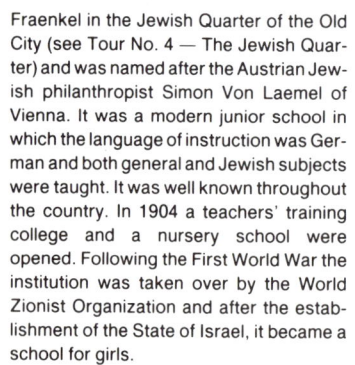

Facade of the Laemel School.

Fraenkel in the Jewish Quarter of the Old City (see Tour No. 4 — The Jewish Quarter) and was named after the Austrian Jewish philanthropist Simon Von Laemel of Vienna. It was a modern junior school in which the language of instruction was German and both general and Jewish subjects were taught. It was well known throughout the country. In 1904 a teachers' training college and a nursery school were opened. Following the First World War the institution was taken over by the World Zionist Organization and after the establishment of the State of Israel, it became a school for girls.

The building is in neo-classic European style combined with oriental elements. The symmetric facade ends in a gable, above which is a stylized palm tree and below it a clock with Hebrew letters as numbers. Underneath two windows is a circle enclosing a Star of David. It now houses a school for special education.

We continue along Press Street in the direction of the Street of the Prophets. At the corner of David Yellin Street was the Hebrew Teachers Training College which existed here between 1921 to 1927 and then the Doresh Zion school which moved here from the Old City. The building at the corner of Prague Street was the community hall, and in the courtyard behind it is a Mameluke tomb, that of Nebi Ukasha, and next to it a mosque. After the First World War, the majority of the inhabitants of Zikhron Moshe moved to the new neighborhoods of Rehavia, Talpiot and Beit Hakerem, and Orthodox religious families moved into the houses as they were vacated. Our tour ends here.

TOUR No. 21

FROM ZION SQUARE TO SHA'AREI HESSED

Details of tour: We will visit the neighborhoods in the western section of the New City built at the end of the 19th century and the beginning of the 20th century. They were built by different communities, and their respective styles are still discernible, especially in the synagogues. Of some of the early buildings only some detail has been kept as a "memorial".
Distance covered: approx. 3 km (2 miles)
Time: approx. 3 hours
Transportation: all bus routes passing through the city center. Return by No 9, 17 Private vehicles will find parking spaces along the route
Starting point: Zion Square
End of tour: Sha'arei Hessed
The sites: 1. Zion Square; 2. Ben Yehuda Street; 3. Schmidt School; 4. Religious Teachers' Seminary; 5. Histadrut building; 6. Talitha Kumi; 7. Artists' House; 8. Beit Ha'am; 9. Knesset Yisrael; 10. Shevet Ahim; 11. Nahalat Zion; 12. Zikhron Ahim and Nahalat Ya'akov; 13. Nahalat Ahim; 14. Neveh Bezalel; 15. Nahalat Zadok; 16. Sha'arei Hessed.

THE TOUR

1. Zion Square The square bounded by Jaffa Road, Ben Yehuda and Salomon Streets, was named for the Zion Cinema completed in 1920, and now replaced by the modern high-rise Bank Hapo'alim building. The Zion Cinema was the center of cultural life in Jerusalem in the 1920s and 1930s, where plays, concerts, lectures and movies were given.

2. Ben Yehuda Street The street ascending from Zion Square to King George Street, the major part of which is now a pedestrian mall, is named for Eliezer Ben Yehuda, who revived Hebrew as a spoken language, and lived and worked in Jerusalem from 1881 to 1922. The land was purchased by the Jewish Colonization Association from the Greek Orthodox Patriarchate, which had planted groves and vineyards on it. The buildings were constructed over a period of twenty years by private individuals, and by companies for residential accommodation, offices and commercial establishments. One of the prominent structures is the **Sansur Building** at the corner of Jaffa Road, Ben Yehuda and Luncz Streets. It was built in 1931 by a Christian Arab merchant from Bethlehem (for whom it is named), in modern European style with rococo embellishments. The three-storey building has long corridors with numerous offices on both sides.

Parallel to and south of Ben Yehuda Street are Shamai Street and Hillel Street,

Zion Square and Sansur Building.

Emblem on facade of Sansur Building.

TOUR No. 21   228

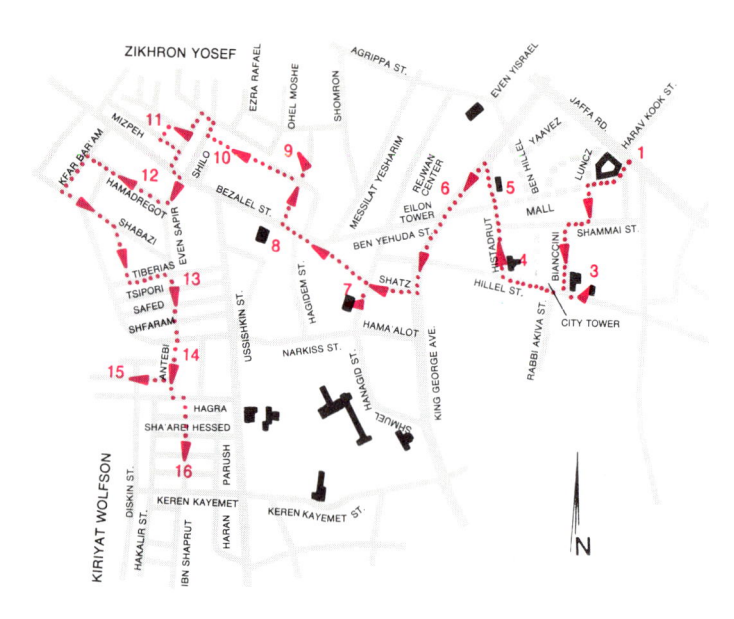

Map of the tour.

which are connected by Bianccini Street. At the corner of Bianccini and Hillel Streets are two buildings separated by a courtyard.

3. Schmidt School This was the first German Catholic institution in Jerusalem. The plot of land bordering on Nahalat Shiva was purchased in 1876 by Father Schneider. At first a small building for the Catholic Girls' school was erected on it, and in 1886 the two present buildings were constructed by the German architect Zandel with German builders. The corner building was a hospice and has a belltower and a chapel. The eastern building was a girls' school, named for Father Schmidt. The three-storey building has Gothic arched windows.

The Italian Synagogue and the Italian community museum are situated in the former German hospice building. The synagogue was brought from Conegliano Veneto in northern Italy, where it was erected at the beginning of the 18th century. Visiting hours (except when services are held): Sun., Tues. 10.00 a.m. to 1.00 p.m. and Wed. 4.00 p.m. to 7.00 p.m. The museum exhibits art treasures, holy arks and religious articles, books and documents relating to Italian Jewry.

We continue along Hillel Street past the Jerusalem City Tower, a high-rise building which houses the offices of the City Engineer, a hotel and shops.

4. Religious Teachers' Seminary 17, Hillel Street. One of the first buildings to be erected in the area at the end of the First World War. It houses a seminary for religious teachers.

We turn into Histadrut Street; on the corner is the former Eden Hotel (today the offices of the Foreign Exchange Dept. of the Finance Ministry).

5. Histadrut building This building erected in the 1920s, the first to serve the Jerusalem Workers' Association, was constructed by members of the Histadrut who came to the country with the third wave of immigrants (Third Aliyah). On the ground floor was the workers' cooperative restaurant; above it the offices of the Jerusalem Workers' Association and the Tel Or hall where movies were screened, plays presented and lectures held.

We continue up King George Street and pass the new Rejwan center and Dr. Mazia House completed in 1986 on the site of Talitha Kumi.

6. Talitha Kumi The stone entranceway, flanked on either side by windows, a gable and a round clock above, is all that is left of Talitha Kumi, the first building to be erected on the barren hilltop during the years 1861 to 1868. The three-storey building had been designed by Conrad Schick. It contained halls, living rooms and service rooms; there were storerooms and stables in a courtyard, and the entire complex was surrounded by a stone wall. It comprised also a girls' school.

The name Talitha Kumi is Aramaic and is taken from Jesus' words to the child whom he resurrected (Mark 5:41) — "I say unto thee, arise"). The school functioned here until 1948 when it moved to its new premises in Beit Jalla. It was then occupied by offices before it was demolished.

We continue along King George Street and pass through the Frances L. Hyatt Garden. For many years this was an abandoned stone quarry, called the Shiber pit after the owner of the plot of land. The nearby building housed the Knesset from 1949 to 1966, and today accommodates the Ministry of Tourism.

We ascend Schatz Street and enter Shmuel Hanagid Street.

7. Artists' House (12, Shmuel Hanagid Street) In 1908 two buildings of the same design were purchased by the Jewish National Fund for the Bezalel School of Arts and Crafts. These two-storey buildings, constructed originally as an orphanage for Arab children, are surrounded by a high stone wall. The walls of the buildings are capped by dentils; the windows are arched and the central windows are deco-

(top) The Italian Synagogue.
(center) Stone gateway of Talitha Kumi.
(bottom) Courtyard of the Schmidt School.

rated with pilasters, and a projecting stone stringcourse runs between the floors. The southern building housed the first museum of Jewish art in Israel and it was founded and directed by Mordechai Narkiss. (Its collections have since been transferred to the Israel Museum.) Today it serves as the Artists' House where exhibitions of the works of Israeli artists are held. In the northern building is the Bezalel School for Arts and Crafts.

The Bezalel Art School functioned here from 1906 to 1929 and since 1935. It was founded by Prof. Boris Schatz who directed it until 1925. Prof. Schatz, a Jewish artist, born in Latvia, founded the Bezalel committee in Berlin in 1905 with the purpose of raising funds to establish an institute to develop art and crafts in order to improve the situation of Jerusalem Jews. Schatz won the support of Theodor Herzl and other leaders of the World Zionist Organization and established in Jerusalem an institution which taught sculpture, painting and crafts.

We continue along Bezalel Street, until we reach HaGidem Street.

8. Beit Ha'am The Gerard Behar Hall is the largest in Beit Ha'am built in 1951, where, in 1961, Eichmann's trial was held. This public building contains an auditorium and the main public lending library.

Opposite Beit Ha'am, on the other side of Bezalel Street, are a number of small neighborhoods.

9. Knesset Yisrael We enter the neighborhood through Yizrael Street and pass by the housing complex of the Tiferet Zvi Kollel. We continue to Shomron Street to Batei Rand.

We turn left into Tabor Street and come to the gate of Knesset Yisrael neighborhood which is divided into three sections, built with funds contributed by American Jews and residents of Jerusalem. The driving force behind this project was Joseph Rivlin, one of the directors of the General Committee. We go through the gate into the courtyard of the first section

(top) The Hyatt Garden.
(center) Facade of the Artists' House.
(bottom) Beit Ha'am.

231 ZION SQUARE TO SHA'AREI HESSED

and find a water cistern in the center surrounded on three sides by two-storey buildings. We continue to the right, along Rama Street, into the next section.

10. Shevet Ahim This tiny quarter was established in 1892 between Bezalel, Shilo and Rama Streets. Its name comes from Psalm 133:1: "Behold, how good and how pleasant it is for brethren to dwell together in unity". It is also symbolical of the fact that Jews from different countries settled here. We continue along Rama Street to Shilo Street.

11. Nahalat Zion The majority of the residents of this neighborhood are immigrants from Iran. The land was purchased in 1891 from Arabs of the village of Lifta by Abraham Antebi, director of the Alliance Israelite Universelle and was sold at cost price, and loans granted to laborers who were prepared to build their own houses. We enter Beersheba Street and come to the water cistern and the public oven. To the left is the Syrian community's Adass Synagogue built in 1900. There are a number of other synagogues in the neighborhood, including that of Raphael Haim Cohen, an immigrant from Iran who established a well-known printing press in Jerusalem.

We return to Shilo Street. On the opposite side, bounded by Giv'on, Beit Zur and Nissim Behar Streets, is the **Neveh Shalom** neighborhood, founded in 1896 on land bought by the Frutiger Company and named for Frutiger's partner Shalom Konstrum from a verse of Isaiah (32:18): "And my people shall dwell in a peaceable habitation [*Neve Shalom* in Hebrew], and in sure dwellings". Its founders were Persian and Yemenite immigrants. It joined up with Shevet Ahim and together with Nahalat Zion and Shevet Zedek forms the area known as Nahlaot.

From Shilo Street, we descend the steps to Bezalel Street and cross over to the other side. Near the crossing a sign over a two-storey building states that this is the Synagogue and Talmud Torah of the community from Urpah in Turkey.

(top) Knesset Yisrael.
(center) Street in Nahalat Zion.
(bottom) Gateway in Nahalat Zion.

12. Zikhron Ahim and Nahalat Ya'akov Zichron Ahim is the neighborhood of the Urpah community built in 1931. We go down Even Sapir Street and turn right to Hamadregot (steps) Street. The steps go down and then up to the other end of the street. Simple one or two-storey dwellings with shared courtyards line the street on either side, and additions made over the years are apparent everywhere.

In the middle of this street we turn left into Nibarta Street and then into Lod Street. We are now in the center of the Nahalat Ya'akov quarter, named for the leader of the Urpah community, who built the first houses in 1927. In the newer section of the neighborhood (near Ussishkin Street) are three-storey buildings. In Lod Street are the buildings of the Dugma religious boys' high school. The buildings go right down to Ben Zvi Boulevard.

13. Nahalat Ahim This predominantly Yemenite neighborhood was established between 1922 and 1924 by Haim Shlomo Iraki. The small, modest apartments are situated in elongated two-storey buildings along Shabazi, Usha, Tiberias, Tsipori, Safed and Shfaram Streets. The synagogue and Talmud Torah are in the center of the neighborhood, in Shfaram Street.

We ascend Mordechai Narkiss Street (after the founder of the Bezalel Museum) to Mevo Yizhar (after Yizhar Armoni who fell in battle during the War of Independence, as attested by the plaque at the beginning of the lane) and climb the steps to Israels Street.

14. Neveh Bezalel The streets in this neighborhood bear the names of Jewish artists: Israels (Holland), Antolkosky (Russia), Hirshberg (Poland, a teacher at Bezalel). It was founded in 1908 by the staff of Bezalel at the initiative of Boris Schatz. The buildings are in the European style of that period, each house with its own garden. Of late, many of these houses have been renovated and turned into modern villas.

(top) Cistern in a courtyard in one of the building complexes in Nahalat Ahim.
(center) Argentine House, Nahalat Zadok.
(bottom) Gateway to Sha'arei Hessed.

ZION SQUARE TO SHA'AREI HESSED

15. Nahalat Zadok We enter Nahalat Zadok Street and walk down to the high-rise apartment buildings overlooking Ben Zvi Boulevard. The land was purchased in 1906 by Abraham Antebi and a street in the neighborhood bears his name.

The neighborhood, named for the then Chief Rabbi of France, Zadok Cohen, was built from 1908 to 1927. The first residents were mainly merchants and government officials. The single-storey houses are built on both sides of the streets, with gardens in the front. Recently, Argentine House was opened as a meeting place for immigrants from South America.

16. Sha'arei Hessed The first neighborhood to be established in the area was built by the Sha'arei Hessed General Philanthropic Association, founded in 1870 to collect funds on behalf of the needy in Jerusalem. The land was purchased in 1908, building begun the following year and the 200 apartments in single-storey houses were completed by 1937. The square units are divided by narrow streets; each house has a front garden.

We enter Yeshayahu Bar Zakkai Street, cross Sha'arei Hessed Street and at the corner we can see the Sha'arei Hessed Beit Midrash and Synagogue, a renovated two-storey building. At the next corner is the Hassidic synagogue of Sha'arei Hessed. Many houses have been renovated and some expanded, all within the confines of a plan to preserve the original character of the neighborhood.

Diskin Street runs along the boundary of the neighborhood and on its other side are the high-rise apartment blocks of Kiryiat Wolfson. The houses are built on the slope of the hill running down to Ben Zvi Boulevard and the Sacker Park opposite the Knesset. At the entrance to the building opposite the junction of Diskin and Keren Kayemet Streets is a paved square above which is a sculpture by the Israeli artist Yaakov Agam.

Our tour ends here.

(top) Street in Sha'arei Hessed.
(center) View of Kiriyat Wolfson.
(bottom) "The Beating Heart", kinetic sculpture by Yaakov Agam in Kiriyat Wolfson.

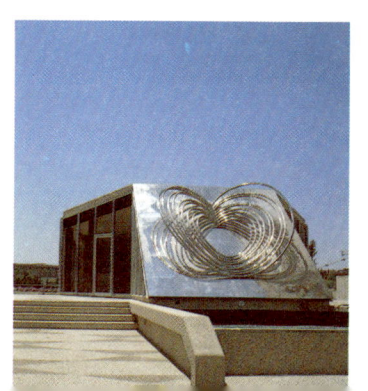

TOUR No. 22

FROM REHAVIA TO THE GERMAN COLONY

Details of tour: The tour passes through the neighborhoods of Rehavia, Talbieh, and the German Colony. As we walk along the streets, we shall notice how the architechtural styles of the houses vary from one neighborhood to the other.
Distance covered: approx. 3 km (2 miles)
Time: approx. 3 hours
Transportation: Buses No 4, 4A, 7, 8, 9, 14, 18 and 19
Parking for private vehicles can be found along the route of the tour
Starting point: Corner Keren Kayemet–King George V Avenue, by the Jewish Agency building
End of tour: Emek Refaim Street
The Sites: 1. Rehavia; 2. Talbieh (Komemiut); 3. German Colony.
Please note that the encircled numbers in the text correspond with the numbers printed in black on the map.

THE TOUR

1. Rehavia, Jerusalem's third garden suburb, after Beit Hakerem and Talpiot, was built in 1922. The neighborhood was founded during the British Mandate as a carefully-planned suburb. Each plot of land was allocated to a single family for a house and a garden. The streets were lined with trees and public parks were laid out. The land on which Rehavia was built was called *Janziriyeh* (Arabic for "iron chain"), and was acquired by the Palestine Land Development Corporation from the Greek Orthodox Church in 1921. Today, Rehavia has about 250 houses and about 3,000 residents. Most of the streets are named for Jewish sages and poets who lived during the Golden Age in Spain. The neighborhood was built in two stages:

Rehavia A, bounded by Ussishkin and Keren Kayemet Streets and King George V Avenue, was constructed between 1924 and 1929, according to a plan drawn up by the architect Kauffmann, who designed all the garden suburbs of Jerusalem. Among the first settlers of Rehavia were members of well-known families of professionals and merchants, native Jerusalemites and Jewish Agency officials. The Hebrew Gymnasium, the second modern high school in the country, was built on the edge of the neighborhood in 1928. Across from it is the Kuzari Park, which divides the neighborhood into two equal parts.

Rehavia B lies between Ramban, Gaza and Jabotinsky Streets. Built during the years 1931 to 1935, its earliest residents were teachers at the Hebrew University, German immigrants, professionals and others.

Apartment blocks were also erected in the area: Workers' Housing A (built in 1931–2), and Workers' Housing B (built in 1934–5).

Some of the buildings are in the style typical of Central Europe at that time. The buildings were designed by well-known Jewish architects who immigrated to Israel from Europe, such as Haecker, Kauffmann and Krakauer. Many buildings are no longer used for the purpose for which they were originally built.

Our tour of Rehavia begins at Keren Kayemet Street near the Jewish Agency buildings (see Tour No. 23). We walk along Keren Kayemet Street unitl we reach the Hebrew Gymnasium ①. En route, we see a few one and two-storey structures which date to the first years of the neighborhood. The Gymnasium building was designed by the architect Kornberg, who immigrated from Vienna and settled in Jerusalem

REHAVIA TO THE GERMAN COLONY

where he designed many buildings. After several years in various temporary quarters, the Gymnasium moved to its present home in 1929. Its founder and first principal, Dr. Metman, also founded the Herzlia Gymnasium in Jaffa in 1906. Among the first teachers were Yitzhak Ben-Zvi, the second president of Israel, and his wife, Rachel Yanait. For several decades, the Gymnasium was Jerusalem's only high school. In 1961, its name was officially changed to the Yitzhak Ben-Zvi Municipal High School A.

We walk down to the Kuzari Park across from the Gymnasium and reach Alharizi Street. House No. 22 ② is built in a Spanish style. This was the home of Dov Joseph, who served as the military governor of Jerusalem during Israel's War of Independence and later became Minister of Supply and Rationing and Minister of Justice. We continue along the path in the park opposite the house, which leads us to the entrance of the Ben-Zvi Institute ③. The Institute is a research center for the study of the history of Jewish settlement in Israel and the history of Jewish communities in Eastern countries. The Institute organizes conducted tours, lectures and courses all over Israel, and publishes periodicals and books. The buildings are on the site of the former Womens' Labor Movement farm, and among them is a bungalow which served as the Ben-Zvi family residence.

Continuing through the Kuzari Park to its southernmost end, we reach Ramban Street. Here there is a childrens' playground ④, named Eliezer Park, after the Jerusalemite architect Eliezer Yellin, who was one of the first builders of Rehavia, and the man who suggested the name Rehavia. On a memorial plaque is inscribed: "And the sons of Eliezer were, Rehabia the chief" (I Chronicles 23:17).

(top) Former residence of Dov Joseph.
(bottom) Entrance to the Ben Zvi Institute, the former residence of the President of Israel.

(top) The Hebrew Gymnasium, the city's first modern high school.
(bottom) Jason's tomb.

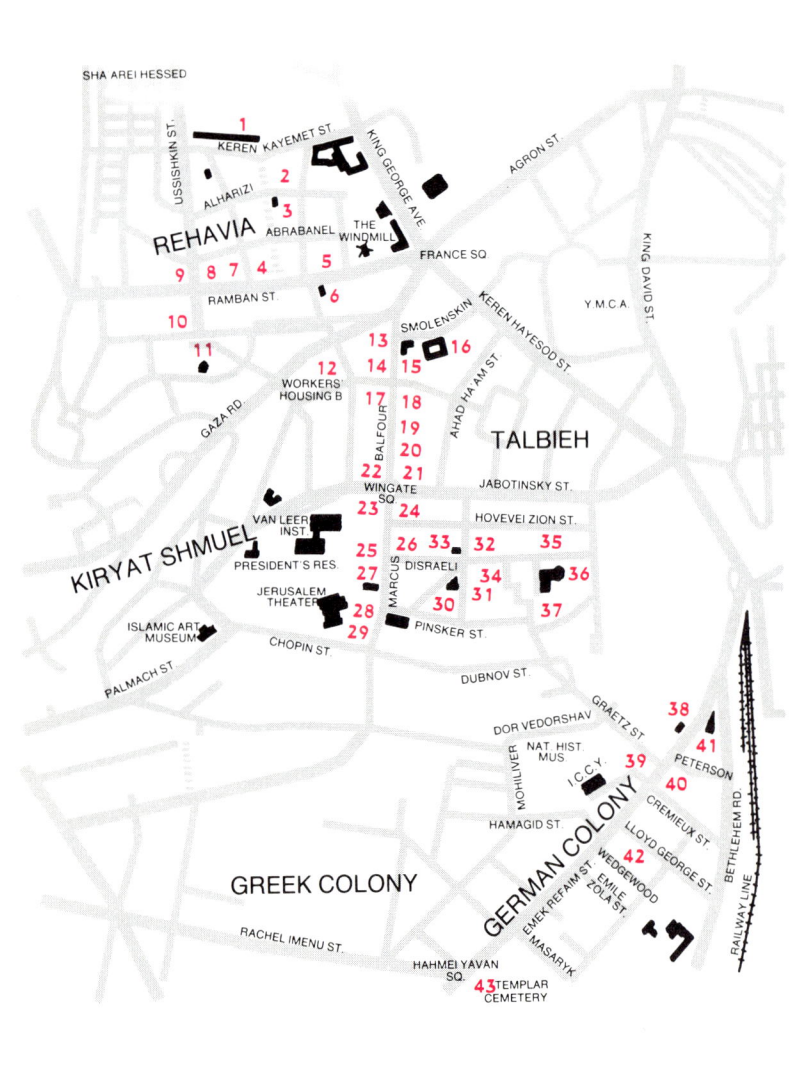

TOUR No. 22

Map of the tour.

His former home, at No. 14 Ramban Street⊙, was the first house to be built in the neighborhood, where, together with his architect partner Haecker, Yellin built many houses.

Opposite Yellin's house, at 21, Ramban Street on the corner of Arlosoroff Street, is a branch of Bank Leumi ⊙ which was the house of Dr. Bonem. It was built according to blueprints drawn up by the architect and artist Leopold Krakauer in 1935. The cubical concrete structure, with concrete awnings over the windows and balconies, was built in the Bauhaus style in favor in Germany in the 1920s. We continue along Ramban Street to the corner of Ibn Ezra Street. Here ⊙ is the home of Judge Gad Frumkin, which bears the name of the Hebrew newspaper "Havatzelet", founded by his father, Dov Frumkin.

At No. 30 Ramban Street stood the house of Arthur Ruppin, a leader of Zionist agricultural settlement ⊙. His name still appears on the gate. The house of Menahem Ussishkin ⊙, one of the leaders of the Hovevei Zion in Russia and head of the Jewish National Fund, is at 32, Ramban Street, on the corner with Ussishkin Street which bears his name. We turn down Ussishkin Street until we reach Molho Square on Ben-Maimon Boulevard. The corner house ⊙ used to be the residence of Israel's Prime Ministers, and the last to live there was Golda Meir. We continue onto Radak Street and turn right onto Alfasi Street. Here we reach Jason's Tomb ⊙, a Hasmonean burial complex, with a triangular lintel. The tomb complex is fenced off and the gate is kept locked, but we can see the outside of the tomb. The site was discovered and reconstructed in 1956 and contains two burial chamber niches. On the walls of the tomb were found drawings of ships, a Greek inscription, and several Aramaic inscriptions which include an epitaph to Jason, who seems to have been a merchant and shipowner.

We go back up to Alfasi Street, turn down Radak Street, and walk up Gaza Road to the corner of Arlosoroff Street ⊙. Here is the Workers' Housing Project B, built in 1934.(Project A was built in 1931 on Ibn Shaprut Street – see Tour No. 21.) The white, two-storey concrete buildings are arranged around a shared garden. The design, impressive in its simplicity, assures privacy to all the residents. The architect R. Kochinski, immigrated from Germany in the 1930s and made his home in Jerusalem.

At the edge of Rehavia B, on Radak and Arlosoroff Streets which border the neighborhood of Talbieh (Komemiut) there are a number of houses which belonged to Christian Arabs, and an Italian convent (opposite the Van Leer Institute). On the southwest, Rehavia borders the neighborhood of Kiryat Shmuel, a religious neighborhood whose construction was begun in 1928, named after Rabbi Shmuel Salant, who served as Jerusalem's Chief Rabbi for 70 years until his death in 1909. We continue along Gaza Road to the corner of Balfour Street, the beginning of the Talbieh neighborhood.

2. Talbieh (or Komemiut) is a lovely, prestigious neighborhood built during the British Mandate period. Its luxurious stone buildings are typical of upper-class Arab houses, and were erected between 1924 and 1937 by Christian Arabs from Bethlehem, Beit Jallah and Ramallah, on land purchased from the Greek Orthodox Church. The area was first known as "Nichophoria", after a priest named Nichophorus (see Tour No. 23). The land was acquired from the Church by Constantine Salame, a Christian Arab merchant and building contractor, and divided into plots which were sold to well-known Arab families and to Armenian families. A few Jewish families rented houses or apartments here, among these, Professor Martin Buber lived at 3, Hovevei Zion Street; Reuben Mass at 11, Marcus Street. From 1936, Reuben Mass operated at this address his publishing house, which he brought with him from Germany. There are also luxurious villas. Most of them are one or two stories high, and were originally intended for rental. During the British Mandate period this was a popular area for the residences of high government officials and British officers. A number of houses were also used as

TOUR No. 22

consulates, some of which remain to this day. During Israel's War of Independence the residents abandoned their houses and were replaced by institutions and Jewish refugee families. Some of the houses have ramained unchanged, to others, additional stories have been added and new buildings have been built on vacant lots. The neighborhood remains prestigious, and its residents include the Prime Minister, other government ministers, and the Sephardi Chief Rabbi. Several important public buildings were built on the fringes of the neighborhood during the 1970s and 1980s, such as the Van Leer Institute, the National Academy of Science, the President's residence and the Jerusalem Theater (See Tour No. 24).

Our tour of Talbieh begins on Balfour Street, which used to be known as Embassy Row. The corner house, 2, Balfour Street is the villa of Hanna Salame ⑮, built in 1932 by the Jewish architect Zoltan Hermet who immigrated from Hungary. The two-storey structure, notable for its semi-circular concave facade, was once the Turkish consulate. Later, American consular officials lived here, and in the 1950s, it was the home of the Guatemala Embassy. The next building, at 4, Balfour Street was built in 1936 as a one-storey building with a shingled roof and housed the Swiss consulate ⑬. Later, the building was sold to the Hebrew University, which added a storey to the building and opened Hillel House, the students' club. In the 1970s the building was sold to the Rubin Academy of Music, which added a third storey. The Academy's central building is located nearby, at 7, Smolenskin Street, the former house of Salman Schocken, which was designed by the architect Mendelsohn ⑯. The opposite corner building, 3, Balfour Street or 9, Smolenskin Street, is the Prime Minister's residence

(top left) Villa of Hanna Salameh.
(top right) Schocken Library.
(center left) The Belgian Consulate.
(center right) Montserrat Institute building.
(bottom left) Dr. Anis Jamal's villa.
(bottom right) Dr. Klabian's villa.

⑮, built during 1936 to 1938. The building is notable for its horizontal-rectangular shape, its rounded corners and its concrete awnings, and it bears the mark of the German Bauhaus school of architecture.

The Schocken Library at 6, Balfour Street ⑦ was built by the noted architect Mendelsohn, who lived in Jerusalem from 1939 to 1941. The library is open to visitors Sunday through Thursday mornings. The opposite building, No. 7 Balfour Street, home of Dr. Kleiber, was the residence of the Sephardi Chief Rabbi Nissim during the years 1955 and 1972, and was built by the architect Kauffmann ⑱. The building at No. 15 housed the Turkish consulate ⑲. House No. 19 was a post office ⑳, and was built by the architect Hermet. It is noteworthy for its simple, straight lines (the name Claremont appears on the gate). The house was rented to British government officials, and in the 1960s was the home of Moshe Sharett when he was the Prime Minister of Israel. Zalman Shazar lived in the building across the street (No. 20) before he was Israel's third President.

Around Orde Wingate (Salameh) Square are three three-storey corner houses which were owned by Constantine Salameh: 21, Balfour Street ㉑ is an apartment house with a convex shape, built by the architect Hermet. No. 22 Balfour Street is a luxurious villa surrounded by a large garden ㉒ which was built by the French architect Lucien Carvo (who also built the French consulate on Emile Botta Street). The building has a symmetrical facade with classical columns supporting a flat roof sheltering a balcony. In the center is an octagonal fountain. The foyer has an open gallery, a wide staircase, plaster decorations and a wooden ceiling. The walls and floors of two of the rooms are faced with Italian Carrara marble in various shades of grey and white. Since 1948, it houses the Belgian consulate.

The three-storey building at 2, Marcus Street ㉓, owned by the Salameh brothers, was also built by the architect Hermet. All four of the Salameh houses were built of rose-colored stone brought from the quarries of Bethlehem.

The one-storey building at 1, Marcus

Street ㉒ is one of the first to be built in the neighborhood, in 1926. It has a shingled roof, ornamented windows, and a door with a decorated lintel. The steps and the banisters which ascend in a funnel-shape to the veranda, and the ornamental iron door, are characteristic of a number of buildings. The house was built by Al-Karami and was the residence of Antonio Katan, a manufacturer of plumbing supplies during the British Mandate period.

Marcus Street is named after David Marcus, a Jewish officer in the American army who came to Israel, became a commander of the Israel Defense Forces and was killed in Israel's War of Independence. There are several other interesting buildings on Marcus Street. The Montserrat Institute building at No. 4 ㉓ has four stories and was built in two phases, the first two floors in 1924, and the upper two stories in the 1960s, in a different style. The house was rented to Father Bonaventura Aubach from the Montserrat monastery in Spain. He opened a Bible research institute named after the monastery, where several books of the Bible were translated into Catalan. The Institute existed until 1941.

The two lower stories of the structure are built in neo-Renaissance style. Stone arches extend above the doors and windows, and the symmetrical facade has an ornate main entrance at its center. On either side of the entrance stand pillars with Corinthian capitals. The second-floor balcony above the door has an elaborate wrought-iron railing.

The corner house, 9, Marcus Street, (1, Disraeli Street) is the Hashme villa ㉘ which was built as a two-storey structure in 1926. In the 1960s, two additional floors were added in a different architectural style. The yard is surrounded by a stone wall above which is a stylized wrought-iron fence and gate. The steps to the main entrance and the stone banisters blend in with the Art Nouveau style of the balconies and windows.

On the front of the house opposite (10, Marcus Street) ㉗ is carved the inscription "Eben-Ezer" and underneath it, in Hebrew, "Hitherto hath the Lord helped us, I Samuel 7:12, 1925". The owner of the house was Elias Samuel, a graduate of the Schneller Institute (see Tour No. 20). The two houses on the end of Marcus Street were built for rental by the Bisharah brothers: house No. 16 ㉖ is notable for its row of arches with stylized stone carvings. House No. 18 ㉕, built in 1926, is surrounded by a large garden, and is built in a luxurious style: vaulted balconies lined with rows of arches, pillars and decorations of colored Armenian ceramic tiles. The house is called "Villa Harun Al-Rashid" and was the residence of high Israeli government officials. The nearby Jerusalem Theater was built only in the 1970s (see Tour No. 24).

We turn eastwards onto Pinsker Street. At the corner is the villa of Sherover, who was the first contributor to the Jerusalem Theater. The villa was built in the 1960s, and its modernistic style is seen in the cement wall covered with delicate mosaic decorations. We continue to the left, to 6, Oliphant Street (corner of Alkalay Street), where there is a two-storey corner building of red stone ㉙. This is the Matosian villa, which was built between 1927 and 1929 by the Armenian builder, a graduate of the Schneller Institute, who also built part of the Y.M.C.A. building. The building is in the style of the 1930s, characterized by right-angled blocks and rows of arches. It has two luxury apartments and a basement. British officials lived here.

The villa opposite, on the corner of Disraeli and Alkalay Streets ㉚, is today the Moadon Ha'oleh (Immigrants' Club). The house was built by Dr. Anis Jamal. The two buildings on the other street corners are Hadad house, at 9, Disraeli Street ㉛, with two wings, between which is a sunken patio. The house at No. 7, the Jelad house ㉜, has several interesting architectonic features: the railing on the roof has stepped, diagonal teeth, the entry pillars and the stone banisters are ornate, the doors and windows are vaulted and the walls are decorated with colored Armenian ceramic tiles. The wealthy merchant Jelad built the house to be rented. In 1927, it was rented by the Peel Commission, the British royal commission that first recommended the partition of Palestine. Since 1948, the building has been occupied by the children's institution of Motza, managed by the Youth Aliyah organization.

We descend to house No. 13 ⓔ which was the residence of an official in the British Mandatory government. The building is impressive, with arched windows, and a spiral staircase leading to a round balcony. House No. 19 ⓕ was built by an Armenian doctor, Dr. Klabian, as a family villa. In the center of its facade is a triangular gable decorated with wooden carvings. Other impressive buildings lie along Hovevei Zion, Lev Ha'ivri and Jabotinsky Streets. Those interested in seeing them may walk along Lev Ha'ivri Street which is at the corner of Disraeli Street, and then return.

We cross to the other side of the street. The corner house ⓖ behind the stone wall is a country home set in a garden of fruit trees. Behind the adjacent stone wall is a hospital for the mentally ill, which uses buildings which were formerly a monastery of Capuchin monks. The building of the monastery was begun in the 1930s, but not completed. The British army rented the buildings and set up a prison for German and Italian prisoners, and later for captured members of the Jewish underground. Since 1949, the General Sick Fund hospital for the mentally ill has been located here. We go up to an alley named Maneh Street and reach another building ⓗ which was owned by the Jamal brothers and is similar to the Immigrants' Club already mentioned. Today the building houses the Jerusalem branch of the Association of Americans and Canadians in Israel. We can cross through the yard (after asking permission) to Pinsker Street, which has numerous modern villas built in the 1980s. Opposite us is the Rose Garden, a public park planted by the British and used until today for official receptions. The planted park has been maintained by the Jerusalem municipality since 1949 and also has a playground for children.

We descend along Graetz Street, at the corner of the park, and reach Emek Refaim Street, the main street of the German Colony. The houses along Graetz Street were built by Arabs during the Ottoman period. The multi-storey apartment house of Mishav was constructed in the 1970s.

3. The German Colony, originally built as an agricultural settlement between 1872 and 1910, was named Rephaim because it was situated in the Rephaim Valley of the Bible (II Samuel 5:22) where the Philistines were defeated by David. It lies between Bethlehem Road and Emek Refaim Street. Its first settlers were a group of Protestants from southern Germany who were members of the Tempelgesellschaft (Temple Society), or Templars for short. This was the Templars' fourth settlement in Israel (the first were in Haifa, Jaffa and Sharona). They

House at 16, Emek Refaim Street.

House and garden in the Germany Colony.

strove to establish a small "Kingdom of God" in Israel with Jerusalem at its center. The settlers built their homes in the style common in their homeland: one- or two-storey houses with red-tiled roofs. Around the house, within the fenced-in yard were the farm buildings. The tall trees create the atmosphere of a rural village.

The area was declared a historical preservation area in 1973 by the Jerusalem Municipality and the houses continue to serve as residences.

In our tour we will follow the various styles in the development of the German Colony. The ground was prepared for building in 1872, and the first to build his home was a farmer named Franck. Over the doorway of his house at 6, Emek Refaim Street ㊳ is carved the year of its construction, 1873, and the inscription "Eben-Ezer" (as on the Samuel house in Talbieh, above). In his house he set up a steam-operated flour mill, which was Jerusalem's second mill. The two adjacent houses, Nos. 8 and 10, were built in 1874. Four houses were built in 1875 and another, at No. 16 ㊴, in 1877. Above the door, a German inscription appears in Gothic script: "Arise, shine, for thy light is come, and the glory of the Lord is risen upon thee" (Isaiah 60:1). In the spring of 1878 the headquarters of the Temple Society and its school ㊵ were transferred from Jaffa to Jerusalem. The school, called the Lyceum, was built at No. 3, and in 1882 another building was added beside it. The community center or *Gemeindehaus* ㊶ at No. 1 was built in a neo-Romanesque style. In 1883, 15 houses lined the main street, reminiscent of a German "street village" or *Strassendorf*. Fruit trees and vegetable gardens were planted between the houses, and the residents also raised animals in the early years. Cross streets were built between the newer houses to the parallel street which connected them (Smuts Street today). We turn onto Lloyd George Street, where the Semadar Cinema ㊷ is located. We turn left on Smuts Street (to houses No. 6,9, and 18) and then proceed right on Cremieux Street to Bethlehem Road. Along the way, we enter some of the courtyards to see the basements which were converted into workshops. Most of the German agricultural settlers later engaged in trades and found work in the city as builders, carpenters, fitters, blacksmiths, bakers and gardeners. Some of them moved into the city; the Fast family built the hotel bearing their name opposite the Jaffa gate. In 1910, the German colony had 400 inhabitants living in family houses. This was the largest and most important of the Templar settlements in Israel. In the Colony's cemetery ㊸ at 39, Emek Refaim Street are buried Christoff Hoffman, who founded the Templar sect, and Eberle, one of the founders of the Colony in Jerusalem. Altogether, there are some 250 graves. A visit to the cemetery can be arranged by telephoning the caretaker at 285928. The adjacent Protestant cemetery is still used today. During the Second World War, the British evacuated the Germans, who were enemy subjects, some of them supporters of the German Nazi party. The colony became a military security zone. In 1948 new immigrants were settled in the houses. Since then, new buildings have been constructed on vacant lots and apartments have been added to some of the houses. At the corner of Bethlehem Road and Lloyd George Street is the Convent of the Borromean Sisters (their order is named after its founder Borromeus, an Italian monk who lived in the 16th century). The convent was built in 1894 by German nuns. They opened an old age home, and later added a hospice (St Charles) and a girls' school.

We continue along Lloyd George, Smuts and Wedgewood Streets to Emek Refaim Street. Along the way we can see several buildings that were built by wealthy Arabs in styles similar to those found in Talbieh. We may visit the International Cultural Center for Youth and the Natural Science Museum. The tour ends on Emek Refaim Street, where there are stops for buses No 4, 4A, 14 and 18.

The International Cultural Center for Youth (I.C.C.Y.) at 12A, Emek Refaim Street organizes classes, lectures and exhibitions. It has evenings of singing and dancing which are open to the public and for tourists. The objective of the establish-

Convent of the Borromean Sisters.

The I.C.C.Y. building.

ment is to encourage international understanding and mutual friendship among youth. It is supported by the Jerusalem Municipality and by the Ministry of Education.

The Natural History Museum is at 6, Mohiliver Street. It is open Sunday through Thursday from 9.00 a.m. to 1.00 p.m. and on Monday and Wednesday from 4.00 p.m. to 6.00 p.m. There is an entry fee. It is also open Saturday mornings, when entry is free. During the summer it is open mornings only. Guided tours for groups can be arranged in advance by calling 631116 or by writing to P.O.B. 7028, Jerusalem 93112.

Within the grounds are located the Pedagogical Center for Natural History, a botanical garden, and the Natural History Museum. The museum was set up in 1949 in the former home of an Armenian merchant, which was built in the 19th century and has since passed through many hands. The museum displays stuffed animals and plants from different parts of Israel, including several extinct species, insects and birds. Models and moving displays are used to demonstrate how various parts of the human body function. The evolution of animal species and early man is illustrated with models. At first the museum was part of the nature center, and in 1962, it was established as a separate institution. It is supported by the Jerusalem Municipality as well as by the Ministry of Education and Culture.

For those wishing to extend their tour there are several other neighborhoods and points of interest in the area.

Geulim (Baka) is a residential area on the south side of the railway line founded during the British Mandate period by Arabs. It is still known by the name it was given then — Baka. After Israel's War of Independence it was populated by Jewish immigrants from the Arab countries and in the course of the years many houses have been added. The older houses are interesting for their variety of styles and architectural influences from Italian Renaissance to Bauhaus.

The **Greek Colony**, which lies between Rachel Imenu and Eliezer HaModa'i Streets and Bethlehem Road, was founded during the British Mandate period by Greeks and Arabs. In 1948 the Arab residents abandoned their houses and were replaced by immigrant families. A few of the villas are occupied by embassies and consulates.

Katamon (Gonen), a residential area situated between Palmach and Agnon

Streets, was also founded in the British Mandate period, by prosperous Arabs, near the Monastery of St Simeon, and hence its name Katamon ("beside the monastery"). During the War of Independence fierce battles were fought here and its inhabitants fled. After the war it was settled by refugees from the Jewish Quarter of the Old City. Its name was changed to Gonen and its streets given names connected with the War of Independence. On Givat Haportzim, beside the monastery, a public park has been laid out in memory of the fighters who fell. Close to it is an Iraqi tank which took part in the fighting.

St Simeon Monastery is situated between Aharoni Street and Hama'apilim Street. The stone building has a silver dome and a bell tower and is encircled by pine trees. At the entrance gate is a Greek inscription referring to the monastery's construction in 1859. St Simeon, who is said to be buried in the monastery, is referred to in Luke 2:25 as the just and devout man who took the infant Jesus into his arms when he was presented at the Temple. The monastery was constructed on the ruins of a Georgian monastery of the 13th century. In 1885 a summer residence was built beside it for the Greek Patriarch. The poet Saul Tchernichowsky lived here at the end of his life. Today the building houses a home for the handicapped run by the Alyn organization.

Near the monastery, on the other side of Agnon Street is the Goldstein Youth Village, an educational institute founded in 1950.

TOUR No. 23

FROM THE RAILWAY STATION TO RATISBONNE MONASTERY

Details of tour: Our tour begins at the Railway Station, which was built at the same time as the railway line from Jaffa at the end of the 19th century, to serve the increasing number of pilgrims traveling to Jerusalem. We shall also visit the Y.M.C.A. and some nearby churches as well as Jewish religious institutions including the Chief Rabbinate and synagogues in Agron and King George Streets. The tour ends at Ratisbonne Monastery, the first building constructed in this neighborhood.
Distance covered: approx. 3 km (2 miles)
Time: approx. 4 hours
Transportation Buses No 5, 6, 7, 8, 21, 48
Parking lot at the Liberty Bell Garden for private vehicles
Starting point: Railway Station
End of tour: Ratisbonne Monastery
The sites: 1. Railway Station; 2. The Khan; 3. St Andrew's Church; 4. Ketef Hinnom; 5. Liberty Bell Garden; 6. King David Hotel; 7. Y.M.C.A.; 8. Convent of the Soeurs du Rosaire; 9. Center for Conservative Judaism; 10. Terra Sancta College; 11. Hechal Shlomo; 12. The Great Synagogue; 13. The National Institutions; 14. Yeshurun Synagogue; 15. St Pierre de Ratisbonne Monastery.

THE TOUR

1. Railway Station At the David Remez Square (named for the first Israeli Minister of Transport) is the station of the first railway line in Palestine which ran from Jaffa to Jerusalem, inaugurated in 1892. The concession for the construction of the railway track was granted by Sultan Abdul Hamid in 1888 to Joseph Navon, who founded a company in France which bought the concession. In 1890 work was begun on laying the track and building the station, a water tower, storeroom and other facilities. The railway was an important factor in transportation to Jerusalem and competed with the coaches plying between Jaffa and Jerusalem. In 1922 the British Mandatory Government bought the Railroad Company from the French shareholders. The narrow-gauge track was changed, new engines and carriages added and storerooms built. The railway was also used to haul goods from the ports of Jaffa, Tel Aviv and Haifa, and for carrying potash from the Dead Sea Works for export. The original structure of the two-storey station has remained intact except for some small architectural changes.

2. The Khan Opposite the Railway Station are a number of buildings set around a small courtyard. These now form the Jeru-

The Khan.

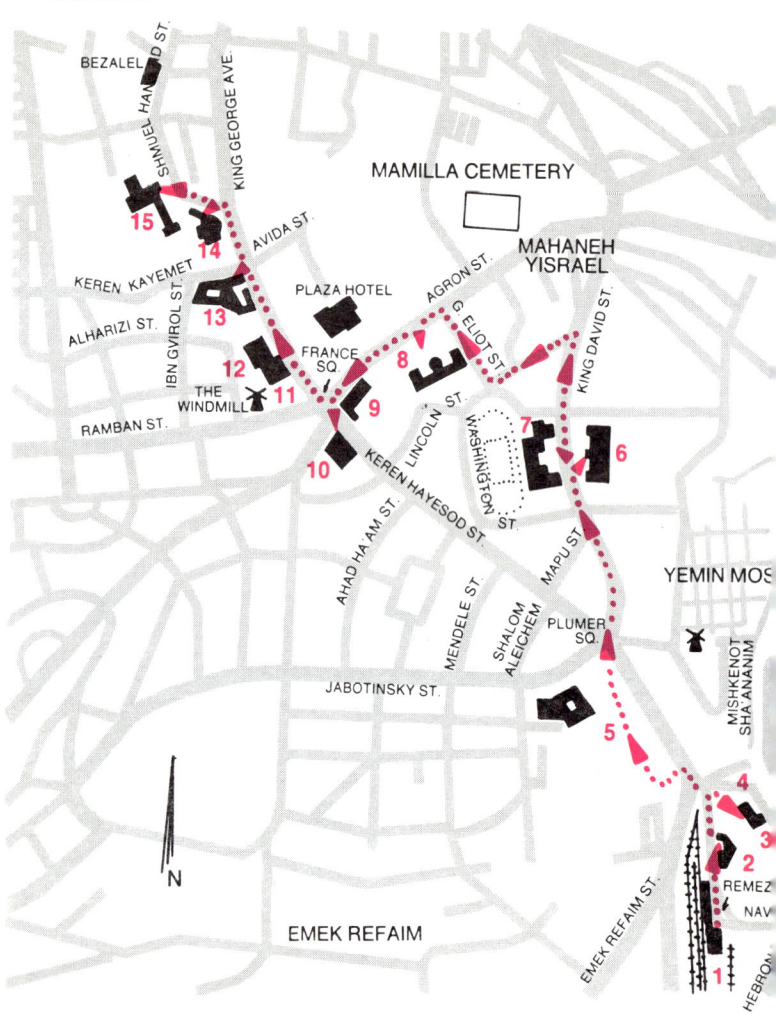

Map of the tour.

salem Khan complex comprising a theater, night club, restaurant, and small exhibition hall. The southern building, partly hewn out of the face of the hill, was apparently built in the Mameluke period as a station for merchants *(Khan)* making their way from the south of the country. In the Ottoman period, the building continued to provide shelter for travelers, their beasts and goods. When a caravan arrived at night, it rested here till the gates of the Old City were opened at sunrise. In the second half of the 19th century the Greek Orthodox Patriarchate, who owned the land, turned the building into a factory for the production of silk goods. The walls of the main hall were blocked up and painted black, and silk worms were bred there, fed on leaves of mulberry trees, grown by the Greeks, nearby. The silk thread was woven in the other rooms and exported to Europe through Damascus. Production ceased at the end of the 19th century and the building was turned into a beer cellar serving residents of the nearby German Colony. In 1967 it became a center for cultural events. In 1972 the Jerusalem Foundation renovated the site, and since then it has been the home of the Jerusalem Khan Theater, with a hall seating 400. Folklore evenings and folkdancing are held in the nightclub.

Near the Khan is the British Consulate in a building which in part was a 16th-century Ottoman observation post. A stone archway supports a square building, to which a further building with a red-tiled roof was added. The courtyard also serves the nearby Scottish hospice and church.

Silver plaque bearing a fragment of the Priestly Blessing.

3. St Andrew's Church We continue along Remez Street and walk up a side street to the right leading to the buildings of the Scottish Church and Hospice. There is a beautiful view from here eastward to the Hinnom Valley, Mount Zion, the western outer wall of the Old City, the Citadel, the towers of the Patriarchate buildings in the Christian Quarter, the Mount of Offense and in the background the Judean Desert.

Oriental and western elements have been integrated in the church building designed by the British architect Holliday, with the assistance of the Israeli architect Ben Dor. A stone cross adorns the top of the tower and the building is crowned with a white dome. The church was built in 1927 as a memorial to the Scottish soldiers who fell in the battle for Jerusalem in the First World War. The dedication ceremony was attended by General Allenby as recorded on the plaque "in commemoration of the liberation of Jerusalem on 9th December 1917". It is dedicated to St Andrew, patron saint of Scotland.

In the floor of the church is an inscription in memory of the Scottish King, Robert Bruce, who before his death in 1392

St Andrew's Church. Below, the burial cave where the plaque shown on the left was found.

4. Ketef Hinnom (In Hebrew: the "Shoulder of Hinnom"). The hill on which St Andrew's Church is built is the watershed between the Hinnom and Refaim Valleys: it rises to 755 m (2477 ft) above sea level (80 m–262 ft above the Hinnom Valley). The name Ketef Hinnom (in Hebrew) derives from the passages in Joshua (15:8; 18:16) describing the border between the tribes of Judah and Benjamin. The hill is situated at the junction of the Jerusalem–Bethlehem road and the road to Hebron. The Roman commander Pompey set up his camp at this strategic position in 63 BCE as told by Josephus. At the time of the Great Revolt in 70 CE, Titus set up the siege wall and one of his camps nearby. Burial chambers were uncovered on the northern slope of the hill when the road to the Scottish Church was being built. During the archaeological excavations carried out in 1940, remains from the Byzantine period were discovered and in 1970 potsherds were found on the eastern slope, from the First Temple period up to the Ottoman period. As a result, further archaeological excavations were carried out from 1975 to 1980 which uncovered a Byzantine church, a crematorium used by the Roman Legion, burial caves and on the surface, dating to the Second Temple period and First Temple period, burial caves which were also used in the Babylonian period. In one of the caves was found an ossuary, a hollow space where bones and skulls, and burial offerings were collected. The cave showed evidence of continuous use from the First Temple period up to the late Roman period. Most of these caves had been pillaged, but one was found intact with many metal, ivory and glass objects, coins, pottery vessels, and silver and gold jewelery. Among the outstanding items are two small cylindrical silver plaques rolled up into tiny scrolls (11 × 39 mm — ⅖ ×1 ½ in) dating to the 7th century BCE. They were apparently worn appended to a cord. Engraved on the metal was a text almost identical with the Biblical verses in Numbers 6:24–26 known as the Priestly Blessing, written in ancient Hebrew script — the most ancient Biblical text found yet. The discovery has provided proof that the Priestly Blessing was in use in the First Temple period. This is also evidence that in that period it was customary to wear an object bearing passages from the Pentateuch, similar to those contained in the phylacteries.

We go down into the exposed area, walk along the rockface east of the church and reach the burial cave where the artifacts were discovered. The entrance to the east leads to eight ledges with head rests where the dead were laid. To the right can be seen the opening to an ossuary.

5. Liberty Bell Garden We return to David Remez Street, cross the intersection to the western side of King David Street, go through the gate and enter the public garden, with its sports facilities for children, youth and adults. It has well-tended lawns and many benches. On a paved section in the center public events are held (such as folk dancing performances, the Hebrew Book Week Fair); at the end of the covered path is a raised platform on which is a replica of the Liberty Bell from Philadelphia, USA, commemorating the Declaration of Independence of the United States on 4th July 1776. The garden was dedicated on the bicentennial of this event. There is also an arts workshop, an open amphitheater and a playground for

Replica of the Liberty Bell of Philadelphia.

small children. At the western corner of the garden are two railway coaches housing the Train Theater.

On the other side of King David Street is the Bloomfield Garden which reaches to the Montefiore Windmill (see Tour No 14). These two gardens enable us to have an uninterrupted view of the landscape up to Mount Zion and the Old City wall. All the land from the Railway Station up to the King David Hotel and westward up to Talbieh was the property of the Greek Orthodox Church from the middle of the 19th century. It was called Nichophoria after the Archimandrite of the Greek Orthodox Patriarchate. The Greeks sold the plots of land during the Mandatory period on which were built the King David Hotel, the Y.M.C.A., the Hagana Veterans' Housing block and the Omaryya School (originally an Arab college, then a Jewish high school and now the Beit Hayeled Elementary School). In the 1970s the Omaryya area was purchased by the Jerusalem Municipality and the Liberty Bell and Bloomfield Gardens were laid out. The road junction near the northern entrance to the Liberty Bell Garden is named Plumer Square, for the British High Commissioner (1925 to 1928) who encouraged the development of Jewish settlement in Palestine. Near the intersection is the King Solomon Hotel.

6. King David Hotel We continue up King David Street, passing by an arched apartment house, and cross Abba Sikra Street (the leader of the Sicarii who is said to have helped to get Rabbi Yohanan Ben Zakkai out of besieged Jerusalem, hidden in a coffin, in 70 CE). The site of the Roman siegewall built by Titus is not far from here. To the west of this street is the nine-storey building of the King David Hotel, built in 1930 according to the design of the Swiss architect, Emile Vogt. We enter the spacious lobby where the influence of Assyrian and Hittite styles — popular in the time of King David — is discernible. Other halls have been decorated in Hellenistic-Syrian and Phoenician styles. In the southern wing of the building were the British Mandatory Government offices which were blown up by members of the Irgun Zvai Leumi underground units on 22nd July 1946 with explosives hidden in milk cans brought into the basement of the building. The wing destroyed in the explosion was rebuilt after the establishment of the State in 1948 and a further two stories added to the hotel.

7. Y.M.C.A. Visiting hours: every morning except Sunday. Entrance to the building is free; admission fee to the tower. The tour takes approximately one hour; guided tours are available.

This is the property of the international

King David Hotel.

Y.M.C.A. building.

organization of the Young Men's Christian Associations, which has two buildings in Jerusalem (the other in Nablus Road). It was constructed between 1928 and 1933 and was designed by the American architect Q.L. Harmon (who designed the Empire State Building in New York) and financed by another American, James Newbig Jarvie of Montclair, New Jersey. The construction work was carried out by Jews and Arabs, and the pupils of the Bezalel School of Arts were invited to decorate it. The architect was influenced by Byzantine and Muslim buildings, and incoporated decorations, and inscriptions taken from Judaism, Christianity and Islam, in Hebrew, Arabic and English. The triangular Y.M.C.A. symbol expresses the aims of the Association: the development of the body, the mind and the spirit.

The building has three main sections. The belltower 46.3 m (151 ft) high, is decorated with six-winged seraphim as described in Isaiah's vision (6:2). The square tower is topped with a stone cupola surrounded by an open balcony with four turrets. There is a covered gallery from which one has a panoramic view of Jerusalem and its environs. In the northern wing is a 650-seat concert hall. The southern wing has a swimming pool, sports hall and library. The halls at the end of each of the wings have domes. The walls are embellished with reliefs related to the New Testament and the building has several chapels dedicated to Christian saints. The wings have four floors, and there are 82 guest-rooms (three star) in the two floors of the central section. The football stadium is the home ground of the Betar Jerusalem team. Weekly chamber music concerts are held in the auditorium; hymns are played on the chimes on special occasions.

On the facade of the building are a number of inscriptions: on the top of the wall of the northern wing, in Hebrew: "The Lord our God, the Lord is One"; on the southern wing in Arabic: "There is no other God but Allah"; on the wall of the northern hall in English: "In essence unity, in non-essence liberty, in all things charity"; on the southern hall in German: "The only temple in the world is the body of man".

On the capitals of the arched pillars in the portico are carvings in stone of trees, flowers and animals. At the entrance to the central section on the ground floor of the tower there is an arch supported by low pillars whose capitals are decorated with legendary creatures representing the four evangelists (Matthew is represented by an angel, Luke by a bull, Mark by a lion and John by an eagle). On either side of the entrance are red stone pillars and on their capitals are statues of a woman bearing a pitcher (the Samaritan woman); there is also an inscription in English of the passage of Isaiah's prophecy (9:6) of the coming of the Messiah. The ceiling of the passageway leading from the entrance consists of interlocking stone arches, and on the inlaid stone floor is the cross of Bethlehem and in the center, a reproduction of the Madaba map of Jerusalem. On the walls are inscriptions in English, acknowledging the donor, and Archibald C. Harte, Secretary General of the Association who "inspired the gift of the building". In the center of the impressive entrance hall is a 17th-century Arab style wooden ceiling brought from Damascus. The concert auditorium has a golden dome with a dozen windows and an exquisite chandelier suspended from the ceiling.

We leave the Y.M.C.A. and walk along Lincoln Street to the north, cross Hess Street and go down George Eliot Street

Convent of the Soeurs du Rosaire.

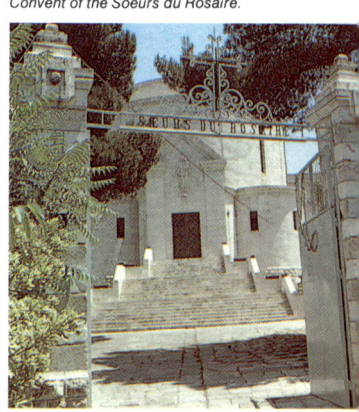

along the wall of the American Consulate and come out on Agron Street.

8. Convent of the Soeurs du Rosaire. At 14, Agron Street, is a circular building with the Virgin and Child on the facade; this is the chapel of the Convent. Beyond it is the two-storey convent, built in 1880, belonging to the Catholic Order of the Holy Rosary founded in Nazareth by a Christian Arab by the name of Taunus. Here, the nuns take care of the education of girls who come daily from East Jerusalem. The Order has another convent in Beit Hanina, a clinic in the Old City and an orphanage in Ein Karem.

We walk up Agron Street to the top of the hill.

9. Center for Conservative Judaism. This is the headquarters of the Conservative Judaism Movement in Israel and also its Jerusalem center. On the ground floor are the Movement's offices, rooms for study and the synagogue. Above the *bimah* at the end of the hall is an inscription: "Its ways are ways of pleasantness, and all its paths are peace." The community numbers a few score families, mainly immigrants from North America. The center organizes study groups in Mishna, Talmud, Jewish studies, Hebrew language and literature, Jewish history, etc. On the second floor is a youth hostel, used by thousands of members of the Movement visiting Israel throughout the year.

The Supersol (supermarket) building, across the street, was constructed on the site where a large building was begun by a Dutch noblewoman in the 19th century, in which she proposed to accommodate 144,000 Jews whom she believed would return to their homeland immediately, as predicted in Revelations (7:2–4). She had come under the influence of the messianic movements popular among Christians at the time, believing in the imminent return to Zion and the coming of the End of Days. She built a house for herself, which was also not completed for lack of funds. The remains of the unfinished building can be seen behind the Plaza Hotel, on the edge of Independence Park.

We cross over to the building at the corner of France Square and 2, Keren Hayesod Street.

10. Terra Sancta College This four-storey building has a statue of the Virgin Mary in the front facing the street. Belonging to the Franciscan Order, it was built to the plans of the Italian architect Barluzzi and inaugurated in 1927. A College for Christian Arabs was opened during the British Mandate and there is a church and the monks' quarters. After the War of Independence, a number of departments of the Hebrew University were transferred here from Mount Scopus, and the University Publishing House, the Magnes Press, as well as the offices of the Friends of the

Terra Sancta College.

The Windmill commercial center.

Hebrew University, the Research and Development Authority, and the headquarters of the World Union of Jewish Students, are still in the building. The British Council Library and the Dante Alighieri Society for Italian Culture are also housed here. The building is a mixture of styles — Italian Renaissance and oriental. We can go through the entrance hall to the courtyard, to the wing containing the chapel, and after receiving permission, climb the steps to the roof for a view of the surroundings.

We cross the road to the Kings Hotel at the opposite corner and behind it in Ramban Street is the Mill, a commercial center opened here in 1987. It was built around an abandoned windmill which functioned during the years 1860 to 1880. From 1939 to 1941 the Jerusalem architect Eric Mendelsohn lived here.

11. Hechal Shlomo At 58, King George Street is an impressive 11-storey high building crowned with a dome. This is the headquarters of the Chief Rabbinate of Israel, named for the father of the philanthropist Isaac Wolfson. Plans for the building were initiated by a former Chief Rabbi, Isaac Herzog, and it was erected from 1953 to 1958. The building contains the offices of the Chief Rabbinate, the Rabbinical Courts, convention halls, a library, a museum of Jewish ritual objects, a diorama exhibition depicting episodes in the history of the Jewish people, and a small synagogue whose fittings were brought from Padua, Italy. The colored stained-glass windows were designed by the British artist David Hillman. The building is

Hechal Shlomo.

open to visitors on Sunday–Thursday from 9.00 a.m. to 1.00 p.m. and on Friday and holiday eves to 12.00 noon. There is an entry fee to the museum.

12. The Great Synagogue Visiting hours: weekdays — 9.00 a.m. to 12.00 noon. The building next door to Hechal Shlomo is the Great Synagogue, opened in 1983. The square is named for Dr. Maurice Jaffe, the driving force behind the construction of the building. In the center of the facade are five stained-glass windows, and a tower above which are two stylized Tablets of the Law. The inscription beside the entrance reads: "This house of prayer is dedicated by Sir Isaac and Lady Wolfson to the memory of all those who died so that we, the Jewish people, may live. To the six million victims of the European Holocaust and all those Jewish men and women who sacrificed their lives for and in defense of the State of Israel".

The architect was A. Friedman and the windows were designed by R. Haim. The internal part of the building is modern, functional and most impressive. The entrance hall is decorated with marble-covered walls and candelabra. Two marble stairways lead up to the synagogue hall rising 20 m (66 ft) to the roof. Further stairs lead up to the women's gallery which can also be reached by a stairway on the outer side of the building. The main hall has about 1,000 seats for men and 700 for women. The red velvet-covered seats can be adjusted and lowered for Tisha Be'Av prayers. The *bimah* is built of marble and behind it is a podium for the choir. The walls are decorated with the symbols of the Twelve Tribes and paintings depicting Biblical events. Most impressive are the windows facing east, depicting wings of seraphs, arms and eyes. The windows bear verses from Proverbs (15:3): "The eyes of the Lord are in every place"; I Chronicles (29:11): "Thine, O Lord is the greatness, and the power, and the glory, and the victory, and the majesty"; Isaiah (6:3): "Holy, holy, holy is the Lord of hosts"; and Exodus (3:1): "I am that I am". Abraham, Isaac and Jacob are represented, as well as the Rainbow in the Cloud, the Burning Bush, the Ten Commandments; Isaiah's vision (2:3): "For out of Zion shall go forth the law, and the word of the Lord from Jerusalem"; and an allegorical picture shows roots in the ground soaked with blood and tears from the suffering of Jews with the passage: "Fear not, O Jacob, my Servant" (Isaiah 44:2).

13. The National Institutions At the corner of Keren Hayesod and Keren Kayemet Streets is a complex of buildings around three sides of a courtyard. These are the main offices of the Jewish Agency for Israel and the World Zionist Organization: the head offices of the Jewish National Fund and the Keren Hayesod (Foundation Fund). The building was designed by the architect Y. Rettner and it was built from 1929 to 1931. After the War of Independence the Knesset held its first six sessions in the auditorium and Dr. Chaim Weizmann was sworn in as first President of the State of Israel. In the wing at the back of the building, bordering on Ibn G'virol Street were the offices of the Prime Minister and the Cabinet until the Government buildings were erected at Kiryat Ben-Gurion.

14. Yeshurun Synagogue We continue along King George Street and turn into Shmuel Hanagid Street. On the corner, at the left, is a semi-circular building — the Central Synagogue Yeshurun Organization. The organization was established in 1924 at the initiative of Chief Rabbis Kook and Uziel with the aim of spreading Hebrew culture. The present building was erected in 1934 (designed by the architects Friedman and Rubin) and in addition to the synagogue hall there is a library and reading-room.

15. St Pierre de Ratisbonne Monastery
We continue along Shmuel Hanagid Street and go in through an iron gate to a courtyard in the middle of which is an elongated fortress-like building. The front of the building is 90 m (295 ft) long and at each end there are square towers from which 20 m (66 ft) wings extend. The style is late Italian Baroque and is reminiscent of palaces built in northern Italy and southern France. Construction was carried out over the years 1874 to 1897 on land purchased by the Greek Orthodox Church and this was the first building to be erected in this area.

The monastery was built by an apostate Jew, Alphonse Ratisbonne, born in Strasbourg, who lived in Jerusalem from 1855 till his death in 1884. He founded the Order of Fathers of Our Mother of Zion to which this monastery belongs. He also founded the women's order of Soeurs de Sion which built convents in the Old City (see Tour No.6) and in Ein Karem, where he is buried. The orphanage which Ratisbonne founded in the Old City moved to this building in 1876; the orphans were Armenian, Maronite and a few Jews. They were taught handicrafts, electrical engineering and agriculture, and their tuition included religious studies and French language and literature. The Catholic Scouts of Jerusalem were originally based here. The right wing served as offices for the institute's directorate and the left wing as the pupils' dormitories; the center section housed the

The National Institutions.

Interior of the Yeshurun Synagogue.

Ratisbonne Monastery.

church and the monks' accommodation. On the ground floor were workshops and classrooms.

The flat roof is surrounded by a carved stone parapet and in its center is a tower in which there is a statue of Ratisbonne holding a cross in one hand and a Gospel scroll in the other. He was canonized by the Catholic Church and named St Pierre de Sion. In the front of the courtyard on the cover of the water reservoir is a bronze statue of Mary and the infant Jesus. There is also a two-tiered circular tower with a cupola built in the 1830s by the Egyptian ruler Ibrahim Pasha, as part of the system of communication towers between Jaffa and Jerusalem.

In the backyard of the monastery were sports grounds and fields, orchards, a vegetable garden, a pig pen, a cow shed, a chicken coop and stables. The area was sold off to Jewish builders in the 1930s and they erected the apartment buildings of Gan Rehavia and Rosh Rehavia, and a high school for Christian girls (today the Evelina de Rothschild School and the Municipal Pedagogic Center). A cemetery in which monks were buried from 1892 to 1951 is in the southern section of the courtyard. Rooms have been rented out as offices and part of the government archives is also here.

The church has remained as originally built with its 27 × 12 m (89 × 39 ft) wide and 20 m (60 ft) high hall, in neo-Gothic style with vaults supported by interlocking arches. The stained-glass windows depict the lives of the saints. There is a central altar and other altars, recesses and statues along the walls, marble plaques with memorial inscriptions, a wooden statue of Alphonse Ratisbonne and stylized antique furniture.

During the First World War the building served as a hospital for Turkish troops and then as headquarters of an Austrian unit. When the British entered Jerusalem an Indian unit of Allenby's troops bivouacked here. The building was soon returned to the owners and continued to fulfill its original function. During the War of Independence, the pupils living in East Jerusalem were no longer able to reach the building and the settlers evacuated from the Etzion Bloc were temporarily housed here. After the war part of the building was rented to the Ministry of Education and the Hebrew University.

Our tour ends here. Public transport can be found in King George Street.

TOUR No. 24

THE PRESIDENT'S RESIDENCE AND VICINITY

Details of tour: The tour includes the President of the State's residence and nearby sites. Not all are open to visitors — details below. As the Islamic Art Museum is closed during the lunch hour and on Fridays it is suggested that visits to other sites be planned accordingly.
Time: approx. 3 hours
Distance covered: approx. 1 km
Transportation: Bus No 15
Starting point: Van Leer Institute
End of tour: Hansen Hospital
The Sites: 1. Van Leer Institute; 2. Israel Academy of Science and Humanities; 3. The President's residence; 4. L.A. Mayer Memorial — Institute for Islamic Art; 5. Jerusalem Theater; 6. Hansen Hospital.

THE TOUR

1. Van Leer Institute We take the No. 15 bus from Binyanei Ha'uma or Jaffa Road in the city center to Albert Einstein Square to visit the Van Leer Institute building in its pleasant garden setting.

The Van Leer Jerusalem Institute was founded in 1956, built and supported by Polly Van Leer as a "center for the study of social problems arising in our complex world, in which information develops rapidly". The Institute is non-political, although the subjects of the research carried out there are of a political nature. It deals with events in the Middle East, Israel-Arab relations, relations between Jews and Arabs in Israel, intercommunity relations in Israel, educational problems and studies in Jewish history, The Institute publishes research papers and organizes colloquies, lectures, concerts and exhibitions.

The circular building was designed by the architects Reznik and Posner; the lecture hall has 250 seats and the meeting room 100; the library has 20,000 volumes and a reading room; there are research rooms, offices and a cafeteria.

2. Israel Academy of Science and Humanities The building next door to the Van Leer Institute is the Israel Academy of Science and Humanities. The only section open to visitors is the information bureau where information leaflets can be obtained and publications of the Academy can be purchased. The Academy was established in 1958 and moved to this building in 1962. It initiates and encourages research projects and publications in the natural sciences and the humanities (history of the Jewish people, Jewish philosophy, Bible, Hebrew literature, Jewish languages, and history of Jewish art).

Since 1932 the Academy has run an academic center in Cairo, Egypt.

3. Residence of the President of the State The permanent residence of the President of the State was built on the

Van Leer Institute.

present site in 1971. The first President, Chaim Weizmann, held his functions from his home at Rehovot from 1949 to 1952. The second President, Itzhak Ben-Zvi, lived and worked in a modest wooden structure in the center of Rehavia from 1952 to 1963; Zalman Shazar, the third President from 1963 to 1973, spent the last two years of his term of office in the new residence.

The President of the State of Israel is elected by the Knesset for a period of five years, and can be reelected for a second term only. The President's residence is open to the public annually during the Festival of Sukkot.

The decorative fence is the work of the artist Bezalel Schatz, and the building was planned by the architect E. Elhanani. It contains the President's bureau, a reception hall and a residential section. The hall is decorated with works by Israeli artists.

We continue our tour along HaNassi Boulevard and turn into HaPalmach Street. On the right is a building faced with reddish stone which is the L.A. Mayer residence for retired academics, built with the assistance of Mrs. Solomons, who also established the Islamic Art Museum.

4. L.A. Mayer Memorial — Institute for Islamic Art Visiting hours: Museum: Sunday to Thursday 10.00 a.m. to 1.00 p.m.; 3.30 p.m. to 6.00 p.m. (closed Friday); Saturday 10.30 a.m. to 1.00 p.m.; eve of holidays 10.00 a.m. to 1.00 p.m. Library: Sunday, Monday, Tuesday, Thursday 8.30 a.m. to 2.00 p.m.; Wednesday 8.30 a.m. to 6.00 p.m.; Friday and eve of holidays 8.30 a.m. to 12.30 p.m. Entry fee.

At the corner of HaPalmach and HaNassi Streets is a building faced with reddish Jerusalem stone, whose rounded facade has five arched openings and long, narrow windows on the second floor. The Institute includes a research library and the Islamic Art Museum. It was established by Mrs. Bryce-Solomons in memory of Prof. L.A Mayer, of the Hebrew University of Jerusalem, a scholar of Islam.

The Museum has 5,000 artifacts from Islamic countries from various periods. A special section is devoted to Iranian Islamic art from its inception in the 7th century. The art of Turkey, India, Egypt, Syria and Iraq are represented; ceramic objects (utensils, statuettes and tiles); a collection of glass vessels, and objects fashioned in metal; pages of caligraphy and miniatures; and a comprehensive collection of figures of the ancient Turkish shadow theater. In the East and West Room are many exhibits reflecting the cultural relations and mutual influences of countries of Europe and the Muslim Oriental countries between the 13th and 15th century. Permanent exhibitions show the historical development of Islamic art, and stress production techniques.

In the archives and research library tens of thousands of slides and photographs on Islamic archaeology are at the disposal of researchers. The material is also available to institutions and publishing houses in Israel and overseas.

The President of the State's residence.

Institute for Islamic Art.

The activities of institute include guided tours and lectures for school children, university students, army units and organized groups.

We come out into HaPalmach Street along whose length runs the **Merhavia** neighborhood founded in 1938. Its name derives from Psalm 118:5: "I called upon the Lord in distress: the Lord answered me, and set me in a large place [merhavia]".

From the museum we turn left into Chopin Street (east of HaPalmach Street); on the left side of the road is the Israel Bar Association and the Jerusalem Law Center. Next door is the Ohel Nehama Synagogue, with a pyramid-like roof.

5. Jerusalem Theater — Center for the Performing Arts The entrance to the new wing is from Chopin Street; the main entrance to the building is from Marcus Street. The high stone building has rounded corners that recall the folds of a stage curtain. The architect was Michael Nadler. The paved courtyard in front of the main entrance overlooks southern Jerusalem. The abstract stone sculptures by Yehiel Shemi in the courtyard, on the building's facade and in the lobby, provide a sense of stage scenery. Exhibitions are held regularly in the entrance lobby, and there is a restaurant and a book shop. The entrance serves both wings which include four halls: the Sherover Theater with 950 seats was the first to be opened in 1971; the Henry Crown Symphony Hall with 750 places — the permanent concert hall of the Jerusalem Symphony Orchestra; the Rebecca Crown auditorium which seats 450; and a small hall with 100 seats.

The new wing housing the latter three halls was opened in 1986. The Center hosts cultural events in all the performing arts from Israel and abroad. Movies are screened regularly.

We continue along Chopin Street to Marcus Street and go down the hill to No. 17.

6. Hansen Hospital This is a hospital, named for a famous researcher of leprosy, for persons suffering from this disease. Built during the years 1885 to 1887, it was planned by Conrad Schick and financed by German Protestants. The two-storey building encompasses an internal courtyard; the front of the building faces south. The external courtyard is enclosed by a stone wall, and the gate facing Gedaliah Alon Street is closed.

In the past there was a farm here worked by the patients. Today, there is only a small number of patients in the hospital which functions under the jurisdiction of the Ministry of Health, and visits are only possible by permission of the Ministry.

Our tour ends here.

Jerusalem Theater.

Hansen Hospital.

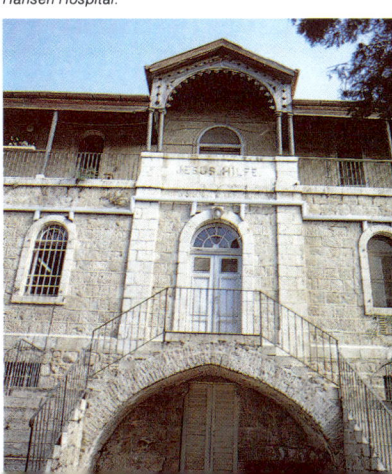

TOUR No. 25

SITES IN WEST JERUSALEM

Details of tour: The tour includes sites in the western part of the city, but should be divided into separate excursions as bus No 11 reaches only site No 7 and sites No 6 and 8 are reached on foot (or by private vehicle) from the Central Bus Station.
Transportation: Buses No 5, 6, 12, 17, 18, 20, 21, 24 and 99; No 11 to Givat Shaul; No 28 to the Biblical Zoo
Parking lots at each site for private vehicles
Starting point: Central Bus Station
The sites: 1. The Military Cemetery; 2. Mount Herzl; 3. Yad Vashem Memorial; 4. Hadassah Medical Center, Ein Karem; 5. ;Model of Jerusalem in the Second Temple period at the Holyland Hotel; 6. Romema; 7. Givat Shaul; 8. Lifta.

EXCURSION BY BUS OR CAR

En route to the first site of the tour, the Military Cemetery, buses leaving the Jerusalem Central Bus Station travel along Herzl Boulevard. To the left is Etz Hayim, a religious housing tenement on the corner of Jaffa Road and Herzl Boulevard, opposite the Central Bus Station. It is named for Etz Hayim Talmud Torah founded in 1928. The **Maimon Neighborhood**, further on, is a housing estate bordering on Kiryat Moshe. It was established in 1936 and named for Rabbi Y.L. Maimon, first Minister for Religious Affairs of the State of Israel.

At the first intersection we see to the right the **Rav Kook Institute** — an Orthodox religious research institute and publishing house which functions under the auspices of the World Zionist Organization. It is named for Abraham Isaac Hacohen Kook, the Ashkenazi Chief Rabbi from 1919 to 1935, and includes a library, archives and conference hall.

Nearby are the buildings of the Jewish Institute for the Blind. Originally founded in the Old City in 1892 it moved to the New City in 1907.

The Institute is on the outskirts of **Kiryat Moshe** — a garden suburb named for Moses Montefiore, founded in 1925 by religious Jews. A tree-lined boulevard leads to a small park at the end of which is a synagogue. In the nearby Merkaz Harav Yeshiva, religious studies are carried out in the spirit taught by Rabbi Kook, for whom it is named.

At the corner of Kiryat Moshe and Herzl Boulevard are the apartment blocks of the Teachers' Union and staff of the Jerusalem Bus Company, built in the 1930s. Opposite are four hotels built in the 1980s. Further along the right side of the road is the small Shoshanat Zion neighborhood established in the 1930s by Jewish immigrants from Persia, which is now part of Kiryat Moshe.

The main road brings us to **Beit Hakerem** — the first suburb to be built in west Jerusalem. Established in 1922 by teach-

Teachers' Training Seminary, Beit Hakerem.

ers, white collar workers and writers, the name was taken from the biblical site mentioned in Jeremiah (6:1) believed to have been situated in the vicinity of the nearby Arab village of Ein Karem. The first houses were built on a rocky hill, and many trees were planted. The large stone-faced building at the top of the hill is the Hebrew Teachers' Training Seminary founded in 1913 in Zikhron Moshe and transferred to the present site in 1928.

We pass through Denmark Square, with its monument recalling how the Danes ferried Jewish refugees from Nazi Germany, in fishing boats, during the Second World War.

The **Hapoalim (Workers') Neighborhood** was founded in 1929 by a group of building workers. They built their own houses, and the streets bear the names of their trades. The neighborhood eventually linked up with the southern section of Beit Hakerem.

To the right of the road, a little further along, are the houses of **Yeffe Nof**, built in 1929 by merchants who traded in the New City.

Between Beit Hakerem and Yeffe Nof is a neighborhood set up in 1950, named **Harel** for the Harel Brigade of the Palmach fighting units. It is on the outskirts of the **Jerusalem Forest**, created in the 1930s and maintained by the Jewish National Fund on the slopes of the Hill of Remembrance, Mount Herzl and Har Nof. Pines, cypress cedar, carob and acacia trees flourish there. A narrow road, about 7 km (4⅓ miles) long, runs through the forest, spans the Revida wadi and climbs up to Har Nof, reaching Givat Shaul. From the fork at the stream, the road runs west along the slope of Mount Herzl and emerges at the Hill of Remembrance. Another entrance to the forest is through Yeffe Nof, and this road leads to the Jerusalem Forest Recreation Center, with its sports facilities and swimming pool. Remains of Crusader period farms have been uncovered in the forest.

We continue along Herzl Boulevard and to the left we see the new **Sha'arei Zedek Hospital** complex opened in 1980 and **Givat Mordechai,** a religious neighborhood situated between Shahal and Heller Streets, named after Rabbi Mordechai Ebel. Founded in 1955, it has been expanded across Bezek Street with apartment buildings occupied by non-religious residents. Above the hospital is the **Bayit Vegan** garden suburb built in 1928 by religious families. After the establishment of the State, the suburb expanded and a number of Orthodox religious educational institutions were set up, among which are Boys' Town, the vocational high school *yeshiva*, the Netiv Meir High School Yeshiva, the Harry Fischel Institute for Training Rabbis and Rabbinical Court Judges, the Institute for Science and Technological Research According to the Halacha, the Talmudic Encyclopedia Research Institute, and the Jerusalem Girls' Higher Education Institute (Ha-Mikhlalah).

A small housing tenement at the southern extremity of Bayit Vegan is called **Bnai Brith**, having been established with the assistance of that organization in 1929.

THE TOUR
1. Military Cemetery
Transportation: Buses No 13, 18. 20
Parking lot for private vehicles
Distance covered: approx. 1 km (⅔ mile)
Time: approx. half an hour

The main military cemetery for those who fell in the wars of Israel is situated on the northern slope of Mount Herzl. To the right of the entrance are an office, toilets

Denmark Square.

and stone benches; to the left an underground memorial hall. The graves have been laid out in sections according to wars and major battles.

Among the first graves is that of Avshalom Feinberg, a member of Nili, an underground organization which spied for the British against the Turks during the First World War, who was murdered in Sinai. His remains were found in 1967 and brought here for burial. Then follow the sections where soldiers are buried who fell in the Second World War, the War of Independence (1948), the Sinai Campaign (1956), the Six Day War (1967) the Yom Kippur War (1973), the Lebanon War (1982) and other military operations.

At the fork in the path is a memorial, symbolizing a ship, to the 140 members of the 402nd Jewish Transport Unit who disappeared in the Mediterranean Sea during the Second World War in 1943. On the monument is the verse from Psalm 68:22.

"The Lord said: I will bring again from Bashan, I will bring my people again from the depths of the sea".

Nearby is another stone memorial to the 23 sailors, members of the Palmach fighting units, who in 1941 set out to attack Nazi outposts in the Lebanese port of Tripoli and were lost at sea.

Further along, a stone block with an aperture in the form of a Star of David is a memorial to the Palestine Jewish fighters in the British army who fell in the Second World War.

Paths lead to sections where the fallen during the War of Independence are buried. The lower path (starting from the fork in the main path) leads to a memorial to those who fell in the Old City of Jerusalem. It is constructed in the form of an alley covered by an arched roof with the inscription: "And gather them from the coasts of the earth" (Jeremiah 31:8) and "And your bones shall flourish like an herb" (Isaiah

THE MILITARY CEMETERY ON MOUNT HERZL

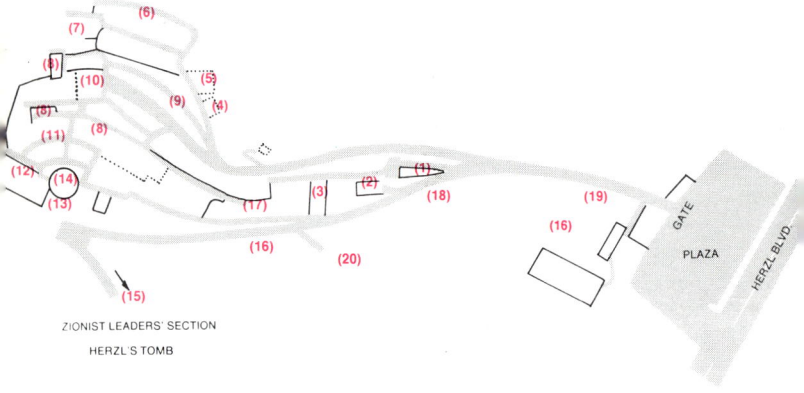

ZIONIST LEADERS' SECTION

HERZL'S TOMB

1. Ship Memorial
2. Memorial to 23 Sailors
3. Nebi Daniel Convoy
4. Jerusalem Old City Fighters
5. Missing in Action
6. Six Day War
7. Police Section
8. War of Independence
9. "Their Graves Are Unknown"
10. "HaLamed-Hay"
11. Kastel Fighters
12. Sinai Campaign
13. "State on the Way"
14. Paratroopers' Memorial
15. Zionist Leaders
16. Yom Kippur War
17. "Follow Me"
18. Palestine Jewish Volunteers
19. "The War after the War"
20. Lebanon War

66:14). Nearby is a memorial to the sailors of the Israeli submarine "Dakar" which mysteriously disappeared in 1968, presumably in Egyptian waters. Despite numerous joint Israeli-Egyptian attempts and American assistance, its whereabouts have never been located.

The soldiers who fell in the Six Day War are buried in two sections: at the end of the lower path and above the steps to the left of the entrance. The upper path leads to Mount Herzl.

2. Mount Herzl

Transportation: Buses No 13, 18, 20, 27, 39, 40 and 99
Parking lot for private vehicles
Visiting hours: Weekdays — summer: 9.00 am to 6.15 pm; winter: 9.00 am to 4.45 pm
Time: approx. 1 hour

This is a national memorial named after Theodor Herzl, visionary of the Jewish State and founder of the World Zionist Organization. It contains his tomb as well as that of pre-state and Israeli leaders, the Herzl Museum, the Mount Herzl Institute, and park. From this hill (834 m, 2376 ft high) there is a marvelous panoramic view of Jerusalem and the surrounding hills.

National ceremonies are held here. On the eve of Independence Day, the Speaker of the Knesset officially declares the end of the Memorial Day for the fallen in Israel's wars, and the opening of the Independence Day festivities.

We enter through the main gate and walk along the paved area to the building at the left — the Mount Herzl Institute. The lecture hall contains sculptures of Herzl, and pictures and books from his Vienna residence. We descend the stairs at the right of the building to the Herzl Museum opened in 1960. It contains selections from the Herzl archives (photographs, documents, correspondence, books and personal effects). Herzl's study has been reconstructed here. Explanatory pamphlets can be purchased in several languages.

(top) Memorial to the "Dakar" crew.
(center) Entrance to Mount Herzl cemetery.
(bottom) Herzl's tomb.

We walk up the main path to Herzl's tomb. When he died in 1904, Theodor Herzl was buried next to his father in Vienna, and in his will instructed that he should lie there until "the Jewish people will bring my body to Eretz Israel". His remains were reinterred here in 1949.

From the nearby observation point is a view of the western suburbs of Jerusalem, the Hebrew University, the Israel Museum and the government offices at Kiryat Ben Gurion. We continue along the path to the section of the graves of the leaders of the World Zionist Organization (Nahum Sokolow, David Wolffsohn, Berl Locker) and the Herzl family (Theodor's parents and sister). The observation point here overlooks the Jerusalem Forest, the vicinity of Motza and Ramot Alon. Below is the Military Cemetery.

We walk along the path in a northwesterly direction and come to the tombs of leaders of the State (Eliezer Kaplan, Joseph Sprinzak, Levi Eshkol, Itzhak Ben Zvi, Zalman Shazar and Golda Meir). Further along the path are the graves of Zeev and Johanna Jabotinsky whose remains were brought here from the USA in 1964. The nearby observation point gives us a view of the Hill of Remembrance, the Jerusalem Forest, Ein Karem, and the Hadassah Medical Center; above are the moshavim Ora and Aminadav, and the Kennedy Memorial. The path brings us back to the entrance and into Holland Square. At the corner of the square is a red steel sculpture dedicated to Jerusalem by the American sculptor Alexander Calder.

3. Hill of Remembrance — Yad Vashem Memorial

Distance covered: approx. 1 km (²⁄₃ mile)
Time: approx. one hour
Transportation: Buses No 18, 20, 27, 39, 40 — to Mount Herzl and then by foot. No 99 enters the site

Map of Yad Vashem.

Buildings
1. Main entrance
2. Cafeteria
3. Admin. building, Archives and Library
4. World Center for Holocaust Teaching
5. Book shop and information
6. Historical Museum
7. Hall of Names
8. Synagogue
9. Art Museum
10. Auditorium
11. Hall of Remembrance
12. Memorial Cave
13. Valley of Destroyed Communities

Memorials
A. To Czerniakov Jewish Community
B. "Hope"
C. Yad Vashem Menorah
D. Wall of Remembrance: "Warsaw Ghetto Uprising" "The Last March"
E. "Job"
F. Auschwitz Monument
G. "Ultima"
H. Soldiers, Partisans and Ghetto Fighters
I. Victims of the Death Camps
J. "Silent Cry"
K. "Korczak and the Children of the Ghetto"
L. Pillar of Heroism
M. The Boat

YAD VASHEM
MARTYRS AND HEROES REMEMBRANCE AUTHORITY

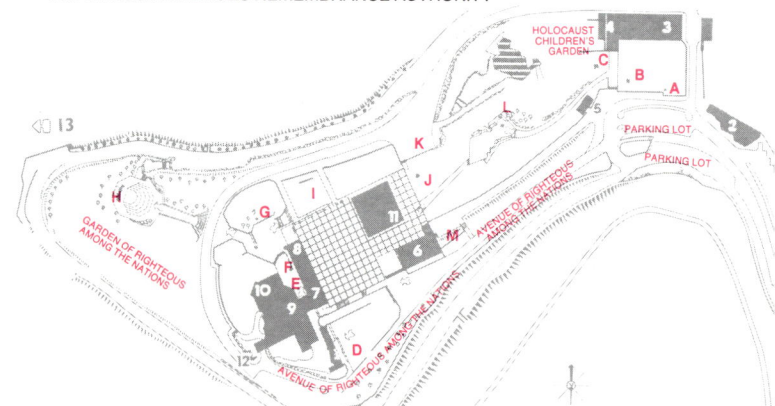

Avenue of Righteous Among the Nations.

Parking lot at the site for private vehicles
Visiting hours: Sun. to Thurs. 9.00 am to 5.00 pm, Fri. and eves of holidays 9.00 am to 2.00 pm. The Hall of Names, the archives and offices are open to 1.00 pm.

To the west of Mount Herzl a path about 800 m (875 yd) long leads to the Hill of Remembrance (806 m — 2644 ft high) on which are the buildings of the government memorial to the Holocaust Martyrs and Heroes, and the research institute on the Holocaust. In 1953 the Israel Government decided to establish the Martyrs and Heroes Remembrance Authority to be called "Yad Vashem" based on Isaiah 56:5: "Even unto them will I give in mine house and within my walls a place and a name... I will give them an everlasting name, that shall not be cut off". The site was opened in 1957; the official memorial celebration is held in the square annually on the eve of Holocaust Day. There are buildings where research is carried out, museums, a synagogue and memorials with tree-lined parks between the buildings. The wrought-iron entrance gate is a stylized reminder of a concentration camp gate (the work of the sculptor Roman Halter).

The first building to the right is the administration building which houses a reference library of thousands of books, a reading room and the Holocaust archives on microfilm: newspapers, diaries and drawings of concentration camp prisoners, lists of people who disappeared and who escaped, and every detail of the legal proceedings against Nazi war criminals. Four works of art are in front of the building: a monument in memory of the Czerniakow community by Mordecai Kafri; "Hope" by Ilana Gur; the six-branched Yad Vashem *menorah* by Zehara Schatz.

The shop where books and souvenirs are sold serves also as information bureau. A detailed guide with a map can be purchased there.

We walk along the Avenue of Righteous Among the Nations. On both sides of the path are trees, beneath each one a plaque with the name of a person or organization, from different countries, who helped to save Jews from the Nazis. We reach the boat in which Danish fishermen smuggled Jewish refugees to Sweden in October 1943. Nearby is the Historical Museum. An exhibition of thousands of documents relates the events of the Holocaust in chronological order: the rise of the Nazi Party to power, attacks on Jews, destruction of communities, the physical annihilation, uprising in ghettos and concentration camps and rescue activities. We continue to the assembly square opposite the Wall of Remembrance built of red bricks with two reliefs, the work of the sculptor Nathan Rapoport: "The Warsaw Ghetto Uprising" and the "Last March". Below them is the phrase from Ezekiel: "In thy blood, live" (16:6).

The Avenue of the Righteous Among the Nations leads to the Memorial Cave in which have been gathered hundreds of "tombstones" of individuals and communities contributed by families from all over the world in memory of their loved ones. The path ascends to four buildings surrounding a courtyard in which stands a statue of Job by Nathan Rapoport and the "Auschwitz Monument" by Elsa Pollak, an Auschwitz survivor. The four buildings include the auditorium; a museum with art works executed by the inmates of the concentration camps; the Hall of Names with records of two million victims out of the six million who perished in the Holocaust; the synagogue in which remains of synagogues destroyed by the Nazis have been gathered, its western wall built of stone blocks similar to those of the Western Wall.

We continue down to the Garden of the Righteous Among the Nations with its open plaza where stands a monument to the soldiers, partisans and ghetto fighters by Bernie Fink. It consists of six granite blocks, in two groups, arranged in such a way that their inner edges form a window in the shape of a stylized Star of David. The blocks represent the six million Jews murdered in the Holocaust. From here we have a view of the Valley of the Destroyed Communities with memorials to some 5,000 communities.

We return to the path leading to a large square. To the left is a blue marble sculpture, "Ultima", by Eli Ilan, and the metal memorial to victims of the concentration and death camps by Nandor Glid with shouting figures entangled in a barbed wire fence. Bordering on the square is the central memorial building — Ohel Yizkor (Hall of Remembrance) built of basalt

(top) The "Pillar of Heroism"; (center) 'Korczak and the Children of the Ghetto"; (bottom) Memorial to the child martyrs.

stone, with a concrete roof and a stylized iron entrance gate created by the sculptor David Palombo. The names of 22 death camps are inscribed on the floor and a flame in a broken bronze cup burns in memory of the victims. The ashes of some of the dead brought from the death camps have been interred under the floor. The exit gates were designed by Bezalel Schatz.

We walk back along the path in the direction of the entrance and pass by the sculpture "Silent Cry" by Lea Michelson depicting a Jew at prayer. We reach a square with a metal "Pillar of Heroism" by Buki Schwartz, 21 m (69 ft) high, in memory of the Holocaust victims, ghetto fighters, partisans, underground fighters, soldiers, and the activists who brought "illegal immigrants" to Palestine after the Second World War. The pillar can be seen from afar. The path continues to the park dedicated to the memory of the children who perished in the Holocaust with its sculpture of "Korczak and the Children of the Ghetto" by Boris Saktsier depicting Janusz Korczak embracing frightened children. We enter the impressive memorial designed by Moshe Safde, with its myriad tiny lights and voices intoning the names of the child martyrs. Our visit to Yad Vashem ends here.

4. Hadassah and Hebrew University Medical Center: Ein Karem

Transportation: Buses No 19, 27 and 99
Parking lots at site for private vehicles

A guided tour (for a fee) of the Chagall Windows, lasting about an hour, takes place on Sunday through Thursday from 8.30 am to 1.45 pm, every half hour; Friday 9.30 am to 12.30 pm. Leaflets in English, Hebrew, German, Spanish and French are available.

The Hadassah complex at Ein Karem was erected on the initiative of Israel's first Prime Minister David Ben Gurion and the Hadassah Medical Organization. It was inaugurated in 1961 and incorporated all the departments of the Hadassah Hospital scattered throughout the New City of Jerusalem after its evacuation from Mount Scopus in 1948. In the center of the complex is the circular main building of the hospital surrounded by the Medical School, School of Dentistry, Pharmacy and Psychiatry, and the synagogue. The School of Nursing is situated to the west of the main building and opposite is the maternity ward. The doctors' and staff's living quarters are to the east of the main building.

The Medical Center with its 800 beds and over 75 departments and out-patients clinics is the largest center in Israel for medical treatment, teaching and research. Over 400,000 patients are treated here annually. Some 2,400 students of the School of Medicine have graduated over the years.

We end our tour with a visit to the synagogue.

The **Chagall Windows** (visiting hours above). The synagogue was consecrated in 1962, to mark Hadassah's 50th anniversary, in the presence of Marc Chagall, the French Jewish artist. Its design with the *bimah* below floor level was inspired by the first verse of Psalm 130:1: "Out of the depths have I cried unto thee, O Lord". The

Hadassah Medical Center.

Hadassah synagogue.

building is faced with reddish Jerusalem stone, and light filters through the stained windows created in France by Chagall. The twelve stained glass windows (each 3.5 m — 11 ft high and 2.5 m — 8 ft wide) symbolize the Twelve Tribes in groups of three, in accordance with events on their trek from Egypt through the wilderness. They represent the twelve sons of Jacob, heads of the tribes, and the blessings of Jacob in Genesis 49. They are painted in 12 bright greens, yellows, blues and reds, recalling the colors of the ephod worn by the High Priest, and are arranged in groups of three — Reuben, Simeon and Levi; Judah, Zebulun and Issachar; Dan, Gad and Asher; Naphtali, Joseph and Benjamin.

5. Model of Jerusalem in the Second Temple Period at the Holyland Hotel

It is recommended to view the model before visiting the archaeological excavation at the Western Wall.

Transportation: Buses No 21, 21A, 99
Parking lot at the site for private vehicles
Visiting hours: Every day. Admission fee
Time: At least half an hour.

There is a cafeteria and souvenir shop which sells booklets which may also be borrowed at the ticket office.

The model of Jerusalem at the end of the Second Temple period shows Jerusalem in all its glory just before the Roman siege in 66 CE. It is built on a scale of 1:50. The model was constructed from the same materials used for construction in that period. The reconstruction is based on descriptions of the city by Josephus, and from the Mishna and the Talmud, descriptions given by Greek and Roman writers of the period and on archaeological finds.

The model was planned by Michael Avi-Yonah, Professor of Archaeology at the Hebrew University who was an expert on the subject, designed by Hava Avi-Yonah and built by A. Sheffler and completed by R. Brotzen. It was erected on the initiative of H. Kroch, the late proprietor of the Holyland Hotel.

Model of Jerusalem.
(top) The Temple; (center) the upper city.
(bottom) the lower city.

Since the model was built it has undergone a number of modifications based on more recent research. The mosaic map on the wall opposite the entrance can be of assistance in understanding the model. A map of Jerusalem in the Second Temple period showing the city's walls today can be purchased at the souvenir shop. We can view the model from four points and relate to the present-day situation of the city.

1. From the north (from Shivtei Yisrael Street near Mea She'arim) a view across the three walls: the nearest wall is the third and last, built in the time of Agrippa I (41–44 CE). Building ceased at the order of the Romans, but was completed by the rebels (in 66). In the corner can be seen the octagonal Psephonus Tower, 35 m (115 ft) high, whose presumed location was north of the Russian Compound. The only gate in the wall was the Women's Gate, assumed to be located near the Tombs of the Kings (outside the wall at that time and thus not included in the model).

The New City — the Bezetha suburb — lies between the Third and Second Walls. The second wall extended from the Phasael tower to the north, then apparently turned east (where the Damascus Gate stands today) and continued to the south to the Antonia Fortress. Beyond this wall are the Pool of the Towers, and nearby Hyrcanus' tomb (near the Hill of Golgotha), Alexander Yannai's tomb (opposite the Rockefeller Museum) and to the south the Bethesda Pool.

2. From the west (by Jaffa Gate) we see three towers (in the vicinity of the Citadel): Phasael, Hippicus and Miriamne. To the south, surrounded by a wall, is Herod's palace (today the Armenian garden), and nearby, to the east, is the upper market. East of the marketplace is the presumed location of the Hasmonean palace, then the palace of the High Priest Annas, and the Herodian theater (today the Jewish Quarter). Further to the east is the Western Wall, marked with a red arrow on the wall of the Temple Mount. At the southwest extremity of the city can be seen the palace of the High Priest Caiaphas, and then King David's Tomb with its pyramidal roof on Mount Zion. The First Wall extended from the towers to the east up to the Temple Mount wall; it encompassed the upper city to the north, the west and the south, continued around the lower city and to David's City.

3. From the south (from the Kidron Valley, and to the west to the Siloam Pool) the lower city can be seen, with its small houses — apparently a poorer residential area. To the east can be seen David's City on the eastern hill. To the north, the Temple Mount wall continues in the western section of which (at the Western Wall) can be seen Robinson's Arch and Wilson's Arch. In the central Tyropoeon Valley, the Stadium built by Herod has been reconstructed on its presumed location. To the east is the western wall of David's City, on which there are a number of buildings (from south to north): a synagogue (named for Theodotos of the Vettenas family, the palaces of the kings of Adiabene and the tomb of Hulda the Prophetess. In the southern wall are the Hulda Gates (the triple and double gates) with the wide stairway leading up to them (not mentioned by Josephus, but uncovered during excavations).

4. From the east (from the western slope of the Mount of Olives) is a view over the eastern wall in which are the Shushan Gate, the Temple and the Antonia fortress. We can see the porticoes (pillar-lined passages along the three walls of the Temple Mount) and the royal portico, the basilica, above the southern wall, the Tadi Gate in the center of the northern wall, and to the north west the Antonia fortress with its four towers and the rampart. From the eastern gate (the Beautiful Gate) steps ascended to the women's gallery, in whose four corners were the chamber of wood, the chamber of the Nazirites, of the lepers and of the oils. Fifteen semi-circular steps lead up to Nicanor's Gate through which the worshipers entered. Beyond it was the priests' gallery where stood the external altar, the slaughter house and the laver. From there twelve steps ascended to the front of the Temple, where there were two pillars on each side of the entrance.

As we leave the parking lot we have a view of western suburbs of Jerusalem: Ramat Denya and Manahat, with the mosque and minaret of the abandoned Arab village of Malha. The village was established in the 16th century. Its Arab inhabitants fled in 1948. Jewish immigrants settled in their place and new buildings were added. The village took the name of Biblical Manahath mentioned in I Chronicles 1:40. To the south can be seen the neighborhood of Gilo, Beit Safafa and Givat Hamatos (Aircraft Hill). To the east, Talpiot and below, the neighborhoods of Gonen, Givat Mordechai, the Eilon Tower and the Wolfson complex. Below is the Rephaim Valley.

A visit to the grounds of the Holyland Hotel (with permission) is worthwhile. Ancient inscriptions and archaeological finds can be seen, and of particular interest is the Merneptah inscription (the Egyptian king who conquered Israel in the 13th century BCE) in which it is believed that the name "Israel" appears for the first time outside the Bible.

From the Central Bus Station we can also walk to Romema or Lifta.

6. Romema, a neighborhood near the central bus station, was founded in 1921. Beside it is the 830 m (2720 ft) high summit on which the Jerusalem reservoir was built. The street names — "Hazvi", "Ariel", Ha'or", "Torah MiZion" — are those of newspapers which were published in the city. Its name is taken from Psalm 118:16 "The right hand of the Lord is exalted [*romema* in Hebrew]". The houses nearest to Jaffa Road were those of wealthy Arabs, built on the edge of the neighborhood. In the heart of the neighborhood is a circular plaza with a monument commemorating the capture of Jerusalem in 1917 by the British forces commanded by General Allenby.

The Israel Television studios and the Jerusalem Post newspaper are in Romema as are Shikun Harabbanim quarter and an industrial estate which developed after 1948. Behind this area the upper Romema neighborhood was built, in which is the central Magen David Adom (First Aid) station.

Biblical Zoo To get to the Biblical Zoo we take bus No 28 from Binyanei Ha'uma (Convention Hall) and travel as far as Yirmeyahu Street. We then walk a short distance to reach the Zoo. Visiting hours: 8.00 am–7 pm; Friday, Saturday and eve of holidays 8.00 am–5.00 pm. Entrance fee (tickets must be bought in advance for Saturdays and holidays).

The Municipal Zoo of Jerusalem houses many species of animals and birds that were common in the Holy Land in Biblical times. The verses in which they are mentioned in the Bible are given for each one of them. The founder of the Zoo, Professor Shulov, established it in 1941 on Mount Scopus. It was moved several times before reaching its present location.

7. Lifta An abandoned Arab village on the outskirts of Jerusalem below upper Romema, on the eastern bank of the Nephtoah (a tributary of the Sorek stream). The spring is identified with the "waters of Nephtoah" on the border between the territories of the tribes of Judah and Benjamin (Joshua 15:9; 18:15). Lifta was established in the 16th century beside the spring.

The village was abandoned in 1948, and after the foundation of the State of Israel, immigrant families settled there. Today there are few residents. A new road has been built leading to the Ramot Alon cross-

View of Lifta.

roads. It is possible to stroll round the village, the spring and the olive press restored by the Nature Reserves Authority, between the fruit trees.

8. Givat Shaul A neighborhood in the western outskirts, established in 1910 and named after the Sephardi Chief Rabbi Yaakov Shaul Eliashar who was one of its principal founders. Its first builders were of Yemenite origin, and later families from Mea She'arim and the Old City moved in. An industrial zone developed there after the foundation of the State. On its outskirts the new Ezrat Nashim mental hospital was built. The Har Menuhot cemetery was established close by. Burial began there in 1951 and it has been the main Jewish cemetery for Jerusalem ever since. Today there are about 50,000 graves. In the year it was established, some of the graves from a temporary cemetery at Givat Ram were transferred here, excluding those of soldiers, whose graves were moved to Mount Herzl.

Har Nof, near Givat Shaul, is a new neighborhood. Building was begun in 1981 by the Jerusalem Contractors' Association. The neighborhood is planned to house 16,000 residents, half of whom are

Monument in Romema commemorating the capture of Jerusalem in 1917 by the British.

already living there. Most of the residents are ultra-Orthodox Jews, some of them new immigrants from the USA and France. The neighborhood takes its name from the hill on which it was built, west of Kfar Shaul. Its summit (808 m — 2650 ft) is in the Jerusalem Forest which surrounds the neighborhood on three sides.

TOUR No. 26

GIVAT RAM AND VICINITY

Transportation: Bus lines are given with the sites where required
The Sites: 1. North Givat Ram (Binyanei Ha'uma-Convention Center, Hilton Hotel, Wohl Rose Garden, the Menorah, the Knesset, HaKirya — David Ben-Gurion Government Center, Beit Yad Labanim); 2. Hebrew University Campus; 3. Israel Museum; 4. Monastery of the Cross.

FOREWORD

Givat Ram is the name given to the ridge south of the Central Bus Station at the entrance to Jerusalem, consisting of three hills.

The northern hill — between Shazar, Wolffsohn, Ruppin and Ben Zvi Boulevards, is 830 m (2723 ft) above sea level. To the north are Binyanei Ha'uma, the Hilton Hotel, the National Insurance Institute, the Zionist Archives, the Ministry for Foreign Affairs, Yad Labanim and Beit Hahayal (Soldiers' Hostel). In the center — the Supreme Court building (under construction), the Rose Garden and the Bank of Israel. To the south are the Government buildings, the Menorah and the Knesset. On its eastern slopes is the Sacker Park.

During the War of Independence the Israeli defense units used the buildings as a base for operations and called it the Officers' Hill (the initials of which in Hebrew constitute the word Ram, the source of its present name — Givat Ram).

Archaeological excavations in the area have revealed remains of a Second Temple period quarry, a kiln for firing roof tiles and clay pipes used by the Tenth Roman Legion, a 6th century church and monastery. A temporary cemetery existed here from 1948 to 1951.

On the western hill, 780 m (2560 ft) high, between Ruppin Boulevard and the Hovevei Zion valley, is the Hebrew University Campus, set up in the 1950s. To the east is the Neveh Sha'anan neighborhood, built in 1929 and nearby Neveh Granot and Nayot built in the 1960s.

The southern hill, south of Ruppin Boulevard and east of Neveh Sha'anan is 786 m (2579 ft) high. The Israel Museum was built here in 1965.

THE TOUR

1. Givat Ram

Distance covered: approx. 2 km (1¼ miles)
Time: approx. 2 hours (including a visit to the Knesset)
Starting point: The square opposite the Central Bus Station
End of tour: Ben-Gurion Government Center (HaKirya).

A high square, rough stone pillar stands in the Shein Square and at its apex the single Hebrew word *Nizkor*, "We shall remember". This is a memorial to the Jerusalemites who fell in battle during the 1948 War of Independence.

We walk through the underground passageway and come out at **Binyanei**

Binyanei Ha'uma.

Wohl Rose Garden.

The Menorah opposite the Knesset.

Ha'uma (literally "Buildings of the Nation") erected in 1950 by the World Zionist Organization as a Convention Center. It consists of one large auditorium seating 3000, several smaller lecture halls, a spacious foyer and broad passageways used for exhibitions. The Zionist Congress is held here every four years, as well as conventions, concerts and artistic events. The Central Zionist Archives are housed here since 1987. To the south is the **Hilton Hotel**, opened in 1972.

After visiting Binyanei Ha'uma we go south to the **Wohl Rose Garden**, used for state occasions, where more than 400 varieties of roses from all over the world can be seen. Walking through the park we are dazzled by the wealth of colors. We continue to the south and come out opposite the Knesset, descend the steps and turn left to the Menorah Square.

At the southeast extremity of the Rose Garden is a large bronze seven-branched **Menorah** (candelabrum). Standing 5 m (16½ ft) high and 4 m (13 ft) wide it was created by the Anglo-Jewish sculptor Benno Elkan, and was presented by the British Parliament in 1956.

On the seven branches of the candelabrum *(menorah)* are depicted in relief figures and events which marked the history of the Jewish people. On the central branch: Moses with the tablets of the law on Mount Sinai; Rachel weeping over her sons; Ruth the Moabite; the vision of the End of Days; the Warsaw Ghetto uprising. On the extreme right branch: Jeremiah; the wars of the Maccabees; a Hassid; the reconstruction of Jerusalem by Nehemiah. On the second right branch: Hillel the Elder; Hananiah ben Teradyon being burned at the stake; the Kabbala; Aharon the Priest and his two sons. On the third right branch: Bar Kochba; the Messiah; Jacob struggling with the angel. On the extreme left branch: Rabbi Yohanan ben Zakkai fleeing burning Jerusalem for Yavneh; Judah and Maimonides; Jews weeping for Zion by the rivers of Babylon. On the second left branch: Ezra the Scribe; Job; the Talmud; King Solomon seated in his garden. On the third left branch: David holding Goliath's head; the modern return to the Land of Israel; Abraham.

To the north of the Knesset Square the road leads to the Knesset gates and to the east is a path leading to a small cemetery (see foreword) which may be visited.

The Knesset (Israel's Parliament) Visiting hours: guided tours by Knesset personnel take place on Sundays and Thursdays from 8.30 am to 2.30 pm. On Mondays, Tuesdays and Wednesdays from 11.00 am until 1.00 pm visitors can listen to debates from the visitors' gallery when the Knesset is in session. Passport or identity card must be shown at the entrance.

TOUR No. 26

Transportation: Buses No 9, 24 and 99. Parking along the streets in the vicinity for private vehicles.

The Knesset compound is the permanent site of the Israeli parliament, built with funds provided by the James de Rothschild family and dedicated on 30th August 1966. The monumental structure in a combination of Classical and modern style is faced with the reddish Jerusalem stone. Only the top floor can be seen from the front; three more floors are visible from the slope on the Ruppin Boulevard side. The main entrance is on the highest level.

The first session of the Knesset was held on February 14, 1949 (Tu Bishvat 5709). Over a period of 16 years the Knesset was located in the building which now houses the Ministry of Tourism (see Tour No. 21). The Knesset has 120 members. It is a legislative body which elects the President of the State, approves the Cabinet and supervises its activities, approves the annual state budget, imposes taxes, appoints the State Comptroller, etc. The work of the Knesset is controlled by the Speaker (elected by the Knesset members) with the assistance of his deputies. There are nine permanent committees: Foreign Affairs and Defense; Constitution, Law and Judiciary; Education and Culture; Finances; Economic Affairs; Labor; Interior; Public Services and the Knesset Committee.

Tour of the Knesset: We enter through a side gate after a security check by the Knesset guard. The main gate is the work of the sculptor David Palombo (who also designed a gate to the Hall of Remembrance at Yad Vashem). In the foyer are the information desk and the entrance to the visitors' gallery.

We pass through a wide passage leading to the reception area, where the focus is on the Marc Chagall Hall, with his three tapestries telling the history of the Jewish People, his wall mosaics and mosaic floor.

From the reception hall we descend into a wide passageway opening on to the plenary chamber and the gallery (336 seats). The seats of the Knesset Members and the Cabinet Ministers are laid out in the form of a *menorah*, the symbol of the State. On the wall behind the Speaker's podium are stone reliefs, the work of the sculptor Danny Caravan. Above the podium hangs a portrait of Theodor Herzl. In the center of the visitors' gallery is the seat reserved for the President of the State when he visits the Knesset on special occasions.

We descend to the third floor where we pass the Speaker's bureau (at the right) and the Knesset cafeteria and restaurant. On the second floor are the offices of Cabinet ministers and the Cabinet's meeting hall, with frescoes by the Reuven Rubin and Mordechai Ardon.

The synagogue on the ground floor was designed by the architect David Cassuto, and the Holy Ark is from an Italian synagogue. On the same floor are the nine Knesset Committee rooms and the editorial offices of "Reshumot" — the official publication of the legislation passed by the Knesset; any law adopted by three readings in the Knesset is required to be published in "Reshumot" for it to take effect.

We leave the Knesset and walk along Eliezer Kaplan Street (the first Minister of Finance) the main street of HaKirya (Ben-Gurion Government Center).

HaKirya (Ben Gurion Government Cen-

(top left) View of the Knesset.
(top right) HaKirya.
(center right) Yad Labanim.
(bottom right) Hebrew University campus.

GIVAT RAM AND VICINITY

ter) is the government offices complex comprising the Ministry of Finance; the Ministries of Labor and Social Affairs, of the Interior and of Immigrant Absorption; the Prime Minister's offices and the Government Archives; opposite is the Bank of Israel.

Beit Yad Labanim (Soldiers' Memorial) (Aluf Street, corner Ben Zvi Boulevard) Visiting hours: Sundays to Thursdays 8.30 to 11.30 am.

Built between the years 1974 and 1977 as a memorial to Jerusalem soldiers who fell in action. The entrance is between two structures on a bridge over a water conduit with a monument of steel pipes by Bezalel Schatz. A path leads to an assembly area with 600 seats. A memorial hall built in the form of a pyramid is divided into two sections, the inside coated with goldplated aluminium, with projecting geometrical forms. An eternal flame burns inside the hall where stands a glass sculpture with the pyramid motif, by J. Hadany. The names of the fallen are inscribed on the Wall of Remembrance.

We descend to the ground floor where there is a mosaic map of Jerusalem, a lecture hall, archives, offices and toilets.

Beit Hahayal (Soldiers' Hostel) next to Beit Yad Labanim. Visiting hours: Sundays to Thursdays, 8.30 am to 4.00 pm and Fridays to 12.00 pm.

The building offers the facilities of a hostel, swimming pool and other sports to soldiers.

2. Hebrew University Campus Visiting hours: the library is open 9.00 am to 2.00 pm and Friday to 12.00 pm. Guided tours between 9.00 to 11.00 am leave from the Administration Building.

The Hebrew University Campus was constructed from 1954 to 1958 on the southern hill of Givat Ram. From 1948 to 1958 various university departments were in different buildings scattered throughout the city until they were all grouped here. When the campus was restored on Mount Scopus and expanded from 1968 to 1984 various departments were transferred there.

We go in through the main gates and see the buildings surrounding the lawns. The entire complex covers an expanse of 500,000 sq m (125 acres) and a road runs round the periphery enclosed by a fence. It was funded by contributions from philanthropists and today houses the Departments of Natural Sciences and Life Sciences, the Jewish National and University Library, the Hebrew Language Academy, the Academy of Music, the Ort Engineering school, the Administration Building, the synagogue, student dormitories, the student club and sports facilities, and a small amphitheater. Beyond the fence is a 16,000 seat stadium. The new botanical gardens are also beyond the fence (opposite Neve Sha'anan and Nayot).

We walk along the path in front of the buildings and come to the **Jewish National and University Library** situated in the center of the campus. It has three floors above ground and three more below. Opened in 1960, the building contains the largest Judaica library in the world, the largest library in the Middle East with over 2 million volumes, 60,000 periodicals, rare manuscripts, and publications in many languages, related to Judaism and the Holy Land.

The library was founded in 1892 as a Hebrew library whose first books were collected in Palestine and overseas. It was set up by the B'nai B'rith organization. In 1925 it was moved to the library building on Mount Scopus and from 1948 to 1960 the books were kept in a number of buildings throughout the city.

The main entrance to the building is on the ground floor where there is an exhibition hall and the catalogue and lending room. On the first floor are Judaica, Oriental Studies, periodicals, music and general reading rooms and a foyer with the famous stained-glass triptych by Mordechai Ardon (installed in 1985) — the colorful depiction of Isaiah's prophecy of the End of Days. On the second floor are the bibliographical services, the collection of maps and the national phototech. On the upper ground floor are the institute for photocopies of manuscripts, archives of famous Jewish personalities, collections of autographs, portraits and manuscripts. On the lower ground floor are the bindery departments and photocopying services.

3. The Israel Museum Visiting hours: the Museum — Sunday, Monday, Wednesday, Thursday 10.00 am to 5.00 pm; Tuesday 4.00 pm to 10.00 pm; Friday, Saturday and eve of Festivals 10.00 am to 2.00 pm. Shrine of the Book — 10.00 am to 10.00 pm daily. Entry fee. Guided tours in English to the Shrine of the Book take place on Sundays at 1.30 pm and on Tuesdays at 3.00 pm, to the Judaica and Jewish Communities sections on Thursdays at 3.00 pm.

Transportation: Buses No 9, 24, 99. Parking lots are provided at the site for private vehicles.

The Israel national museum was established in 1965 on the southern ridge of Givat Ram, facing Ruppin Boulevard and the Knesset. All the collections of the Bezalel Museum of Art and Folklore as well as those of the Israel Antiquities Department were transferred to the Museum. Designed by the Israeli architects Dora Gad and Eli Mansfeld it consists of a number of building units, new ones added as required, and thus the Museum has grown fourfold since it was first erected. The Shrine of the Book is a separate structure.

The Museum has four wings: the Art Exhibition Wing (including the Billy Rose Sculpture Garden); the Biblical and Archaeological Museum; the Shrine of the Book; the Youth Wing. Additional sections include the archaeological garden, the library, graphics department, ethnology, design, glass, ancient Hebrew script, archives and an auditorium. There are souvenir shops and a cafeteria. The Museum organizes approximately 25 exhibitions each year, lectures, concerts and movies, and publishes catalogues and pamphlets.

Our tour begins at the **Shrine of the Book** situated at the right of the path leading from the entrance to the Museum. Built in the form of the lid of an ancient clay vessel in which scrolls were kept, it was created to house the ancient letters and manuscripts discovered in the Judean Desert near the Dead Sea, dating from the first century BCE to the second century CE. The white dome and a black slab of polished basalt standing opposite symbolize the War of the Sons of Light and Darkness referred to in one of the Dead Sea Scrolls.

We descend the steps behind the wall to the entrance square, and enter the cave-like structure, walk along a narrow tunnel with niches where are displayed fragments of the documents and artifacts from the period of Bar Kochba (132 to 135 CE) discovered between 1947 and 1961 in the Judean Desert and in the Dead Sea area. At the end of the tunnel are two clay vessels in which the Dead Sea Scrolls were found.

The passage ends in steps ascending to a circular hall capped with the white dome consisting of a series of circles creating the effect of the inside of a lid to a vessel. In the center of the hall is a round platform and in the glass-fronted display cases around the hall the Dead Sea Scrolls can be seen.

The first Scrolls were discovered in caves at Qumran in the Judean Desert in 1947 by Beduin shepherds who sold them to antique dealers. That year three scrolls were purchased by Prof. Eliezer Sukenik from an antique dealer in Bethlehem and four others were sold to the head of the Syrian community in the Old City of Jerusalem, found their way to the USA, and in 1955 were brought back to Israel through the generosity of the Gottesman family. Six scrolls are on show, each with sectional photographs and explanations.

They comprise: the Apocrypha Scroll to Genesis, written in Aramaic with a description of the Patriarchs; the Scroll of the Book of Isaiah, containing only the latter third of the Book of Isaiah; the Thanksgiving Scroll, thanksgiving hymns of the Dead Sea sect (40 in all); the Scroll of the War between the Sons of Light and the Sons of Darkness, a description of the struggle between the Sons of the Judean Desert Sect — the Sons of Light — and the Sons of Darkness, the forces of evil; the Scroll of Serekh ha-Yahad, the manual of discipline of the Judean Desert Sect; the Scroll of the Commentary on the Book of Habakkuk, a commentary alluding to events that occurred during the history of this sect.

On the circular platform in the center of the hall is a drum-like structure tapering off to what looks like the handle of a rubber stamp. Within the drum is a facsimile of the Isaiah Scroll, the only book of the Bible found complete, dating to approximately 100 BCE; it is almost identical to the Masoretic text. At first the original scroll was on display, but when it began to show signs of disintegration it was replaced by the facsimile. All the other scrolls on show are the originals.

We descend the steps to the basement

View of the Israel Museum.

Interior of the Shrine of the Book.

where we can view glass vessels, textiles, baskets, metal utensils and phylacteries discovered in a cave in the Hever Valley, in the Judean Desert.

We leave the Shrine of the Book and walk along the path to the right (passing the souvenir shop and toilets) and return to the main path. Opposite is the Schenker Antiques Garden with Byzantine period mosaics. To the east we see the Goldie Weisbrod Exhibition Hall and we come to the **Ruth Youth Wing**, pass through the play area and enter the hall. There are workshops for children and youth, a library and exhibition rooms.

We return to the main path with its olive trees and in the archaeology garden see fragments of an ancient aqueduct, sarcophagi, sculptures, capitals of pillars, most of which are from Roman times. To the right is the Sculpture Garden. In the Crown Square are a number of sculptures by Jacques Lipschitz, and by B. Schwartz and remains of ancient synagogues in the Galilee, and near the Museum entrance "Blue Trees", a metal sculpture by M. Kadishman.

In the entrance foyer is an information bureau, a souvenir and book shop, and to the right a cloakroom (cameras must be deposited here as photographing inside the museum is prohibited).

The exhibition hall is opposite the cloakroom. Steps to the right lead to the library foyer which also has exhibitions from time to time. The library contains books and manuscripts on art, reading rooms and copying equipment and a Graphics Department.

The **Zaks-Abramov Israel Art Section** (reached through the exhibition hall) displays the works of Israeli artists. The **Design Section** is reached through the Israeli art section. The **Israeli Art** section has permanent exhibitions of the works of leading Israeli painters and sculptors.

From the entrance hall we descend the stairs to an exhibition hall from which there are three possible directions: behind the stairs to the **Numismatics hall** (102) where selections of Israeli coins are on display we pass by the auditorium to other sections (Asian art, ethnic art etc.); or to the left to the Bronfman Biblical and Archaeological Museum; or, opposite the stairs to **Jewish Art and Ethnography.** In the first hall are ceremonial objects and ritual Jewish art.

We descend a few steps to the reconstructed synagogue of Vittorio Venetto (northern Italy) built in 1701; a *sukka* from southern Germany dating to the 19th century, built of colored wood and decorated with illustrations of houses and landscapes; the reconstructed synagogue of Horb (Southern Germany, 1735), built of wood decorated with paintings and illustrations.

We walk through the Jewish Festivals hall and pass on to the hall depicting the Jewish life-cycle. There is an exhibit showing a German Jewish family at home (19th century) and the living-room of a Moroccan Jewish family. The hall at the side has a display of prints and graphic art. The following halls are devoted to clothes and jewelry worn by different Jewish communities throughout the world.

From here there is the **Impressionist art** section (the main entrance is through the ethnic art hall) with classic works of the European artists from 1874 to 1893 such as Pissarro, Renoir, Sisley, Cezanne, van Gogh and others.

Stairs descend to halls displaying European art from the 15th to 19th century. There are exhibits of an 18th-century English dining-hall, a Venetian and a French drawing-room.

We move into the **ethnic art** section: art from Africa and Oceania, South America pre-Columbian art and Asian art. From here it is possible to reach the Numismatics section (102) and the auditorium.

The Bronfman Archaeology wing displays finds from archaeological excavations from all periods of the history of the Holy Land, presented in chronological order from prehistoric times to the present day — Rooms 301 to 315.

We go down steps to the hall with cultures of neighboring countries (Room 316): finds from Egypt, Anatolia, Iran, Mesopotamia, Greece and Cyprus. From here there is a passage to the Youth Wing and out to the main pathway.

GIVAT RAM AND VICINITY

The **Billy Rose Art Garden** to the west of the main square, was designed by the Japanese-American landscape architect Isamu Noguchi and it spreads on four crescent-shaped terraces. The several score sculptures include works by Jacques Lipschitz, Shlomo Koren, Benny Efrat, Picasso, Henry Moore, Isamu Noguchi, Robert Indiana, Vitkin and Danziger. At the southern edge of the garden stands a row of seven giant circular stones, reminiscent of millstones, quarried at Mizpeh Ramon. Entitled "Negev", this is the work of sculptress Magdalena Abakanowicz, and was erected at the site in 1987. From the garden there is a panoramic view to the west of the Hebrew University, Mount Herzl, Bayit Vegan and the Holyland Hotel. To the south can be seen Gilo and Beit Jalla. Close to the Israel Museum the Bible Lands Museum is under construction. The building and its approximately 2,000 exhibits, collected over a period of 40 years, were donated by the collector Dr. Elie Borowski. They span 5,000 years and reflect the cultures of Mesopotamia, Iran, Anatolia, Syria, Lebanon, Greece, Rome and Byzantium, and many illustrate descriptions found in the Bible.

We leave the Israel Museum and visit the neighborhoods in the area. **Neveh Sha'anan**, on the slope below the Art Garden, was founded in 1929 by a group of religious Jews. The name derives from Isaiah 33:20: "Look upon Zion, the city of our solemnities: thine eyes shall see Jerusalem a quiet habitation [in Hebrew *neveh sha'anan*], a tabernacle that shall not be taken down; not one of the stakes thereof shall ever be removed, neither shall any of the cords thereof be broken". **Neveh Granot** founded in 1963 and named for Abraham Granot, former President of the Jewish National Fund. **Nayot** was founded in 1962 and named for a settlement mentioned in I Samuel 19:18.

4. Monastery of the Holy Cross Visiting hours: Monday to Friday 9.00 am to 4.00 pm; Saturday to 2.00 pm. Entrance fee.

Transportation: Buses No. 19, 24 and 99. Parking lot in Yehoshua Yevin Street (below Nayot) for private vehicles.

The monastery is in the Valley of the Cross between Rehavia and the Israel Museum. A square belltower and a brown dome with a cross at its peak stand out over the high wall. The structure looks more like a fortress than a monastery. According to tradition, it was here that the tree grew from which the cross of Jesus was taken. And, legend goes further, it is said that this same tree was an offshoot of the Tree of Life that grew in the Garden of Eden, grown from a twig planted by Seth, son of Adam, at the head of Adam's tomb.

The monastery is the property of the Greek Catholic Church. It was built in the sixth century in the reign of Emperor Justinian. It is not known who built the monastery. Some say it was the work of the 5th century king of Georgia, Tatian, who had it built on land that had been given to the first Christian king of Georgia some years earlier. Others ascribe it to Constantine and

Billy Rose Art Garden.

Monastery of the Holy Cross.

Helena. It was destroyed by the Persians in 614 and once again by the Fatimid caliph Hakim in 1009. It was rebuilt by a Georgian monk in the 11th century. Between the 12th and 15th centuries scores of Georgian monks, poets and scholars inhabited the monastery, and among them was their national poet Shota Rustaveli, who left a self-portrait and an inscription on one of the pillars inside the church. In the 17th century, the Greek Orthodox Church purchased the monastery and renovated it, and most of the art works were painted then. In the 19th century (1855–1908) one of the most important theological seminaries in the eastern Christian world was located here. In this period, too, the tower, living quarters, dining halls and kitchen were built, and it served as a hospice for Christian pilgrims.

In 1969 the Monastery was completely renovated with the aim of turning it once again into a theological seminary.

In 1972 a study mission from the Republic of Georgia visited the monastery in the hope of finding early Georgian artifacts and manuscripts, especially of their national poet Shota Rustaveli, but they were disappointed. The monastery is lit up at night and is one of the most beautiful sites of Jerusalem.

Many legends relate to the monastery. One of them tells that Valerius, the commander of the Emperor Justinian's army, after conquering Rome, took possession of the ritual vessels taken from the Second Temple as trophies, had them returned to Jerusalem, and at first placed them in the Nea Basilica. A few years later, when the Emperor feared that the city might fall into the hands of his enemies, he ordered the vessels to be transferred to the Monastery of the Cross where the monks, to make doubly sure, buried them. When the monastery was captured by the Muslims all the monks were killed and not one was left who knew the whereabouts of the vessels from the holy sanctuary.

Pilgrims began to visit the Monastery of the Cross during Crusader times, and all their accounts describe its singular beauty. The monastery was destroyed in the reign of Baybars and was turned into a mosque, but was returned to the Georgians in the 14th century. It changed ownership in 1858 when the Greek Orthodox Church took it over, and it has remained in its possession ever since.

As we enter the monastery through a low, narrow opening we find ourselves in a paved stone courtyard. To the left, stairs lead to a flat roof. Beyond the stairs is a garden with vines and fruit trees. To the right are the monks' quarters (closed to visitors), to the left the dining hall. We go out to a balcony and ascend to two rooms in which are displayed artifacts belonging to the Greek Patriarchate. In the passage are portraits of Greek priests and 18th-century paintings.

The church is built in traditional eastern Byzantine style — a basilica with a central dome supported by six square pillars. The floor is covered with mosaics decorated with birds. Part of the floor dates from the 6th century, but most of it from the 17th century. An opening at the end of the hall leads to a passage and to the altar and the spot where the holy tree grew.

Our tour ends here.

TOUR No. 27

EIN KAREM

Details of tour: The tour takes us through the lanes of this picturesque village, nestling in a deep valley surrounded by steep mountains and adorned with olive and cypress trees. We will visit churches, and tour the village.
Distance covered: approx. 3 kms (2 miles)
Time: approx. 3 hours
Transportation: Bus No 17 from Jerusalem
Parking at start of tour for private vehicles
Starting point and end of tour: The main square of Ein Karem
The Sites: 1. Church of St. John the Baptist; 2. Sisters of Zion Convent; 3. Tour of the village; 4. Church of the Visitation; 5. Russian Convent; 6. St John in the Desert Monastery.

FOREWORD

Ein Karem, a former Arab village south east of Mount Herzl, now an attractive suburb of Jerusalem, lies 650 m (2133 ft) above sea level in a valley below the slopes of four mountains. The original inhabitants were mostly farmers who sold their produce in Jerusalem.

The village is named for the spring (*ein*) in its center whose sweet water is used for watering the gardens, and vineyards *(Karem)* and it is believed that this was the Beth-Haccerem mentioned in Jeremiah, and it has been identified with "the city of Juda" where John the Baptist was born to the elderly Zacharias and Elisabeth (Luke 1:39). Considered holy by Christians since the 4th century, pilgrims called it "the house of Zacharias" and later built churches and monasteries in the area. It was here that the Virgin Mary visited her cousin Elisabeth.

The present inhabitants (approximately 2,000) are immigrants from various countries since 1949 — North Africa, Asia and Eastern Europe — as well as native-born Israelis. Most residents work in Jerusalem; a number of artists have opened studios here.

The road winds down from Mount Herzl below the outskirts of the suburb of Kiryat Hayovel. To the right is the Ein Karem valley; above, the slopes of the Hill of Remembrance and the Jerusalem Forest with its recreation center. To the west we can see the Hadassah Medical Center, and to the right, in the valley, the Ein Karem Agricultural School. Among the first houses can be seen the Judean Regional College; the road turns to the right and we then reach the village center. The parking lot is at the road junction.

THE TOUR

1. Church of St John the Baptist Visiting hours: daily 8.00 a.m. to 12.00 noon; 3.00 to 5.00 p.m. Sunday from 9.00 a.m.

We go up a street to the gate of the Spanish Franciscan Monastery named for St John the Baptist. In front of the church are displayed a statue of the goddess Venus found on the site as well as a wine press and two tombs, which indicate that the site was inhabited and probably inhabited in the Roman period. We enter the stone-paved courtyard with steps leading

Interior of St John the Baptist Church.

up to the church. To the right, in front of the stairway, are the basement windows with grilles, through which we can see the remains of a mosaic decorated with peacocks, partridges and flowers, of the 6th century Byzantine church. The mosaic, which bears a Greek inscription: "Hail martyrs of the Lord", was uncovered in 1885 at the time the foundations of the church were being sunk. The church is believed to have been first built in the 4th century CE, and destroyed in the 6th century by the Samaritans, who killed the monks whose graves were discovered in 1102 when the Crusaders built the present monastery. After the Arab conquest the monastery was turned into a *khan* (caravanserai). The Franciscans were granted possession of the site in 1485; Spanish monks began to settle in 1674 and the monastery was expanded in 1897.

The wooden church door is decorated with paintings and inscriptions referring to the contribution of Spain toward its construction in 1845 and of Argentina in 1964. The church one can visit today was built in 1674. Six square supporting pillars divide the hall into three aisles, the central one ending in an apse in front of which is the high altar dedicated to St John the Baptist. On the right is an altar dedicated to Elisabeth. The walls are covered with white ceramic tiles with blue decorations. The apse has statues of St Francis and St Clare, of Elisabeth and Zacharias, and in the center a statue of Mary.

On the left are steps leading down to a natural cave, known as the Grotto of the Birth of St John, where, according to tradition, John was born. On the lintel is a Latin inscription: "Blessed be the Lord God of Israel; for he hath visited and redeemed his people" (Luke 1:68), the first words of the prophecy uttered by Zacharias at the birth of his son. In the crypt there is an altar and on the walls are verses in a number of languages describing the life of John and the history of the monastery.

2. Convent of the Soeurs de Sion (Sisters of Zion) We return to the road junction and continue along the main road from where we turn right and then take the first lane to the left. We walk under the arched roof of an ancient structure — probably a *khan*. We continue to walk up the path until we reach a stone wall with dentils at the top. On the green iron gate is the sign "Soeurs de Notre Dame de Sion". A nun on duty will open the gate in answer to the bell. Inside the enclosure are the convent, a church, a hospice, a fruit and vegetable garden and a graveyard. The convent was built in 1860 by Alphonse Ratisbonne, who is buried here. He founded the Order of the Sisters of Zion (whose convent is on the Via Dolorosa in the Old City) and an order of monks (the Ratisbonne Monastery; see Tour No 23).

We walk up the path to the convent building and notice the semicircular apses of the church topped by a cross and pointed dentils. We enter the passageway to the long church hall, whose ceiling consists of interlocking vaults supported by pillars along the walls. The apses have two stained glass windows depicting Moses and the Prophet Elijah. We walk around the building on its western side and come to a path leading to a structure in the garden in which there is a statue of the Virgin and Child, behind which is an observation point. The view is magnificent: on the horizon to the north is Nebi Samwil and below, Mevasseret Zion with Ma'oz Zion opposite; beneath them Motza Ilit, Beit Zayit, the Agricultural High School and the Sorek River Dam; to the east are the hills of Har Nof and the Hill of Remembrance; to the south is the Russian Convent with the green roof of its belltower. We can see the Church of the Visitation and the Hadassah Medical Center. Below the observation point is the convent's well and vegetable garden and in the courtyard are fruit trees, flowers and a pond with goldfish.

We walk down a path between tall pine trees to the graveyard, where Alphonse Ratisbonne is buried.

We return to the gate where our tour of the convent ends.

3. Tour of the Village We go down the street to the right of the convent and continue to the left, passing by housing lots with gardens and trees, in the center of which are one- or two-storey buildings. In spring the entire area is one big carpet of wild flowers and the trees are heavy with fruit. The houses have arches, pillars and architectural ornaments. These were the dwellings of wealthy Christian Arabs whose Greek Orthodox Church is situated at the bottom of the hill.

The road runs through the center of the village past the Broshim School for special education. We turn right in Hamayan Street (Street of the Fountain) and come to the spring of Ein Karem, named Mary's Spring in memory of the Virgin's visit. A mosque with a hexagonal minaret and a dome characteristic of the end of the Mameluke period (11th century) style, is built above the spring. The water flows westward along a canyon down to the Beit Hakerem Valley in the direction of the Sorek River. In the western valley were most of the agricultural lands of Ein Karem and the laborers lived nearby. Today these lands are cultivated by the pupils of the Agricultural School in the center of the village. According to the Mishna, large stone blocks were brought to the Temple from the Beit Hakerem Valley for the construction of the altar. It was here that Abraham camped when Melchizedek, King of Salem, came to meet him. The copper scroll which was found in the Judean Desert describes a treasure trove in Beit Hakerem.

4. Church of the Visitation Visiting hours: daily 9.00 a.m. to 12.00 noon; 3.00 p.m. to 5.00 p.m.

We turn to the west from the Ein Karem Spring along the slope of the southern bank of the river. We pass by the Soeurs du Rosaire Orphanage (built in 1910) and the locked gate of the Russian Convent. We climb up steep, wide stairs and come to the wrought iron gate of the Church of the Visitation. The courtyard, with an arcade on one side, is decorated with ceramic plaques bearing in 42 languages Mary's hymn of thanksgiving that she is to become the mother of the Lord, which came to be known as the "Magnificat" in Christian liturgy (Luke 1:46-55). This

(top) General view of Ein Karem.
(center) Church of the Visitation.
(bottom) Tiles bearing the "Magnificat".

Franciscan Church was built in 1955 and designed by the Italian architect Barluzzi. It has a square belltower, a lower chapel beside the well and an upper church with a triangular roof. On the outer wall is a colored mosaic depicting Mary riding on a donkey on her way from Nazareth to Ein Karem, accompanied by angels, and the Latin text describing her visit to her pregnant cousin Elisabeth (Luke 1:39), hence the name of the church. We enter the chapel built on the site where it is believed the house of Zacharias and Elisabeth stood. On the walls are paintings of the events in the life of Zacharias and Elisabeth and of the birth of John. According to legend, when the Roman soldiers were hounding mothers and children in their search for the baby John, he disappeared miraculously into a rock, which is preserved behind a grille. We ascend to the church which has 80 seats and an organ. The semicircular apse has a triangular roof decorated with colored geometric designs; paintings depict events in the life of Jesus and his disciples.

We return to the square in front of the spring and climb the steep path to the Handicapped Children's Home run by the Sisters of St Vincent, whose church and main institutions are in Mamilla Road. The Home is situated in a stone building erected in 1886 and renovated in 1981.

5. Russian Convent From the Handicapped Children's Home we continue up the path to the main gate of the Russian Convent. (The convent is closed to visitors but most of it can be seen from the outside). The major part of the southern slopes of the hill down to Ein Karem, enclosed by a stone wall, was purchased by the Provoslavic Russian Church in 1871. The convent, called Gorny or Mar Zacharias, was built here. In the center of this area was built the Zacharias Church with its great belltower and small cottages providing housing for the nuns. In 1882 a vineyard was planted here, and the nuns grew vegetables and bred chickens. That year, too, a hospice was built for pilgrims from Russia. At the beginning of the 20th century, another church was begun, but building ceased with the outbreak of the Russian Revolution, and the vestiges of the building can be seen to the south near the road that leads to Hadassah Medical Center.

The Ein Karem Youth Hostel can be reached from the path to the Handicapped Children's Home. We return to the parking lot where our tour ends.

6. Monastery of St John in the Desert Although not in Ein Karem, this monastery can be reached from here by car along the road that runs northwest. It is also possible to take bus No 52 from the Street of the Prophets in the city center to Even Sapir.

We take the left road at the Karem intersection, signposted Even Sapir. We travel along this road till just before the entrance to the settlement a sign points to a 2 km (just over 1 mile) dirt road which leads to the entrance to the monastery courtyard. This Franciscan monastery was built in the mid-19th century on the site where according to Luke (1:80) "the child [John] grew, and waxed strong in spirit, and was in the deserts till the day of his shewing unto Israel." The buildings are on the side of the hill sloping down to the Sorek Valley. In the monastery garden is a spring held holy by Muslims, and called Ain el-Habis (the Spring of the Hermit). Details of visiting hours can be obtained from the Church of the Visitation.

> **TOUR No. 28**
>
> # SITES IN THE NORTHEAST OF THE CITY
>
> **Details of tour:** We will visit sites on Mount Scopus, and the Rockefeller Museum.
> **Transportation:** Buses No 9, 4A and 99 from the city center; Bus No 28 shuttles between Givat Ram and Mount Scopus campuses
> **The sites:** 1. The Hebrew University Campus. 2. Hadassah Hospital Center. 3. The Jerusalem War Cemetery. 4. The Rockefeller Museum.

THE TOUR

1. Hebrew University Campus on Mount Scopus Rising 829 m (2720 ft) above sea level, Mount Scopus constitutes the northern section of the Jerusalem mountain ridge, the center of which is the Mount of Olives. According to Josephus (*Antiquities* 11:8,5) it was on Mount Scopus that the High Priest met Alexander the Great when he entered Jerusalem.

Jewish and non-Jewish burial caves have been found on the mountain, and it was here that the Roman Thirteenth and Fifteenth Legions camped prior to the conquest of Jerusalem in 70 C. E.

The idea of the establishment of a Hebrew University in Jerusalem was first put forward in 1882 by Zvi Hermann Shapiro, one of the early members of the Hovevei Zion organization. In 1913 the World Zionist Organization appointed a committee to implement the proposal and it set about arranging the purchase with funds provided by Y.L. Goldberg and other Russian Zionists, of a plot of land on the top of Mount Scopus. The land was bought from Sir John Grey Hill who owned a villa there. The cornerstone was laid in 1918 by Dr. Chaim Weizmann. The official opening took place on April 1st, 1925.

In the university's first academic year 164 students studied at the Institutes of Jewish Studies, Chemistry, and Microbiology. Up to 1948 other faculties were opened in the new buildings as they were erected, including the David Wolffsohn National Library, the Rosenblum Department of Humanities and the Einstein Mathematics Institute.

When the War of Independence broke out in 1948, Mount Scopus was cut off from Jerusalem and remained as an Israeli enclave in Jordanian-held territory. A convoy bringing food and replacements for the policemen guarding the installations was brought up every two weeks under United Nations protection. Up to 1958 the University departments were scattered throughout the city, and in 1967 they were brought together at the Givat Ram Campus; since 1968 most of them have been returned to Mount Scopus.

Mount Scopus: The Departments of Social Sciences, Business Administration,

View of the Hebrew University campus on Mount Scopus.

Social Work, Law, Humanities, School of Education, School for Overseas Students, the Center for Pre-Academic Studies, the Martin Buber Adult and Further Education Center, the Truman Center for the Advancement of Peace and the Academy of Arts.

Givat Ram: The Departments of Mathematics and Natural Sciences, School of Applied Science and Technology, the Jewish National and University Library, the School of Library Sciences, the Institute for Advanced Studies.

Ein Karem: The School of Medicine, School of Pharmacy, School for Public Health and Community Health, the School of Dental Medicine.

Rehovot: The faculty of Agriculture, School of Nutritional Science and Home Economics.

In 1987, 18,800 students were registered at the Hebrew University, 5,500 working towards their second and third degrees. Thirty percent of the students are studying the Natural Sciences. Since its establishment the university has granted 60,000 B.A., M.A. and Ph.D. degrees.

Before visiting the university campus we will look at the surrounding landscape from Mount Scopus. We leave the bus at the stop before it enters the campus and follow the sign to the Observation Point. At the bottom of the slope, to the right of the signpost, are two burial plots: the tomb of the Bentwich family whose head was one of the leading personalities of British Jewry and an active Zionist, and the burial plots of members of the American Colony in Jerusalem (see Tours No 10 and 11).

The Observation Point can be reached by car by an internal road, at the end of which is a parking lot. To the north we see the Temple Mount and the Old and New City of Jerusalem spread out below, to the west, as far as the eye can see, with the Judean mountains in the background. We can make out Herodion to the south, Nebi Samwil to the north west.

We take the road to the east and come to the western gate at the end of Churchill Street. We go through the gate and reach, on the left, the Botanical Garden, and to the right the Faculty of Social Sciences, housed in seven triangular four-storey buildings, joined by covered passages. The path is named for the Hebrew poet Avigdor Hameiri, who wrote the famous poem "From the Peak of Mount Scopus." Further along is the Administration building with a painting by L. Polichovski of the Hebrew University's opening ceremony.

A guided tour in English is conducted daily (except Saturdays and holidays) at 11.30 a.m., leaving from the Administration building, and lasts approximately 45 minutes.

The reconstruction program of the Hebrew University campus on Mount Scopus began after the Six Day War. A number of the original buildings were renovated, new ones erected alongside, and the campus has now more than doubled. To the west of the faculty buildings are student dormitories and the School for Overseas Students. The basement serves the dual purpose of underground parking lot and air-raid shelter. Between the buildings are paved squares, flower-beds and lawns. The open-air theater has been renovated and a high tower built. We continue along the path which crosses a bridge over the internal road and come to the Rosenblum building which houses the Law Faculty. The building was erected during the British Mandate and repaired after 1967. The original library, the Wolffsohn building, was renovated and taken over by the Law Faculty. Further along the path we come to a paved square surrounded by buildings: to the left, the Frank Sinatra Student Center and, to the right, part of the former Archaeology building.

The steps going down to the right lead to a large courtyard surrounded by buildings: to the right are the main library and the Humanities Department buildings, the main auditorium, and the School of Education, situated in octagonal buildings joined together.

We turn left and walk up to another square. To the right is the Buber Adult Education building and to the left the Archaeological Institute. To the right of the square is the Truman Institute faced with reddish stone. The Institute carries out research for the advancement of peace.

Exterior of the Rothberg Amphitheater.

To the east is the Rothberg Amphitheater. It was designed by the architect Kornberg (who planned many of the buildings constructed during the Mandatory period). We ascend the steps to the square between the two buildings of the Institute for Contemporary Jewry, both of which were built during the Mandate and rebuilt after 1967. The one to the right was the Einstein Mathematics Institute, with Pythagoras' theorem inscribed above the entrance. Further along are the Auditorium and lecture halls, the Tower Square, and opposite, the Bezalel School of Arts buildings.

We continue along the closed-in glass passage and return to the first courtyard and from there to the main entrance. On the way we pass a grilled window above which is an inscription indicating this to be the Second Temple Period family tomb of "Hanania bar Yohanan the hermit".

We reach the Botanical Garden (by taking the road to the east) in which there are trees and shrubs native to the Holy Land. On the slope of the garden is the tomb of Nicanor from Alexandria who built the Second Temple doors. In modern times the writer Y.L. Pinsker and the head of the Jewish National Fund, Menahem Ussishkin, were buried here.

2. Hadassah Hospital Center on Mount Scopus Guided tours, lasting about 1 hour, take place on weekdays at 9.00, 10.00 and 11.00 a.m.

The Women's Zionist Organization in America, Hadassah, was founded in 1912 by Henrietta Szold. It has 370,000 members organized in 600 chapters throughout the U.S.A. It has established many institutions in Israel related to health and education. Hadassah's first project in this country was the establishment in 1913 of a Mother-and-Child Care Center in the Old City of Jerusalem. In 1918 it began setting up hospitals and clinics, the first project being the reopening of the Rothschild Hospital in Jerusalem after the First World War.

Among Hadassah's projects in Jerusalem are the Hadassah Youth Center on Mount Scopus (the former Nursing School) where members of the Hadassah-supported American Jewish youth movement Young Judea spend a year on a study-work program in Israel; the Hadassah University Hospital on Mount Scopus; the Hadassah Medical Center at Ein Karem. Both these medical institutions were established by the Hadassah Medical Organization which is affiliated to the Hadassah Women's Organization.

The hospital on Mount Scopus was built in 1939, according to the plans of the architect Erich Mendelsohn who immigrated to this country from Germany in 1933 and has many other buildings to his credit.

The Hadassah Hospital, the foremost and most modern medical center in the Middle East, received patients from many countries and during the Second World War treated soldiers of the Allied Forces serving in the area. The hospital ceased functioning after the treacherous Arab attack on a convoy of medical personnel making its way up to Mount Scopus on April 13th, 1948, in which 78 persons were killed, including doctors, nurses, patients, laboratory technicians and research workers. After 1948 all the hospital's departments were transferred to the Jewish sector of Jerusalem. The area remained in no-man's land from 1948 to 1967. In 1961 the various departments were brought together again at the new Medical Center in Ein Karem. After the Six Day War, the center on Mount Scopus was rebuilt and now serves as the regional hospital for residents of the northern and eastern areas of the city, as well as for the residents of Judea and Samaria.

Although the hospital building was

abandoned over a period of 19 years, its original external structure was preserved. In the course of the renovations (1968 to 1974) it was decided to introduce changes in its internal structure and new wings were added. The stone-faced building follows the topography of the area. Three domes are to be seen at the entrance. The architectural style has oriental motifs. The area covered by lawns opposite the entrance serves as the roof of the car park, and on it is a 6 m (19½ ft) high sculpture "The Tree of Life", the last work of the sculptor Jacques Lipshitz. The roots of this "tree" depict Noah, above him Abraham with his son Isaac and an angel hovering over them holding up a burning bush. Beside him is Moses and the Ten Commandments. At the top of the sculpture is a phoenix with figures arising from flames. The complex work culminates in a seven-branched candelabrum.

The hospital wards contain 300 beds; there is the Guggenheim convalescence building, the area maternity unit and emergency unit for premature babies which deal with over 15,000 patients each year. On the ground floor are the tourist section, auditorium and a room in memory of Henrietta Szold, founder of Hadassah. In the grounds of the building is a memorial to Presidents of Hadassah.

3. The Jerusalem War Cemetery (British Military Cemetery) At the side of the road below the Hadassah Hospital is the cemetery where soldiers of the Allied Forces who fell in Palestine during the First World War are buried. On both sides of the entrance are the emblems of the units whose soldiers are buried here, including that of the Jewish Legion — the Royal Fusiliers. Facing the entrance is a memorial to the Australian forces who fought in the War.

The cemetery includes 2500 graves and is divided into four sections by two perpendicular paths. At the end of the path, at the top of the hill, is a memorial chapel. Above is a statue of St George standing victorious on the head of the dragon. On the lintel above the entrance to the room are the words (from the Book of Maccabees): "We therefore remember you in our prayers as it becometh us to think upon our brethren". On the walls on either side of the chapel are the names of the soldiers who fell in action and have no known graves, and a verse from Deuteronomy: "But no man knoweth of his sepulchre unto this day" (34:6). At the end of the northern section (to the left) are the graves of 24 Jewish soldiers, most of whom fought in the ranks of the Royal Fusiliers. At the far left, near the fence beside the road, are the graves of

(left) Entrance to the War Cemetery. (right) Hadassah Hospital with "Tree of Life" in the foreground.

enemy soldiers, of sixteen Germans and three Turks.

The road which turns down to the left passes the Hyatt Regency Hotel which opened in 1987. It is the largest hotel in Jerusalem. Opposite the hotel can be seen the government buildings (Kiryat Hamemshala) which were constructed after 1967. Above them is the Police Headquarters, the first building to be constructed there. It faces Nablus Road where there are several bus stops.

4. Rockefeller Museum

Transportation: Buses No 23 and 99 from Katzir Street, beside the government buildings.

Visiting hours: Sunday to Thursday 10.00 a.m. to 5.00 p.m.; Friday, eve of holidays and Saturday 10.00 a.m. to 2.00 p.m. Admission fee. Guided tours in English on Sunday and Friday at 11.00 a.m.

This was the first archaeological museum in Palestine, established by the British Mandatory Government between 1930 and 1938 with funds donated by the American millionaire John D. Rockefeller Jnr. The building is faced with white stone and most outstanding is its octagonal tower. The English architect Austin St Barbe Harrison combined the style of Christian churches with oriental elements and symmetrical galleries on both sides of

Hyatt Hotel and government buildings on the left.

the tower. There is a central courtyard with a pond, around which the exhibition halls are built. At the front of the building are offices of the Israel Government Department of Antiquities, storerooms, the library, archives and workshops.

The Museum displays finds from excavations made in Palestine prior to the establishment of the State. Among the treasures are prehistoric works of art found in caves on Mount Carmel, in the Judean Desert and in Jericho; the Seti I stele from Beth Shean; ivories from Samaria; the Lachish letters and Hebrew

Roman altar outside the Rockefeller Museum.

Rockefeller Museum.

seals from Megiddo and Lachish. The majority of the items are numbered and catalogues can be borrowed at the entrance. The exhibition halls are arranged in chronological order, or by subject as follows:

The entrance hall (the tower): temporary exhibitions.

The southern octagonal hall: items from the Beth She'an excavations dating to the Late Canaanite (Bronze) period; the basalt Seti I victory stele, the basalt statute of Ramses III.

The southern gallery: exhibits from the Stone Age — skulls of the prehistoric "Carmelite and Galilee man", an elephant tusk, flint tools and prehistoric art works (200,000 to 4,000 BCE); Chalcolithic period sarcophagi in the form of dwellings (4,000 to 3,000 BCE), bronze utensils, tombstones, statuettes, ivories, scarabs and seals from various sites dating to the Bronze Age (3,000 to 1,200 BCE).

The southern hall: carved wooden panels from the el-Aksa Mosque dating to the Umayyad period.

Coins found in Palestine, from all periods.

The western hall: stucco decorations and statues from the Umayyad palace at Hirbat Mifajr, near Jericho, from the 8th century CE.

Ornaments from various periods.

The northern hall: marble lintels from the Church of the Holy Sepulcher carved in the Crusader period, 12th century CE.

The northern gallery: finds from the Israelite period (Bronze Age I and II: 1,200 to 586 BCE) including Megiddo ivories, Samarian ivories from Ahab's palace, the Lachish Letters, Hebrew signet rings (from Lachish, Beth Shemesh, Megiddo, Tel Beth Mirsim, etc.); finds from the Babylonian and Persian periods (586-332 BCE), the Helenistic I period (332-142 BCE) and II — the Hasmonean periods (152-37 BCE), the Roman I period (Herod, 37 BCE-70 CE), II (70-180 CE), III (180-324) including lamps, inscriptions, reliefs of Nabatean altars from Transjordan; ossuaries and statuettes from the Byzantine period (324-640), the early Arab period (640-1099) and the Crusader period (1099-1291). In the eastern corner is a reproduction of a burial cave from Jericho in the Middle Canaanite II period.

The northern octagonal hall: carved stone seven-branched *menorah* (from Eshtamoa), inscription and mosaics from Second Temple period synagogues and synagogues from the Mishna and Talmudic periods.

The internal courtyard: capitals, carved ossuaries from the Roman period, inscriptions and architectural elements from various periods.

A pamphlet is given to visitors free of charge at the entrance.

TOUR No. 29

SITES IN THE SOUTHEAST OF THE CITY
TRIP BY CAR OR BUS

The tour is by car, taxi or bus (bus numbers are given in the text for each part of the tour). The interval between buses allows enough time to enjoy the view at the observation points and visit the sites.
Time: approx. 2 hours by private vehicle; approx. 3 hours by bus
The Sites: Gilo; Talpiot; Arnona; Ramat Rachel; East Talpiot; the Promenade; Abu Tor (Givat Hananya) Observation Point.

THE TOUR

We take bus No 31 or 32 opposite the Central Bus Station and travel along Jaffa Road, King George Avenue, Ramban, Gaza, Herzog, Pat and Dov Joseph Streets to the terminus at the Gilo Forest Park.

Note: private vehicles are not allowed to enter Jaffa Road (one way street); drive from Binyanei Ha'uma along Ben-Zvi and Hazaz Boulevards to Herzog Boulevard and then follow the bus route described above.

In Jaffa Road the bus passes the former site of the Sha'arei Zedek Hospital (to the right), Sha'arei Yerushalayim and Sha'arei Zedek neighborhoods (to the left), Batei Sayidoff and the Mahaneh Yehuda Market (to the right), the Mahaneh Yehuda neighborhood, the Sundial building and the regional offices of the Ministry of Health (to the left), the Etz Hayim Yeshiva, Mahaneh Yehuda Police Headquarters, the Alliance Israelite Universelle building, the Clal building, the Even Yisrael neighborhood (to the right) and Ezrat Yisrael neighborhood (to the left).

In King George Street the bus passes the Rejwan Center building, Talitha Kumi, the Eilon Tower, Yeshurun Synagogue (with the Ratisbonne Monastery behind it), the Jewish National Institutions, the Great Synagogue and Hechal Shlomo. From Ramban Street we travel through Rehavia and along Gaza Road passing Workers' Housing B and Kiryat Shmuel to our left. To the right of the intersection of Gaza Road and Herzog Boulevard we can see the Monastery of the Cross. On Herzog Boulevard we pass the Nayot and Givat Mordechai neighborhoods (to the right), Rassco, Givat Haveradim and Gonen E (to the left); Pat Street passes through Gonen H (to the right) and Gonen C (to the left).

Gonen is the Hebrew name of the Katamon neighborhoods built in this area after the War of Independence for new immigrants who had been temporarily housed in huts and tents in Talpiot (now an industrial area). The tenements were hastily built to provide housing as quickly as possible with the restricted funds available at the time. The two-storey houses were built partly with rough stone and partly with building blocks and cement. Each building includes four small apartments which, over the years, the tenants have expanded.

The road to Gilo passes over a bridge above the railway track which follows the Refaim Valley. To the left is the **Pat** neighborhood (named after the Jerusalem Hagana units commander), which, up to the Six Day War, was on the armistice line between Israel and Jordan; next to it is the Arab village of Beit Safafa, divided by the railway line. It is first mentioned in a 12th century Crusader document. Some of its land was sold to German Templars who set up a village there in the 19th century.

Mekor Hayim is a garden suburb (the fourth to be built in Jerusalem) along Mekor Hayim Street. The land was purchased in 1924 by the Israel Land Development Company. Its houses were built in 1926 with funds provided by Hayim Hacohen (an active member of the Mizrahi Party in Cracow, Poland at the time). The name also alludes to the Torah — "it is a tree of life *[Hayim]* to them that grasp it." The original houses are being torn down and replaced by housing tenements and industrial complexes. The road climbs up the steep, rocky slope at the top of which the suburb of Gilo has been built.

Gilo Building of this suburb began in 1970 and it was named for the Biblical settlement on the border of the territory of the tribe of Judah. The name is recalled in that of the Arab village of Beit Jalla on the slopes of the ridge to the south, west of Bethlehem.

From Gilo we have a panoramic view of the surroundings: to the north we can see the western suburbs of Jerusalem and the villages of Ora and Amminadav; the city center; the Old City wall and the mountain ridges of the Mount of Olives and Mount Scopus. To the east are the hills of the Judean desert and Herodion in the form of a truncated cone; to the south are Bethlehem and Beit Jalla, surrounded by olive groves, Mount Gilo (with the Nature Preservation Society's Field School) and the Cremisan Monastery below, with its vineyards and pine groves. The signpost at the entrance to the Gilo Forest Park has a map depicting the sites in the vicinity. A visit to the park is recommended. The spring, Ein Ya'el, at the bottom of the ridge, can be reached by a path from the park.

Mar Elias Monastery.

Gilo is a suburb planned for 40,000 housing units of which 5,000 have already gone up, housing 16,000 residents. The style of the houses is varied: cottage-type houses, apartment blocks, terraced housing, etc. Some of the buildings are prefabricated and have arches and projections reminiscent of buildings in the Old City. Most of the streets are named after fragrant shrubs, e.g., myrrh, rosemary, etc.

We leave Gilo on bus No 30 which turns to the east along the Bethlehem–Jerusalem road. On the hill to the right at the intersection is the Tantur International Ecumenical Center — a Christian theological institution which was expanded after 1967. The road turns north (left) and reaches an intersection with a sign pointing to Herodion (13½ km — 8⅓ miles) on a new road going south.

On the continuation of the main road to Jerusalem we pass **Mar Elias Monastery** (to the right), built like a fortress on a ridge from which both Jerusalem and Bethlehem can be seen. According to tradition the prophet Elijah slept here on his flight from Queen Jezebel's wrath (I Kings 19:2,3). Another tradition claims that a Greek bishop called Elias was buried here in 1345. The most plausible version is that it was the burial site of St Elias, a 5th-century Patriarch of Jerusalem. Originally, Elias was a monk from Egypt. Many miracles are attributed to Mar (St) Elias, who is said to respond to the prayers of barren women and ailing children. To this day, many children are vowed to Mar Elias, and the monastery bearing his name is considered to be a protector of travelers. The monastery seems to have been erected in the 6th century. It was destroyed by an earthquake and rebuilt in the Crusader period.

The hill to the east of the monastery is called Givat Arba (the Hill of the Four) in memory of the four persons killed by gunfire from this spot in 1956 (see below).

Opposite the entrance to the monastery is a stone bench set up in memory of the English painter William Holman Hunt by his widow Edith on the spot from which he drew many of his works. On either side of the bench are engraved in Hebrew and

Greek the words of King David: "God is my strength and power: and he maketh my way perfect" (II Samuel 22:33).

A few score meters north of the bench, among olive trees, is a memorial to the pilot Dan Givon who crashed here during the Six Day War.

We continue along the road and reach the former border with Jordan, marked by a yellow-painted pillbox at the right. Such reinforced concrete shelters were built by the British forces during the Mandate at the outskirts of Jewish quarters to fend off attacks of Arab marauders. Along the Hebron Road which we enter here, housing tenements were built in the 1950s. We leave the bus at the first intersection and go up Ein Gedi Street in Talpiot to the No 7 bus stop, where we can take the bus to its terminus at Kibbutz Ramat Rachel, as an alternative to walking there.

Talpiot, the first garden suburb in Jerusalem, was built in 1922. Its name derives from Song of Songs 4:4: "Thy neck is like the tower of David builded for an armoury [Talpiot]". Its founders were government officials, merchants and writers, among whom were Eliezer Ben Yehuda, Joseph Klausner, S.Y. Agnon and Leib Jaffe. The original buildings were single family houses surrounded by gardens, but only a few of these remain. The high trees give the neighborhood a special character; the new buildings have several apartments, but none has more than four floors. Beit Agnon (at 16, Klausner Street), the home of the Israeli writer S.Y. Agnon who was awarded the Nobel Prize for Literature, has been designated by the Jerusalem Municipality as a center for the study of his works and for the preservation of his library. The house is open to visitors during morning hours.

Up till 1967 Talpiot was on the armistice line between Israel and Jordan and both Talpiot and nearby Arnona suffered from attacks during the riots in Mandatory times and during the War of Independence. Founded in 1931, **Arnona** was named for the Arnon River, which can be seen from here on the eastern side of the Dead Sea. We walk through the streets of Talpiot, visit Beit Agnon and continue through

Proto-Aeolian capital found at Ramat Rachel.

Arnona to Kibbutz Ramat Rachel. This should take about half an hour. Some of the streets are named after the settlements in the Etzion Bloc, not far from here. On the outskirts of Talpiot is a cemetery where are buried Muslim Indian soldiers who served with the British forces in the First World War and fell in the battle for Jerusalem in 1917.

Kibbutz Ramat Rachel was founded in 1926. It was named Rachel because of its proximity to the tomb of the Biblical matriarch. The founding members worked in nearby quarries, in building and paving roads in Jerusalem, as well as in the Potash Works at the Dead Sea. They built the neighborhoods of Talpiot, Beit Hakerem, and Rehavia and many buildings throughout Jerusalem. Even after they built their own houses, the members continued to work outside the kibbutz, mainly because of the lack of agricultural land. Today its economy is based on its guest house, youth hostel and swimming pool, as well as its orchards and chicken coops.

The kibbutz was attacked during the 1929 Arab riots and completely destroyed. It was rebuilt and a large security structure built, which also served as the dining hall and is now part of the guest house. From 1936 to 1939 it was subject to many attacks and during the War of Independence in 1948 it was shelled by Egyptian forces, was conquered and retaken three times and almost completely destroyed. The Egyptian forces and the Jordanian Legion were finally repelled, but during the battle many kibbutz members were killed. Its valiant stand prevented the advance of enemy forces into the Jewish sections of Jerusalem. After the war the kibbutz was rebuilt to the north of the original site and

Memorial to fighters of the Jerusalem Brigade.

over a period of 19 years manned the border which ran along three sides, facing Jordanian entrenchments. During the Six Day War these outposts were taken by the Jerusalem Brigade of the Israel Defense Forces. Near the gate to the kibbutz is a memorial to the eleven soldiers of this division who fell in battle near the Arab village of Sur Baher, which can be seen to the east. This village was a source of constant harassment to Ramat Rachel, Talpiot and Arnona during the riots of the 1930s and during the War of Independence. To the north, across the valley, we can see the suburb of East Talpiot (see below) built after the Six Day War.

The road passes the entrance to the kibbutz and comes to an intersection where the road to the left leads to Sur Baher and to the right to the guest house, recreation area and swimming pool. The latter road ends at the peak of the hill (828 m–2716 ft high) on which stands a water tower (a plaque on the water tower recalls the memory of the four participants in an archaeological conference at the kibbutz in 1956 who were killed by shots fired from the Jordanian outpost on the hill to the north). An ancient tell was excavated in 1959 and some of the finds are on show at the Israel Museum. Eight levels of habitation have been uncovered from the Israelite period (8th century BCE) up to the early Arab period (8th century CE). Of particular interest are the ruins of the royal fortress of one of the last kings of Judah which was surrounded by a retaining wall 5–7 m (16½–23 ft) thick. It had columns with capitals of the proto-Aeolian type (a reproduction of one is to be seen on the path) and stone-carved window sills. All these fit the description in Jeremiah (22:13–15) and are similar to the Israelite royal palace discovered in Samaria. Seals of "Yahud", the Judea province of the Persian period have been found, attesting to the existence of a regional headquarters here. Jews inhabited this area during the Second Temple period up to the destruction of the city in 70 CE. On the slope of the hill burial caves from this period have also been discovered. The site is generally identified with the "Beth Haccerem" mentioned in the Books of Jeremiah and Nehemiah. After the destruction of the Temple, the Tenth Roman Legion was stationed here, and in the Byzantine period (5th century) a monastery and church called **Kathisma** ("resting place" in Greek) were built with funds provided by a rich Jerusalem matron to sanctify the spot where, according to legend, the Virgin Mary rested on her way to Bethlehem.

We enter the **Mitzpeh Rachel** Observation Point through the recreation and sports center built on the original site of the kibbutz. The security building is now part of the modern guest house, with a view of Bethlehem and its environs to the south. The old sculpture depicting Rachel defending her sons, erected to mark the rebuilding of the settlement after it had been destroyed in the War of Independence, has been restored. From the southern side of the area there is a view of Gilo, Mar Elias, Bethlehem, Herodion and the Judean desert.

We take the No 7 bus to Hebron Road and get off at the second intersection. To the left are the houses of the Geulim (Baka) neighborhood and to the right the huts and tents of Allenby Barracks that accommodated British soldiers during the Mandate Period and is now used by the Israeli Border Police. From here we take the No 8 or 48 bus in the direction of East Talpiot.

Near the bus stop, to the north of Allenby Barracks, on the field alongside the Convent of St Clare, was the first airfield in Jerusalem, built by the German army in the First World War and used by its military airplanes from 1916. After the British conquest of Jerusalem, the airfield was used by the British forces until 1922.

The **Convent of St Clare**, belonging to the Franciscan Poor Clares order of nuns, is surrounded by a high stone wall. It was erected in 1888 to 1912 (the order was founded in the 13th century by St Clare, a disciple of St Francis of Assisi). The first convent of the order in Palestine was established in Acre and destroyed by the Mamelukes in 1291. The convent is not open to visitors.

We take the No 8 or 48 bus and pass **North Talpiot**, a small neighborhood bound by Albeck and Caspi Streets. It was founded in 1935 as an offshoot of Talpiot mainly by immigrants from Germany. From here there is a fine view of the Old City and the surrounding hills.

The bus route continues past Kiryat Hatefutsot and Kiryat Moriah, two educational institutions established by the Education and Youth and Hechalutz Departments of the World Zionist Organization for the training of Jewish teachers and youth leaders from abroad, and serving as hostels for thousands of Jewish youth visiting Israel on short-term educational programs.

To the east is **Havat Halimud** — an educational institution established by Rachel Yanait Ben-Zvi (wife of Israel's second President). It originated in 1920 as a "Women Workers' Farm" next to the Ben-Zvi family's hut in Rehavia, where flowers and vegetables were grown. When it was moved to its new quarters, livestock were added and young girls were trained for cooperative life on agricultural settlements, which they later joined. The farm was badly hit during the War of Independence and seven students were killed; the inhabitants were evacuated and the Israel Defense Forces set up an outpost there. After the establishment of the State it was handed over to the Hebrew University which opened a genetics experimental station. The farm was transferred to Ein Karem where an agricultural school was established.

We leave the bus at the nearby road junction, cross the road and walk to the east until we reach the memorial to the men of the Jerusalem Brigade who fell while taking the Jordanian outpost during the Six Day War in 1967. Nearby is the Sherman Park with an Observation Post to East Talpiot, Sur Baher, Herodion and the Judean desert. We enter the park and walk to the wooden hut from which a half meter (1½ ft) wide path delineates the course of a tunnel which runs 7 m (23 ft) below. In the center of the hut is an air vent to the tunnel which served as a water conduit. On the floor of the hut is a colored mosaic map showing the water conduit which ran from springs in the Hebron mountains to Solomon's Pools, and the lower conduit which continued to the Temple Mount in Jerusalem. On the map can be seen the sites through which the conduit passed; Solomon's Pools are 760 m (2495 ft) above sea level and the Temple Mount 740 m (2428 ft). Part of this conduit, 14 kms (8¾ miles) long, can still be seen in many places along its course. This great engineering feat was built during the reign of Herod and was in use up to the time of the Mandate (the Turkish authorities introduced a 10 cm — 4 inch pipe), when in 1920 more modern methods of piping water to Jerusalem were introduced. The tunnel uncovered in this area is 370 m (403 yd) long. It is open at both ends and can be entered (with torches). It is not possible to walk the entire length because it has been blocked by a landslide.

Mosaic map of the conduit in Sherman Park.

Government House can be seen from here, set in a grove of olive and pine trees. The building was erected by the Mandatory Government in 1930 on the summit of a hill called Jebel Mukabir (785 m — 2543 ft high) as the official residence of the British High Commissioner. It was planned by the English architect Austin St Barbe Harrison who designed the Rockefeller Museum. After the establishment of the State of Israel the building was in the demilitarized zone and was used as headquarters for the United Nations observers serving in the area. On the first day of the Six Day War it was captured by Jordanian forces but was retaken and after the war returned to the United Nations.

East Talpiot is one of the outlying suburbs of Jerusalem built up after the Six Day War on the former strategic outposts held by the Jordanians. Building began in 1972 on the hilltop of east Talpiot, south of Government House and in the valley between them; 6,000 units have been planned to house 24,000 people. The streets have been named after Jewish heroes sentenced to death by the British Mandatory Government. The houses of the Beduin tribe, Es-Sawahra can be see to the east and the village of Sur Baher to the south.

Entrance to Government House.

From the **Promenade** there is a most impressive panoramic view of the southern section of the Old City and its environs. The stone-paved Promenade runs parallel to the road from North Talpiot to the Government House pine grove. From here we have a clear view of the structure of David's City, the location of the Kidron Valley, the Temple Mount, Mount Zion, and the buildings on the Mount of Olives and Mount Scopus. The 800 m (875 yd) long Promenade has a large observation bal-

View from the Promenade: in the background to the left, Givat Shapira, to the right, Mount Scopus; in the center, Temple Mount; in the foreground to the left, City of David excavations, to the right, Silwan.

cony above a cafeteria and there are benches along its length. The entire area has been landscaped with beautiful gardens, and has parking bays for cars. The Promenade is to be extended northwards and will continue to Abu Tor. It was built by the Jerusalem Foundation with funds provided by the Haas family and was designed by the architects Aaronson and Halprin and laid out during 1982 to 1987.

The **Peace Forest** was planted from 1967 by the Jewish National Fund along the border between Abu Tor and Government House. It covers an area of 500,000 sq m (125 acres) along the Azal stream (a tributary of the Kidron) below the Promenade and to the north. In the forest are pine, cypress, oak, cedar, and terebinth trees as well as shrubs and flowers.

A memorial was erected in the forest to the 11 Israeli sportsmen who were murdered by Arab terrorists in 1972 at the Olympic Games of Munich. Another plaque recalls the men of the Jerusalem Brigade who fell in battle during the Yom Kippur War in 1973. There is a recreation section and a place where visitors may plant trees.

If we have a car we can continue along the road that runs behind Government House. We travel in an easterly direction, pass the high radio aerial used by the United Nations, and turn left near the Mishkenot Haro'im (The Shepherds) restaurant. We continue along the road to the left on a section which, in relationship to the fence at the side of the road, seems to go downhill, but is in fact on an incline. This section of the road has been dubbed the "magic road" because of this illusion; when you reach the top of the section, cut the motor and the car will roll back to the beginning of the section of the road. The road crosses the Kidron Valley, continues along to the Mount of Offense and reaches the Jerusalem-Jericho Road. We can take this road to the Mount of Olives to the observation point above the Jewish cemetery (see Tour No. 12). We can also return to the Promenade and take the No 8 or 48 bus along Hebron Road as far as Navon Square.

We walk along En Rogel Street to the **Abu Tor Observation Point** (Givat Hananya) on the roof of No. 5 (which houses a cafeteria, restaurant and nightclub). Before 1967, the site was on the border, which divided the neighborhood; the western, upper, section was in Israeli territory and was inhabited mostly by new immigrants, and the eastern section was in Jordanian-held territory. It is possible that the hill (770 m — 2525 ft high) on which the houses were built is the "top of the mountain that lieth before the Valley of Hinnom" mentioned in Joshua (15:8) along which ran the border between the tribes of Judah and Benjamin. According to Josephus, the siege wall built by the Romans ran along the hill. Here, too, was the tomb of the High Priest Annas (Hananya) and hence the Hebrew name of the neighborhood. According to a Christian tradition, here was the summer residence of the High Priest Caiaphas, with whom the Jews took counsel before handing over Jesus to the Romans (John 18:13,24), and thus the hill on which this house stood was named the "Hill of Evil Counsel". On the crest of the hill remains of a Byzantine monastery, church and burial caves have been found. In medieval times a church was built upon the ruins and today is under the jurisdiction of the Greek Orthodox Church. The Arabic name Abu Tor was the nickname of a hero in Saladin's army who, according to a Muslim legend, rode a bull *(tor)*. On the northern slope of the hill, the **Beit Yosef** neighborhood was built in 1887, named for Yosef Navon, one of its founders, but was abandoned because of its isolation from the main city. During the War of Independence, half of Abu Tor was wrested from Iraqi forces and in the Six Day War the other half was taken by the Jerusalem Brigade. Hamefaked (commanding officer) Street which leads to Navon Square is named for the commanding officer Micha Paykes who was killed in this battle. On the slope to the right of the road is a park in which is a memorial to the 17 men who fell in battle. A clubroom for blind people stands in the park.

Our tour ends here and buses can be taken from the bus stop opposite the Railway Station.

TOUR No. 30

GIVAT SHAPIRA — NEVEH YA'AKOV
TRIP BY CAR OR BUS

The tour is by car, taxi or bus (bus numbers are given in the text for each part of the tour). The interval between buses allows enough time to enjoy the view at the observation points and visit the sites.
Time: approx. 2 hours by private vehicle; approx. 3 hours by bus

THE TOUR

We take Bus No 4 on Yehuda Hanassi Street in Gonen to Givat Shapira. It travels along the following route: Emek Refaim; Keren Hayesod; King George; Strauss; Yehezkiel; Eshkol Boulevard; Sheshet Hayamim; Nablus Road and into Givat Shapira through Hahagana and Bar Kochba Streets. We walk up one of the paths to the park in the pine grove on the crest of the hill.

Givat Shapira (French Hill), named for the late Minister of Religious Affairs, Haim Moshe Shapira, one of the leaders of the National Religious Party, was begun in 1971, and its 2,000 units house over 10,000 residents in 6-8 storey tenement houses, or in terraced houses on the eastern slope (the Tsameret Habira complex). The neighborhood has a shopping center and well-developed public amenities. The hill in the center rises to 835 m (2740 ft) above sea level and was originally known as French Hill after the British General, French, commander of General Allenby's forces during the First World War, who built a house there.

A memorial to the eight soldiers of the Harel Brigade who fell fighting on the hill during the Six Day War is situated on Givat Hamivtar opposite Givat Shapira. A small fortress from the period of the Second Temple has been uncovered in archaeological excavations carried out on the summit of the hill. Also found were Second Temple period burial caves and the ruins of two farm buildings dating to the Byzantine period. Remains of another fortress have been discovered near the reservoir in the southern part of the neighborhood.

From the crest of the hill we have a view to the west of Nebi Samwil, the northwestern suburbs of Jerusalem, the buildings on the western mountain ridge at the entrance to the city, the south-western suburbs and Mount Herzl. To the south we can see the Old City, the Rockefeller Museum and the government buildings complex in eastern Jerusalem. The Mount Scopus campus can be seen to the southeast, and to the east the Arab villages of Isawiya and Anata (Biblical Anathoth, the birthplace of the Prophet Jeremiah), the road to Ma'aleh Adumim and on the ridge above, the village of Michmash. To the north we see part of the Givat Ze'ev neighborhood, the road to Neveh Ya'akov and the village of Hizma (Biblical Azmaveth).

We go northwest down Bar Kochba Street to the intersection with Nablus Road, and take bus No 25 to Neveh Ya'akov.

The bus passes through the Arab suburb of **Shu'afat.** The name is considered to be a corruption of the name Jehoshaphat, and it is possible that in the First Temple

Givat Shapira: modern sculpture in foreground.

period this was the site of the priestly city, Nob. The suburb began as a small village which sprung up around the mosque, seen to the west of the road. During the War of Independence the village was taken in the battle for the road to the beleaguered Jewish settlement of Neveh Ya'akov. Under Jordanian rule the village developed and after 1967 many Arabs settled in what became a modern suburb of Jerusalem.

As the road continues we pass Tel el-Ful, whose summit rises 840 m (2755 ft) above sea level, identified as the Biblical Gibeah of Saul (I Samuel 10:26) (Givat Shaul). In the archaeological excavations carried out there six fortresses have been uncovered in layers dating to periods from the 11th century BCE to the 1st century CE. The excavations were carried out by the American School of Oriental Studies between the years 1922 to 1933 and in 1964 by the Theological Seminar of Pittsburg. The most ancient of these fortresses may date to the Philistine period, and after that fortresses were built by Hezekiah and the Hasmonean kings. The uppermost fortress was built by Herod and was conquered by Titus at the time of the destruction of Jerusalem. This latter fortress is mentioned by Josephus as Gibeah of Saul. In 1966 King Hussein of Jordan began building a palace, the remains of which can be seen on the tell. We can leave the bus and climb to the top of the tell (after receiving permission from the military authorities).

There is a turning to the west which leads to the Arab village **Beit Hanina** and the continuation of this side road reaches an intersection: the road to the south leads Ramot Allon, to the southwest to Beit Iksa and to the west to the road to Givat Ze'ev which passes below Nebi Samwil (see Tour No. 31).

The main road continues to the north and we pass by a military camp to the right in a pine grove. This was the site of the Jewish settlement of Neveh Ya'akov (named for Rabbi Ya'akov Reines, one of the founders of the Mizrahi Movement). The land was purchased from the inhabitants of Beit Hanina in 1924 by the Jewish Settlement Association of the Young Mizrahi Federation, and a few score *yeshiva* students established a settlement named Kfar Ivri. Each settler set up a house on a holding of 2,500 sq m (0.6 acre) on which they planted vegetable and flower gardens and orchards, and built stables, cow sheds, and chicken coops. In 1935 immigrant families from Germany joined the settlers (bringing the total to 126) and a *yeshiva* was set up. The settlers supplemented their income with work in Jerusalem and sold their produce there. They also set up a summer holiday center. At the beginning of Israel's War of Independence the settlement was subject to constant Arab attacks and when it became impossible to fend them off, the settlers decided to abandon it.

Tel el-Ful, identified with Biblical Gibeah.

Dahiyat el-Barid is a neighborhood established in 1954 by workers of the Arab Postal Union on the road to Ramallah near the military camp. After 1967 the neighborhood expanded and became a suburb of Jerusalem.

The **Nusseiba** neighborhood consists of two-storey buildings opposite the entrance to Neveh Ya'akov. It was set up by a group of Arabs in 1978 with 500 apartments.

We continue along the main road and turn east into Neveh Ya'akov Boulevard. On the hill north of the crossroads is Metzudat Kfir, headquarters of the Israel Defense Forces Central Command. We take the side road into **Neveh Ya'akov,** established in 1970 as the northeastern suburb of Jerusalem on the former site of the settlement of that name. A total of

4,500 housing units with most modern community facilities have been planned for the inhabitants who consist of Jerusalem-born families and immigrants. We leave the bus at the shopping center and walk through the streets, look at the variety of building styles and view the surroundings — to the east, the deep gorges of the Michmash river and its tributaries; to the northeast, the houses of the Arab villages of Jaba (Geba), Hizma (Azmaveth) and the Jewish settlement of Michmash.

From Neveh Ya'akov we return by bus No 48 which passes to the south through **Pisgat Ze'ev** (named for Ze'ev Jabotinsky), a neighborhood begun in 1982 and designed for 12,000 housing units. The road continues to the intersection from which a road leads south to Ma'aleh Adumim, and another to the west to another crossroads on Nablus Road near Givat Shapira. A two-lane highway from this intersection leads to the west to Ramot Allon. Bus No 48 travels through Nablus Road, Eshkol Boulevard, Yirmeyahu Street, to Binyanei Ha'uma (and then follows the route of bus No 8 to East Talpiot).

The sites north of Neveh Ya'akov are not included in this tour but can be visited by car or bus from Jerusalem.

The main road we took to Neveh Ya'akov continues north and passes the industrial complex at Atarot and the Jerusalem Airport (bus No 41 leaves Jaffa Gate on weekdays from 6.30 to 8.30 a.m. and returns to Jerusalem from 3.00 to 4.00 p.m.).

The **Atarot Industrial Complex** was established after the Six Day War and comprises wholesale warehouses and light industries.

The **Jerusalem Airport** was first built as a British military airport during the First World War. After 1948 the Jordanians expanded it into an international airport, part of which was on the lands of the Jewish settlement of Atarot. It was named Kalandia after the nearby Arab village. From 1967 it became the official airport of Jerusalem and was incorporated within the municipal boundary.

The cooperative village (*moshav*) of **Atarot** was founded in 1923, but its lands were first purchased in 1912 by the Israel Land Development Company and registered in the name of David Yellin, who was a Turkish national and a member of the Jerusalem Municipality (under Turkish law land could not be sold to foreign nationals). A farm was set up in 1914 with the name of Kalandia (some of the land was purchased from the nearby Arab village). The handful of settlers lived there and worked the land, but the exceedingly harsh conditions caused a large turnover among the workers. In 1923 the Jewish National Fund purchased the major part of the land and with the aid of the Keren Hayesod (Foundation Fund), a cooperative village called Atarot was established. The name was taken from the Book of Joshua (16:5 and 18:13), Ataroth-Addar on the border of the land of the tribe of Benjamin. The nearby spring provided water, and the settlement ex-expanded, but had to be abandoned in 1948. Most of the members set up farms in the abandoned German colony of Wilhelma near Lod airport and named the settlement Bnei Atarot.

TOUR No. 31

RAMOT ALLON — NEBI SAMWIL
TRIP BY CAR OR BUS

The tour is by car, taxi or bus (bus numbers are given in the text for each part of the tour). The interval between buses allows enough time to enjoy the view at the observation points and visit the sites.
Time: approx. 2 hours by private vehicle; approx. 3 hours by bus

THE TOUR

We take bus No 35, 36 or 37 opposite the Central Bus Station to Ramot Allon travelling along Jaffa Road through the Street of the Prophets, Strauss, Yehezkiel and Shmuel Hanavi Streets and Golda Meir Boulevard. No 35 turns into the eastern section of Ramot Allon, No 36 to the western part and No 37 to the upper eastern bloc of houses.

Ramot Allon (named for Yigael Allon) is a northwestern suburb of Jerusalem built beside two tributaries of the Sorek River, separated by a gorge in which the approach road, Golda Meir Boulevard, has been built. The differences in height between the lower and upper levels of the suburb reach up to 100 m (328 ft). The architectural style of the buildings varies greatly: there are rectangular buildings, several stories high with large numbers of apartments; red-roofed cottages set in pretty gardens; and the so-called Ramot Polin — a group of beehive-like houses on the upper eastern slopes. Building of the suburb began in 1971 on the eastern section and developed, as planned, to the western side — there are altogether 10,000 housing units. The main road continues down to the coastal plain through Beit Horon. A wide road runs from the lower end of the suburb to Nablus Road and to the Givat Shapira intersection. A short road joins the suburb to the western entrance to Jerusalem, Sha'arei Yerushalayim Street, below the abandoned village of Lifta.

From the highest point of the suburb there is a breathtaking view of the north and west, the Hadassah Medical Center in Ein Karem, Beit Zayit, Motza, Beit Iksa, Mevasseret, Ma'oz Zion and the Kastel.

On the summit of the hill on which the eastern section of the suburb rises (769 m — 2523 ft), remains have been found of an ancient fortress which existed here from the Canaanite to the Roman periods. Remains of a Crusader stronghold have been uncovered on the summit of the western section.

We leave the bus at the top of the eastern section and visit the pentagonal cubes of the "beehive" neighborhood (designed by the architect Y. Haecker). We can then walk through the streets and take bus No 36 or 37 from a stop on one of these streets, to the western section.

To continue our tour we shall take bus No 71 (which goes to Giv'at Ze'ev). We travel down to the Nebi Samwil intersection and then climb a steep, narrow path up to the summit of the mountain (885 m–290 ft high), on the top of which is

View of Ramot Allon.

Nebi Samwil. The road that passes by Nebi Samwil to the north goes to Givat Ze'ev and continues to the coastal plain via Beit Horon.

Nebi Samwil (the Prophet Samuel in Arabic) is a rectangular structure with a mosque whose minaret can be seen from afar. The building was erected in the 16th century over a burial cave believed to contain the tomb of the Prophet Samuel, although the Bible clearly states that Samuel was buried at Ramah (I Samuel 25:1) which has been identified with the village of Er-Ram, some 5 km (3 miles) north of Jerusalem.

The tradition connecting Samuel's burial place with this site began in the Byzantine period. In 530 CE Emperor Justinian ordered a church, St Samuel, to be built here, and this tradition was passed on to the Arab conquerors. The Crusaders carried on the Byzantine tradition and called the site Mitzpeh or Ramah and even Shilo, and built the St Samuel de Shilo Church. The hill was given the name of Montjoie (the "Mount of Joy") because it was from this spot that the Crusaders viewed Jerusalem's walls for the first time.

In the 11th century the Karaites were given permission to set up a synagogue; both the building and the land around it were purchased in the 12th century by a group of Jerusalem Jews, who also erected a synagogue and a few houses. Pilgrims visted the site and celebrations were held there. In the 16th century, the site was taken over by the Muslims. The cave was sealed up, the minaret built and Jews were allowed to enter for a fee. Jews still make pilgrimages to the site, especially on 25th Iyar, the traditional date of Samuel's death.

At the end of the 19th century Jews began to purchase land in the vicinity. A few immigrant families from the Yemen settled there and began to work the land; they lived there until the First World War. In 1896 a group of Jews from Jerusalem set up a settlement, Nahalat Israel-Ramah which lasted until 1921.

We go through the square and into the hall which is the transept of the building built in the form of a cross. Through an iron grille we can see the elongated hall of the Crusader church which has been turned into a mosque. In the center is a cenotaph; this is the tomb of Samuel according to the Muslims. We turn right into the passageway, the former northern portico of the church. We descend the steps into the cave below the hall, originally a burial chamber hewn out of the rock. The tomb in this chamber is considered holy by Jews who come here to worship. We return to the entrance hall from which we ascend a steep staircase to the roof. From here it is also possible to climb to a balcony surrounding the minaret, from which we have a panoramic view: to the south and southwest we see Jerusalem, the northern section of the Hebron mountains and the coastal plain; to the west, the western section of the Beth-El mountains, the coastal plain and part of the coast; to the north, Givon (El-Jib) and the northern part of the Beth-El mountains; to the east; the eastern section of the Beth-El mountains, the northern Judean desert and the Gilead mountains. On our return journey we can make out on both sides of the steep road the former Jodanian fortifications which existed here up to the Six Day War.

Our tour ends here. We return along the same route. Private vehicles can drive along Sha'arei Yerushalayim Street which leads from the Ramot intersection to the main entrance to Jerusalem.

Nebi Samwil.

TOUR No. 32

ORA — AMMINADAV — KENNEDY MEMORIAL
TRIP BY CAR OR BUS

The tour is by car, taxi or bus (bus numbers are given in the text for each part of the tour). The interval between buses allows enough time to enjoy the view at the observation points and visit the sites.
Time: approx. 1 hour by private vehicle; approx. 2 hours by bus

THE TOUR

We take bus No 50 from the Street of the Prophets and travel to the Central Bus Station, along Herzl Boulevard, Hanke Street in Kiryat Hayovel, through Kiryat Menahem, Ora and Amminadav.

Kiryat Hayovel, situated west of Bayit Vegan, was founded in 1954 on the lands of the former Arab village of Beit Mazmil. The name commemorates the 50th anniversary *(yovel)* of the establishment of the Jewish National Fund in 1904.

Kiryat Menahem, to the west of Kiryat Hayovel, was founded in 1958 and named for the philanthropist Menahem Bressler. Nearby is **Kfar Selma** (the Swedish Village), an institution for the care of the handicapped. Founded after 1948 with donations from supporters in Sweden and maintained by the Ministry of Health, it was named after the Swedish writer Selma Lagerlof.

Ir Ganim, a neighborhood south of Kiryat Menahem, was founded in 1950. The large, crowded tenement houses have turned the neighborhood into a problem area, bringing it within the Project Renewal rehabilitation program. A municipal sports center was built there in 1984.

The road turns off from Kiryat Menahem at the intersection to Ora and continues along the foot of Mount Ora, 839 m (2753 ft) high. A church is perched on its summit, with a square tower and a cupola on an octagonal drum. It was built by an English missionary, Miss Carey, with the purpose of uniting the three monotheistic religions and thus bringing about the redemption of the world. A pilgrims' hostel was built alongside the church. Today it serves as a boarding school for girls. The church is in a closed military area. Close by is the small Arab village of Jura. **Ora** (similar in sound to the name of the Arab village) is a cooperative *(moshav)* founded in 1950 by immigrants from Yemen who breed chickens. Some of the residents work in Jerusalem.

The road continues to the cooperative settlement of **Amminadav**, named for the father of Nahshon, the chief of the tribe of Judah (Numbers 1:7) and founded by immigrants from North Africa on the same day as nearby Ora.

We leave the bus at its terminus at Amminadav and continue on foot to the summit of the hill 842 m (2762 ft) above sea level, and come to the round **Kennedy Memorial** (Yad Kennedy), built in the form of a tree stump whose roots spread out onto a paved square. Inside, as we enter, is a bust of John F. Kennedy, the President of the United States who was assassinated in 1963, to whose memory it was built in 1966 with funds donated by Jewish communities in the USA. Designed by the Israeli sculptor Dov Feigon, the circular hall is divided into sections for each of the states of the USA, and the official emblems of a different state appear on the window of each section.

Nearby is a Jewish National Fund tree-planting area and camping grounds. There is a view toward the south of the northern section of Mount Hebron, the Etzion Bloc, the villages of Husan and Beitar (Battir), the Gilo mountain ridge with the Gilo Field School, the suburb of Gilo and the Refaim valley; to the southeast is the Bar Giora mountain ridge, the settlements of Mevo Beitar, Tsur Hadassah, Bar Giora and Ness Harim; to the west: the Sorek valley which passes through the Judean hills to the coastal plain; to the north: the Shmuel Hanavi mountain ridge with the Nebi Samwil minaret standing on the summit.

A path descends from below Kennedy Memorial to the northwest and reaches the Hirbet Se'adim nature reserve. The path passes through a pine forest to the Hadassah Medical Center in Ein Karem.

Our tour ends here.

Kennedy Memorial.

Interior of Kennedy Memorial.

TOUR No. 33

BETHANY (EL-AZARIEH)

The tour is by car, taxi or bus.
The bus to El-Azarieh leaves from Nablus Road bus station which can be reached from the Central Bus Station by buses No 1, 27
Time: approx. 1 hour by private vehicle; 2 hours by bus

THE TOUR

We take bus No 43 from the main bus station on Nablus Road. The bus crosses the Jehoshaphat Valley and skirts the Jewish cemetery, passing between the Mount of Olives and the Mount of Offense to the south. We reach an intersection: the road to the right passes through Ras el-Amud and ends at the entrance to the Beit Abraham Catholic hostel; a second road descends to the right, reaches the Kidron Valley and then goes up to the hill on which Government House stands, continues to the west below East Talpiot up to Sur Baher and ends at Bethlehem.

The bus travels along the road to Jericho and continues through the village of Bethany, today known as El-Azarieh, i.e., the place of Lazarus in Arabic. The majority of the inhabitants settled here after 1948 and most of them are employed in Jerusalem.

Bethany was the hometown of Martha, Mary and Lazarus who were the beloved friends of Jesus and here Jesus performed the miracle of Lazarus' resurrection (John 11:43–44). It could also be the site of Ananiah mentioned in the Book of Nehemiah (11:32). Archaeological excavations have uncovered Second Temple burial caves, and a number of sites holy to Christians are in the vicinity.

We leave the bus at the eastern end of the village. To the right is the silver-domed Greek Orthodox Church built in the 19th century on the remains of a Crusader church. It can be visited only with permission from the Greek Patriarchate in Jerusalem. In the center of the church is a rock, traditionally the site of the meeting between Jesus and Mary of Bethany (John 11:32).

We walk along the road in a westerly direction (towards Jerusalem) and to the

(left) View of El-Azarieh (Bethany): in the background, center, remains of a Crusader monastery can be seen; on the left, the Church of St Lazarus. (right) Entrance to the tomb of St Lazarus.

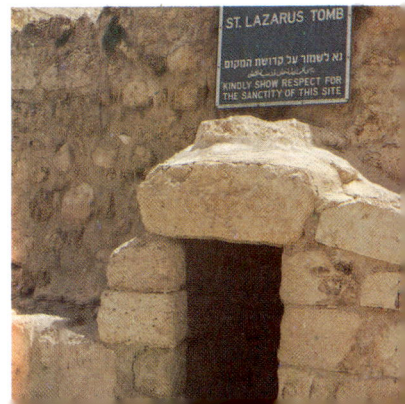

right we see a rock on which Jesus is said to have rested. Further along the road to the right is a Russian Monastery of the Bethany Order of the Resurrection of Jesus. Beside the courtyard a path descends about 600 m (655 yd) to an abandoned Jordanian army camp, which was built partly from tombstones uprooted from the Jewish cemetery on the Mount of Olives. The camp has been preserved as a memorial and can be visited. We follow the road to the west until it turns left and nearby we see the Franciscan Church of St Lazarus. The facade has a gable decorated with mosaics, and the church has a silver dome on a circular drum and a square bell tower. It was built in 1954 by the Italian architect Barluzzi. Inside are paintings illustrating scenes from Jesus' visit to Bethany; the resurrection of Lazarus; his meeting with Mary, and his meeting with Martha in the house of Simon the leper. The interior of the dome is decorated with 48 gilded plates with mosaic illustrations of doves. Both altars, at the north and the south, are in the form of sarcophagi and have carved scenes of the death and resurrection of Lazarus. In the courtyard is a sculpture of Pope Pius VI, commemorating his visit there in 1964. There is also a mosaic with a geometric design dating to the Byzantine period, remains of Byzantine churches and an oil-press.

The road climbs behind the church to an ancient burial cave. We descend the steps leading to a two-storey structure inside which is the burial site of Lazarus. According to tradition the tomb is empty because Jesus resurrected Lazarus here (John 11:17–44). Near the cave is the Nebi el-Uzeir Mosque, built in the 16th century and named for a Muslim saint. The mosque is closed to visitors.

We climb the steps up to the remains of a Crusader monastery destroyed by Saladin when he entered Jerusalem in 1187. The monastery was built on the site of the house where Jesus visited Simon the leper (Mark 14:3).

On the road going up to the Mount of Olives there is a new Greek Orthodox Church built in 1965 on the ruins of a Crusader church. It is open on special occasions only. Remains of buildings from the Second Temple period can be seen at the side of the road.

On the crest of the hill above the village are a convent, an orphanage and a church of the Order of St Vincent de Paul. The road continues up to the summit of the Mount of Olives and 1 km (3/5 mile) further along reaches **Bethphage** ("house of figs") closely associated with the last days of Jesus (Matthew 21:1). A narrow road leads to the site and then continues to the Pater Noster Church (see Tour No. 12).

On Palm Sunday the procession begins at Bethphage and ends at the Church of St Anne in the Old City. In Crusader times the processions began at Bethany and ended at the Temple Mount, entering through the Golden Gate (the Gate of Mercy) which was opened especially for the occasion. Under Ottoman rule the Armenians and then the Franciscans continued this tradition, but the procession ended in the Jehoshaphat Valley.

We return to the main road and take bus No 43 back to town.

Index

A

Abba Sikra Street 249
Absalom's Tomb (Monument) 10, 23, 161
Academy of Science and Humanities 239, 255
Aceldama see St Onuphrius
Adass Synagogue 231
Adler Street 194
Adonyahu HaCohen Street 209, 210
Aftimos Market 111
Agnon Street 243, 244
Agony, Church of the 165, 166
Agrippa Street 216, 218
Agron Street 174, 179, 182, 251
Aharoni Street 244
Ahavat Zion Synagogue 70
Ahva neighborhood 221, 225
Ala ed-Din Street 72, 80
Albright American School of Archaeology 150
Alexander Nievsky Church 94, 97, 110
Alfassi Street 237
Alharizi Street 235
Alkalay Street 240
Allenby Barracks 292
Alliance Israelite building 215, 219, 220
All Nations, Church of see: Agony, Church of the
Aluf Street 273
Americans and Canadians Association 241
American Colony 147, 148
American Institute, Mt. Zion 137
Amminadav 290, 301
Amos Street 224
Anata 296
Anglican School 187
Annas, Church of the House of 113, 117
Antebi Street 233
Antonia Fortress 26, 34
Ararat Street 71, 115, 119
Araunah the Jebusite Road 137
Arbelim Synagogue 205
Archaeological Garden see: City of David
Archangels Church 113
Ari Synagogue 71
Arlosoroff Street 237
Armenian Catholic Church 92
Armenian Garden 113, 115, 131
Armenian Mosaic 185, 196
Armenian Patriarchate Road 52, 116
Armenian Quarter 90, 104, 112, 120, 143
Armon Hanatziv (Government House) 140, 144, 293-295, 303
Arnona 289, 291
Artists' House 227, 229
Ascension Church 155, 158, 159
Ascension Church (Russian) 142
A-Sheikh Road 160
Ashkenazi Compound 52, 60, 61

Assumption Church 166, 167
Atarot 298
Atonement, Gate of (Bab Hitta) 24, 33
A-Tur 155, 158
Augusta Victoria Hospital 142, 157, 167
Austrian Hospice 91, 141
Austrian Post Office 123

B

Badryya 85
Bak (Nissan) neighborhood 185, 196
Baka see Geulim
Balfour Street 237, 239
Bank Leumi 182
Barclay's Bank 216
Barclay's Gate 33, 41
Bar Kochba Street 296
Barkuk Street 83
Baruchoff Street 217
Bar Zakkai Street 233
Batei Mahseh 52, 55, 57, 144
Batei Neitin 202
Batei Sayidoff 221, 222
Batei Ungarn 202
Batei Warsaw 202
Bath, Gate of the 24, 36
Bayt Vegan 259
Beersheba Street 231
Behar (Nissim) Street 231
Beit Abraham Catholic Hostel 303
Beit Avraham 204
Beit Avraham Metivta 223
Beit David 185, 186
Beit Davidoff 208
Beit Ha'am 227, 230
Beit Habad Market / Street 72, 74, 85, 93-95, 109, 110
Beit Hahayal (Soldiers' Hostel) 273
Beit Hakerem 259
Beit Hamaaraviim 84
Beit Hanina 297
Beit Hillel Synagogue 70
Beit Jalla 290
Beit Safafa 289
Beit Simhayoff 208
Beit Ya'akov 221
Beit Yad Labanim (Soldiers' Memorial) 273
Beit Yehudayoff Hefetz 207
Beit Yisrael 205, 206
Beit Yisrael Square / Synagogue 205, 206
Beit Yosef 295
Ben Addaya Road 157
Ben Maimon Boulevard 237
Ben Matityahu (Yosef) Street 219
Benny's Ascent 137
Ben-Shimon Street 179

INDEX

Ben Yehuda Street 216, 227
Ben Zvi Boulevard 232-233, 273, 289
Ben-Zvi Institute 235
Bergheim houses 197
Bet-El Street / Synagogue 57, 59, 69
Bethany (El-Azarieh) 303, 304
Bethesda Pool 86, 88, 89
Bethlehem Road 241, 242, 243
Bethphage 160, 304
Bezalel Street 230, 231
Bezetha 88, 89, 104, 151
Bible Society 197, 199
Bikur Holim Hospital 52, 71, 185, 188, 216
Binyanei Ha'uma (Convention Center) 268, 270
Bir Ayyub (Job's Well) 19
Bloomfield Garden 174, 249
B'nai Brith Street 184, 190-192
Botta (Emile) Street 178
British Consulate 247
Builders of Jerusalem Park 130-131
Bukharan Quarter 205, 207-210
Bukharim Street 208-210
Butchers' Market 74

C

Caiaphas, House of 89, 121, 131, 132
Calvary see Golgotha
Cardo 52, 54, 61, 63, 69, 92, 94, 95, 141, 146
Casa Nova Hospice 104, 107, 109
Cemetery, Armenian 136
Cemetery, British Military 286
Cemetery, Catholic (Mt. Zion) 131
Cemetery, Har Menuhot 269
Cemetery, Jewish (Mt. of Olives) 162, 163
Cemetery, Protestant 137
Cenacle (Room of the Last Supper) 90, 121, 131-134
Central Command Street see Pikud Merkaz Street
Central Hotel 186
Central Valley (Tyropoeon) 47, 48, 131, 136, 141
Chagall Windows 265, 266
Chain, Gate of the (Bab es-Silsileh) 34, 36, 37, 38, 78
Chopin Street 257
Christ Church 113, 120
Christian Community Center 200
Christian Quarter 86-112, 140, 141
Christian Quarter Road 103, 108, 111, 162, 169, 200
Christians' Street 103, 112, 120
Cinematheque 168, 171
Citadel 48, 115, 121-130, 138, 143, 144, 151, 162
Citadel Museum 124
City of David 10-20, 48, 49, 78, 113, 162, 294
City Tower 162, 228
Clal Center 162, 215, 220-221
Collège des Frères 106, 140, 199
Condemnation and Imposition of the Cross,
Church of the 90, 91
Conservative Judaism Center/Synagogue 251
Convent of the Lentils see Deir el-Adass
Coptic Khan 104, 111
Coptic monastery 95
Coptic Patriarchate 95, 104, 110
Copts, Street of the 108
Cotton Merchants' Gate (Bab el Qattanim) 24, 35, 36, 79
Cotton Merchants Market 35, 72, 79, 83
Cradle of Jesus 38
Cremieux Street 242

D

Dahiyat el-Barid 297
Damascus Gate 48, 52, 62, 82, 85, 138, 140-141, 144, 146, 147, 151-154, 173, 185, 196, 198
Daniel Park see Gan Daniel
Davidka 185, 186
David Street 37, 52, 62, 63, 74, 85, 103, 121
David's (King) Tomb 55, 121, 132, 134-135
Deir el-Adass (Monastery of the Lentils) 82, 142
Deir es-Sultan 95, 110
Dimitri Street 107
Diskin Street 233
Disraeli Street 240, 241
District Health Office 215, 219,
Dome of the Rock 24, 27, 30, 34, 141, 161
Dominus Flevit Church 161, 163, 164
Dormition Abbey and Church 121, 131-133, 145, 162
Dung Gate 23, 47, 49, 63, 78, 138, 144, 146

E

Ecce Homo, Church / Arch 91
Ecole Biblique et Archeologique Française 151
Eilon Tower 289
Ein Karem 265, 279-282
El-Aksa Mosque 24, 27, 38-41, 45, 47, 49, 51, 144, 161
El-Azarieh see Bethany
Eleona Church see Pater Noster Church
El-Hanka Street 93, 109
Elijah Synagogue 58
El-Khalidyya Street 79, 83, 84, 85
Emek Refaim Street 234, 241, 242, 296
En Rogel 10, 19, 168
Eshkol Boulevard 212, 213, 296
Eshkolot Cave 211, 212
Es-Sarayya Street 72, 84, 85
Ethiopian Church 185, 186, 191
Ethiopian Consulate 185, 194
Ethiopian Patriarchate 104, 109
Ethiopia Street 185, 190, 191
Etz Hayim Street 218, 220
Etz Hayim Yeshiva 61, 215
Evelina de Rothschild School 254
Even Sapir 282
Even Shetyyah see Foundation Stone

INDEX

Even Yehoshua Street 202
Even Yisrael 215, 216
Eye Hospital 214
Ezra Street 205-208
Ezrat Nashim Hospital 269
Ezrat Yisrael 215, 216, 289

F

Feil Hotel building 197, 199
Finnish Messianic Center 202
First Wall 125, 129
Fishel Lappin Building 81
Fistul Street 208
Flagellation, Chapel of the 90
Foundation Stone 24, 28, 30, 34
France Square 251
Franciscan Biblicum Studium 91
Franciscan Convent 104-106, 121, 168
French Consulate 140, 143, 178
French Hill see Givat Shapira
French Hospital, St Louis 140, 197, 200
Frères Street 107

G

Galed Street 56, 57
Gan Daniel 197, 199
Gan Rehavia 254
Garden Tomb 147, 152
Gaza Street 237, 289
Generali Building 182
German Colony 144, 234, 237, 238-243
German Evangelical School 185, 193-194
German Hospice 52, 66, 67
Gesher Hahayim Street 222
Gethsemane 89, 157, 165-167
Geula Quarter 210
Geulim (Baka) 243
Gihon Spring 10, 14-17
Gilo 144, 162, 268, 289, 290, 301
Givat Arba 290
Givat Hamivtar 213
Givat Hananya 168, 289, 295
Givat HaTahmoshet (Ammunition Hill) 211, 213
Givat Ram 270-277
Givat Shapira (French Hill) 296
Givat Shaul 209, 259, 269
Gobat School 121, 137, 177
Golda Meir Boulevard 299
Golden Gate (Mercy Gate) 24, 32, 33, 162, 304
Goldstein Youth Village 244
Golgotha 89, 96, 97, 100, 101
Gonen see Katamon
Gordon's Calvary see Garden Tomb
Government House see Armon Hanatziv
Graetz Street 241
Great Synagogue 245, 252
Greek Catholic Patriarchate 104, 106
Greek Colony 243
Greek Monastery Street 108
Greek Orthodox Church 303

Greek Orthodox Monastery 121, 136
Greek Orthodox Patriarchate 104, 108, 111
Greek Orthodox Patriarchate Museum 104, 107, 178
Greek Patriarchate Road 107
Grunzberg Street 184
Gulbenkian Library 113, 116
Gymnasium, Hebrew (Yitzhak Ben-Zvi Municipal High School) 234, 235

H

Ha'Ayyin Het Street 201
Habad Street / Synagogue 52, 70, 115
Habakkuk Street 205
Habrecha Street (Pool Street) 178
Hadassah Community College 193
Hadassah Medical Center (Ein Karem) 265-266, 279, 302
Hadassah Medical Center (Mt. Scopus) 283, 285-286
Hadassah Technical College 193
HaDegel Street 83
HaEmek Street (Valley) 143, 169
HaGai Street (El Wad Street) 35, 52, 62, 66, 72, 78-82, 91, 92, 141
HaGidem Street 230
Hagiz (Moshe) Street 225
Hahagana Street 296
Hahatsotsrot Street 55
HaKaraim Street 69
Hama'apilim Street 245
Hama'aravim Lane 179
Hamayan Street 281
Hammam Ashifa 72, 79
Hammam el-Ein 72, 78, 79
Hammam es-Sultan 92
HaNassi Street 255, 257
Hanke Street 301
Hansen Hospital 255, 257
HaOphel Road 162, 167
Haram esh-Sharif see Moriah, Mount; Temple Mount
Harat Sa'adyya 72, 81
Harel Brigade Street see Hativat Harel Street
Har Nof 259, 269
Hashalom Road 162
Hashalshelet Street (Street of the Chain) 52, 55, 62, 72, 74-79, 83
Hativat Harel (Harel Brigade) Street 211
Hativat Yerushalayim Road (Jerusalem Brigade Road) 52, 130, 137, 171, 172, 174
Hatsabaim Street 94, 110
Hatsanhanim (Paratroopers) Street 140
Haturim Street 221
Havatzelet Building 72, 83
Hayehudim Street 52, 60, 63, 69
Hayei Olam Yeshiva 83, 84
Hazan (David) Street 209
Hazanowitz Street 191

INDEX

Hazaz Boulevard 289
Hebrew Union College 140, 143, 174, 179
Hebrew University (Mt. Scopus) 142, 214, 282-285
Hebrew University (Givat Ram) 270, 273, 274
Hebron Road 168, 171, 177
Hebron Street (Old City) 72, 83
Hechal Shlomo 162, 252
Helene Hamalka Street 184, 193, 201
Herod family tomb 174, 178
Herodian residential quarter 52, 69
Herod's Gate 82, 83, 142
Heroism, Hall of 183
Herut Square 185, 186
Herzl Boulevard 258-263, 301
Herzog Boulevard 289
Heshin Street 184
Hess (Moshe) Street 179
Hessed-El Synagogue 70
Hezekiah's Tunnel / Pool 10, 16, 17, 169, 199
Hezir family, Tomb of 10, 20, 21
Hillel Street 181, 227, 228
Hilton Hotel 162
Hinnom Valley 131, 136, 140, 146, 168-173, 247, 248
Holocaust Chamber 121, 131, 135
Holy Cross, Monastery of the 277, 278
Holyland Hotel 255, 266, 268
Holy Sepulcher Church 29, 62, 86, 90, 94, 95-104, 110, 141, 143, 162
Holy Trinity Cathedral 183
Hovevei Zion Street 241, 243
Hulda Gates 26, 44, 48, 51
Hulda the Prophetess, Tomb of 160
Hurva Synagogue 52, 60, 69, 162
Huzot Hayozer (Artisans' Quarter) 168, 170
Hyatt (Frances L.) Garden 229
Hyatt Regency Hotel 287

I

Ibn Gvirol Street 253
Ibn Jarah Street 82
Ibn Shaprut Street 237
Immigrants' Club 241
Imrei Binah (Warsaw Kollel) Yeshiva 144
Inspector, Gate of the (Bab en-Natir) 34, 35, 81
Institute for the Blind 258
Intercontinental Hotel 155, 161
International Cultural Center for Youth 242
International Evangelical Church 185, 188
Ir Ganim 301
Iron Gate (Bab el-Hadid) 24, 35, 80
Isaiah House 180
Islamic Art Institute / Museum 255-257
Islamic Museum (Old City) 24, 41
Israel Museum 274-276
Italian Hospital 185, 202
Italian Synagogue 227, 228

J

Jabotinsky Street 241
Jaffa Gate 52, 63, 71, 74, 85, 103, 107, 112-113, 120-123, 130-140, 181, 267
Jaffa Road 174, 181, 182, 215, 216, 221, 227, 258, 268, 289
Jason's Tomb 237
Jehoshaphat (Valley and Tomb) 10, 20-23, 86, 151, 303
Jerusalem Brigade Road see Hativat Yerushalayim Road
Jerusalem Forest 259, 269, 279
Jewish Agency 234
Jewish Quarter 52-71, 141, 162

K

Kalandia 298
Kamenitz Hotel building 185, 187
Kamra Mosque 105, 140
Kapah (Yehia) Street 205
Karaite Cemetery 168, 172
Karaite Synagogue 52, 68
Katamon (Gonen) 243, 244, 245, 289
Kathisma 292
Katzir Street 287
Kennedy Memorial 301, 302
Kerem Avraham 221, 224
Kerem neighborhood 221, 223
Keren Hayesod Street 174, 251, 253, 296
Keren Kayemet Street 233, 234, 253, 296
Ketef Hinnom 248
Khalidi Library 72, 76
Khan, The 245-247
Khan es-Sultan 72, 75
Khan Tankizyya 79
Kidron Valley 10, 12, 14, 15, 20, 78, 89, 136, 143, 149, 151, 161, 166, 168, 267
King David Hotel 143, 249
King David Street 179, 249
King George Avenue 215, 216, 227, 229, 234, 252, 254, 289, 296
Kings Hotel 252
Kirami Street 72, 84, 85
Kirya Ne'emana 185
Kiryat Hamemshala (government offices) 287
Kiryat Hayovel 301
Kiryat Menahem 301
Kiryat Moshe 258
Kiryat Shmuel neighborhood 237
Kishla 113, 115, 143
Knesset 270, 272
Knesset Yisrael neighborhood 230
Koresh Street 182
Kuzari Park 234, 235

L

Laemel School 66, 221, 225
Last Supper, Room of see Cenacle
Latin Patriarchate 104, 106, 107, 162
Lazarist Convent 180

INDEX

Lev Harova (Heart of the Jewish Quarter) 61
Liberty Bell Garden 245, 247, 248
Library, Jewish National and University 274
Lifta 268
Lions' Gate *see* St Stephen's Gate
Lithostrotos 90, 91, 92
Lloyd George Street 242
Lohamei Harova Street 61
Luncz Street 227
Lutheran Church 162
Lutheran Youth Hostel 113, 118, 119

M

Ma'aleh Hashalom Road 135
Maalot Yehuda Halevy 52, 66
Madrassa Ashrafyya 78
Madrassa el-Arghunyya 80
Madrassa el-Fakhryya 41
Madrassa el-Manjikyya 81
Madrassa et-Tankizzyya 72, 77
Madrassa el-Uthmanyya 24, 36
Madrassa Hasanyya 81
Madrassa Jawharyya 80
Madrassa Muzhiryya 80
Madrassa Tashtimuryya 72, 75
Mahanaim House 185, 195
Mahaneh Israel neighborhood 174, 179
Mahaneh Yehuda market, street, neighborhood 168, 215, 218, 221, 289
Maimon neighborhood 258
Malha *see* Manahat
Malkei Yisrael Street 223
Mamilla 140, 143, 168-170, 180, 181
Mamunyya School 82, 142
Manahat (Malha) 268
Marcus Street 239, 240, 257
Mardigian Museum 113, 116
Mar Elias Monastery 290
Maronite Church 113, 119, 120
Mary Magdalene Church 144, 161, 164, 165
Mary's Spring 281
Mayer (L.A.) Memorial Museum *see* Islamic Institute
Mazkeret Moshe 215, 217
Mea She'arim 197, 202-204, 225
Medical Association, Israel 185, 189
Mekor Baruch 221, 222
Mekor Hayim 289, 290
Menachem Zion Synagogue 61, 71
Mercy Gate *see* Golden Gate
Merhavia neighborhood 257
Mevo Yizhar 232
Micrographics Museum 192
Ministry of Agriculture 184
Ministry of Commerce and Industry 180
Ministry of Education 195, 196
Ministry of Tourism 229
Misgav Ladach Street 52, 66, 67, 75
Mishkenot Sha'ananim 131, 143, 174, 176
Mishkenot Yisrael 215, 217

Mishmeret Hakehuna Street 57, 58, 59, 71
Mitchell Garden 143
Moghrabi Gate (Moors' Gate) 24, 27, 41, 66
Mohliver Street 243
Molho Square 237
Monbaz Street 184-185, 193
Montefiore Windmill 174, 249
Morasha (Musrara) 141, 197, 200
Moriah, Mount *see* Temple Mount
Mormon University 142, 157
Mosque, Hankat el-Mulawyya 82
Mosque of Omar 39, 41
Mosque of the Forty Martyrs 39, 41
Mount Herzl 258, 261-263
Mount (or Hill) of Offense 19, 144-145
Mount of Olives 19-20, 141, 142-143, 155-167, 267, 303
Mount Scopus 141, 283-287
131-137, 144, 177
Mount Zion Hotel 171
Mujir ed-Din, Tomb of 167
Muristan 104, 108, 110
Musayoff Street 210
Music Center 171, 176
Music, Rubin Academy of 237
Muslim Quarter 72-85, 142, 143
Musrara *see* Morasha

N

Nablus Road 141, 142, 149, 151, 152, 167, 196, 213, 214, 287, 296, 298, 303
Nahalat Ahim 227, 232
Nahalat Shiva 227, 228
Nahalat Ya'acov 227, 231
Nahalat Zadok 227, 233
Nahalat Zion 227, 231
Nahalat Zvi 205, 206
Narkiss Street 232
Nathan HaNavi Street 201
Natural History Museum 243
Nature Preservation Society 184
Navon (Joseph) Bey house 185, 188
Nayot 277
Nea Church 49, 51-52, 55-57
Nebi el-Uzeir Mosque 303
Nebi Samwil 296, 300-302
Nebi Ukasha tomb, mosque 185, 226
Neveh Bezalel 227, 232
Neveh Granot 277
Neveh Sha'anan 277
Neveh Shalom 231
Neveh Ya'akov 297, 298
New Gate 104, 106, 108, 140, 200
Nibarta Street 232
Nicanor, Tomb of 285
Notre Dame de France 141, 162, 197, 200
Nusseiba neighborhood 297

O

Ohalei Simha neighborhood 221, 223

Ohel Moshe 215, 217-218
Ohel Shlomo 221, 222
Old Yishuv Court Museum 52, 54, 70, 71
Oliphant Street 240
Omar ibn el-Khattab Square 112, 120, 122, 140
(El) Omaryya College / Mosque 34, 90, 111
Ophel 10, 23, 48, 49, 50, 173
Ophel Archaeological Garden 42, 47
Ophel Road 10, 23
Ophira Street 212
Ora 301
Or Hahayim Street / Synagogue 52, 70, 71
ORT School 185, 194
Our Lady of the Spasm, Church of 92
Ovadia Street 224

P

Palace Hotel building 179, 180
Palmach Street 243, 256, 257
Palombo Museum 121, 135
Paratroopers Memorial 167
Paratroopers' Street see HaTsanhanim Street
Pasha's house 185, 188
Pater Noster Church 160, 161
Pat neighborhood 289
Patriarchate Road 112
Peace Forest 295
Pelagia Cave 160
Perlman houses 202
Pharaoh's Daughter, Tomb of 20
Phasael Tower 125, 127, 267
Pikud Merkaz, Kikar (Central Command Square) 147
Pines Street 225
Pinsker Street 240, 241
Pisgat Ze'ev 298, 300
Plugat Hakotel Street 52, 63-65, 75
Police Headquarters 214, 287
Police Station (Mahaneh Yehuda) 215, 219
Pontifical Biblical Institute 140, 174, 179
Porat Yosef Yeshiva 54, 67, 69
Post Office, Central 182
Praetorium 90, 91
Prague Street 226
President's Residence 255, 256
Pri Hadash Street 225
Prime Minister's Residence 239
Probst building 185, 194
Promenade (Talpiot) 294
Prophets, Street of the 78, 119, 141, 185-196, 216, 225, 282
Prophets, Tomb of the 163

R

Rabbi Diskin building 84
Rabbi Kook Street 185, 193
Rabi'a al-Addawyya, Tomb of 160
Rachel Imenu Street 243
Rachel Yanait Ben-Zvi Center 64, 71
Rachtman (Moshe) building 83

Radak Street 237
Railway Station 245, 295
Rama Street 231
Ramat Denya 268
Ramat Rachel Kibbutz 289, 291-293
Ramban Street 235, 237, 252, 289
Ramban Synagogue 52, 59, 60
Ramot Allon 298, 299
Ramparts Walk 121, 138-154
Rashedyya High School 142
Rashi Street 222, 223
Ratisbonne Monastery 245, 253, 254
Rav Kook Institute 258
Redeemer, Church of the 94, 104, 110
Red Minaret Street 142
Rehavia 234, 241
Rejwan Center 229, 289
Remembrance, Hill of 262-265, 279
Remez (David) Street 245, 247, 248
Resurrection, Russian Monastery 304
Ribbat Ala ed-din el-Basir 80
Robinson's Arch 47, 48
Rockefeller Museum 142, 162, 283, 287, 288
Romema 268-269
Rose Garden 241
Rose Garden, Wohl 271
Rothschild House 56, 57
Ruhama neighborhood 223
Ruppin Boulevard 270, 274
Russian Compound 78, 162, 174, 181, 184
Russian Convent (Ein Karem) 279, 281, 282

S

Sa'adyya Street 82
Sacker Park 233
Salah ed-Din Street 143, 148
Salahyya Theological School 89
Salameh Square see Wingate Square
Salant Street 202, 203
Salomon Street 181, 227
Sanhedria neighborhood 211, 212
Sanhedria Tombs 211
Sansur Building 227
Sapir Center 71
Schatz Street 229
Schmidt School building 227, 228
Schneller Compound 162, 197, 223, 224
Schocken Library 239
Scottish Hospice and Church 247
Sephardi Educational Center 55, 57
Sephardi Orphanage 215, 217
Sephardi Synagogues, Old City 52, 57
Sha'ar Hapinah neighborhood 205
Sha'ar Haprachim Street 82
Sha'arei Hessed 227, 233
Sha'arei Yerushalayim 221, 222
Sha'arei Yerushalayim Street 299, 300
Sha'arei Zedek Hospital (new) 259, 289
Sha'arei Zedek neighborhood 221, 222
Shaul Hamelech Street 212

Sheikh Jarrah 214 224
Sheraton-Plaza Hotel 143
Shevet Ahim 227, 231
Shiloah *see* Siloam
Shilo Street 231
Shivtei Yisrael Street 147, 150, 194, 195, 199, 200-202, 221, 224, 267
Shlomo Hamelekh Street 199
Shlomzion Hamalka Street 181
Shmuel Hanagid Street 229, 253
Shmuel Hanavi Street 147, 206, 211
Shomrei Hahomot Building 72, 78
Shomron Street 217
Shrine of the Book 274
Shu'afat 297
Shunei Halahot Street 64, 65
Sikra Street 178
Siloam, Pool 10, 12, 16-19, 78, 136, 146, 267
Siloam Road 16, 173
Silwan 19, 145, 173
Simon the Just, Tomb of 206, 211, 214
Sisters of Zion, Convent 90, 91, 141
Sisters of Zion, Convent (Ein Karem) 279, 281
Slonim Street 202
Smolenskin Street 239
Smuts Street 242
Soeurs du Rosaire, Convent 245, 251
Solomon's Pools 146
Solomon's Stables 24, 27, 38, 43
Spafford Baby Home 82, 142, 148
St Abraham Monastery 98
St Andrew Church 140, 144, 172, 245, 247, 248
St Anne Church 86, 88, 89, 143, 304
St Antony Church 110
St Clare Convent 292, 293
St Etienne 147, 151, 167
St Francis Convent 136
St Francis Street 105, 109
St George Cathedral 147, 150
St George Monastery 111
St George Street 147, 211
St Helena, Chapel of 95, 96, 103
St Helena's Street 103, 111
St James Cathedral 116
St James Street 52, 71, 118
St John in the Desert Monastery 279, 282
St John the Baptist Church 104, 111
St John the Baptist Church (Ein Karem) 279-280
St Joseph Convent and School 185, 189
St Lazarus Church and tomb 303, 304
St Longinus Chapel 103
St Louis Hospital *see* French Hospital
St Mark Church and Convent 113, 118
St Mark's Road 119
St Mary la Latine Church 110
St Mary la Grande Church 108
St Mary of the German Knights 66
St Nicodemus Church 83
St Onuphrius Monastery 168, 172, 173

St Paul Church 197, 201, 202
St Paul Hospice 147, 152
St Paul Monastery 142
St Peter in Gallicantu 121, 131, 135, 136, 145
St Savior Monastery / Church 104-106, 141
St Simeon Monastery 244
St Stephen Church 167
St Stephen's Gate 34, 55, 86, 87, 138, 141-143
St Thomas Church 113, 118
St Veronica's house 93
St Vincent de Paul Convent 143
Stambuli Synagogue 57, 59
Stations of the Cross 90-101
Strauss Street 189, 216, 224, 296
Street of the Chain *see* HaShalshelet Street
Street of the Prophets *see* Prophets, Street of
Sukkat Shalom 215, 217
Suleiman Fountain 77
Sultan's Pool (Birket es-Sultan) 168, 170, 173, 177
Sundial Building 215, 218, 219
Supersol Building 251
Suq Khan ez-Zeit (Beit Habad Market) 74
Swedish Theological Institute 191

T

Tabor Street 215, 230
Tachkemoni School Street 192, 223
Takyya 72, 83
Talbieh (Komemiut) 234, 237, 238, 239, 240, 241
Talitha Kumi 227, 229
Talpiot 140, 144, 162, 289-293, 303
Tanus building 143
Teachers' Seminary, Religious 227, 228
Tel el-Ful 294
Temple Mount 24-41, 45, 47, 49, 54, 60, 66, 72, 74, 75, 77, 80, 83, 134, 146, 161, 304
Terra Sancta College 251
Thabor House 185, 190
Theater, Jerusalem 240, 255, 257
Third Wall 72, 104, 106, 141, 143, 147, 182, 199
Ticho House 185, 192, 193
Tiferet Israel Street / Synagogue 52, 67, 68, 69
Tiferet Yerushalayim Square 55
Tombs of the Kings 50, 141, 147-149
Tourjeman Post Museum 147
Tower of David *see* Citadel
Town Hall / Municipality 140, 197, 199
Tribes, Gate of the (Bab el-Asbat) 24, 33, 86
Tsahal (IDF) Square 140, 143, 197, 199, 200
Tsanhanim Street (Paratroopers Street) 199

U

United States Consulate 180
Ussishkin Street 232, 237

V

Van Leer Institute 255, 256
Via Dolorosa 86, 89-103

Viri Galilaei Church   157-159
Visitation, Church of the   279, 281, 282

W

Wallenberg (Raoul) Street   188
Warren's Shaft / Gate   14-15, 44, 48
Watson House see Lutheran Youth Hostel
Wedgewood Street   242
Western Wall   24, 26, 27, 41-52, 66, 78
Western Wall Observation Point   52, 66
White Fathers, Monastery of the   88
Wilson's Arch / Shaft   44, 46, 48, 77
Wingate (Salameh) Square   239
Wittenberg House   81, 202
Wohl Rose Garden see Rose Garden
Wolfsohn Gardens   171
Womens' Gate   24, 30
Writers' House (Beit Hasofer)   56

Y

Yad Sarah   192
Yad Vashem   262-265
Yam Suf (Red Sea) Street   213
Yeffe Nof   259
Yegia Kapaim   221, 225
Yehezkiel Street   205, 206, 210, 296
Yehuda Halevy steps   52
Yehuda Hanassi Street   296
Yehudit Street   219, 223

Yellin (David) Street   225, 226
Yemin Moshe   131, 137, 143, 174, 176-178
Yeshayahu Street   225
Yeshivat Hakotel   54, 67, 145
Yeshurun Synagogue   245, 253
Yirmeyahu Street   268, 298
Yissa Bracha Street   208
Yizrael Street   230
YMCA   143, 162, 249, 250
Yoel Street   205
Yohanan Ben Zakkai Synagogue   58, 59
Yohanan Migush Halav Street   182, 196
Youth Hostel, Ein Karem   282

Z

Zawyya el-Afghanyya   83
Zawyyat el-Hunud   82
Zechariah Harofeh Street   205
Zechariah, Tomb and Cave of   20, 22, 167
Zedekiah's Cave   43, 141, 142, 147, 154
Zibenberg Museum   71
Zikhron Ahim   227, 232
Zikhron Moshe   221, 225, 226
Zikhron Tuviya Street   218
Zion Gate   52, 54, 55, 132, 137, 138, 143, 144, 146
Zion Park (Beit Shalom Park)   138, 146
Zion Square   227
Zoo, Biblical   268

Acknowledgments

We would like to thank the following persons and organizations for their assistance in the preparation of the Guide:
- Baruch Brendl for his valuable remarks regarding achaeology matters
- Professor N. Avigad for the use of the two illustrations of the Herodian quarter from his book *Discovering Jerusalem* (1983)
- The Israel Museum for the illustrations of the Shrine of the Book and the Billy Rose Art Garden

For giving us permission to reproduce drawings and maps:
- The Citadel Museum of the History of Jerusalem for the drawing of the Citadel
- Yad Vashem Memorial for the map of the Hill of Remembrance
- M. Ben Dov for the map of the Ophel Archaeological Garden
- S. Zechariah for the map of the Muslim Quarter

For additional photography:
- A.A.M. van der Heyden
- David Harris
- Zev Radovan
- Israel Sela

CHRONOLOGICAL TABLE

PREHISTORY

BCE — *Flint instruments of the Pleistocene period found in the area of Jerusalem give earliest indication of human habitation.*

CANAANITE PERIOD

ca. 3200	*First settlement on the eastern hill.*
19th–14th cent.	*Mentioned as Canaanite city-state in Egyptian texts (Execration Texts and Letter of Tell el-Amarna).*
1250	*In the Bible, Melchizedek is mentioned as king of Salem (Jerusalem) in Genesis 19:19.*
	Adoni-Zedek, king of Jerusalem, leads coalition of five Amorite kings during conquest of Canaan by Joshua. He is defeated and killed (Joshua 10:1). However, Jerusalem remains in the hands of the Jebusites (a Canaanite people) until the time of David (Judges 19:11–12)
	David captures Jebusite citadel of Zion and makes it the City of David (II Samuel 5:6–10). He brings the Holy Ark to Jerusalem, making it the religious as well as the political center of the Israelite kingdom.

FIRST TEMPLE PERIOD 1000–586

	Construction of the First Temple and royal palace by Solomon on the eastern hill turns Jerusalem into holy royal city.
925	*After Solomon's death the kingdom is split in two: the northern Kingdom of Israel (capital Samaria) and the southern Kingdom of Judah of which Jerusalem remains the capital.*
722	*Fall of Samaria to the Assyrians leads to flux of refugees swelling the population of Jerusalem.*
705–702	*Hezekiah prepares the city in anticipation of an Assyrian assault: reinforces its walls and cuts the Siloam Tunnel to assure water supply in case of siege.*
597	*Nebuchadnezzar, king of Babylon, seizes the Kingdom of Judah and exiles King Jehoiachin and 10,000 captives.*
586	*After two-year siege, Nebuchadnezzar captures Jerusalem, destroys the Temple, exiles large part of the population and kills King Zedekiah.*

SECOND TEMPLE PERIOD 538 BCE–70 CE

538	*Cyrus, king of Persia issues decree allowing Jews to return and to rebuild the Temple.*
	Return from Babylonia. City walls rebuilt by Nehemiah.
332	*Conquest of Alexander the Great. After his death, rule of Ptolemaic dynasty of Egypt. Period of prosperity.*
198	*Rule of Seleucids of Syria.*
	As a result of internal struggle for power, Antiochus Epiphanes IV seizes the city. Construction of Akra (fortress) and stationing of garrison in the city. Intensive Hellenization. Leads to rebellion of Jews led by Judah Maccabee.
167	*City recaptured and purified. Establishes autonomous Jewish state. Jerusalem capital of Hasmonean kingdom.*

ROMAN PERIOD 63 BCE–326 CE

63	*Roman rule.*
37	*Herod transforms aspects of Jerusalem. Extensive building program.*
CE	
29	*After crucifixion of Jesus by the Romans, Jerusalem becomes focus of Christian reverence.*
66–70	*Jewish revolt, Jerusalem besieged by the Romans. After lengthy siege, the city is destroyed by Titus together with the Temple.*
	Jerusalem, however, remains central; when it shows signs of nationalist aspirations, the emperor Hadrian resolves to raze it completely.
132	*Establishes Roman colony on the site named Aelia Capitolina. Jews are barred.*
132–135	*Second Jewish Revolt led by Bar Kochba.*